PROMOTING PHYSICAL ACTIVITY

A GUIDE FOR COMMUNITY ACTION

U.S. DEPARTMENT OF HEALTH AND HUMAN SERVICES

Public Health Service

Centers for Disease Control and Prevention

National Center for Chronic Disease Prevention and Health Promotion

Division of Nutrition and Physical Activity

CENTERS FOR DISEASE CONTROL
AND PREVENTION

Human Kinetics

Library of Congress Cataloging-in-Publication Data

Promoting physical activity : a guide for community action / U.S.
    Department of Health and Human Services, Public Health Service,
    Centers for Disease Control and Prevention, National Center for
    Chronic Disease Prevention and Health Promotion, Division of
    Nutrition and Physical Activity.
        p.　cm.
    Includes bibliographical references and index.
    ISBN 0-7360-0152-2
    1. Health promotion--Social aspects--United States.　2. Physical
fitness--Social aspects--United States.　3. Medicine, Preventive-
-Social aspects--United States.　I. Centers for Disease Control and
Prevention (U.S.).　II. National Center for Chronic Disease
Prevention and Health Promotion (U.S.).　Division of Nutrition and
Physical Activity.
    RA427.8.P767　1999
    613.7'.0973—dc21　　　　　　　　　　　　　　　　99-17119
　　　　　　　　　　　　　　　　　　　　　　　　　　　　CIP

ISBN: 0-7360-0152-2

This book is published for the U.S. Department of Health and Human Services, Public Health Service, Centers for Disease Control and Prevention, National Center for Chronic Disease Prevention and Health Promotion, Division of Nutrition and Physical Activity, by Human Kinetics Publishers.

Photo credits: Photos © PhotoDisc, Inc., except where otherwise noted. Photos on pages 63, 76, 91, 97, 132 © CLEO Photography. Photos on pages 99, 128, 188, 199, 204 © Human Kinetics. Photos on pages 53, 173, 185, 205 © Mary Langenfeld/ Langenfeld Photo. Photo on page 67 © Robert Skeoch/The Picture Desk.

Suggested citation: U.S. Department of Health and Human Services, Public Health Service, Centers for Disease Control and Prevention, National Center for Chronic Disease Prevention and Health Promotion, Division of Nutrition and Physical Activity. *Promoting Physical Activity: A Guide for Community Action.* Champaign, IL: Human Kinetics, 1999.

Printed in the United States of America　　　10　9　8　7　6　5　4

Human Kinetics
Web site: www.HumanKinetics.com

United States: Human Kinetics, P.O. Box 5076, Champaign, IL 61825-5076
800-747-4457
e-mail: humank@hkusa.com

Canada: Human Kinetics, 475 Devonshire Road, Unit 100, Windsor, ON N8Y 2L5
800-465-7301 (in Canada only)
e-mail: orders@hkcanada.com

Europe: Human Kinetics, 107 Bradford Road, Stanningley
Leeds LS28　6AT, United Kingdom
+44 (0) 113 255 5665
e-mail: hk@hkeurope.com

Australia: Human Kinetics, 57A Price Avenue, Lower Mitcham, South Australia 5062
08　8277 1555
e-mail: liahka@senet.com.au

New Zealand: Human Kinetics, P.O. Box 105-231, Auckland Central
09-523-3462
e-mail: hkp@ihug.co.nz

Contents

Part III Strategies for Planning and Implementing Your Intervention

Part IV Resources for Action

A National Call to Action

Families need to weave physical activity into the fabric of their daily lives. Health professionals, in addition to being role models for healthy behaviors, need to encourage their patients to get out of their chairs and start fitness programs tailored to their individual needs. Businesses need to learn from what has worked in the past and promote worksite fitness, an easy option for workers. Community leaders need to reexamine whether enough resources have been devoted to the maintenance of parks, playgrounds, community centers, and physical education. Schools and universities need to reintroduce daily, quality physical activity as a key component of a comprehensive education. And the media and entertainment industries need to use their vast creative abilities to show all Americans that physical activity is healthful and fun. . . .

We Americans always find the will to change when change is needed. I believe we can team up to create a new physical activity movement in this country. In doing so, we will save precious resources, precious futures, and precious lives. The time for action—and activity—is now.

Donna E. Shalala, 1996
Secretary of Health and Human Services

Preface

Welcome to the world of physical activity promotion! *Promoting Physical Activity: A Guide for Community Action* is a resource for professionals and volunteers who wish to promote physical activity in almost any setting: a community, a workplace, a school setting, a health care facility, an agency or organization, or a religious institution. The ultimate goals of this book are to provide direction and assistance in program planning and to serve as a flexible blueprint for action for professionals who are on the front lines of intervention in any setting. Our mission is to help you succeed in getting more Americans moving!

This guide is for you whether you have just become interested in promoting physical activity but are not sure where to begin, or you are experienced in physical activity or health promotion but need new ideas to improve or expand existing programs. Whether you have a staff of one and very few resources or a staff of hundreds with resources to spare, you'll find that this publication includes advice and examples from an array of experiences and perspectives that you can apply to your situation. It's a practical guide to community *action*, fostering physical activity as a quality way of life. And you don't even have to know a great deal about physical activity to use this book.

Promoting Physical Activity: A Guide for Community Action is for anyone interested in promoting behavior change—any professional, in nearly any field—whether you're working with individuals one at a time; a small class; a scout troop; a retirement community; the entire school district staff; all the employees of a nationwide corporation; or an entire neighborhood, city, county, or state. Regardless of your situation, this guide will show you how to get started and, better yet, where you can go for additional ideas and resources. This book may prove to be a timeless treasure, for it summarizes the most basic information about physical activity promotion, the social marketing approach to program planning, and effective behavior change theory and translates the information into practical everyday suggestions for busy program planners. The best-case scenario is that by reading this book you will have found a friend—a user-friendly resource you can turn to again and again for ideas, regardless of the behavior you are targeting for change.

You will discover that there are some things you can do to increase the likelihood that people in your community will change their behavior and become more physically active. The first step is to stop creating "expert-driven" programs and instead to put the people you're trying to reach with behavior-changing messages and services into the driver's seat. Stop targeting and reaching only the already-active, and instead design strategies that will help those who want to be more active discover that they can do it. Help them build "self-efficacy."

The key to success is reaching people where they are and equipping them with the knowledge and skills they need to carry out a physically active lifestyle. Give them safe opportunities to practice those new skills, surround them with a supportive environment, and address some of the biggest physical or political barriers to their being successful. Do all that, and people can change if they want to—and sometimes even if they don't.

How to Use This Book

Although this guide systematically takes you through planning or revising a physical activity promotion program, you need not read the book from cover to cover. Instead, get familiar with its contents, mark the chapters or pages that interest you most, and start there. Not all chapters will apply to everyone. You might need to read some parts of the book more closely than others. It's a resource tool. Pick it up anytime. Keep it handy on your shelf. Photocopy the pages you like best. While research findings will certainly change with each passing day, the book keeps the door open to the future, with endless resource possibilities: places you can turn for continued inspiration, partnership potential, educational resources, or just good advice. The world of physical activity promotion is here at your fingertips. Here's what each part has in store:

• Part I, "Foundations for Physical Activity Promotion," explains the scientific basis for promoting physical activity—including the benefits and risks associated with an active lifestyle—and how to meet current physical activity recommendations.

• Part II, "Strategies for Changing Physical Activity Behavior," takes you through the process of profiling your target audience, the basics of behavior change, and specific intervention strategies that focus on the individual and the environment.

• Part III, "Strategies for Planning and Implementing Your Intervention," shows you how to set program objectives and measure program success, find partners in your community that will complement your promotion efforts, and design interventions focused specifically on worksites and school settings.

• Part IV, "Resources for Action," is devoted entirely to additional resources for physical activity program planning. You'll find addresses and phone numbers of agencies and organizations across the country that are interested in promoting physical activity, excerpts from the *1996 Surgeon General's Report on Physical Activity and Health,* and many other helpful resources that will make physical activity promotion easier for you.

If you are starting a new program, you may want to work through the guide from the beginning to get the best overview. If you are trying to strengthen an ongoing program, chapters 3 through 6 provide valuable keys to successful programs and chapters 9 and 10 give site-specific ideas for action. The Glossary of Physical Activity Terms and the Glossary of Program Planning Terms in the back of the book will also help you learn or review concepts related to physical activity promotion.

What You Won't Find In This Book

This book will not provide you with a cookie-cutter model program that will fit anyone, anywhere. Only the people who make up your target audience can tell you what physical activity message is best for them. By reading this book, you won't learn how to promote physical activity to one specific demographic group, such as people with disabilities, the elderly, the obese, women, or a specific ethnic group, though the book does point you to some excellent outside resources that might help you plan such programs.

This guide does not contain clinical, diagnostic, or treatment guidelines for physical activity or physical rehabilitation. It is not intended for use with frail persons or persons with serious chronic diseases, nor is it intended to assist with patient care. This publication is not an inclusive listing of physical activity promotion programs or resources currently available or under development. The programs, resources, and references in this guide are not necessarily endorsed by the Centers for Disease Control and Prevention.

Tips for Additional Resources

Although this guide attempts to provide most of the basic information you might need to initiate and manage a physical activity program, it is by no means comprehensive. You undoubtedly will have questions that the guide does not answer. For assistance, turn to the following resources.

- "Read More About It" boxes throughout the book and the lists of suggested readings at the end of each chapter will direct you to relevant references if you want more in-depth information on a given topic.
- The reference list at the end of the book is organized by chapter to help you locate reference citations easily as you work within an individual chapter.
- The Combined Health Information Database (CHID) is a computerized database that will keep you current on the journals, books, manuals, reports, teaching guides, and other published and unpublished resources in all areas of health promotion, including physical activity. Be sure to contact the CHID staff to tell them about your program ideas and accomplishments. By sharing your program descriptions, others will learn from your experiences. For information about CHID or how to contact CHID staff, see resource A in part IV of this book.

Acknowledgments

Principal Author

Barbara Duvekot Latham, RD, MPH
Division of Nutrition and Physical Activity
National Center for Chronic Disease Prevention and Health Promotion
Centers for Disease Control and Prevention
Atlanta, GA

To Colleagues Within the Centers for Disease Control and Prevention:

Agency for Toxic Substances and Disease Registry
Division of Health Education and Promotion
  Jamie W. Purvis, EdD, PhD

National Center for Chronic Disease Prevention and Health Promotion
Centers for Disease Control and Prevention
Atlanta, GA

  Division of Adolescent and School Health
  Janet Collins, PhD
  Wanda Jubb, EdD, CHES
  Marlene K. Tappe, PhD, CHES
  Howell Wechsler, EdD, MPH

  Division of Adult and Community Health
  J. Nell Brownstein, PhD, MA
  Greg Heath, DHSc, MPH
  Catherine A. Hutsell, MPH
  Dyann Matson-Koffman, MPH, DrPH, CHES
  Diane Orenstein, PhD

  Division of Nutrition and Physical Activity
  Teri Barber, MA
  David Brown, PhD
  Charlene Burgeson, MA
  John Davis, RD, MPA
  Fred Fridinger, DrPH, CHES
  Elizabeth Howze, ScD
  Richard Killingsworth, MPH, CHES
  Bruce Leonard, MPH
  Carol Macera, PhD
  Refilwe Moeti, MA
  Michael Pratt, MD, MS, MPH

  Technical Information and Editorial Services Branch
  Christine S. Fralish, MLIS
  Rick L. Hull, PhD
  Brenda Mazzocchi
  Reba A. Norman, MLM
  Emma Stupp

Office of Communication

  Division of Health Communication
  Galen E. Cole, PhD, MPH

Special thanks to those who contributed significantly to this publication for their technical expertise and willing assistance!

Barbara Ainsworth, PhD, MPH
Department of Epidemiology and Biostatistics
Department of Exercise Science
University of South Carolina
Columbia, SC

George I. Balch, PhD
Prevention Research Center
University of Illinois at Chicago
Chicago, IL

David Cotton, PhD, MPH
Macro International Inc.
Atlanta, GA

Carolyn E. Crump, PhD
Center for Health Promotion and Disease
Prevention
University of North Carolina
Chapel Hill, NC

Chris Dropinski, CLP
Boulder Parks and Recreation
Boulder, CO

Patricia Dubbert, PhD
Department of Veterans Affairs Medical
Center
University of Mississippi School of Medicine
Jackson, MS

Linda Dusenbury, MS, RN
California Department of Health Services
Sacramento, CA

Martin Fishbein, PhD
Annenberg Public Policy Center
Annenberg School for Communication
University of Pennsylvania
Philadelphia, PA

Manny Harageones
Escambia County Schools
Pensacola, FL

Bess Marcus, PhD
Behavioral Medicine Department
Miriam Hospital
Providence, RI

Joanne Mitten, MHE
Idaho Department of Health and Welfare
Boise, ID

JoAnne Owens-Nauslar, EdD
American School Health Association
Kent, OH

Susan Provence, MAT
South Carolina Department of Health
and Environmental Control
Columbia, SC

Bill Smith, EdD
Academy for Educational Development
Washington, DC

Kathy J. Spangler, CLP
National Recreation and Park Association
Arlington, VA

Susan B. Toal, MPH
Consulting Technical Writer/Editor
Atlanta, GA

Kim Yeager, MD, MPH, FACPM
Yeager and Associates, Inc.
San Diego, CA

For their thorough and thoughtful reviews of preliminary drafts:

Terry Bazzarre, PhD
Science Consultant, Office of Scientific
Affairs and Office of Education and
Community Programs
National Center
American Heart Association
Dallas, TX

Steven N. Blair, PED
Director, Epidemiology
Institute for Aerobics Research
Dallas, TX

Molly J. Burns
Information Coordinator
American Running and Fitness Association
Bethesda, MD

Don Camp
Executive Director
Alabama Governor's Commission on
Physical Fitness
Montgomery, AL

Diana Cassady, DrPH
Cardiovascular Disease Outreach Resources
and Epidemiology
California Department of Health Services
Sacramento, CA

John Cates
Executive Director
California Governor's Council on Physical
Fitness and Sports
University of California at San Diego
La Jolla, CA

Barbara Fraser, MS, RD
Nebraska Department of Health
Lincoln, NE

Sharon Gerberding
Idaho Department of Health and Welfare
District 5
Twin Falls, ID

Marge Hamrell
Chief, Health Promotion
Vermont Department of Health,
Epidemiology and Disease Prevention
Burlington, VT

Carol Johnson
Physical Education
Walton County Wellness Coordinator
Walton County School District
Loganville, GA

Michelle Corzier Kegler, DrPH, MPH
College of Public Health
University of Oklahoma
Oklahoma City, OK

Chris Kimber
Health Education, Division of Family Health
Minnesota Department of Health
Minneapolis, MN

Linda Kotowski, CLP
Past Chairman, National Fitness and
Wellness Coalition
Superintendent of Recreation
Boulder, CO

George Kroeninger
Wellness Administrator
Foothills Park and Recreation District
Lakewood, CO

Patricia Kryzalka
Health Promotion
Eastman Kodak
Rochester, NY

Paula Kun
National Association of Sport and Physical
Education
Reston, VA

Louise Linton
Office of the Director
National Center for Chronic Disease
Prevention and Health Promotion

Centers for Disease Control and Prevention
Atlanta, GA

Brenda Motzinger
Chief, Division of Adult Health
North Carolina Department of Health
Raleigh, NC

Kelly Nebel
PATCH Coordinator
Division of Health Education
Indiana State Department of Health
Indianapolis, IN

Kevin Patrick, MD, MS
San Diego State University
San Diego, CA

Shellie Pfohl
Executive Director
North Carolina Council on Physical Fitness
and Health
Raleigh, NC

Sarah E. Pierce, MPH
University of Texas
Health Science Center
School of Public Health
Houston, TX

Jim L. Purvis
Founder, California Wellness Information
Network
Special Advisor, Governor's Council on
Physical Fitness and Sports
Sacramento, CA

Edward Roubal
Chronic Disease Control
Louisiana Department of Health and Hospitals
New Orleans, LA

Miriam Sutton, MA
Health and Fitness Consultant
Atlantic Beach, NC

Michele Volansky
Westat Corporation
Atlanta, GA

Judith C. Young, PhD
Executive Director
National Association for Sport and Physical
Education
Reston, VA

For editing, design, and production:

Human Kinetics
Champaign, IL

Rainer Martens
President

Lynn M. Hooper-Davenport
Developmental Editor

Jennifer Goldberg and Jennifer Miller
Assistant Editors

Terri Hamer
Permission Manager

John Mulvihill
Copyeditor

Jim Burns
Proofreader

Joan Griffitts
Indexer

Kristine Ding
Production Manager

Nancy Rasmus
Graphic Designer

Francine Hamerski
Graphic Artist

Patrick Griffin, Kimberly Maxey, and Tom Roberts
Illustrators

Dusty Willison
Cover Photographer

Jack Davis
Cover Designer

Versa Press
Printer

Introduction

Americans need a boost in the area of physical activity. They need to be educated about the benefits of physical activity and the risks of remaining sedentary. They need to know how much and what kinds of physical activity will make them healthier and happier. They also need to know how to get started and how to keep going once they've taken the leap. This book shows you how effective physical activity promotion can fill all of these needs.

What Is Promotion?

Promotion can mean different things to different people. We use the term in a broad sense in this publication, to include both efforts to make physical activity a more fundamental part of American life as well as efforts to use publicity to achieve that goal. Physical activity promotion can take many forms. Examples of promotion include the following:

• Initiatives that focus on making physical activity more accessible to a wider range of people, such as creating parks, open areas, and safe and accessible walking and biking trails in cities

• Programs that seek to educate people about the value of physical activity, such as courses that address physical activity and wellness in health care settings, in community colleges, and through parks and recreation organizations

• Initiatives that provide a variety of fitness programs or organized sporting events, such as park district or YMCA/YWCA sports programs, workplace sporting opportunities, and organized youth leagues

• Programs or organizations that provide individuals and communities with the support network they need to continue a physically active lifestyle

Who Is Responsible for Physical Activity Promotion?

Physical activity promotion can happen just about anywhere, and in fact, for it to be successful, it needs to happen just about *everywhere*. We need to create positive environments for people in which physical activity is accessible, safe, affordable, fun, and supported. Worksites, health care settings, communities, schools, and families all need to have the information and resources necessary to create environments that are conducive to a more active lifestyle.

Regular physical activity enhances both personal health and the vitality of our society. Establishing such activity as a habit for all our citizens must be a national priority.

Jimmy Carter

Promotional strategies need to simultaneously target individuals, government policies, and community organizations if the goal is to create lasting behavior change in our communities. Groups like the following must all work together to do their part in making physical activity become a regular aspect of American life (USDHHS 1996):

- State and local governments
- Transportation, health, and community planners
- Architects and engineers
- Behavioral and social scientists
- Exercise specialists and health professionals
- Health clubs
- Community groups
- Businesses
- Schools
- Colleges and universities
- Recreational programs and community leagues
- Social service organizations
- Libraries
- Senior centers and nursing homes
- Places of worship

The key is for all the pieces of the community puzzle to make physical activity a priority by creating real opportunities for physical activity in daily life and by doing whatever they can to remove the barriers that make it difficult for Americans to participate in an active lifestyle.

The Evolution of National Physical Activity Recommendations

What level of physical activity do we want to promote among Americans? How will we measure success? Chapters 1 and 2 will cover these questions in more detail, but first, to understand how far we've come, read the timeline on pages xix–xx, which shows how national recommendations for physical activity have evolved since the 1960s.

Major Milestones in the Development of National Recommendations for Physical Activity

1960s and 1970s Expert panels and committees from a variety of health- and fitness-oriented organizations begin to recommend specific physical activity programs or exercise prescriptions for improving physical performance capacity or health (USDHHS 1996). Numerous recommendations are developed on the basis of substantial clinical experience and scientific research available at the time (for example, see President's Council on Physical Fitness 1965; AHA 1972, 1975; ACSM 1975).

1978 The American College of Sports Medicine (ACSM) releases *The Recommended Quantity and Quality of Exercise for Developing and Maintaining Fitness in Healthy Adults,* which outlines the types of exercise that healthy adults need in order to develop and maintain cardiorespiratory fitness and healthy body composition (ACSM 1978; USDHHS 1996). Guidelines include

- a frequency of exercise training of 3 to 5 days per week,
- an intensity of training equivalent to 60 to 90% of maximum heart rate,
- a duration of 15 to 60 minutes per training session, and
- the rhythmical and aerobic use of large muscle groups through activities such as running or jogging, walking or hiking, swimming, skating, bicycling, rowing, cross-country skiing, and rope skipping.

From 1978 until the early 1990s Most exercise recommendations made to the general public are based on the ACSM's 1978 position statement, even though it addresses only cardiorespiratory fitness and body composition. As a result, many people interpret the statement as if it contains guidelines for overall health.

From the 1970s to the mid-1990s Additional exercise training studies conducted with middle-aged and older persons demonstrate that these persons could achieve improved cardiorespiratory performance and health-related benefits simply by engaging in moderate levels of physical activity. Population-based research during this period also shows that the greater the level of physical activity, the better the health outcomes (USDHHS 1996).

1989 and 1996 The U.S. Preventive Services Task Force (USPSTF), a group of experts convened by the U.S. Department of Health and Human Services' Office of Disease Prevention and Health Promotion, recommends that health care providers counsel all adult patients on the importance of incorporating physical activities into their daily routines to prevent coronary heart disease, hypertension, obesity, and diabetes (Harris et al. 1989; USPSTF 1989, 1996).

1990 The ACSM adds to its 1978 position statement a major objective on the development of muscular strength and endurance and recognizes that activities of moderate intensity may have health benefits other than cardiorespiratory fitness (ACSM 1990).

1991 The Public Health Service (PHS) releases the report entitled *Healthy People 2000: National Health Promotion and Disease Prevention Objectives* (PHS 1991), which outlines a national strategy to improve the health of all Americans. Physical activity and fitness objectives are integral components in this overall national strategy. See page xxi for a complete list of the year 2000 objectives related to physical activity promotion. For an electronic copy of both the year 2000 and year 2010 objectives for the nation, see **http://web.health.gov/healthypeople**.

1993 As a complement to 1991's *Healthy People 2000* report, the ACSM and the Centers for Disease Control and Prevention (CDC) bring together a group of experts to review the scientific evidence on physical activity and to synthesize the data into a broad message on the amount and types of physical activity needed to promote good health and quality of life.

(continued)

(continued)

From these deliberations, the ACSM and CDC formulate the following recommendation directed at people who are mostly inactive:

Every American adult should accumulate 30 minutes or more of moderate-intensity physical activity on most, preferably all, days of the week (Pate et al. 1995a).

The experts emphasize the benefits of a minimum of 30 minutes of moderate-intensity physical activity. This recommended "dose" of daily activity could be achieved in a single session or accumulated in multiple bouts, each lasting at least 8 to 10 minutes (Pate et al. 1995). The experts also suggest that the 30-minute minimum regularly include activities that would develop and maintain muscular strength and joint flexibility.

1993 A consensus statement from the International Consensus Conference on Physical Activity Guidelines for Adolescents emphasizes that adolescents should be physically active every day as part of general lifestyle activities and that they should engage in 3 or more 20-minute sessions of moderate- to vigorous-intensity activities each week (Sallis and Patrick 1994). Likewise, the American Academy of Pediatrics (1992, 1994) issues several statements encouraging active play in preschool children, assessment of children's activity levels, and evaluation of physical fitness. Both of these important documents acknowledge the need for appropriate school physical education curricula and particularly emphasize active play, parental involvement, and generally active lifestyles for youth.

1994 The American Medical Association's *Guidelines for Adolescent Preventive Services (GAPS)* recommends that physicians provide annual physical activity counseling to all adolescents from the age of 12 years as part of a comprehensive preventive services package designed to address numerous adolescent health issues (AMA 1994).

1995 The National Institutes of Health convene a Consensus Development Conference on Physical Activity and Cardiovascular Health, once again bringing together a group of experts who design a call to action (NIH 1996). The core recommendations, similar to those jointly made by the ACSM and CDC (Pate et al. 1995a), call for all Americans to engage in regular physical activity at a level appropriate to their capacity, needs, and interest. The report concludes that children and adults should set a goal of accumulating at least 30 minutes per day of moderate-intensity physical activity. The recommendations also acknowledge that persons already achieving this minimum could experience even greater health and fitness benefits by increasing duration or intensity of activity. For persons with known cardiovascular disease, more widespread use of cardiac rehabilitation programs that include physical activity is recommended (NIH 1996).

1996 The Office of the Surgeon General, U.S. Department of Health and Human Services, releases a landmark document entitled *Physical Activity and Health: A Report of the Surgeon General*, which is produced by the CDC and the President's Council on Physical Fitness and Sports (USDHHS 1996). In an unprecedented effort, this report represents the most comprehensive synthesis of the research to date on physical activity. The report concludes that:

- People who are inactive can improve their health and well-being by becoming even moderately active on a regular basis.
- Physical activity need not be strenuous to achieve health benefits.
- People who are already physically active will benefit even more by increasing the amount (duration, frequency, or intensity) of physical activity.

1997 The CDC releases a set of recommendations for establishing lifelong patterns of physical activity among youth. *Guidelines for School and Community Programs to Promote Lifelong Physical Activity Among Young People* is designed for persons who wish to promote, develop, or deliver physical activity programs for youth. It can be used by professionals within health and education agencies and organizations; by personnel who provide training for professionals in public health, education, recreation, and medicine; by persons who develop youth recreation and sports programs; and by policymakers at the local, state, and federal levels (CDC 1997).

Healthy People 2000: National Health Promotion and Disease Prevention Objectives Related to Physical Activity and Fitness

Objective 1.3 Increase to at least 30 percent the proportion of people aged 6 and older who engage regularly, preferably daily, in light to moderate physical activity for at least 30 minutes per day.

Objective 1.4 Increase to at least 20 percent the proportion of people aged 18 and older and to at least 75 percent the proportion of children and adolescents aged 6 through 17 who engage in vigorous physical activity that promotes the development and maintenance of cardiorespiratory fitness 3 or more days per week for 20 or more minutes per occasion.

Objective 1.5 Reduce to no more than 15 percent the proportion of people aged 6 and older who engage in no leisure-time physical activity.

Objective 1.6 Increase to at least 40 percent the proportion of people aged 6 and older who regularly perform physical activities that enhance and maintain muscular strength, muscular endurance, and flexibility.

Objective 1.7 Increase to at least 50 percent the proportion of overweight people aged 12 and older who have adopted sound dietary practices combined with regular physical activity to attain an appropriate body weight.

Objective 1.8 Increase to at least 50 percent the proportion of children and adolescents in 1st through 12th grade who participate in daily school physical education.

Objective 1.9 Increase to at least 50 percent the proportion of school physical education class time that students spend being physically active, preferably engaged in lifetime physical activities.

Objective 1.10 Increase the proportion of work sites offering employer-sponsored physical activity and fitness programs as follows:

50–99 employees	20%
100–249 employees	35%
250–749 employees	50%
≥750 employees	80%

Objective 1.11 Increase community availability and accessibility of physical activity and fitness facilities as follows:

Hiking, biking, and fitness trail miles	1 per 10,000 people
Public swimming pools	1 per 25,000 people
Acres of park and recreation open space	4 per 1,000 people (or 250 people per managed acre)

Objective 1.12 Increase to at least 50 percent the proportion of primary care providers who routinely assess and counsel their patients regarding the frequency, duration, type, and intensity of each patient's physical activity practices.

Revised physical activity and fitness objectives are currently under development for the year 2010. To view the latest version, please visit this website: **http://web.health.gov/healthypeople/**

Reprinted from PHS 1991.

Suggested Reading

For a list of organizations, agencies, and selected program materials for promoting physical activity, see:

Resource A, for general resources

Chapter 6, for environment-related resources

Chapter 9, for worksite-related resources

Chapter 10, for school-related resources

For an international comparison of perspectives on physical activity public policy and health promotion, read:

Killoran AJ, Fenten P, Caspersen CJ, editors. *Moving On: International Perspectives on Promoting Physical Activity.* London, England: Health Education Authority, 1994. ISBN: 0-7521-0266-4.

To order a copy of this publication, contact

Health Education Authority
Customer Services, Marston Book Services
P.O. Box 269
Abingdon, Oxon, England OX14 4YN

Visit their website at the following address: **http://www.hea.org.uk**

Part I

Foundations for Physical Activity Promotion

It's time to get Americans moving! Promoting physical activity is about helping your community, your worksite, your schools, your family get excited about incorporating physical activity into their daily lives. It's about giving your target population information that will help them understand that an active lifestyle is not only fun but also essential for optimal health and well-being.

In part I, you'll be given the foundations for successfully promoting physical activity: you'll be introduced to the scientific basis for promoting a more physically active lifestyle to members of your community. In chapter 1 you'll learn what you need to teach your target population about the myths related to physical activity, the health benefits of an active lifestyle, the facts and figures related to Americans' physical activity participation rates, and the dangerous health consequences of the continuing sedentariness of Americans.

Chapter 2 will take the scientific message a step further by focusing on how to meet the Surgeon General's 1996 physical activity recommendations. You'll learn what counts as "regular, moderate" physical activity—how much, how often, and how intense—and how people can determine their own physical activity intensity levels. You'll also find safety considerations for a physically active lifestyle.

Chapter 1 Understanding the Power of Physical Activity

The evidence is mounting and is more convincing than ever! People of all ages who are generally inactive can improve their health and well-being by becoming even moderately active* on a regular basis (USDHHS 1996). Those who enjoy being moderately or vigorously active on a regular basis benefit by lowering their risk of developing coronary heart disease, non-insulin-dependent diabetes mellitus, high blood pressure, and colon cancer by 30 to 50% (USDHHS 1996). Active people have lower premature death rates than do people who are the least active.

* For a discussion defining moderate physical activity, see pages 16–17.

People of all ages can improve the quality of their lives through a lifelong practice of moderate physical activity.

Donna E. Shalala, 1996
Secretary of Health and Human Services

Despite the mounting evidence in favor of an active lifestyle, most Americans still remain sedentary. Although our nation has made significant progress over the past decades to control high blood pressure and high blood cholesterol, and to discourage tobacco use, since 1985 we have made little progress in increasing physical activity levels among Americans.

Regardless of your profession or area of specialty, you can do a great deal to foster change and improve the quality of life of people in your community, workplace, organization, or school by helping people become more physically active. This publication will assist you by equipping you with specific ideas and resources that will help make this important objective a reality. Regardless of the desired behavior or environmental change you choose as your goal, you can benefit from this book, which contains some of the best ideas that epidemiologic and behavioral science and the experience of a variety of experts have to offer.

Chapter 1 lays the scientific foundation on which to build a physical activity promotion program by defining the terms and reinforcing the benefits of maintaining an active lifestyle and summarizing what we have learned so far from research scientists regarding

- the benefits of regular, moderate physical activity;
- the risks of maintaining a sedentary lifestyle; and
- the demographic characteristics of the Americans who remain least active.

Leaving Behind America's Physical Activity Myths

For years Americans have heard the message that they should exercise vigorously for at least 20 minutes per day, 3 times per week. They believed that nothing less would do. Even though many people today might be able to recite the recommendation from memory, the vast majority of Americans have not successfully carried out the advice. And it is likely that a good many have given up trying.

Previous efforts by public and private organizations to promote physical activity have emphasized the importance of high-intensity physical activities while saying little or nothing about the benefits of less-intense activities. As a result, many people are convinced that unless they engage in vigorous, continuous activity for at least 20 minutes 3 times a week, they will fail to achieve any health benefits. Rather than do less than this, many people choose to do nothing at all. Unfortunately, as people's perception of the effort required to perform an activity increases, their participation in physical activity seems to decrease (Dishman and Sallis 1994).

Therefore, if people with little confidence in their ability to be physically active were convinced that moderate-intensity activity counts and that "it's easier than you think" to fit activity into the course of a busy day, perhaps the number of people who would be willing to adopt and continue a physically active lifestyle would increase. The box on page 5 lists tips for integrating physical activity into even the busiest of schedules. Perhaps if Americans felt more comfortable with their own ability to fit physical activity into their lives, they'd be more likely to spread the word and really get the ball rolling for a "fitness revolution." After all, studies show that people who have confidence in their ability to be physically active and who receive support from family members and friends are more likely to begin and continue exercise programs (Dishman and Sallis 1994).

Now, after many years, there's good news for all Americans: the scientific evidence now confirms that physical activity doesn't need to be strenuous to

Tips for Getting Moving

With a little creativity and planning, even the person with the busiest schedule can make room for physical activity. For many folks, before or after work or meals is often an available time to cycle, walk, play, or just be active. Think about your weekly or daily schedule and look for or make opportunities to be more active. Every little bit helps. Consider the following list of suggestions:

- Walk, cycle, jog, skate, etc., to work, school, the store, or church.
- Park the car farther away from your destination.
- Get on or off the bus several blocks away.
- Take the stairs instead of the elevator or escalator.
- Walk the dog.
- Play with the kids.
- Take fitness breaks—walking or doing desk exercises—instead of taking cigarette or coffee breaks.
- Perform gardening or home repair activities.
- Avoid labor-saving devices.
- Use leg power—take small trips.
- Exercise while watching TV.

achieve health benefits (USDHHS 1996). If people have been sedentary, they can improve their health and well-being by regularly including even moderate levels of activity throughout the day. And those who are able can achieve lesser but still substantial gains by gradually increasing the frequency (how often), the intensity (how hard), and the duration (how long) of their activities.

Those who already participate in more vigorous activities regularly should be encouraged and supported in their efforts to continue. But strenuous activity may not be a realistic goal for everyone, at least not at first. Many Americans, for whom the term "exercise" conjures up negative images and emotions, can celebrate the good news by setting a new personal goal—that of achieving and enjoying the benefits of a regularly active lifestyle that includes a variety of moderate or vigorous-intensity activities.

More good news is that it's never too late to start an active lifestyle. No matter how old you are, how unfit you feel, or how long you've been inactive, the scientific evidence shows that starting a more active lifestyle now through regular, moderate-intensity activity can make you healthier and improve your quality of life.

In a nutshell, physical activity is something you *do*. Physical fitness is something you *acquire*—a characteristic or an attribute one can achieve by being physically active. And *exercise* is structured and tends to have fitness as its goal.

Michael Pratt, MD, MPH, 1993
CDC Division of Nutrition and Physical Activity

Understanding the Specific Health Benefits
of Being Regularly Active

Regular physical activity of at least moderate intensity and practiced on five or more days of the week, reduces the risk of developing coronary heart disease, hypertension, colon cancer, and diabetes—some of the leading causes of illness and death in the United States (USDHHS 1996). Regular physical activity can improve health and reduce the risk of premature death in the following ways.

- Reduces the risk of dying from coronary heart disease (CHD)
- Reduces the risk of having a second heart attack in people who have already experienced one heart attack
- Lowers both total blood cholesterol and triglycerides and may increase high-density lipoproteins (HDL or the "good" cholesterol)
- Lowers the risk of developing high blood pressure
- Helps reduce blood pressure in people who already have hypertension
- Lowers the risk of developing non-insulin-dependent (Type II) diabetes mellitus
- Reduces the risk of developing colon cancer
- Helps people achieve and maintain a healthy body weight
- Reduces feelings of depression and anxiety

- Promotes psychological well-being and reduces feelings of stress
- Helps build and maintain healthy bones, muscles, and joints
- Helps older adults become stronger and better able to move about without falling or becoming excessively fatigued

The Good News Applies to Everyone

- **Older adults**

  No one is too old to enjoy the benefits of regular physical activity. Evidence indicates that muscle-strengthening exercises can reduce the risk of falling and fracturing bones and can improve the ability to live independently.

- **Parents**

  Parents can help their children maintain a physically active lifestyle by providing encouragement and opportunities for physical activity. Families can plan outings and events that allow and encourage everyone in the family to be active.

- **Teenagers**

  Regular physical activity improves strength, builds lean muscle, and decreases body fat. Activity can build stronger bones to last a lifetime.

- **People trying to manage their weight**

  Regular physical activity burns calories while preserving lean muscle mass—muscle that would have been lost by adhering to low-calorie diets alone. Regular physical activity is a key component of any weight-loss or weight-management effort.

- **People with high blood pressure**

  Regular physical activity helps lower blood pressure.

- **People with physical disabilities, including arthritis**

  Regular physical activity can help people with chronic, disabling conditions improve their stamina and muscle strength and can improve psychological well-being and quality of life by increasing the ability to perform the activities of daily life.

- **Everyone under stress, including persons experiencing anxiety or depression**

  Regular physical activity improves one's mood, helps relieve depression, and increases feelings of well-being.

USDHHS 1996

Read More About It

The Health Benefits of Physical Activity

For a thorough scientific review of the physiological responses to physical activity and the effects of physical activity on health and disease, read chapters 3 and 4 of *Physical Activity and Health: A Report of the Surgeon General* (USDHHS 1996). See also:

Nieman D. 1998 *The Exercise-Health Connection.* Champaign, IL: Human Kinetics.

"How much exercise do you really need?" *Consumer Reports* April 1998:1–4.

Battling the Real American Pastime: Inactivity

Some Americans do participate in daily physical activity, but far too many are less than optimally active. Although Americans have been told over and over that a commitment to regular exercise and a healthy diet can reap health benefits, far too many of them remain sedentary and unmotivated to make a lifestyle change to improve their health and well-being. In your work to promote physical activity, it will help to know what the health risks are to the sedentary population and just how widespread inactivity is. Armed with that information, you'll have a clearer picture of whom to target and the negative consequences of inactivity that you need to communicate to inactive Americans.

Several national data sets have demonstrated that about 30% of American adults report no leisure-time physical activity and an additional 30% are not sufficiently active to achieve health benefits. These data have not changed over the past decade (USDHHS 1996; Jones et al. 1998). State-based Behavioral Risk Factor Surveillance Data 1996 demonstrate that the problem of physical inactivity is widespread throughout the United States, with estimates of no reported leisure-time physical activity ranging from a low of 17.1% in the most active state, Utah, to a high of 51.4% in the least active state of Georgia (CDC 1998).

sedentary lifestyle—a lifestyle characterized by little or no physical activity. In scientific literature, *sedentary* is often defined in terms of little or no leisure-time physical activity.

Inactivity Among Adults

Current research on physical activity and health focuses on leisure-time physical activity. While some adults may have physically demanding jobs, most do not. Because most jobs require minimal amounts of physical activity, the choices made during leisure time represent the majority of health-related physical activity. Health promotion efforts may be effective in changing choices during leisure time, which may incorporate time at work (i.e., during lunch breaks), but are unlikely to be successful in changing the activity level associated with a particular occupation. Because of this, national data sets have collected information on physical activity during leisure time, and have only begun to explore occupation-related activity levels.

Data on adults collected from several sources consistently find that (Jones et al. 1998)

- approximately 60% of adults are not sufficiently active to achieve health benefits and about 30% report no leisure-time physical activity (see figure 1.1);
- participation in leisure-time physical activity decreases as age increases;
- women are less likely than men to engage in moderate or vigorous physical activity; and
- African-American and Hispanic adults are less likely to be physically active than white adults.

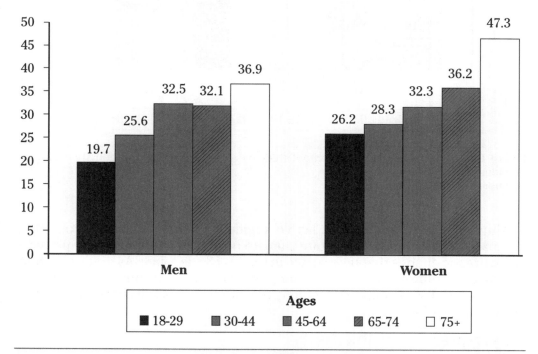

Figure 1.1   Percentage of U.S. adults age 18 and older reporting no leisure-time physical activity during the past month.
Data from BRFSS 1996 (CDC 1998)

Inactivity Among Youth

American youth are also less than optimally active. Results of the 1997 Youth Risk Behavior Surveillance (YRBS) (Kann et al. 1998; USDHHS 1996), a national school-based survey of 9–12th graders, revealed that

- 36% of youth do not engage in vigorous activity consistently or strenuously enough to maintain or improve cardiorespiratory fitness;
- girls are less likely than boys to engage in vigorous activity;
- African-American and Hispanic youth tend to be less vigorously active than white youth;
- participation in physical activity decreases as grade in school increases (see figure 1.2).

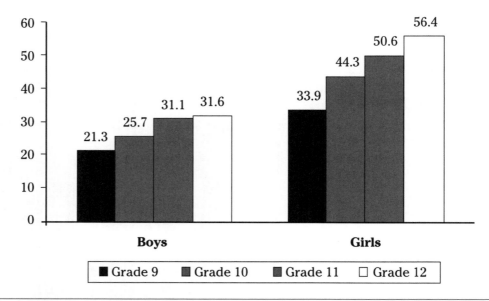

Figure 1.2   Percentage of U.S. high school students reporting no vigorous activity during the previous seven days.
Data from YRBS 1997 (Kann et al. 1998)

Although youth are a more active segment of the U.S. population when compared to adults, the important thing to note about youth activity patterns is the drastic change that takes place in the 11–13 age range. As grade in school increases, a number of factors create personal and environmental barriers to physical activity and make it less likely that adolescents will continue an active lifestyle into adulthood.

Consequences of Inactivity

The closer we look at the health risks associated with physical inactivity, the more convincing it is that the two out of three Americans who are not yet moderately physically active should become active. Premature death and cardiovascular disease are "complications" of physical inactivity that ought to get Americans to take notice. Studies by Paffenbarger and associates (1993) and Blair and associates (1995) showed that previously sedentary or unfit men who became moderately physically active or fit had lower death

rates than those who remained sedentary or unfit (figure 1.3). Research like that ought to be compelling enough to get Americans to be more physically active!

In a study of 11,130 Harvard University alumni, researchers found that people who expended 1,000 kilocalories per week—the equivalent of walking briskly 30 minutes a day, 5 days a week—had about a 24% reduction in their risk of stroke, a leading cause of disability in the United States. Meanwhile, those expending 2,000 kilocalories each week—the equivalent of a one-hour brisk walk, 5 days a week—had a 46% lower risk of stroke than those who did little or no exercise (Lee and Paffenbarger 1998).

High blood pressure, an important risk factor for both coronary heart disease and stroke, has also been associated with inactivity. A 1984 study by Blair and colleagues reported that people with low cardiorespiratory fitness had a 52% higher risk of later developing high blood pressure than their physically fit peers, and studies by Arroll and Beaglehole (1992) and Kelley and McClellan (1994) have shown that both systolic and diastolic blood pressure are reduced by approximately 6–7 mm Hg through aerobic exercise. If physical activity can reduce elevated blood pressure, thereby reducing the risk of cardiovascular disease, and if physical inactivity puts people at risk for developing high blood pressure, then it seems obvious that physical activity, taken in the right "doses" and at the right intensity, is an important key to preventing cardiovascular disease.

Paffenbarger and associates (1993) studied men over an 11-year period. Those who were sedentary at the beginning of the study and took up moderately-intense sports activity had a 23% lower death rate than those who remained sedentary.

Blair and associates (1995) found that men who were in the bottom fifth in terms of cardiorespiratory fitness at the beginning of the study and later improved to at least a moderate level of fitness had a 44% lower death rate than those who remained in the bottom fifth for cardiorespiratory fitness.

Figure 1.3   Two large studies provide evidence that changing from lower to higher levels of physical activity or cardiorespiratory fitness has an effect on subsequent mortality.

Suggested Reading

For a list of organizations, agencies, and selected program materials for promoting physical activity, see:

Resource A, for general resources

Chapter 6, for environment-related resources

Chapter 9, for worksite-related resources

Chapter 10, for school-related resources

Physical Activity and Health: A Report of the Surgeon General

To obtain a copy of the report: U.S. Department of Health and Human Services. *Physical Activity and Health: A Report of the Surgeon General*. Atlanta: U.S. Department of Health and Human Services, Centers for Disease Control and Prevention, National Center for Chronic Disease Prevention and Health Promotion, 1996, order forms are available via telefax by calling toll-free 1-888-CDC-4NRG (1-888-232-4674), or set your Internet browser to the following address: **http://www.cdc.gov/nccdphp/sgr/sgr.htm.** (Also available: an Executive Summary, At-A-Glance Summary, and a set of consumer fact sheets. These items are also reproduced in Resource B of this publication.)

NIH Consensus Conference: Physical Activity and Cardiovascular Health

A copy of the summary report of the NIH Consensus Conference is available by calling toll-free 800-NIH-OMAR (644-6627), by visiting the Internet at the following address: **http://www.text.nlm.nih.gov/nih/nih.html**, or by obtaining a copy of the article with the following citation: NIH Consensus Development Panel on Physical Activity and Cardiovascular Health. *Journal of the American Medical Association* July 17, 1996; 276(3):241–246. The full papers have also been compiled into a book, available from Human Kinetics: A. Leon, editor. *Physical Activity and Cardiovascular Health: A National Consensus.* Champaign, IL: Human Kinetics, 1997. To order, call 800-747-4457 or visit **http://www.humankinetics.com**.

For periodic reviews of current research related to physical activity and fitness, review:

Physical Activity and Fitness Research Digest published by:

The President's Council on Physical Fitness and Sports
Department of Health and Human Services
Humphrey Bldg. Room 738H
200 Independence Ave. SW
Washington, DC 20201
202-272-3421

For more information about BRFSS and YRBS

To understand the Behavioral Risk Factor Surveillance System (BRFSS) and how to interpret these survey data, review the specific physical activity-related definitions used for each category of respondents (Caspersen and Merit 1995; USDHHS 1996). To obtain the most current BRFSS statistics for your state, contact your BRFSS Coordinator at your state health department or visit **http://www.cdc.gov/nccdphp/brfss**.

For the most current information on physical activity levels among youth, contact your state Department of Education to determine whether your state participates in Youth Risk Behavior Surveillance (YRBS), a system that collects data on the health behaviors of high school students. To obtain more information about the YRBS, review Kann et al.1998 or visit **http://www.cdc.gov/nccdphp/dash**.

For more information about the economic impact of physical activity and physical inactivity, read:

Jones, TF and CB Eaton. 1994. Cost-benefit analysis of walking to prevent coronary heart disease. *Archives of Family Medicine* 3: 703–710.

Keeler, EB, WG Manning, et al. 1989. The external costs of a sedentary lifestyle. *American Journal of Public Health* 79: 975–981.

For information about Americans' attitudes toward physical activity read:

Rodale Press Inc. and Parkwood Research Associates. 1995. *Pathways for People II: Americans' Attitudes Toward Walking, Bicycling and Running in Their Communities.* Summary Report. Emmaus, PA: Rodale Press. (May).

Chapter 2 Achieving a Moderately Active Lifestyle

A moderate amount of physical activity is a vital component of a healthy lifestyle for people of all ages and abilities. There is no demographic or social group in America that could not benefit from becoming more active. No matter where you live or work, you can make a significant contribution to improving the health and well-being of your community by helping people become more physically active.

The scientific evidence to date supports the following statements:

1. Those people who do not currently engage in regular physical activity should begin by incorporating a few minutes of physical activity into each day, gradually building up to 30 minutes or more of moderate-intensity activities.

Terms You Need to Know

Physical activity is any bodily movement produced by skeletal muscles that results in an expenditure of energy (expressed as kilocalories) and includes a broad range of occupational, leisure-time, and routine daily activities. These activities can require either light, moderate, or vigorous effort and they can lead to improved health if they are practiced regularly (USDHHS 1996).

Exercise is physical activity that is planned or structured. It involves repetitive bodily movement done to improve or maintain one or more of the components of physical fitness—aerobic capacity (or endurance capacity), muscular strength, muscular endurance, flexibility, and body composition.

Physical fitness is a measure of a person's ability to perform physical activities that require endurance, strength, or flexibility and is determined by a combination of regular activity and genetically inherited ability.

Note: Because people frequently perceive the term "exercise" negatively and the phrase "physical activity" positively (CDC 1995b), in this book we focus on promoting the latter to emphasize that Americans can choose activities they enjoy.

2. Individuals who are now active, but at less than the recommended level of
   - moderate-intensity physical activity on 5 or more days of the week, or
   - vigorous-intensity physical activity on 3 or more days of the week,

should strive to adopt more consistent activity.

3. Persons who currently engage in moderate-intensity activities on 5 or more days of the week may achieve even greater health benefits by increasing the duration or intensity of their activities.

4. People who currently regularly engage in vigorous-intensity activities should continue to do so.

In this chapter, we'll give you the scientific foundation you need to promote physical activity. You'll find answers to these questions that your target population might have as they consider initiating and maintaining a more active lifestyle:

- how much activity is enough?
- how is physical activity intensity measured?
- how can I safely incorporate physical activity into my lifestyle?

The Definition of "Regular, Moderate" Activity

People can improve the quality of their lives through a life-long practice of moderate amounts of regular physical activity of moderate or vigorous intensity.

USDHHS, 1996

The minimum amount of physical activity required for health benefits can be achieved through moderate- or vigorous-intensity activities sufficient to burn approximately 150 calories of energy per day (1,000 calories per week). The time needed to burn 150 calories of energy depends primarily on the intensity of the activities chosen—the more vigorous the activity, the less time is needed. The recommended amount of physical activity can be achieved by engaging in a variety of moderate- or vigorous-intensity activities throughout the day—

including sports and physical conditioning, a variety of occupational activities, transportational activity, home repair, and other unstructured activities (Jones et al. 1998).Therefore, people should be encouraged to select activities that they enjoy and that fit best into their daily lives.

What Is Meant by "Regular" Physical Activity?

A pattern of physical activity is "regular" if activities are performed

- most days of the week, preferably daily;
- 5 or more days of the week if moderate-intensity activities are chosen; or
- 3 or more days of the week if vigorous-intensity activities are chosen.

What Is "Moderate-Intensity" Physical Activity?

A moderate-intensity activity refers to a level of effort equivalent to

- a "perceived exertion" of 11 to 14 on the Borg scale;
- 3 to 6 metabolic equivalents (METs); any activity that burns 3.5 to 7 kilocalories per minute (kcal/min); or
- the effort a healthy individual might expend while walking briskly, mowing the lawn, dancing, swimming, or bicycling on level terrain, for example.

What Is "Vigorous-Intensity" Physical Activity?

A vigorous-intensity activity refers to the level of effort any one activity requires that is equivalent to

- a "perceived exertion" of 15 or greater on the Borg scale;
- greater than 6 metabolic equivalents (METs); any activity that burns more than 7 kcal/ min; or
- the effort a healthy individual might expend while jogging, mowing the lawn with a nonmotorized pushmower, chopping wood, participating in high-impact aerobic dancing, swimming continuous laps, or bicycling uphill, for example.

What Is the Minimum Recommended *Amount* of Physical Activity Needed to Achieve Health Benefits?

General examples of a recommended *amount* of physical activity for a day would include those found in figure 2.1.

- On average, regularly participating in one or more moderate-intensity or vigorous-intensity activities as required to burn a minimum of 150 kcal/ day, 7 days per week, or total of 1,000 kcal/week (Jones et al. 1998).
- The length of time required to burn 150 kcal in a day depends on the intensity of the activities chosen. For example, if someone selects moderate-intensity activities (at 3.5 to 7 kcal/min), the time required to satisfy the minimum recommendation would be generally 30 minutes per day. The more strenuous or vigorous the activities chosen (>7 kcal/min), the less time needed (22 minutes or less) to burn the minimum of 150 kcal during the day.

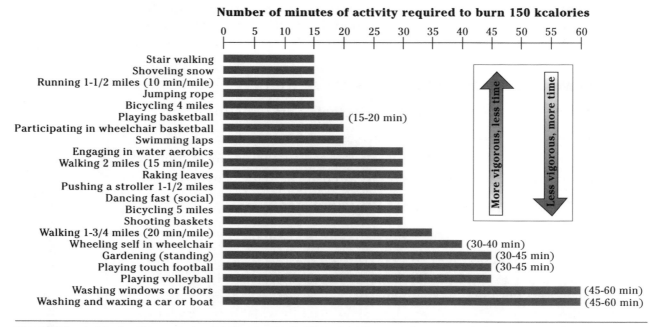

Figure 2.1 Achieving the recommended amount of physical activity can be accomplished by engaging in a variety of moderate- or vigorous-intensity activities. The less vigorous the activity, the more time needed to burn the recommended number of calories. The more vigorous the activity, the less time is needed to burn the same number of calories.
Adapted from USDHHS At-A-Glance 1996

How Many Americans Meet the Current Recommendations?

According to the 1990 National Health Interview Survey, among respondents aged 18 years or older, almost one-third reportedly engaged in moderate activities at least 30 minutes per day or they expended at least 150 kcal/day (or 1,000 kcal/week) in leisure-time physical activities.

While it is encouraging that approximately 32% of U.S. adults in 1990 met current recommended levels of physical activity, more than 60% failed to participate at the recommended levels. Those categorized as less than optimally active were predominantly women, especially women of low educational attainment, of ethnic minorities, and older than 45 years (Jones et al. 1998).

What would help to explain such disparities between genders and socioeconomic subgroups? Perhaps much could be explained by the use of the term "leisure-time physical activity." The proportion of women meeting current moderate-activity recommendations might increase if household and family care activities were counted toward daily totals of physical activity (Jones et al. 1998; Ainsworth et al. 1993b).

If occupational activities were included in national surveys, perhaps differences observed among education subgroups and minority groups would change considerably. Those individuals with lower educational attainment may have jobs that require more physical activity, so that leisure-time physical activity may be irrelevant for these groups (Jones et al. 1998). And in the modern hectic pace of life so common among Americans, if you were to ask any adult, "What physical activities do you do in your leisure time?" he or she might very well reply, "What leisure time?"

Percentage of Americans Who Meet Current Physical Activity Recommendations

U.S. Recommendations for Physical Activity	Adult men	Adult women	Total American adults
1995 CDC-ACSM Guidelines (Pate et al. 1995a) "Every U.S. adult should accumulate 30 minutes or more of moderate-intensity activity on most, preferably all, days of the week."	34.3%	29.8%	32.0%
1996 Surgeon General's Report Guidelines (USDHHS 1996) The report recommends an amount of physical activity sufficient to burn 627.6 kJ/day (150 kcal/day) or 1,484 kJ/week (1,000 kcal/week).	47.7%	29.2%	37.9%

Data from Jones and associates 1998

How to Determine Physical Activity Intensity

The intensity of physical activity is categorized as *light, moderate,* or *vigorous* based on the amount of energy or effort expended in performing the activity. See table 2.1 for a comprehensive chart that lists the intensity levels of many different types of activities.

Individuals can estimate the relative intensity of any physical activity as it applies to their own level of health and fitness by using one of the following methods: the talk test, target heart rate and estimated maximum heart rate, perceived exertion, or MET level.

Table 2.1 General Physical Activities Defined by Level of Intensity

In Accordance with CDC and ACSM Guidelines

Light activity+ less than 3.0 METs* (less than 3.5 kcal/min)	Moderate activity+ 3.0 to 6.0 METs* (3.5 to 7 kcal/min)	Vigorous activity+ greater than 6.0 METs* (more than 7 kcal/min)
Walking casually, less than 3 miles per hour (mph) • walking in the house, in the yard • window shopping, strolling and stopping frequently • casual walking, sauntering, strolling, purposeless wandering	Walking at a moderate or brisk pace of 3 to 4.5 mph on a level surface inside or outside, such as • walking to class, to work, or to the store; • walking for pleasure; • walking the dog; or • walking as a break from work. Walking downstairs or down a hill Racewalking—less than 5 mph Using crutches Hiking Roller skating or in-line skating at a leisurely pace	Racewalking and aerobic walking—5 mph or faster Jogging or running Wheeling your wheelchair Walking and climbing briskly up a hill Marching rapidly—military Backpacking Mountain climbing, orienteering, rock climbing, rapelling Roller skating or in-line skating at a fast pace

* The ratio of exercise metabolic rate to resting metabolic rate. One MET is defined as the energy expenditure for sitting quietly, which, for the average adult, approximates 3.5 ml of oxygen uptake per kilogram of body weight per minute (1.2 kcal/min for a 70-kg individual). For example, a 2-MET activity requires two times the metabolic energy expenditure of sitting quietly.

+ For an average person, defined here as 70 kilogram or 154 pounds. The activity intensity levels portrayed in this chart are most applicable to men aged 30 to 50 years and women aged 20 to 40 years. For older individuals, the classification of activity intensity might be higher. For example, what is moderate intensity to a 40-year-old man might be vigorous for a man in his 70s. Intensity is a subjective classification.

Data for this chart were available only for adults. Therefore, when children's games are listed, the estimated intensity level is for adults participating in children's activities.

To compute the amount of time needed to accumulate 150 kcal, do the following calculation: 150 kcal divided by the MET level of the activity equals the minutes needed to expend 150 kcal. For example: 150 ÷ 3 METs = 50 minutes of participation. Generally, activities in the moderate-intensity range require 25 to 50 minutes to expend a moderate amount of activity, and activities in the vigorous-intensity range would require less than 25 minutes to achieve a moderate amount of activity. Each activity listed is categorized as light, moderate, or vigorous on the basis of current knowledge of the overall level of intensity required for the average person to engage in it, taking into account brief periods when the level of intensity required for the activity might increase or decrease considerably.

Persons with disabilities, including motor function limitations (e.g., quadriplegia) may wish to consult with an exercise physiologist or physical therapist to properly classify the types of physical activities in which they might participate, including assisted exercise. Certain activities classified in this listing as moderate might be vigorous for persons who also must overcome physical challenges or disabilities.

Light activity less than 3.0 METs (less than 3.5 kcal/min)	Moderate activity 3.0 to 6.0 METs (3.5 to 7 kcal/min)	Vigorous activity greater than 6.0 METs (more than 7 kcal/min)
Bicycling less than 5 mph Stationary bicycling—using very light effort	Bicycling 5 to 9 mph, level terrain, or with few hills Stationary bicycling—using moderate effort Unicycling	Bicycling more than 10 mph or bicycling on steep uphill terrain Stationary bicycling—using vigorous effort
Aerobic dancing—stretching and slow warm-up period	Aerobic dancing—low impact Water aerobics	Aerobic dancing—high impact Step aerobics Water jogging Teaching an aerobic dance class
Sitting in the whirlpool or sauna Stretching exercises—slow warm-up	Calisthenics—light Yoga Gymnastics General home exercises, light or moderate effort, getting up and down from the floor Jumping on a trampoline Using a stair climber machine at a light-to-moderate pace Using a rowing machine—with moderate effort Using an exercise rider machine (no tension required)—performing less than approximately 40 repetitions per minute	Calisthenics—push-ups, pull-ups, vigorous effort Karate, judo, tae kwon do, jujitsu Jumping rope Performing jumping jacks Using a stair climber machine at a fast pace Using a rowing machine—with vigorous effort Using an arm cycling machine—with vigorous effort Using a cross-country ski machine Using an exercise rider machine (no tension required)—performing approximately 40 or more repetitions per minute
Weight training—light workout using free weights, Nautilus- or Universal-type weights	Weight training and bodybuilding using free weights, Nautilus- or Universal-type weights	Circuit weight training
—	Boxing—punching bag	Boxing—in the ring, sparring Wrestling—competitive

(continued)

Table 2.1 *(continued)*

Light activity less than 3.0 METs (less than 3.5 kcal/min)	Moderate activity 3.0 to 6.0 METs (3.5 to 7 kcal/min)	Vigorous activity greater than 6.0 METs (more than 7 kcal/min)
Ballroom dancing—very slowly	Ballroom dancing Line dancing Square dancing Folk dancing Modern dancing, disco Ballet	Professional ballroom dancing—energetically Square dancing—energetically Folk dancing—energetically Clogging
Table tennis or Ping-Pong—leisurely	Table tennis—competitive Tennis—doubles	Tennis—singles Wheelchair tennis
Golf—riding a powered golf cart Golf—driving range Playing miniature golf	Golf, wheeling or carrying clubs	—
Playing catch—football or baseball Throwing a baseball	Softball—fast or slow pitch Basketball—shooting baskets Coaching children's or adults' sports	Most competitive sports Football game Basketball game Wheelchair basketball Soccer Rugby Kickball Field or rollerblade hockey Lacrosse
Volleyball—recreational	Volleyball—competitive	Beach volleyball—on sand court

Light activity less than 3.0 METs (less than 3.5 kcal/min)	Moderate activity 3.0 to 6.0 METs (3.5 to 7 kcal/min)	Vigorous activity greater than 6.0 METs (more than 7 kcal/min)
Throwing a frisbee Bowling or lawn bowling Croquet Shuffleboard Horseshoes Pistol or rifle target practice Darts Billiards	Playing frisbee Juggling Curling Cricket—batting and bowling Badminton Archery (nonhunting) Fencing	Handball—general or team Racquetball Squash
—	Downhill skiing—with light effort Ice skating at a leisurely pace (9 mph or less) Snowmobiling Ice sailing	Downhill skiing—racing or with vigorous effort Ice-skating—fast pace or speedskating Cross-country skiing Sledding Tobogganing Playing ice hockey Playing broomball
Swimming—floating	Swimming—recreational Treading water—slowly, moderate effort Diving—springboard or platform Aquatic aerobics Waterskiing Snorkeling Surfing, board or body	Swimming—steady paced laps Synchronized swimming Treading water—fast, vigorous effort Water jogging Water polo Water basketball Scuba diving
Boating—powerboat Yachting	Canoeing or rowing a boat at less than 4 mph Rafting—whitewater Sailing—recreational or competition Paddle boating Kayaking—on a lake, calm water Removing a tarp from a boat Washing or waxing a powerboat or the hull of a sailboat	Canoeing or rowing—4 or more mph Kayaking in whitewater rapids

(continued)

Table 2.1 *(continued)*

Light activity less than 3.0 METs (less than 3.5 kcal/min)	Moderate activity 3.0 to 6.0 METs (3.5 to 7 kcal/min)	Vigorous activity greater than 6.0 METs (more than 7 kcal/min)
Fishing, seated in a boat or while standing along a riverbank Ice fishing	Fishing while walking along a riverbank or while wading in a stream—wearing waders	—
Duck hunting, wading or from a duck blind Hunting with a bow and arrow or crossbow—stationary Pistol shooting or trapshooting—standing	Hunting deer, large or small game Pheasant and grouse hunting Hunting with a bow and arrow or crossbow—walking	—
Horseback riding—walking	Horseback riding—general Saddling or grooming a horse	Horseback riding—trotting, galloping, jumping, or in competition Playing polo
Sitting and playing a board game or video game Sitting while reading, writing, coloring, painting, using a computer	Playing on school playground equipment, moving about, swinging, or climbing Playing hopscotch, 4-square, dodgeball, T-ball, or tetherball Skateboarding Roller-skating or in-line skating—leisurely pace	Running Skipping Jumping rope Performing jumping jacks Roller-skating or in-line skating—fast pace
Sitting and playing most musical instruments	Playing instruments while actively moving; playing in a marching band; playing guitar or drums in a rock band Twirling a baton in a marching band Singing while actively moving about—as on stage or in church	Playing a heavy musical instrument while actively running in a marching band

Light activity less than 3.0 METs (less than 3.5 kcal/min)	Moderate activity 3.0 to 6.0 METs (3.5 to 7 kcal/min)	Vigorous activity greater than 6.0 METs (more than 7 kcal/min)
Gardening and yard work: pruning, weeding while sitting or kneeling, or slowly walking and seeding a lawn Using a riding mower or driving a tractor on firm ground	Gardening and yard work: raking the lawn, bagging grass or leaves, digging, hoeing, light shoveling (less than 10 lbs per minute), or weeding while standing or bending Planting trees, trimming shrubs and trees, hauling branches, stacking wood Pushing a power lawn mower or tiller	Gardening and yard work: heavy or rapid shoveling (more than 10 lbs per minute), digging ditches, or carrying heavy loads Felling trees, carrying large logs, swinging an ax, hand-splitting logs, or climbing and trimming trees Pushing a nonmotorized lawn mower
Using a snowblower	Shoveling light snow	Shoveling heavy snow
Light housework: dusting, vacuuming, sweeping floors, straightening, making beds, cooking or serving food, washing dishes, folding and putting away laundry, sewing, or carrying out light bags of trash Most other household tasks done while sitting or standing	Moderate housework: scrubbing the floor or bathtub while on hands and knees, hanging laundry on a clothesline, sweeping an outdoor area, cleaning out the garage, washing windows, moving light furniture, packing or unpacking boxes, walking and putting household items away, carrying out heavy bags of trash or recyclables (e.g., glass, newspapers, and plastics), or carrying water or firewood General household tasks requiring considerable effort	Heavy housework: moving or pushing heavy furniture (75 lbs or more), carrying household items weighing 25 lbs or more up a flight of stairs, or shoveling coal into a stove Standing, walking, or walking down a flight of stairs while carrying objects weighing 50 lbs or more
Putting groceries away—generally Stocking shelves with food	Putting groceries away—walking and carrying especially large or heavy items less than 50 lbs.	Carrying several heavy bags (25 lbs or more) of groceries at one time up a flight of stairs Grocery shopping while carrying young children *and* pushing a full grocery cart, or pushing two full grocery carts at once

(continued)

Table 2.1 (continued)

Light activity less than 3.0 METs (less than 3.5 kcal/min)	Moderate activity 3.0 to 6.0 METs (3.5 to 7 kcal/min)	Vigorous activity greater than 6.0 METs (more than 7 kcal/min)
Sitting and playing with children Child care: dressing, bathing, feeding, or occasionally lifting young children	Actively playing with children—walking, running, or climbing while playing with children Walking while carrying a child weighing less than 50 lbs Walking while pushing or pulling a child in a stroller or an adult in a wheelchair Carrying a child weighing less than 25 lbs up a flight of stairs Child care: handling uncooperative young children (e.g., chasing, dressing, lifting into car seat), or handling several young children at one time Bathing and dressing an adult	Vigorously playing with children—running longer distances or playing strenuous games with children Racewalking or jogging while pushing a stroller designed for sport use Carrying an adult or a child weighing 25 lbs or more up a flight of stairs Standing or walking while carrying an adult or a child weighing 50 lbs or more
Animal care: feeding domestic animals or sitting and caring for animals	Animal care: shoveling grain, feeding farm animals, or grooming animals Playing with or training animals Manually milking cows or hooking cows up to milking machines	Animal care: forking bales of hay or straw, cleaning a barn or stables, or carrying animals weighing over 50 lbs Handling or carrying heavy animal-related equipment or tack
Light home repair: wiring, plumbing, or repairing appliances	Home repair: cleaning gutters, caulking, refinishing furniture, sanding floors with a power sander, or laying or removing carpet or tiles General home construction work: roofing, painting inside or outside of the house, wall papering, scraping, plastering, or remodeling	Home repair or construction: very hard physical labor, standing or walking while carrying heavy loads of 50 lbs or more, taking heavy loads of 25 lbs or more up a flight of stairs or ladder (e.g., carrying roofing materials onto the roof), or concrete or masonry work

Light activity less than 3.0 METs (less than 3.5 kcal/min)	Moderate activity 3.0 to 6.0 METs (3.5 to 7 kcal/min)	Vigorous activity greater than 6.0 METs (more than 7 kcal/min)
Workshop carpentry	Outdoor carpentry, sawing wood with a power saw	Hand-sawing hardwoods
Light automobile repair Motorcycle or bicycle repair	Automobile bodywork Hand washing and waxing a car	Pushing a disabled car
Occupations that require extended periods of sitting or standing. Tasks frequently requiring movement of little more than hands and fingers. For example: • office work: sitting in meetings or classes, laboratory work, computer terminal work, or standing while sorting or using light office equipment (e.g., photocopying and telefaxing) • sales—while sitting or standing • driving a car, light truck, train, airplane, or heavy equipment that is fully automated with a smooth ride • operating most machinery from a sitting or standing position (e.g., forklift or crane operation) • appliance or automotive repair—light • most light-to-moderate assembly-line work—working with hands	Occupations that require extended periods of walking, pushing or pulling objects weighing less than 75 lbs, standing while lifting objects weighing less than 50 lbs, walking while carrying objects weighing less than 50 lbs, or carrying objects of less than 25 lbs up a flight of stairs. Tasks frequently requiring moderate effort and considerable use of arms, legs, or occasional total body movements. For example: • briskly walking on a level surface while carrying a suitcase or load weighing up to 50 lbs • maid service or cleaning services • waiting tables or institutional dishwashing • driving or maneuvering heavy vehicles (e.g., semi-truck, school bus, tractor, or harvester)—not fully automated and requiring extensive use of arms and legs	Occupations that require extended periods of running, rapid movement, pushing or pulling objects weighing 75 lbs or more, standing while lifting heavy objects of 50 lbs or more, walking while carrying loads of 50 lbs or more, or carrying heavy objects of 25 lbs or more up a flight of stairs. Tasks frequently requiring strenuous effort and extensive total body movements. For example: • running up a flight of stairs while carrying a suitcase or load weighing 25 lbs or more • teaching a class or skill requiring active and strenuous participation, such as aerobics or physical education instructor • firefighting • masonry and heavy construction work • coal mining • manually shoveling or digging ditches • using heavy nonpowered tools

Note: Almost every occupation requires some mix of light, moderate, or vigorous activities, depending on the task at hand. To categorize the activity level of your own position, ask yourself: How many minutes each working day do I spend doing the types of activities described as light, moderate, or vigorous? To arrive at a total workday caloric expenditure, multiply the minutes spent doing activities within each intensity level by the kilocalories corresponding to each level of intensity. Then, add together the total kilocalories spent doing light, moderate, and vigorous activities to arrive at your total energy expenditure in a typical day.

Table 2.1 (continued)

Light activity less than 3.0 METs (less than 3.5 kcal/min)	Moderate activity 3.0 to 6.0 METs (3.5 to 7 kcal/min)	Vigorous activity greater than 6.0 METs (more than 7 kcal/min)
• directing traffic • patient care and nursing	• operating heavy power tools (e.g., drills and jackhammers) • many homebuilding tasks (e.g., electrical work, plumbing, carpentry, dry wall, and painting • farming—feeding and grooming animals, milking cows, shoveling grain; picking fruit from trees, or picking vegetables • packing boxes for shipping or moving • assembly-line work—tasks requiring movement of the entire body, arms, or legs with moderate effort • mail carriers—walking while carrying a mailbag • patient care—bathing, dressing, and moving patients or physical therapy	• most forestry work • farming—forking straw, baling hay, cleaning barn, or poultry work • moving items professionally • loading and unloading a truck

Adapted from Ainsworth BE, Haskell WL, Leon AS, et al. Compendium of physical activities: classification of energy costs of human physical activities. *Medicine and Science in Sports and Exercise* 1993; 25(1):71–80. Adapted with technical assistance from Dr. Barbara Ainsworth.

The Talk Test

The talk test method of measuring intensity is relatively simple. A person who is active at a light- or moderate-intensity level should be able to carry on a conversation comfortably while engaging in the activity. If a person becomes winded or too out of breath to carry on a conversation, he or she is exercising vigorously.

Target Heart Rate and Estimated Maximum Heart Rate

Physical activity intensity can be monitored by determining whether a person's pulse or heart rate is within the target zone during exercise. For moderate physical activity, a person's target heart rate should be 50 to 70% of his or her maximum heart rate. This maximum rate is based on the person's age. An estimate of a person's maximum age-related heart rate can be obtained by subtracting the person's age from 220 (Long et al. 1992). For example, for a 50-year-old person, the estimated maximum age-related heart rate would be calculated as 220 – 50 years = 170 beats per minute (bpm). The 50% and 70% levels would be:

50% level: 170 $\times$ 0.50 = 85 bpm, and

70% level: 170 $\times$ 0.70 = 119 bpm.

Thus, moderate-intensity physical activity for a 50-year-old person will require that the heart rate remains between 85 and 119 bpm during physical activity.

Taking Your Heart Rate

Generally, for someone to determine whether he or she is exercising within the heart rate target zone, the person must stop exercising briefly to take their pulse. You can take the pulse at the neck, the wrist, or the chest. We recommend the wrist. You can feel the radial pulse on the artery of the wrist in line with the thumb. Place the tips of the index and middle fingers over the artery and press lightly. Do not use the thumb. Take a full 60-second count of the heartbeats. Start the count on a beat, which is counted as "zero." If this number falls between 85 and 119 bpm in the case of the 50-year-old person, he or she is active within the target range for moderate-intensity activity.

Perceived Exertion

A third method of determining exercise intensity is perceived exertion. Perceived exertion is based on the physiological sensations a person experiences during physical activity, including increased heart rate, increased respiration or breathing rate, increased sweating, and muscle fatigue. During physical activity, individuals can self-monitor the intensity of their activities by paying attention to the physical exertion they are experiencing and using this information to slow down or accelerate their movements. People can use perceived exertion to pace themselves. This is also the preferred method to assess intensity among those individuals who take medications that affect heart rate or pulse.

An individual can use the Borg Rating of Perceived Exertion (RPE) scale (see page 31) to assign numbers to how he or she feels during physical activity or exercise. Although this is a subjective rating, a high correlation exists between a person's perceived exertion rating times 10 and the actual heart rate during physical activity; so a person's exertion rating may provide a fairly reasonable estimate of the actual heart rate during exercise (Borg 1982). For example, if a person's rating of perceived exertion (RPE) is 12, then $12 \times 10 = 120$; so the heart rate should be approximately 120 beats per minute. Note that this calculation is only an approximation of heart rate, and the actual heart rate can vary considerably depending on age and physical condition. Practitioners generally agree that perceived exertion ratings in the approximate range of 12 to 14 suggest that physical activity is being performed at a moderate level of intensity.

RPE Scale Instructions

While exercising, we want you to rate your perception of exertion, i.e., how heavy and strenuous the exercise feels to you. The perception of exertion depends mainly on the strain and fatigue in your muscles and on your feeling of breathlessness or aches in your chest.

Look at the rating scale; we want you to use this scale from 6 to 20, where 6 means "no exertion at all" and 20 means "maximal exertion."

6	No exertion at all
7	
8	Extremely light
9	Very light
10	
11	Light
12	
13	Somewhat hard
14	
15	Hard (heavy)
16	
17	Very hard
18	
19	Extremely hard
20	Maximal exertion

Borg RPE scale
© Gunnar Borg, 1970, 1985, 1994, 1998

9   corresponds to "very light" exercise. For a healthy person, it is like walking slowly at his or her own pace for some minutes.

13   on the scale is "somewhat hard" exercise, but it still feels OK to continue.

17   "very hard" is very strenuous. A healthy person can still go on, but he or she really has to push him- or herself. It feels very heavy, and the person is very tired.

19   on the scale is an extremely strenuous exercise level. For most people this is the most strenuous exercise they have ever experienced.

Try to appraise your feeling of exertion as honestly as possible, without thinking about what the actual physical load is. Don't underestimate it, but don't overestimate it either. It's your own feeling of effort and exertion that's important, not how it compares to other people's. What other people think is not important either. Look at the scales and the expressions and then give a number.

MET Level

Although the intensity of certain activities is commonly characterized as light, moderate, or vigorous, many activities can be classified in any one or all three categories simply on the basis of the level of personal effort involved in carrying out the activity. Table 2.1 provides one method of characterizing physical activities at different levels of effort based on the standard of a metabolic equivalent (MET). This unit is used to estimate the metabolic cost (oxygen consumption) of physical activity (Ainsworth et al. 1993a).

One MET equals the resting metabolic rate and is defined in practical terms as the energy (oxygen) expended as someone sits quietly, perhaps while talking to someone on the phone or while reading a book. Less than one MET is complete inactivity, such as reclining while watching television or lying in bed—motionless, yet awake. Energy expended that is greater than one MET requires physical activity. The more intense or vigorous the activity, the higher the MET. Any activity that burns 3 to 6 METs is considered moderate activity.

Understanding Intensity Levels

According to exercise scientists, physical activity intensity levels are defined as follows (USDHHS 1996):

- *Vigorous* physical activities generally require sustained, rhythmic movements performed at greater than 70% of an individual's age-related maximum heart rate.

- *Moderate* physical activities generally require sustained, rhythmic movements that are performed at 50 to 70% of an individual's age-related maximum heart rate. *Moderate intensity* is equivalent to:

  —a person's "perceived exertion" of 12 to 14 on the Borg scale

  —any activity that burns 3.5 to 7 kilocalories per minute (approximately 3 to 6 METs)

  —a category of activities such as brisk walking, mowing the lawn, thorough housecleaning, dancing, and recreational swimming or bicycling, just to name a few. See table 2.1 for a more complete list of moderate-intensity activities.

- *Light* or *very light* physical activities are generally performed at less than 50% of age-related maximum heart rate.

Safety Considerations for a Physically Active Lifestyle

Occasionally, we learn about an athlete who died suddenly while jogging or while exercising strenuously. These athletes typically had underlying cardiovascular disease that, when coupled with extremely strenuous activity, resulted in their death. Such events can plant doubts and fears in the minds of people who are thinking about leading a more active lifestyle. "Me? Exercise and end up having a heart attack? No way!" However, sudden deaths due to underlying cardiovascular disease are extremely rare, particularly among individuals participating in moderate physical activity (Pratt 1995).

> Given what we know about the health benefits of physical activity, it should be mandatory to get a doctor's permission NOT to exercise.
>
> *Per-Olof Åstrand, 1986*
> *Karolinska Institute Stockholm, Sweden*

In fact, research suggests that the health risks associated with a sedentary lifestyle *far outweigh* the risks associated with being active (Pate et al. 1995a). Most "apparently" healthy adults of any age may engage in moderate-intensity physical activities such as walking or gardening without a medical evaluation. Even if an individual has several risk factors for cardiovascular disease, he or she can safely begin moderate-intensity physical activities (Patrick et al. 1994).

Persons with known cardiovascular disease or persons who have already experienced a major cardiovascular event, such as a heart attack, stroke, or heart surgery, should have a physical evaluation by their physician before engaging in even a moderate physical activity program. But other than in those cases, most adults do not need to consult their physicians before engaging in

When Is a Medical Evaluation Necessary?

Individuals should obtain a medical evaluation before engaging in *vigorous* physical activity if they (Pate et al. 1995)

- use tobacco.
- currently have some form of cardiovascular disease.
- have two or more of the following risk factors for cardiovascular diseases:
  —high blood pressure,
  —high blood cholesterol,
  —a family history of heart disease,
  —diabetes mellitus, or
  —obesity.
- are men older than 40 years of age.
- are women older than 50 years of age.
- answer "yes" to any of the questions listed in the Physical Activity Readiness Questionnaire (PAR-Q) on page 34. The PAR-Q is a simple screening questionnaire used as a preliminary tool to identify individuals who cannot participate in fitness testing or engage in physical activity without physician clearance.

moderate-intensity physical activity. If, however, they are planning to engage in a new *vigorous* physical activity, then men over age 40 and women over age 50 should also consult a physician first to make sure they do not have heart disease or other health problems.

Common Risks

The most common risk associated with physical activity is injury to the musculoskeletal system—the bones, joints, tendons, and muscles. These injuries are usually not serious, often require no treatment other than a few days of rest, and can be minimized by taking sensible precautions. Most musculoskeletal injuries related to physical activity may be prevented by gradually working up to the desired level of activity and by avoiding excessive amounts of activity at one time.

Therefore, to avoid soreness and injury, people who have not been regularly active and are thinking about increasing their levels of physical activity should be encouraged to start out slowly, incorporating even a few minutes of increased activity into their day, gradually building up to the desired amount of activity, and giving their bodies time to adjust (Pate et al. 1995a).

Tips for Avoiding Activity-Induced Injury

Keeping the following tips in mind can help prevent common injuries associated with participating in physical activity.

- Listen to your body—monitor your level of fatigue, heart rate, and physical discomfort.
- Be aware of the signs of overexertion. Breathlessness and muscle soreness could be danger signs.

Determine Your Readiness to Participate in Physical Activity

Complete the following questionnaire (reprinted from the Canadian Society for Exercise Physiology 1994) to help you determine your readiness to begin or intensify a physical activity program.

Physical Activity Readiness
Questionnaire – PAR-Q
(revised 1994)

PAR - Q & YOU

(A Questionnaire for People Aged 15 to 69)

Regular physical activity is fun and healthy, and increasingly more people are starting to become more active every day. Being more active is very safe for most people. However, some people should check with their doctor before they start becoming much more physically active.

If you are planning to become much more physically active than you are now, start by answering the seven questions in the box below. If you are between the ages of 15 and 69, the PAR-Q will tell you if you should check with your doctor before you start. If you are over 69 years of age, and you are not used to being very active, check with your doctor.

Common sense is your best guide when you answer these questions. Please read the questions carefully and answer each one honestly: check YES or NO.

YES	NO	
☐	☐	1. Has your doctor ever said that you have a heart condition <u>and</u> that you should only do physical activity recommended by a doctor?
☐	☐	2. Do you feel pain in your chest when you do physical activity?
☐	☐	3. In the past month, have you had chest pain when you were not doing physical activity?
☐	☐	4. Do you lose your balance because of dizziness or do you ever lose consciousness?
☐	☐	5. Do you have a bone or joint problem that could be made worse by a change in your physical activity?
☐	☐	6. Is your doctor currently prescribing drugs (for example, water pills) for your blood pressure or heart condition?
☐	☐	7. Do you know of <u>any other reason</u> why you should not do physical activity?

If you answered

YES to one or more questions

Talk with your doctor by phone or in person BEFORE you start becoming much more physically active or BEFORE you have a fitness appraisal. Tell your doctor about the PAR-Q and which questions you answered YES.

- You may be able to do any activity you want—as long as you start slowly and build up gradually. Or, you may need to restrict your activities to those which are safe for you. Talk with your doctor about the kinds of activities you wish to participate in and follow his/her advice.
- Find out which community programs are safe and helpful for you.

NO to all questions

If you answered NO honestly to <u>all</u> PAR-Q questions, you can be reasonably sure that you can:

- start becoming much more physically active—begin slowly and build up gradually. This is the safest and easiest way to go.
- take part in a fitness appraisal—this is an excellent way to determine your basic fitness so that you can plan the best way for you to live actively.

DELAY BECOMING MUCH MORE ACTIVE:

- if you are not feeling well because of a temporary illness such as a cold or a fever—wait until you feel better; or
- if you are or may be pregnant—talk to your doctor before you start becoming more active.

Please note: If your health changes so that you then answer YES to any of the above questions, tell your fitness or health professional. Ask whether you should change your physical activity plan.

<u>Informed Use of the PAR-Q:</u> The Canadian Society for Exercise Physiology, Health Canada, and their agents assume no liability for persons who undertake physical activity, and if in doubt after completing this questionnaire, consult your doctor prior to physical activity.

You are encouraged to copy the PAR-Q but only if you use the entire form

NOTE: If the PAR-Q is being given to a person before he or she participates in a physical activity program or a fitness appraisal, this section may be used for legal or administrative purposes.

I have read, understood and completed this questionnaire. Any questions I had were answered to my full satisfaction.

NAME _____

SIGNATURE _____   DATE _____

SIGNATURE OF PARENT _____   WITNESS _____
or GUARDIAN (for participants under the age of majority)

©Canadian Society for Exercise Physiology   Supported by: Health   Santé
Société canadienne de physiologie de l'exercice   CANADA   Canada   Canada

- Be aware of the warning signs and signals of a heart attack, such as sweating, chest and arm pain, dizziness, and lightheadedness.
- Use the appropriate equipment and clothing for the activity.
- Take 3 to 5 minutes at the beginning of any physical activity to properly warm up your muscles through increasingly more intense activity, such as stretching or jogging. As you near the end of the activity, cool down by decreasing the level of intensity through walking or stretching.
- Start at an easy pace—increase time or distance very gradually.
- Drink plenty of water throughout the day to replace lost fluids. Drink a glass of water before you get moving, and drink another half cup every 15 minutes that you remain active (*Health* 1998).

Tips for People Who Have Been Inactive for a While

- Use a sensible approach by starting out slowly.
- Begin by choosing moderate-intensity activities you most enjoy.
- Gradually build up the duration of the activity, adding a few minutes every few days or so, until you can comfortably perform a minimum recommended amount of activity (150 calories burned per day).
- As the minimum amount becomes easier, gradually increase either the length of time performing an activity or increase the intensity of the activity, or both.

Suggested Reading

For a list of organizations, agencies, and selected program materials for promoting physical activity, see:

Resource A, for general resources

Chapter 6, for environment-related resources

Chapter 9, for worksite-related resources

Chapter 10, for school-related resources

For suggestions on a commonsense approach to starting a physical activity program to minimize the possibilities of injury, read:

Blair SN. *Living With Exercise: Improving Your Health Through Moderate Physical Activity*. Dallas: American Health Publishing Company, 1991.

Kopy Kit Reproducible Resources. Fitness injury prevention: tips for exercising safely. In: *Health and Wellness: Fitness and Nutrition*. Emeryville, CA: Parlay International, 1990.

To learn more about stretching and flexibility exercises, muscular strength and endurance training, and training to improve cardiorespiratory fitness, read:

American Heart Association with the National Heart, Lung, and Blood Institute. *Exercise and Your Heart: A Guide to Physical Activity*. Dallas, 1993.

Hockey RV. *Physical Fitness: The Pathway to Healthful Living*. St. Louis: Mosby, 1996.

Kopy Kit Reproducible Resources. *Health and Wellness: Fitness and Nutrition*. Emeryville, CA: Parlay International, 1990.

McGlynn G. *Dynamics of Fitness: A Practical Approach*. Madison, WI: Brown & Benchmark, 1996.

Miller DK. *Fitness: A Lifetime Commitment*. Boston: Allyn & Bacon, 1995.

Nieman DC. *Fitness and Sports Medicine: A Health Related Approach* (3rd Edition). Palo Alto, CA: Bull Publishing Company, 1995.

To learn more about assessing physical activity levels and physical fitness, read:

Ainsworth BE, Montoye HJ, Leon AS. Methods of assessing physical activity during leisure and work. In: Bouchard C, Shephard RJ, Stephens T, editors. *Physical Activity, Fitness, and Health: International Proceedings and Consensus Statement*. Champaign, IL: Human Kinetics, 1994:146–159.

American College of Sports Medicine. *Guidelines for Exercise Testing and Prescription* (5th Edition). Baltimore: Williams and Wilkins, 1995.

Joint Task Force of the American Alliance for Health, Physical Education, Recreation and Dance and the Cooper Institute for Aerobics Research. *Physical Best—Fitnessgram: You Stay Active*. Dallas: Cooper Institute for Aerobics Research, 1995.

HealthScreen Software

HealthScreen is an advanced computer software program that can be used by health club instructors as well as university professors and students in exercise physiology classes. It provides a systematic method of screening individuals to see if they can participate safely in exercise and fitness programs. The program uses the preexercise screening guidelines developed by the American College of Sports Medicine in 1995. The *HealthScreen* software is available from

Human Kinetics
P.O. Box 5076
1607 N. Market St
Champaign, IL 61825-5076
Phone: 800-747-4457
Fax: 217-351-2674
Website: **http://www.humankinetics.com**

Part II

Strategies for Changing Physical Activity Behavior

In part I, we established the scientific foundation for a physical activity promotion program—the scientific research that suggests what it is we want people to do. The goal is to get Americans moving—to adopt physically active lifestyles. But what can you do to motivate people to choose to be active in their daily lives? What information and skills do people need, and how do you move them toward action? How can you change the environment within your organization, worksite, school, or neighborhood so that it will foster successful behavior change? In part II, we will explore some of the answers to these difficult questions and give you effective strategies for changing your target population's physical activity behavior and getting them committed to a lifelong habit of healthy movement.

Follow along as we introduce the social marketing approach to physical activity promotion: the notion that it is the needs, desires, and intentions of your target population that will guide your program planning.

In chapter 3 you'll be guided through the process of developing a profile of your target audience and assessing its readiness to change its physical activity behavior for the better. Chapter 4 will explain the basics of behavior change theory and will introduce to you the concept of balancing intervention strategies that focus on the individual and on the environment. You'll also be introduced to what we call the intervention puzzle—the seven essential components, that, when put together in a combination tailored to your target population, will result in an effective behavior change intervention.

The last two chapters in part II build on the intervention puzzle theme by covering in much more detail the individual aspects (chapter 5) and environmental aspects (chapter 6) of successful physical activity promotion. No matter what your population's needs are, you'll find in these chapters creative ideas you can put to use in your community now. You'll also find in chapter 6 a comprehensive list of organizations, programs, and agencies across America that can help you create a supportive environment for your unique target population.

Chapter 3 | Targeting Your Efforts

Where does one begin in translating scientific messages into consumer-friendly messages or in developing a program plan responsive to the needs of the community? Let's start by recalling a lesson you may have learned during childhood: Stop, Look, and Listen!

- Stop rushing into problem solving with "one-size-fits-all" strategies and expert-driven solutions.
- Look beyond traditional epidemiologic data and scientific research for guidance in determining your plan of action. Look also to the results of quantitative and qualitative behavioral and market research to vividly describe the very people you intend to reach.

- Listen carefully as members of your intended audience express their attitudes and expectations, their wants and intentions, their perceived motivations and barriers to a desired course of action. Herein lie the greatest clues to determining which pieces of the intervention puzzle will most effectively foster sustainable behavior change.

As people coming from different perspectives interact, they sometimes question the credibility of those who see it differently. To resolve these differences and to restore credibility, one must exercise empathy, seeking first to understand the point of view of the other person.

Stephen R. Covey, 1989

Many successful program planners begin by applying a social marketing approach to program development. Simply defined, *social marketing* is a process that applies business marketing principles and techniques to social and health-related issues with the goal of bringing about behavior change in a well-defined group of people, known as the *target audience* or *target population* (Andreasen 1995; Sutton et al. 1995).

Social marketing is not a theory; nor is it a communication strategy. It is an approach to strategic planning that puts consumers back into the driver's seat by taking into account what matters most to them and by focusing on their perceptions of the problem and its potential solutions. By clearly defining whom you will reach and carefully exploring the characteristics of your target audience, you will be equipped with the information needed to create an *audience profile* that vividly describes the people you intend to reach (Andreasen 1995; W. Smith 1998).

As the social marketing process unfolds, you will discover what matters most to members of your target audience—what they see as benefits to being more physically active, what they think keeps them from being optimally active, whether they intend to do more, and what they believe would help them to do more. At that moment you will be ready to reach into your professional arsenal of educational theories, behavior change models, and intervention strategies to find a number of possible solutions.

However, no one theory or model holds the definitive answers to understanding the complexity of behavior change. Like a road map, it can only guide your way. Perhaps the greatest challenge to program planners is recognizing how to put the puzzle pieces of intervention together—how to draw from a variety of theoretical perspectives to customize or *tailor* a plan of action that will satisfy the needs as well as the desires expressed by the targeted population. While many roads may lead to success, which one you choose depends on your goal. How you get there depends on your target audience. Targeting involves these three customer-driven issues, which will be covered in this chapter:

1. Who should be your target audience?
2. What is that target audience like? What is its profile?
3. How can you tailor your intervention components to make them most effective in reaching, engaging, motivating, enabling, and sustaining the program audience in achieving the program goal?

Keeping Your Eyes on the Goal

Precisely whom do you wish to reach or influence with your physical activity promotion messages, programs, or policies? Selecting the population you desire to reach will be easier if you keep in mind what it is you are trying to accomplish. Your overall vision or mission statement is central to all decision making. It will keep you and your team focused, even when unforeseen opportunities tempt you to take divergent paths.

By posting your mission statement in a prominent location and keeping your program goals clearly in view, each day you can ask your team, "How will the decisions we make today bring us closer to our goal?" Chapter 7 covers in more detail the process of setting program goals and objectives.

Defining Your Target Population

Whatever your goal, your desire may be to design an intervention that will effectively change behavior to some extent. But any intervention, whether its effects are planned or unplanned, will influence some people more than others. By focusing on a specific and narrow segment of the population, you can make strategic program decisions that increase the likelihood that the people who are most likely to hear, interpret, and respond appropriately to your call to action are also the very people you most want to reach.

Targeting takes place either by design or by default.

Sutton et al., 1995

Program planners who choose not to segment a population and precisely target their efforts may inadvertently

- design programs that reach and benefit persons who need it least, such as people who are already maintaining a physically active lifestyle (e.g., providing worksite gyms or vigorous aerobics classes, which often do little more than give already active people a more convenient place to exercise and fail to have a positive effect on sedentary employees); and

- offer people programs they neither want nor need, thus serving everyone poorly and no one well.

Realizing Joe Public Doesn't Live Here Anymore

Clearly defining the population you intend to reach and involving them in strategic program planning is central to the process of social marketing. Yet consumer research-based and targeted approaches to program planning are frequently viewed with skepticism by administrators or public officials who believe it is their mandate to serve the entire population, not just certain targeted segments. Too often these well-meaning officials limit their support to "one-size-fits-all" programs or generic communication strategies, with the intention of reaching "the general public" or everyone in a population all at once.

Unfortunately, "general public" strategies are rarely effective or justifiable (Sutton et al. 1995). In fact, the larger population is so diverse that the public is really anything but general and "the average citizen" or the "typical American household" no longer exist (Francese 1995). Very simply, "Joe Public" doesn't live here anymore; perhaps he never did.

Staggering Your Approach

Whenever you focus your efforts on one population segment, you will miss some others. But perhaps the question is not *whether* you will try to reach nearly everyone in your community or organization, but rather *when* and *how*. By dividing your population strategically into smaller groups of people who share similar characteristics, you can set priorities and choose one or more segmented groups as your initial target audience.

When additional resources become available, you may be able to reach additional groups with interventions tailored specifically to their different needs. Multiple campaigns can occur simultaneously or can be staggered over time.

Success in any one segment will make it easier to reach others, both as you learn what program components are most effective and as you demonstrate to administrators and potential partners the value of investing resources wisely. Eventually, it may be possible to effectively reach nearly everyone in your worksite, school, or community.

Cutting the Population Pie

Defining and segmenting a target audience is the dynamic process of focusing on people who share similar traits, then learning about their characteristics and opinions until it becomes obvious that the larger audience consists of even smaller groups that have more specific traits in common.

There are many ways to divide a population into smaller groups or segments—for example, by certain demographic, geographic, physical, behavioral, or psychographic attributes. Yet, no one characteristic is sufficient to define a target audience. By combining attributes, you will be able to identify people who not only exhibit or express similar desires, needs, motivations, or life situations, but who are also likely to react similarly to a particular intervention or communication strategy. The five major categories of population characteristics are demographic, geographic, physical, behavioral, and psychographic. These characteristics are summarized on page 45 and are more fully explained in the following sections.

Demographic Characteristics

Demographics include race or ethnicity, gender, age or age cohort, marital status, years of education, income, occupation, place and type of residence, and qualities related to family status, such as the number and age of children

Understanding Population Characteristics

Population characteristic	Definition of characteristic	What the characteristic reveals
Demographic	The kind of information the Census Bureau might collect	Who they are
Geographic	Picture maps and clusters	Where they are
Physical	The kind of information you would find in a medical record	Who has special needs; who has a physical incentive or barrier to action
Behavioral	Observable actions; their lifestyle	What they do; what they don't do; what they do instead of the desired behavior
Media use	What they read, listen to, or watch with any regularity	Where they gather information; which channels might reach them
Life path points	The places they go frequently or in the course of a typical day	Where we can find them
Psychographic	Their own expressions and frame of mind; their beliefs, attitudes, and opinions	What they think and their reason why; when they are most teachable and reachable

Adapted from Maibach EW, Maxfield A, Ladin K, Slater M. Translating health psychology into effective health communication: The American Healthstyles Audience Segmentation Project. *Journal of Health Psychology* 1996; 1:261–278.

living in the home or the presence or absence of a spouse in the home. Age cohorts define generations by their year of birth and by the year in which they "came of age" (age 18) (see page 46). Generational ties link otherwise disparate individuals of varying education, income, and life stage by major events that occurred during the group's lifetime and tended to shape their perspectives on life from that time on (Meredith and Schewe 1994).

Understanding a cohort's defining characteristics can help a program planner create services or craft messages that will resonate with specifically targeted consumers. For example, America's oldest citizens at the turn of the millennium want to be rewarded for years of self-sacrifice and hard work, whereas baby boomers who were born in times of great economic prosperity have a tendency to believe that a comfortable living is their birthright (Smith and Clurman 1997).

Geographic Characteristics

Geographic information groups people by topography or political boundaries (e.g., by state, region, county, township, city, neighborhood, school district, or political district lines). Geographic distinctions help one to visualize the extent to which people are either scattered or clustered.

By mapping or clustering groups of people, program planners can make strategic decisions regarding communication or service delivery channels, the allocation of resources in accordance with the density of potential program users, the placement of intervention sites, or the political districts that require advocacy efforts.

Understanding U.S. Cohorts

U.S. population cohort		Born between...	Coming of age (18 yrs) between...	Age range by the year 2000
Depression generation		1912 and 1921	1920 and 1939	79 to 88 years old
World War II generation		1922 and 1927	1940 and 1945	73 to 78 years old
Post-War generation		1928 and 1945	1946 and 1963	55 to 72 years old
Boomers I generation		1946 and 1954	1964 and 1972	46 to 54 years old
Boomers II generation		1955 and 1965	1973 and 1983	35 to 45 years old
Generation X generation		1966 and 1976	1984 and 1994	24 to 34 years old
Millennial generation		1977 and 1994	1995 and 2012	6 to 23 years old

Physical Characteristics

Physical characteristics describe people according to their physical conditions, disease risk factors, or physical challenges. For example, people might be grouped by their diagnosis of heart disease, their degree of obesity, or their reliance on wheelchairs for mobility.

Behavioral Characteristics

Behavioral characteristics describe people according to the things they do—their observable behaviors, such as reading a daily newspaper, working outside of the home, using mass transit, participating in a class, bicycling for pleasure, or frequently shopping in a particular store.

Behavioral data, such as that found in national health or lifestyle surveys, can describe what people most enjoy doing or identify which people are least physically active. Behavioral characteristics also include media use patterns—when and where people are ready to hear a behavior-changing message, what channels reach them, and which channels they apparently trust.

By learning what people do and where they go during the normal course of a day, you discover where you are most likely to find them. These "life path points"—the places people frequent (e.g., grocery store, pharmacy, post office, bank, shopping center, laundromat, or library), the sights familiar to them (e.g., billboard, bus stop poster, or daily newspaper), and their choices in communication channels (e.g., people, print, or electronic)—provide you with valuable insights into how you can reach them most effectively (King 1991). While behavioral characteristics describe what people do, they cannot reveal *why* people do them. That is where psychographic characteristics come into play.

Psychographic Characteristics

Psychographic characteristics include descriptions of people's personality traits, beliefs, opinions, preferences, feelings of self-efficacy, levels of self-esteem, attitudes, willingness to take risks, intentions, and readiness to change. Most importantly, psychographic information provides clues as to why people behave as they do.

Narrowing Your Focus

As you decide upon the one or more population segments you will target with intervention strategies, you might find it helpful to weigh and prioritize a number of criteria in relation to one another and to your program goals (Sutton et al. 1995). As you try to decide which of several population segments or target populations you will try to reach first, ask yourself how each group passes the "Ability" test.

The list on page 48 lists a number of "ability" factors that describe some of the variables you might want to consider before selecting one target audience over another. While each factor has its pros and cons, all may be important to your decision-making process. Certainly, no one factor alone is sufficient to determine the target audience. The relative importance of the ability factors will vary according to your situation; so feel free to add a few more "ability" categories of your own designing. Try drawing a matrix with your most likely target audience segments across the top, and the various ability factors down the side. Now rank each segment by each of the factors to determine which segment rates highest and is a likely target audience to achieve your program's goals.

"Ability" Factors

Impact-ability

How many people must you reach with a behavior-changing message or intervention strategy if you are going to make a difference? How large must the segment be to have a public health significance? How will each potential segment meet these criteria—how large is the population in this segment, and is it large enough to make a difference in the problem you are trying to address?

Benefit-ability

Who would benefit most from intervention? What physical, social, or emotional characteristics might distinguish one group of people as needing intervention or potentially benefiting from it more than others (e.g., higher morbidity and mortality rates, at greater risk, or at a critical time when negative consequences might be avoided)?

Access-ability

How easily, affordably, or practically can you reach the population segment given your current resources? How readily accessible is this segment, considering your influence with this population? Is anyone else reaching this segment effectively and are they potential partners? Remember, there is no such thing as a "hard-to-reach" population, only populations that require more abundant or creative strategies to reach them.

Account-ability

To whom must your program remain accountable? And to what extent do those stakeholders determine the focus of the program (e.g., by job responsibilities, source of funding, policies mandated by the administration, specified program criteria)? Are you in a situation in which your target audience has been determined for you, to some extent, or do you have the freedom to choose any population segment within a defined geographic or political boundary?

Achieve-ability

What is most reasonable and feasible for you, given your particular situation? What practical, political, or financial constraints must you overcome if you choose to address one group of people versus another? And remember, constraints can be overcome with a little creativity and some innovative partnering. Have a "can-do" attitude as you approach this task.

Response-ability

Who is most ready, willing, and able to respond or to take the desired action? This factor ranks groups of people by their readiness to change, their stage of change, their life stage, or their competence in certain skills necessary for change.

Remember that the goal in program planning is not to design your message or service, then search for the population segment most likely and able to respond, but rather to examine the needs of a target population and formulate a call to action that is reasonable and achievable for them. If those you wish to reach do not have the means to follow through desirably, then you must either redesign your communication or intervention strategy to fit their needs or find program partners who can bridge the gap and overcome perceived barriers to action (Balch 1996).

Visualizing Your Intended Audience

Once you have defined your target audience, your next task is to create an *audience profile* that describes them vividly and thoroughly. Imagine your target audience as two or three individuals standing before you. Can you paint a detailed portrait of them in your mind? How would they look? In what surroundings would you find them? What would they be doing in this picture? To paint such a portrait, you must really know your target audience (W. Smith 1998).

Become familiar with your audience's lifestyle and behaviors—what they do or don't do, where they go and how they spend their time, with whom they are likely to interact, and the values, attitudes, and beliefs that greatly determine their actions. The more vividly you can describe your audience, the more likely you will discover what would move them along the continuum of behavior change. Pages 50–52 lists questions that when answered may help you paint a mental portrait of your target audience. Resource C is a sample audience profile that describes the target audience of CDC's "Ready. Set. It's Everywhere You Go" physical activity campaign.

Have You Segmented Enough?

How do you know when you've segmented enough? The degree of segmentation needed depends to a great extent on the nature of the problem you are trying to address. For example, if your goal were to eradicate a deadly disease spreading worldwide and you had available to you an effective vaccine against that disease, then your target audience would include every person in the world deemed at risk. If, on the other hand, you held a cure for a very rare disease that affects only a few hundred people, your target audience would be very small. Herein lies the answer. You will have segmented enough when you have identified a target population small enough to reach, yet large enough to be capable of having public health significance—of making a difference in the problem you wish to address.

If you believe that sedentary individuals in our society could significantly improve the quality of their lives by becoming at least moderately active, then you might become eager to reach each and every sedentary person with this life-changing message. Yet, if you were to include in your target audience every sedentary person in your community, would you have set a realistic or doable goal in your situation? Consider once again the "Ability" factors on page 48. The "target practice" on pages 54–56 may help you in focusing on the target population most right for you.

> You have segmented enough if you have defined a target audience small enough to reach, yet large enough to make a difference.
>
> *Bill Smith, EdD, 1998*

Information to Consider When Profiling a Target Audience

Demographic data

- Age range; age cohort
- Gender
- Ethnicity
- Educational level
- Employment status, occupation
- Marital status
- Presence and number of children in the home

Geographic information

- What geographic places do members of your target audience share in common (e.g., residence, workplace, school, life path points, political boundary, county, state)?
- Can they be clustered within a defined geographic area, or are they scattered?

Current behaviors and lifestyle

- How would you characterize the lifestyle of people within your target audience?
- In what life stage (or stages) are they?
- How physically active are they . . . on the job? at home? at school? during their leisure time?
- What do they do for recreation (e.g., watch television, read, take trips with the family, go to the movies)?
- What competes with the desired behavior (i.e., what are people doing instead of being physically active)?
- What other factors in their lifestyles will support or deter their efforts to be physically active (e.g., residence, occupation, income, tobacco use, social influences)?
- What other health- or physical activity-related messages and programs are currently being targeted at your own intended audience? What specific behaviors are these programs promoting? Do they complement or contradict your own program goals?

Values, beliefs, attitudes

- What would members of the target audience describe as their highest priorities (e.g., personal faith, time with family and friends, home life, work life, health, longevity, quality of lifestyle, financial security)?
- What would they describe as their greatest concerns or problems (e.g., lack of time, job security, child care, crime, finances)?
- What are the predominant needs and wants of your target audience?
- How can physical activity be linked to these overriding priorities, concerns, needs, or wants?
- How important to them is a healthy lifestyle? Do they believe that physical activity is an important or necessary component of a healthy lifestyle?
- Is looking good, feeling good about themselves, being energetic, or some other quality more important to them?
- Do they have a positive or negative self-image or body image?
- Do they see themselves as active, and are those perceptions accurate?
- If less than optimally active, do they intend to increase their physical activity in the foreseeable future?
- What is their level of readiness to change regarding physical activity-related behaviors?

- How physically active do they wish to be and how do their personal goals compare to nationally recommended levels of physical activity?
- Is being active the goal, or will being active simply help them accomplish a different goal—such as spending time with their families or getting a job done?
- What do they believe increased physical activity could do for them? Do they perceive those effects to be positive or negative?
- What is it that motivates them to be (or want to be) physically active?
- What are their personal barriers to physical activity (e.g., lack of time, money, safety, convenience, self-confidence, physical condition)?
- What activities do they believe are most enjoyable or would be fun?
- What does the target audience say would make physical activity less boring or more fun and enjoyable?

History

- What lessons could you learn from previous efforts to reach this target audience with health promotion, physical activity promotion, or other behavior-changing messages and services?

Awareness and knowledge

- How aware is the target audience of the potential risks of a sedentary lifestyle?
- How aware are they of the benefits of moderate physical activity?
- How would they currently define "physical activity" or "exercise"? What comes to their minds when they hear those terms?
- When during the course of a day would members of the target audience be most open or receptive to information about physical activity? At what point during their day are they making decisions concerning physical activity?

Media use

- What are the primary sources of health-related or physical activity-related information for members of your target audience?
- What media channels (e.g., radio, television, or print) do they routinely use?
- How accurate or appropriate is the health- or physical activity-related information that reaches the target audience via each of these channels?
- Considering a typical day, where would the target audience be most likely to see or hear your messages promoting physical activity?

Physical health status

- To what extent are other health-related factors present among members of the target audience (e.g., high blood pressure, high blood cholesterol, tobacco use, uncontrolled blood glucose, obesity, stress, pregnancy, arthritis)?
- Do members of the target audience have any physical conditions that would limit or alter their participation in a variety of physical activities?

Skill and ability level

- To what extent do people within the target audience possess the skills needed to successfully initiate and maintain a physically active lifestyle?

Level of self-efficacy

- How confident are members of your target audience in their ability to be regularly active?
- To what extent do they believe they can improve their levels of physical activity?

(continued)

Information to Consider When Profiling a Target Audience (*continued*)

Cultural and social norms

- How does your target audiences's social culture and climate support or deter being physically active?
- Do certain traditions, customs, folklore, or religious beliefs in your target audience either support or hinder men's, women's, or children's efforts to be physically active?
- How might supportive beliefs and traditions be reinforced while those that hinder physical activity be minimized?

Supportive and reinforcing social network

- What social or peer pressures greatly influence the actions of people within your target audience?
- What do the people who are most important to members of the target audience think they should do in regard to physical activity?
- Who would support their efforts to be physically active and who would deter efforts to change? Consider those in authority over, under, and equal to the target audience (e.g., administrators, community leaders, supervisors, parents, teachers, clergy, health care providers, constituents, staff, clients, friends, family members, coworkers, peers).
- Who are their role models in general? Who are their role models for a physically active lifestyle in particular?
- Who are they most likely to turn to for information regarding health or physical activity?
- What organizations or groups do people within your target audience frequently join? Do any of these organizations have goals complementary to your own? Is there a potential for partnership with these organizations?

Physical environment, facilities, and resources

- What natural resources are available in the local geographic area (e.g., rivers, lakes, trails)?
- What recreational resources are available to the target audience (e.g., safe sidewalks, bicycle paths, walking trails, playing fields, gymnasiums, showers and locker rooms, tennis courts, community recreation centers, a local YMCA or YWCA)?
- Are existing resources accessible and affordable?
- Are current resources acceptable to your target audience (i.e., do members of your target audience feel welcomed and comfortable using these various resources)?
- Are recreational facilities and parks—including playground equipment; tennis, volleyball, or basketball nets and courts; soccer fields, swimming pools—safe, attractive, and well maintained (e.g., free of debris and broken glass, in good repair, well-lighted during early morning and evening hours, periodically patrolled by police or park security)?
- What untapped or underused resources are potentially available in your community or site (e.g., shopping malls closed to walkers, unlighted playing fields, vacant lots that could be converted to recreation space, or highway or transportation funds that could be used to construct bicycle paths)?

Political environment

- What laws, policies, or regulations affecting the environment in which members of your target population live, work, or spend their leisure time either encourages or restricts their levels of physical activity (e.g., curfews, personnel policies, membership rules)?

Listening to Your Population's Changing Needs

No matter how well you think you know your target population, the factors that influence their lives change constantly. Therefore, it becomes essential that you continuously listen to what they have to say.

Regardless of the methods you choose for gathering information, you must look beyond the traditional epidemiologic, demographic, and behavioral data, supplementing your findings with descriptive psychographic data obtained directly from the people who make up your target audience. In any way possible, consider spending time observing and listening to the people whose lives you are trying to impact.

Your best source of information about your target audience comes directly from members of your target audience.

For example, if they belong to certain organizations, periodically ask to attend a meeting; or invite a small group to someone's home, a favorite community gathering place, or a local restaurant to discuss your ideas over a cup of coffee (or some culturally appropriate food). Share ideas and ask for their feedback. Take advantage of every opportunity to assess people's perspective on their problems and their ideas regarding possible solutions.

Primary Sources of Information

Gathering consumer-related information need not be costly nor time-consuming. A number of formal and informal methods can be used to gather target audience input without burdening program resources.

Formal methods of data collection include surveys conducted by mail, telephone, or in person; central location intercept interviews conducted by stopping and asking the opinion of people who fit your audience description as they go about their normal business; and focus groups. Formal consumer-based research is often conducted with the help of a reputable marketing firm.

Target Practice: An Exercise in Focusing Your Efforts

For the next few minutes, think of yourself as the social marketer brought onto a team of health promotion, education, and community planning experts. Your assignment is to define a problem, select a target population, and consider alternative strategies for intervention. Where would you begin? The following are a series of questions that will guide you through the basic steps in narrowing your focus and selecting a target population.

What is your goal? For all Americans to achieve a physically active lifestyle. To get Americans moving! For specific and measurable objectives, consider the *Healthy People 2000* or the upcoming *Healthy People 2010* objectives.

What is the problem? And is it a problem worth solving? Americans have made little progress in increasing their levels of physical activity since 1985. Currently, too many Americans are less than optimally active. According to the Surgeon General's report on *Physical Activity and Health*, regular physical activity that is performed on 5 or more days of the week reduces the risk of developing some of the leading causes of illness and death in the United States (USDHHS 1996).

What is the magnitude of the problem? More than 60% of American adults fail to participate in recommended levels of activity (Jones et al. 1998) while 36% of youth fail to engage in vigorous activity consistently enough to maintain or improve cardiorespiratory fitness (Kann et al. 1998).

Consider the *impact-ability* factor: How many people do we have to reach to make an impact that has public health significance? What would the statisticians say about calculating accurately the level of significance? If statisticians are not readily available, then very roughly we might estimate that if more than 60% of the population need to do something to improve their levels of physical activity, perhaps we should target 15 to 25% of the total population, realizing that not everyone will respond to our call to action.

Who has the problem? Adults and youth. Both men and women? Of any particular age? All youth, or just certain youth? In other words, what characteristics of a population best describe those who have the problem? See page 45 for characteristics that describe a target population.

Consider the *benefit-ability* factor: Who would benefit most by an intervention? Who is most in need or at greatest risk for the problem? Those who are *most* sedentary have a greater risk than their active counterparts of developing chronic diseases, including cardiovascular disease, hypertension, non-insulin-dependent diabetes, and colon cancer.

Those who are *least* active in American society include the following:

- Among adults, levels of physical activity tend to decrease as age increases and as educational attainment decreases; women tend to be less active than men; African-American and Hispanic adults tend to be less active than white adults.

- Youth reveal a similar pattern, in that participation in physical activity decreases as grade in school increases, girls are less likely than boys to engage in vigorous activities, and African-American and Hispanic youth tend to be less vigorously active than white youth.

- Among youth, the period of greatest risk of inactivity is 11 to 13 years of age.

What are possible solutions to the problem? Which behaviors or social and environmental factors are the greatest determinants of the problem behavior? A brief look at research data or the current literature can direct your thinking at this point. Even a brainstorming session to come up with possible solutions can be a worthwhile place to start. Your preliminary solutions could address individual behaviors by trying to increase people's awareness, knowledge, motivation, and skills; or you could focus on fostering an environment supportive of change by addressing social norms, access to resources, policies that mandate change; or a combination of these many factors. (See chapter 4, pages 80–81, for more information on the many pieces of an intervention puzzle.)

Where can you make the most difference? Of those many behaviors or factors that contribute to the problem, which one or two represent your *best* opportunity to make a difference in the problem? For example, those who are most sedentary would benefit more than any other group by becoming at least moderately active on a regular basis. Those who are irregularly active could achieve greater overall health benefits if they were to become regularly active. Those who already engage in moderate-intensity physical activity regularly might be able to achieve greater health benefits by increasing the intensity of their activities, including some vigorous activities as well as some strength and flexibility activities in their weekly routines.

Again, what scale of change is needed to make a difference in the overall problem and how many people are potentially affected by each possible solution? For example, how many people would need to change their physical activity behaviors, becoming regularly active, to create a significant shift in physical activity rates? You can narrow your menu of possibilities by ranking them according to their potential impact or their estimated reach. Some options may be eliminated because they do not pass the impact test—they would not affect sufficient numbers of people to make a dent in the problem.

Another consideration is the *achieve-ability* factor: What is reasonable for your organization to do, given your unique strengths as well as your limitations? What practical, political, or financial constraints would you have to overcome if you were to address this possible solution? What creative approaches and innovative partnerships would potentially ease those constraints?

Consider the *response-ability* factor by asking: Who is most ready to respond, or to do something about the problem? How many people does this represent? Are the numbers sufficient? According to the Stages of Change model, people vary considerably in their willingness or readiness to commit themselves to an active lifestyle. As you think through possible solutions, rate each by asking how likely is it that people are willing or ready to do it. Who among the most sedentary is willing to become at least moderately active? Who among the irregularly active is ready to heed the advice to do more? Who would be willing to increase the intensity of their activities in order to achieve a greater perceived benefit? Often simple, easy-to-do behaviors with few obvious problems are a reasonable place to start as you consider a variety of possible solutions (W. Smith 1998).

Separate the "Doers" from the "Non-Doers". Who already does the desired behavior and who doesn't? By comparing the Doer versus Non-Doer groups, you can compare similarities and differences and discover the best predictors of the desired behavior. What are the Doers doing that makes them so successful in carrying out the desired behavior? How does that differ from what the Non-Doers are currently doing?

(continued)

(continued)

	Benefits	**Barriers**
Desired behavior		
Competing behavior		

What are the Non-Doers doing *instead* of the desired behavior? What are the competing behaviors? Are Non-Doers of optimal physical activity sitting in front of the television or their computers? Are they sitting in their automobiles or behind a desk? Do they take the elevator rather than the stairs, a car rather than a bicycle? What are they doing throughout the day *instead* of being active?

For every group of people, both competing behaviors and desired behaviors have their benefits and barriers. At this point you might ask the target audience what is it that makes the competing behaviors easier or preferable to the desired ones? What would help them to be more active? What are their barriers to change—what is keeping them from being more active? And who, among the people who are important to them, would support their efforts to be more active? Who would not?

Once you have analyzed epidemiologic data, as well as descriptive lifestyle and market research data, by separating those who *do* from those who *don't,* you might discover that the Less Than Optimally Active group has certain characteristics that set them apart from the Regularly Actives. These differences offer valuable insights to the program planner. The Doer/Non-Doer analysis helps you determine whether the behavior is dependent upon certain knowledge, attitudes, motivations, skills, social supports, or some other physical or political factors.

You will be well on your way to understanding—from the perspective of those you intend to reach—which components of a comprehensive program provide the greatest opportunities for change toward the desired behavior, and what perceived benefits of doing the desired behavior, of being more physically active, outweigh the benefits of being inactive.

By now, you are well on your way to tailoring an intervention plan that matches the needs as well as the desires of the target population. (For more information about tailoring an intervention, see page 79.)

W. Smith 1998

When budgets are tight, first consider how you might downsize your target audience, alter your goals, or find partners to supplement portions of your program plan. But through it all, hold fast to your plans to conduct consumer-based research. To keep research costs to a minimum, consider working with local businesses, and with the public health, education, communication, and business departments within local colleges and universities. You might involve workplace retirees, school parent/teacher groups, professional organizations, voluntary organizations, and local business leaders in helping you gather or process the information you need.

As a last resort, several focus groups, each conducted with 8–10 members of your targeted population gathered in someone's living room, or in a "town meeting" at a church or in a community center, would certainly provide more valuable information than if you were to eliminate consumer opinion entirely. Resources C and D (pages 291–303) provide examples of the types and amounts of information you can obtain regarding your population's attitude, beliefs, and behaviors from survey and focus group research.

If you think you cannot afford market research, consider the alternative—an expert-driven approach, in which professionals make crucial intervention decisions with little or no input in the planning process from those whom the intervention is intended. How can professionals hope to meet expressed needs unless they provide opportunities for the targeted population to express them? To increase your likelihood of success and to use limited resources more widely and strategically, your program simply cannot afford to *not* do consumer-based research.

Secondary Sources of Information

Increasingly, secondary resources are becoming available, including Internet sites, reference books, marketing research journals, or formative research conducted by other organizations on populations nearly identical to your own. A host of professionals who have had extensive experience in working with your target audience provide yet another secondary resource. There is a great deal to be learned from people who have been successful in delivering messages or services to your target population.

Take time, as well, to meet with formal and informal community or group leaders—people who are admired and respected by members of your target audience. Your own staff or volunteers may know the target audience so well that they can provide valuable guidance as to the places to begin gathering the data most pertinent to your audience segment. However, no secondary source of information can ever substitute for direct contact with members of the target population.

> Almost always, the data you collect raises as many questions as it answers. But at some point, you just have to say, "I'm going to stop asking questions and I'm just going to do something. I'll monitor what happens and I'll make the changes necessary for it to work."
>
> *W. Smith, 1998*

Segmenting Populations by Stage of Change

Within any population, people will vary considerably in their readiness or willingness to change. James Prochaska and his colleagues (1992) have described how people move through a series of five separate stages as they evaluate information and its relevance to their lives, make a commitment to take action, strengthen their intention to change, and eventually make progress toward their goal of adopting or altering a specific behavior. This theory, called Stages of Change, is illustrated on page 59. Read more about the stages of change in chapter 5.

Those who are classified in the Contemplation or Preparation stages are most ready to change for a specific behavior. For example, they are already thinking about becoming more physically active, they may be making definite plans to take action in the near future, or they may be trying out an activity or two, but are not yet doing it on any regular basis. By targeting these ready and willing population segments, your program may enjoy results more quickly than if you were to target those who are either ambivalent or resistant to change (i.e., Precontemplators).

If you know how many people within your target population fall within each Stages of Change category, you can then evaluate whether reaching one or more stages successfully will have significant enough impact on the problem you are trying to address.

The data in the table on page 59 is based on the national Healthstyles survey (a national consumer survey conducted by the Porter Noveli company in Washington, DC). This market research data was averaged over a three-year period, 1995–1997 (Maibach et al. 1996). From this data, it appears that 36.0% of the population is in the Maintenance stage for regular moderate-intensity physical activity. Even though the Maintenance group is the largest single segment of people classified by the Stages of Change model, targeting this segment would do little to solve the national problem of physical inactivity, since people in Maintenance have already achieved an active lifestyle to some extent. In contrast, by choosing the segments of people who are in Contemplation and Preparation, you would be targeting 42.5% of the U.S. population, segments that, with appropriate assistance, are far more likely to make a difference in improving national physical activity rates.

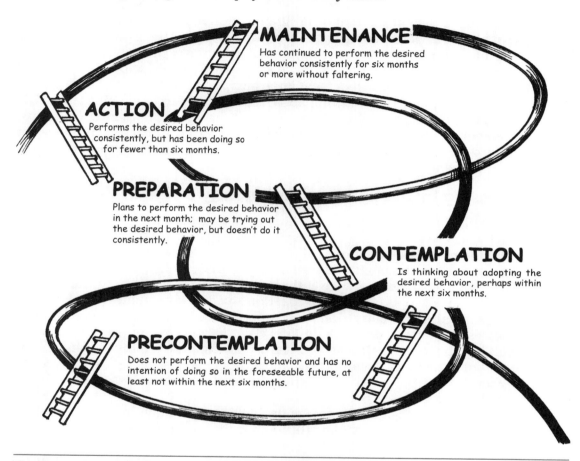

MAINTENANCE
Has continued to perform the desired behavior consistently for six months or more without faltering.

ACTION
Performs the desired behavior consistently, but has been doing so for fewer than six months.

PREPARATION
Plans to perform the desired behavior in the next month; may be trying out the desired behavior, but doesn't do it consistently.

CONTEMPLATION
Is thinking about adopting the desired behavior, perhaps within the next six months.

PRECONTEMPLATION
Does not perform the desired behavior and has no intention of doing so in the foreseeable future, at least not within the next six months.

The Stages of Change model.

Estimated Percentage of the U.S. Population by Stage of Change for Achieving Regular, Moderate-Intensity Physical Activity

Stage of Change	Percentage
Precontemplation	14.0%
Contemplation	13.9%
Preparation	28.6%
Action	7.4%
Maintenance	36.0%

Source: Basil et al., unpublished

Assessing Individual Stage of Change

To assess an individual's or small group's readiness to change, you might try inserting brief staging questions, such as those in the questionnaire on page 61, within a company newsletter, on an event registration form, or on a patient information questionnaire in a physician's office. The box on page 62 gives instructions on how to score the questionnaire. You could then use the results to customize the information or programs offered, providing different strategies matched to the different stages along the continuum (see pages 106–111 for more information about moving people along the Stages of Change continuum).

From a practical point of view, while many people might appreciate learning the results of your assessment and knowing where they fit along the Stages of Change continuum, they may not appreciate nor understand being labeled as "Precontemplators" or "Preparers." Rather than using the theoretical terms, you might want to create your own descriptive terms for each of the stages of change—terms or labels that your target audience might perceive as positive and motivating.

Assessing Institutional or Community Stage of Change

Classically, Prochaska's Stages of Change model has been used to describe individual behavior change. However, the principles that differentiate individuals by their intention to adopt a desirable behavior may be applied to group, organization, or community as well (Abrams 1991; McLeroy et al.1988).

To designate stage of change at the institutional level and at the community level, you need to assess an organization's or the community's intention to change as well as its ability to achieve a specific behavioral goal. Organizational needs assessment might include interviews or surveys of employees at all levels of the organizational structure, examination of the worksite's or community's physical environment, and its policies governing its employees or citizens to identify potential barriers as well as motivators to successful behavior change.

Indicators of stage of change might include, for example, evidence of an institution's or community's level of commitment to some ideal or practice; the level of their intention to fulfill some desired course of action toward institutional change; or the extent to which they meet the criteria for an organizational or community award or designation as having achieved some other exemplary status.

In practice, Stage of Change theory and more traditional organizational development theories complement each other, and they may have a greater potential to achieve health-enhancing change when they are combined (Glanz et al. 1997; Goodman et al. 1997; Abrams et al. 1986).

Sample Physical Activity Questionnaire to Determine Stage of Change

Moderate physical activity or exercise includes such activities as walking, gardening, and heavy housecleaning. For moderate activity to be regular, it must add up to 30 or more minutes per day and be done at least 5 days per week. For example, in one day you could achieve your total of 30 minutes by taking a brisk 10-minute walk, raking leaves for 10 minutes, and washing your car for 10 minutes.

For each question below, mark Yes or No.

		Yes	**No**
1.	I currently participate in moderate physical activity.	A. ___	B. ___
2.	I intend to increase my participation in moderate physical activity in the next six months.	C. ___	D. ___
3.	I currently engage in regular moderate physical activity.	E. ___	F. ___
4.	I have been participating in moderate physical activity regularly for the past six months.	G. ___	H. ___
5.	In the past, I was regularly physically active in moderate activities for at least three months.	I. ___	J. ___

Complete the following questions. (Note: If you are not currently physically active or do not exercise at all, please write 0 [zero] to the questions below.)

6. How many days per week are you physically active or do you exercise?   ____ days per week

7. Approximately how many minutes are you physically active or do you exercise each day?   ____ minutes per day

8. How long have you been physically active or exercising at this level?   ___ years, ___ months

This scale was developed by Dr. Bess Marcus, Brown University Medical School, The Miriam Hospital Division of Behavioral Medicine. It has been reproduced with minor adaptations with permission. The full-length scale developed by Dr. Marcus also includes a section that asks persons to report on the extent to which they participate in vigorous activity: "vigorous" is substituted for "moderate" in the questionnaire. The section on vigorous physical activity starts with the following definition: "Vigorous physical activity or exercise includes hard activities such as jogging, aerobics, swimming, and biking. For vigorous activity to be regular, it must last at least 20 minutes each time and be done at least 3 days per week."

Questionnaire Scoring Instructions to Determine Stage of Change

If lines **B** and **D** are checked   →   Precontemplation *(not active, currently has no intention of being active)*

If lines **B** and **C** are checked   →   Contemplation *(not active, but intends to be soon)*

If lines **A** and **F** are checked   →   Preparation *(trying, but not yet regularly active)*

If lines **A, E,** and **H** are checked   →   Action *(regularly active, but for less than six months)*

If lines **A, E** and **G** are checked   →   Maintenance *(regularly active for six months or more)*

If line **I** is checked   →   Perhaps relapse *(if the score indicates a relapse, also designate the person's current stage)*

Examples of Community Stage of Change

If you were to assess a variety of institutions in your community for their stage of change in regard to physical activity promotion, you might come across the following examples.

- A worksite that is considering a change in employee health benefits to include physical activity incentives might be in **Contemplation.**
- A worksite whose administration is already taking the appropriate steps to institutionalize a cost-effective physical activity program might be in **Maintenance.**
- A school district that is piloting a model physical activity program in one of its schools may be in **Preparation** for adopting the program districtwide.
- A community that is in the construction phase in converting old railroad ties into pedestrian and bicycle pathways has demonstrated a commitment to **Action.**

If you keep in mind a specific desired behavior and your program goal, then by focusing on criteria for success, as well as indicators for measuring progress (e.g., "have met 7 out of 10 criteria for excellence; have obtained 3 out of 5 infrastructure categories," etc.), you can determine the stage of the various businesses or organizations in your community, or several entire communities, by their readiness to change, based on the strength of their intentions and evidence of their commitment to reach a desired endpoint.

Assessing Larger Populations

To assess stage of change on a statewide or nationwide population basis, you may wish to include stage-related questions in a written and telephone survey or surveillance instruments or in targeted intercept interview questionnaires administered to large and statistically representative samples of the population.

Segmenting Populations by Life Stage

People's willingness or ability to adopt and maintain behaviors such as a physically active lifestyle may vary considerably throughout life. By characterizing the times in life when people and families are in greatest transition, it may be possible to match behavioral interventions with stages of the life cycle (King 1991). Stressful transitional periods mark those times when consumers are most likely to try something new, when they become information seekers and are open to life-changing messages.

Major life transitions include graduating from school or training, leaving home or school to join the workforce, getting married or remarried, becoming parents with the birth or adoption of a child, moving to a new location, losing a job or changing careers, experiencing a major illness, learning about a life-threatening diagnosis, becoming a caretaker, retiring, or losing a loved one (Mergenhagen 1995).

First, move away from the notion that consumers are best segmented by age. Consumers' needs originate more from levels of personal growth and from levels of social development achieved in family, job, and other social circles. Age is primarily a coincidental factor, not a determining factor. When you divide a market by age, you're going against the grain of life's realities.

V. Thomas and D.B. Wolfe, 1995

In a target population characterized on the basis of life stage, the chronological age of the population is secondary to life events. For example, new mothers could be in their 20s, 30s, or 40s, yet all would share certain life-stage characteristics common to new parents. A couple in their mid-40s might be facing the parenting challenges of raising toddlers, adolescents, or grandchildren. In this case, 45-year-old parents of preschool-age children could have more in common with 25-year-old parents of preschoolers than with 45-year-old peers whose children are attending college.

Taking the "Screen Test"

The final test that will help you put the whole picture together and tell you how well you have completed the targeting phase of program planning is what we will call the Screen Test, imagining a scenario created by the decisions you have made to this point. Before you can select strategies appropriate to your target audience, you must consider three variables: (1) the precise action or desired behavior you are striving to achieve, (2) the actor—any person from your target audience who is to perform the desired action, and (3) the specific circumstances or context in which that action is to take place (W. Smith, personal communication 1998).

Imagine members of your target audience doing what it is you want them to do in the context of circumstances relevant to their lives. By looking at all three variables together, you may determine whether you have defined your target audience specifically enough, whether you have described the desired behavior precisely enough, and whether you have profiled the audience thoroughly enough to be able to describe a realistic set of circumstances in which the desired behavior is to take place.

Change any one variable, and everything would change. Different strategies would be needed to address the new scenario. For example, if you have selected as your target audience youth between the ages of 9 and 14 years, the actor would be one girl or boy between the ages of 9 and 14 years. The desired action might be for the actor to select at least one activity from a variety of activities that he or she enjoys, and to engage in these activities for at least 30 minutes each day after school. The circumstances? What if the child lived in a depressed neighborhood in the inner city? The action required of this child and the strategies needed to achieve the desired action would be very different from those of a child who must go to an after-school program until his parents return from work, or from a latchkey child who must care for his siblings, or from the child who goes home to help with the chores on a rural farm or to a wealthy suburb with a lovely park just down the street.

The three variables in relation to each other make all the difference in deciding which strategies would be most effective. What if the actor changed, and now you wanted a 17-year-old youth to be active after school? That creates a much different scenario, with different competing behaviors requiring different program strategies. So double-check before you continue in strategic program planning. Have you been specific enough in defining the actor (your target population), the desired action, and the circumstances? If so, you're ready for the next step—deciding on your intervention strategies from your arsenal of behavioral theories and behavior-change models, and tailoring the intervention to the characteristics unique to your target audience.

Tailoring Your Intervention to Suit Your Audience

Tailoring an intervention is the process of customizing a plan of action by matching program components to the needs and wants of the target population. When you begin to understand the intended audience's compelling reasons for carrying out or not carrying out the desired behavior, the strength of their intention or commitment to change, their mastery of the skills necessary to adopt and maintain change, and the absence or presence of social and environmental constraints to change, you will have identified the information necessary to develop an effectively tailored intervention (Fishbein 1995; Balch 1996).

For example, according to Fishbein (1995), if the target audience *has not* yet formed a strong intention to change—that is, they have not made a commitment to being regularly physically active—your intervention plan may focus on strengthening their commitment by

- addressing gaps in knowledge,
- correcting misconceptions in their beliefs and outcome expectations,
- building self-efficacy,
- motivating the target audience by linking the desired behavior (e.g., regularly engaging in physical activities) to whatever it is they value highly, and
- creating supportive social norms.

If, however, the target audience *has* formed a strong intention and members have made a strong commitment to change (e.g., to being regularly physically active), but they are not successfully acting upon that intention, your intervention plan may focus on identifying and minimizing barriers to being regularly active by

- improving the skills people need to adopt and successfully maintain the desired change (the physically active lifestyle),
- providing opportunities to practice new skills,
- increasing social support, and
- overcoming environmental constraints.

Once you have a clear idea of who your target population is and what their interests and needs are, you're ready to begin on the path toward behavior change. The next chapter will explain how you can use behavior change theory to move your population toward the goal of a regularly active lifestyle.

Suggested Reading

For a list of organizations, agencies, and selected program materials for promoting physical activity, see:

Resource A, for general resources

Chapter 6, for environment-related resources

Chapter 9, for worksite-related resources

Chapter 10, for school-related resources

To learn more about the process of social marketing, review:

Andreasen AR. 1995. *Marketing Social Change: Changing Behavior to Promote Health, Social Development, and the Environment.* San Francisco: Jossey-Bass Publishers.

Kotler P, Roberto EL. *Social Marketing: Strategies for Changing Public Behavior.* New York: The Free Press/Macmillan, 1989.

Lefebvre RC, Flora JA. Social marketing and public health intervention. *Health Education Quarterly* 1988; 15(3):299–315.

Sutton SM, Balch GI, Lefebvre RC. Strategic questions for consumer-based health communications. *Public Health Reports* 1995;110:725–733.

To learn more about using focus groups, read:

Breitrose P. *Focus Groups: When and How to Use Them: A Practical Guide.* Palo Alto, CA: Health Promotion Resource Center, Stanford Center for Research in Disease Prevention, Stanford University School of Medicine, 1988.

Krueger RA. *Focus Groups: A Practical Guide for Applied Research* (2nd Edition). Newbury Park, CA: Sage Publications, 1994.

Morgan DL, editor. *Successful Focus Groups: Advancing the State of the Art.* Vol. 156. Newbury Park, CA: Sage Focus Editions, 1993.

A Guidebook—Listening to Your Audience: Using Focus Groups to Plan Breast and Cervical Cancer Public Education Programs (1994) is available from:

AMC Cancer Research Center
1600 Pierce Street
Denver, CO 80214

To learn more about the characteristics of various age cohorts and generational marketing, read:

American Demographics monthly publication published by Intertech Publishing. Or, visit their website at **www.demographics.com.**

Mitchell, Susan. *American Generations: Who They Are, How They Live, What They Think.* (2nd Edition). Ithaca, NY: New Strategist Publications, 1998.

Walker Smith J, Clurman A. *Rocking the Ages: The Yankelovich Report on Generational Marketing.* New York: Harper Business, 1997.

For a valuable review of the literature regarding physical activity interventions, read:

American Journal of Preventive Medicine. November 1998. 15(4): 255–440.
To obtain a copy of this special issue, contact the publisher, Elsevier Science, toll-free at 888-437-4636 or via fax 212-633-3913.

King AC, Blair SN, Bild DE, et al. 1992. Determinants of physical activity and interventions in adults. *Medicine and Science in Sports and Exercise* 24(6 Suppl): S221–S236.

Chapter 4 Understanding the Basics of Behavior Change

Fundamental to the success of any health promotion program is a clear understanding of behavior, behavioral theory, and the process of behavior change. The more clearly you understand what factors most influence the desired behavior (i.e., being regularly physically active) and the environmental context in which those behaviors occur, the better prepared you will be to design interventions that foster the behavior changes you hope to achieve (Glanz et al. 1997). Let's review the basics of behavioral theory and the behavior change process.

Behavior is something observable. It is an action that can be described, characterized, and defined. *Behavioral theories* provide an explanation about the complexity of factors that influence a behavior one way or another at any given point in time—the *determinants* of a particular behavior. Theories can help you to understand the nature of the desirable behaviors you wish to promote as well as the undesirable ones you wish to replace. For example, behavioral theories that focus on the determinants of behavior, such as the Health Belief Model (Becker 1974), Social Cognitive Theory (Bandura 1986), and the Theory of Reasoned Action (Ajzen and Fishbein 1980), try to explain why some members of a given population do some particular thing, while other members of the same population do not.

In order to change behavior . . . it is first necessary to understand why people behave as they do. The more one knows about the variables underlying a person's decision to perform or not to perform a given behavior, the more likely it is that one can develop successful behavioral intervention programs.

M. Fishbein et al., 1992

Behavior change is a dynamic process rather than a one-time event. Various models and theories that attempt to describe the process of behavior change suggest how individuals progress through stages of change (Prochaska et al. 1992), how people learn and adopt new ideas (Adult Learning Theory by Knowles 1984), how new ideas diffuse and are adopted throughout populations (*Diffusion of Innovations,* Rogers 1983), and how ecological systems or levels of social structure can support the process of behavior change (Gottlieb and McLeroy 1994).

No one behavioral theory or model holds the definitive answer to understanding all of the great complexities of behavior change. Yet, like a road map, theories guide your way by suggesting pathways that may lead you to your destination effectively—a destination consistent with your program goals.

As a program planner, what can you do to facilitate the behavior change process among members of your targeted population? In this chapter we will examine environmental and personal barriers to behavior change and suggestions for overcoming them. Next, we will consider the need to balance individual intervention strategies with environmental intervention strategies in a comprehensive multi-level approach to behavior change. By blending the major behavioral theories of the late 20th century, we will identify the essential components of behavior change that, when pieced together in accordance with the needs of the target population, create an intervention puzzle based on a comprehensive public health approach to behavior change.

Then in the two chapters that follow, we will take a closer look at each of the many intervention puzzle pieces — those that comprise individual-based intervention strategies in chapter 5 and environmental strategies in chapter 6.

Overcoming Barriers to Behavior Change

Given the health benefits of regular physical activity, we have to wonder why two out of three Americans are continuing to choose to risk their health and the quality of their lives by remaining sedentary. There are many barriers that keep Americans from being, or becoming, regularly physically active. Understanding common barriers to regular physical activity and creating strategies to overcome them may allow us to reach people who find it difficult to fit physical activity into their daily lives.

Environmental Barriers

In his book *The American Way of Life Need Not Be Hazardous to Your Health,* John Farquhar (1987) points out that advances in technology have affected all aspects of our lives and have generally resulted in decreased levels of activity. Too often, our environment provides us little incentive to become physically active. For example, how many of the communities in which we live have walking trails and bicycle paths? How many neighborhoods have sidewalks and safe access to playgrounds or parks? In office buildings, how easy is it to find the staircases? Are they convenient and inviting, let alone safe? For decades, community decisions affecting land use have favored the automobile and economic development rather than creating pedestrian- or bicycle-friendly environments.

The growing urbanization and mechanization of modern life have made it easier for us to become physically lazy and sedentary. We drive rather than walk; we take an elevator rather than climb stairs; we push a button on an electric dryer rather than bend down and reach up to hang clothes on a clothesline. Whereas exercise was once an inevitable part of living, today we must consciously plan to get the exercise needed to maintain good health.

John Farquhar, 1987

Personal Barriers

Aside from the many technological advances and conveniences that have made our lives easier and less active, many personal variables, including physiological, behavioral, and psychological factors, may affect our plans to become more physically active. In fact, the 10 most common reasons adults cite for not adopting more physically active lifestyles are (Sallis and Hovell 1990; Sallis et al. 1992)

- do not have enough time to exercise,
- find it inconvenient to exercise,
- lack self-motivation,
- do not find exercise enjoyable,
- find exercise boring,
- lack confidence in their ability to be physically active (low self-efficacy),
- fear being injured or have been injured recently,
- lack self-management skills, such as the ability to set personal goals, monitor progress, or reward progress toward such goals,
- lack encouragement, support, or companionship from family and friends, and
- do not have parks, sidewalks, bicycle trails, or safe and pleasant walking paths convenient to their homes or offices.

The quiz on pages 100–101 can help people identify the types of physical activity barriers that are undermining their ability to make regular physical activity an integral part of their lives. The quiz calculates a score in each of seven barrier categories. The strategies on pages 71–72 can then be used to help overcome some of the most common fitness barriers: lack of time, social influences, lack of energy, lack of willpower, fear of injury, lack of skill, lack of resources, weather conditions, travel, family obligations, and retirement years.

Suggestions for Overcoming Physical Activity Barriers

Lack of time

- Identify available time slots. Monitor your daily activities for one week. Identify at least three 30-minute time slots you could use for physical activity.
- Add physical activity to your daily routine. For example, walk or ride your bike to work or shopping, organize social activities around physical activity, walk the dog, exercise while you watch TV, park farther from your destination, etc.
- Make time for physical activity. For example, walk, jog, or swim during your lunch hour, or take fitness breaks instead of coffee breaks.
- Select activities requiring minimal time, such as walking, jogging, stair climbing.

Social influence

- Explain your interest in physical activity to friends and family. Ask them to support your efforts.
- Invite friends and family members to exercise with you. Plan social activities involving exercise.
- Develop new friendships with physically active people. Join a group, such as the YMCA or a hiking club.

Lack of energy

- Schedule physical activity for times in the day or week when you feel energetic.
- Convince yourself that if you give it a chance, exercise will increase your energy level; then, try it.

Lack of willpower

- Plan ahead. Make physical activity a regular part of your daily or weekly schedule and write it on your calendar.
- Invite a friend to exercise with you on a regular basis and write it on *both* your calendars.
- Join an exercise group or class.

Fear of injury

- Learn how to warm up and cool down to prevent injury.
- Learn how to exercise appropriately considering your age, fitness level, skill level, and health status.
- Choose activities involving minimal risk.

Lack of skill

- Select activities requiring no new skills, such as walking, climbing stairs, or jogging.
- Exercise with friends who are at the same skill level as you are.
- Find a friend who is willing to teach you some new skills.
- Take a class to develop new skills.

Lack of resources

- Select activities that require minimal facilities or equipment, such as walking, jogging, jumping rope, or calisthenics.
- Identify inexpensive, convenient resources available in your community (community education programs, park and recreation programs, worksite programs, etc.).

(continued)

Suggestions for Overcoming Physical Activity Barriers *(continued)*

Weather conditions

- Develop a set of regular activities that are always available regardless of weather (indoor cycling, aerobic dance, indoor swimming, calisthenics, stair climbing, rope skipping, mall walking, dancing, gymnasium games, etc.).
- Look on outdoor activities that depend on weather conditions (cross-country skiing, outdoor swimming, outdoor tennis, etc.) as "bonuses"—extra activities possible when weather and circumstances permit.

Travel

- Put a jump rope in your suitcase and jump rope.
- Walk the halls and climb the stairs in hotels.
- Stay in places with swimming pools or exercise facilities.
- Join the YMCA or YWCA (ask about reciprocal membership agreement).
- Visit the local shopping mall and walk for half an hour or more.
- Bring a small tape recorder and your favorite aerobic exercise tape.

Family obligations

- Trade babysitting time with a friend, neighbor, or family member who also has small children.
- Exercise *with* the kids—go for a walk together, play tag or other running games, get an aerobic dance or exercise tape for kids (there are several on the market) and exercise together. You can spend time together and still get your exercise.
- Hire a babysitter and look at the cost as a worthwhile investment in your physical and mental health.
- Jump rope, do calisthenics, ride a stationary bicycle, or use other home gymnasium equipment while the kids watch TV or when they are sleeping.
- Try to exercise when the kids are not around (e.g., during school hours or their nap time).

Retirement years

- Look upon your retirement as an opportunity to become more active instead of less. Spend more time gardening, walking the dog, and playing with your grandchildren. Children with short legs and grandparents with slower gaits are often great walking partners.
- Learn a new skill you've always been interested in, such as ballroom dancing, square dancing, or swimming.
- Now that you have the time, make regular physical activity a part of every day. Go for a walk every morning or every evening before dinner. Treat yourself to an exercycle and ride every day during a favorite TV show.

Balancing Individual
and Environmental Approaches

Ultimately, societal behavior change involves individual behavior change. Whether those individuals are students, employees, citizens, constituents, decision makers or presidents, each is surrounded by interpersonal networks comprising families, friends, colleagues, and acquaintances. Small groups of people form larger organizations and institutions. Institutions are subsystems of communities, and together communities form society as we know it. Each layer of social structure—whether individual, interpersonal, institutional (or organizational), community, or societal—affects the others above or below it, from the inside outward or the outside inward.

Change one level and multiple levels may experience the change. For example, if employees of a large company reorganize into new project teams (group level), the effects may be felt throughout the organization (Abrams 1991). The newly formed social interactions will influence not only the individuals who make up the new teams, but also the local workplace climate—the local daily behaviors—and perhaps eventually the entire workplace environment, setting the tone and norms for acceptable behavior within the organization (organizational level). Likewise, if school district administrators (organizational level) decide to build a swimming pool in each of their district's schools, and they pass a ruling that allows community residents to use the facilities during after-school hours, the effects will be felt outward to the community level as well as inward to the interpersonal and individual levels.

To get the bad customs of a country changed and new ones, though better, introduced, it is necessary first to remove the prejudices of the people, enlighten their ignorance, and convince them that their interests will be promoted by the proposed changes; and this is not the work of a day.

Benjamin Franklin, 1781

Targeting Multiple Levels of Social Structure

Each of the five major levels of social structure described on page 74 and illustrated in figure 4.1 calls upon different strategies and methods of intervention—from individual cognitive and behavioral approaches to policy, environmental, and community organizational approaches. For change interventions to be successful, each level must be supportive of the change (Gottlieb and McLeroy 1994).

Even if you target people at one level of social structure, you may need to direct complementary interventions across levels to effect that change. For example, if you were to target key decision makers within an organization, you could use the inter-level influences to your advantage by applying pressure from above, from below, and within the level you are targeting. The most effective and comprehensive interventions may occur when individual and environmental strategies are directed at several levels of social structure simultaneously (Abrams 1991; Gottlieb and McLeroy 1994).

Examples and Focus of Intervention Strategies by Level of Social Structure

Level of Social Structure	Defined as . . .	Interventions focus on trying to . . .
Individual level	individual members of a target audience, such as the consumer, client, student, employee, homeowner, resident, health care provider, teacher, decision maker, gatekeeper, an individual business or community leader, CEO or president, one legislative representative or senator.	increase awareness, knowledge; assess attitudes, opinions, values; increase motivation; strengthen intentions and commitment; enhance readiness to change; build skills; foster self-efficacy, self-esteem; promote trial behavior.
Interpersonal or group level	small groups of individuals who share something in common; social network. A family, circle of friends, one's peer group, classmates, co-workers, colleagues, neighbors.	create or enhance social networks, social support, group dynamics; address peer influence, group or social norms; assess and modify local organizational or workplace climate (many smaller "climates" impact the bigger organizational "environment").
Institutional or organizational level	an organization, institution, agency, or association that crosses group lines; one facility, health clinic, health department, hospital, school, business, neighborhood, church or synagogue. A state or national organization or agency whenever the focus is inward—internal to the organization itself.	address organizational structure, organizational leadership (formal and informal), authority and management styles; modify the organizational environment (made up of many "climates"), its policies, benefit and incentive programs, internal communication networks; address the organizational "culture" or expectations.
Community level	an interagency task force, council, coalition, or larger entity that crosses organizational lines; a school district, county or regional health departments or other government agencies, the combined business community, combined neighborhood associations, collectively the formal and informal community leaders. Includes organizations whenever the focus is external to members of the organization itself—when the client is the community.	address social norms, customs, traditions; enhance community resources; account for area economic conditions, social and health-related services; enhance inter-organizational communication; build partnerships; impact upon community development, city and regional planning; make use of mass media (e.g., radio, television, print media).
Societal or public policy level	crossing multiple community or organizational lines to affect a broad spectrum of the population or society-at-large; regional, state or national levels of organizations and agencies; multi-regional regulatory boards, political parties, the Congress or Senate.	enact or enforce legislation, policies, regulations, guidelines, standards, position and consensus statements, Surgeon General reports, land use and zoning laws; provide legal or monetary incentives and social reinforcements; enforce negative incentives such as taxes, fines, penalties.

Adapted from Lefebvre et al. 1987, King 1991, and McLeroy et al. 1992.

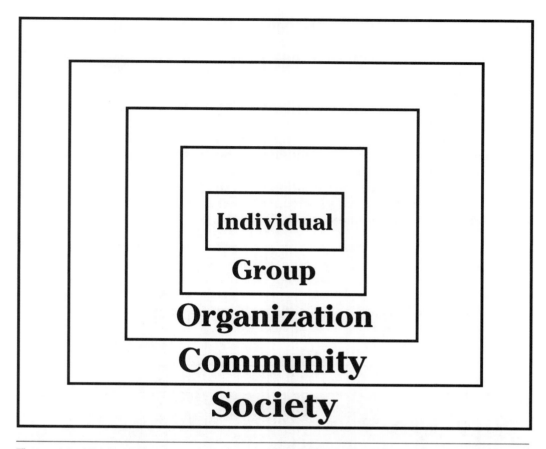

Figure 4.1   This is the key to success: our interventions should strengthen the ability of each level of social structure to support the initiation and maintenance of a physically active lifestyle.

Consider how every other level either helps or hinders your desired behavioral outcome. How does each level of social structure contribute to sedentary behavior or to promoting an active lifestyle? How can physically active lifestyles be produced and maintained in this society? (Abrams 1991; King 1991; King et al. 1995).

Understanding the Dynamic Relationship Between the Individual and the Environment

A person's social, physical, and political environment plays a significant role in fostering individual behavior change by making active lifestyle options more readily accessible, affordable, comfortable, and safe (Green and McAlister 1984; King 1991; King et al. 1995). Environmental changes can help people avoid relapse while encouraging behavior change among those who are "late adopters" or least ready to change (Rogers 1983). Confidence in one's ability to adopt and maintain a desired behavior (i.e., self-efficacy) seems greater when the environment is responsive to one's needs.

While environmental factors have a tremendous influence in shaping individual behaviors, people are rarely passive victims in the process. There is a great deal that individuals can do to create and change their own environments (Bandura 1986). Alone, individuals can rearrange and restructure their personal environments to build in positive reinforcements, cues for action, and social support for their desired lifestyle, whether at home, at work, at school, or as active members of community organizations.

When united, individuals can become active citizens who in partnership with public agencies, private organizations, and local businesses can do much to effect change in the very dynamics of a community. For example, people can begin to revitalize a community by working with community officials and local business owners to close portions of the downtown area to motorized traffic, enlarge sidewalk space, and provide safer crosswalks; create narrow, tree-lined streets and divert traffic flow; and modify zoning ordinances and improve mass transit opportunities (Burden 1997). And everyone's attitudes may be so affected by their revitalized surroundings that the positive effects will spill over into individual behavior change—people may start walking and bicycling more and driving their automobiles less (USDOTFHA 1994a,b).

The process of learning involves change. It is concerned with the acquisition of habits, knowledge, and attitudes. It enables the individual to make both personal and social adjustments. Since the concept of change is inherent in the concept of learning, any change in behavior implies that learning is taking place or has taken place.

from L.D. Crow and A. Crow, 1963

One can safely say that a strong dynamic relationship exists between individuals and their environments and that both are necessary components to create and sustain behavior change. Regardless of the individual's level of awareness and knowledge, training, or motivation, if people who have been equipped for behavior change are then sent back into an unhealthy and unsupportive environment, their lifestyle change may be short lived.

Therefore, individual-based behavior change interventions (emphasizing personal responsibility for action), and environmental support interventions (focusing on social, physical, and regulatory components of change) naturally and effectively complement each other. In fact, research shows that behavior change is more likely to endure when both the individual and the environment undergo change simultaneously (Lasater et al. 1984; Abrams 1991). Together, the two approaches create synergy, having a far greater influence on individuals, organizations, communities, and society as a whole than program planners would be able to achieve by implementing either individual or environmental strategies alone. The next two chapters will cover in much more detail what you can do at the individual and environmental levels to effect behavior change and get your community moving—and having fun while they're doing it!

Read More About It

Major Behavior Change and Learning Theories

Adult Learning Theory

Knowles MS. *The Adult Learner: A Neglected Species* (3rd Edition). Houston: Gulf Publishing Co., 1984.

Social Learning Theory, also known as the Social Cognitive Theory

Bandura A. *Social Foundations of Thought and Action: A Social Cognitive Theory.* Englewood Cliffs, NJ: Prentice-Hall, 1986.

Brower, AM, Nurius, PS. *Social Cognition and Individual Change: Current Theory and Counseling Guidelines.* Newbury Park, CA: Sage Publications, 1993.

Theory of Reasoned Action

Ajzen I, Fishbein M. *Understanding Attitudes and Predicting Social Behavior.* Englewood Cliffs, NJ: Prentice-Hall, 1980.

Health Belief Model

Becker, MH. The health belief model and the personal health behavior. *Health Education Monographs* 1974; 2:324–473.

Janz NK, Becker MH. The health belief model: a decade later. *Health Education Quarterly* 1984; 11:1–47.

Rosenstock IM, Strecher VJ, Becker MH. Social learning theory and the health belief model. *Health Education Quarterly* 1988; 15:175–183.

Transtheoretical Model, also known as the Stages of Change

Prochaska JO, DiClemente CC, Norcross JC. In search of how people change. *American Psychologist* 1992; 47:1102–1114.

Prochaska JO, Norcross JC, DiClemente CC. *Changing for Good.* New York: William Morrow & Co., 1994.

Diffusion of Innovations

Rogers EM. *Diffusion of Innovations* (3rd Edition). New York: The Free Press/ Macmillan Publishing Company, 1983.

Identifying the Essential Components
of a Behavior Change Strategy

If you were to review a great many of the behavioral theories and models of behavior change shaping interventions today, certain themes and building blocks (theoretical constructs) would emerge consistently and would therefore seem to be most relevant to effective behavior change. Among the most basic components in a behavior-changing intervention are the building blocks of high self-efficacy, a strong intention and readiness to change, a supportive social network, and a nurturing environment.

Recently, leading behavioral scientists convened to reach consensus on the essential and necessary components of behavior change. At the end of their deliberations, they concluded that for individuals to begin performing a given behavior, one or more of the following eight determining factors must be true (Fishbein et al. 1992).

1. They must believe that the advantages (i.e., the benefits, positive antici-pated outcomes or expectations) of performing the behavior outweigh the disadvantages (i.e., the costs, negative anticipated outcomes or expectations); in other words, they have a positive attitude toward performing the behavior.

2. Their emotional reaction to performing the behavior must be more positive than negative.

3. Performing the behavior must be consistent with their self-image; perfor-mance does not violate personal standards or values that might activate negative self-sanctions (i.e., guilt, self-reprimand).

4. They must have revealed a strong commitment to perform the behavior, or they will have formed a strong positive intention to do it.

5. They must possess or demonstrate the skills necessary to perform the behavior.

6. Their self-efficacy to perform the desired behavior must be high; they must believe they are capable of performing the behavior under a number of different circumstances.

7. They must perceive more social (normative) pressure to perform the behavior than not to perform it.

8. The environment must be free of constraints that would make it impos-sible for the behavior to occur; the environment should provide oppor-tunities to perform the desired behavior.

Participants of the consensus workshop viewed three of these factors—having a strong positive intention (#4), having the essential skills (#5), and having a supportive environment (#8)—as necessary and sufficient for a behavior to occur. The remaining five variables were viewed as important influences on the strength and direction of a person's intention to perform any specified behavior (Fishbein 1995).

While the consensus views of major theorists may have provided a basic recipe for successful behavior change, the seemingly difficult task of deciding the order and the amounts of each ingredient is still yours as an intervention planner.

Recipe for an Effective, Tailored Intervention

Ingredients

- Awareness
- Knowledge
- Motivation
- Readiness to change
- A strong personal commitment or intention to perform the desired behavior*
- The skills needed to establish and maintain the desired change*
- Strong self-efficacy specific to the desired behavior
- Opportunities to practice skills and new behaviors in a safe environment
- Strong social support
- A supportive environment free of any constraints to change*

* According to a consensus report by the National Institute of Mental Health (Fishbein et al. 1992), these three factors are viewed as necessary and sufficient for producing behavior change.

Directions

In the order and amounts suggested by the target audience profile, add to your proposed intervention plan an emphasis on strategies that effectively increase people's awareness, knowledge, motivation, self-efficacy, and readiness to change. Season by enhancing with the skills needed to establish and maintain the desired lifestyle changes, even when temptations and challenging situations are stirring. Toss in plenty of opportunities to practice new skills in a safe setting, where constructive guidance is available and where imperfections or failed attempts are permitted. Surround the new behavior with significant social support and place it within a nurturing environment, one that is supportive of the desired behavior and free of social, physical, or political barriers to behavior change. Test periodically to see if further encouragement and assistance are needed (particularly during those times prone to relapse). Garnish with rewards and recognition (Fishbein 1995).

Piecing Together an Intervention Puzzle

If a variety of theories and behavioral models are fundamental to designing any successful intervention plan, how do you translate theoretical determinants and processes of change into everyday advice for the intervention planner? What would a comprehensive intervention founded on theoretical principles look like?

Visualize an interlocking puzzle in which each piece represents an important component of a comprehensive behavior-changing intervention, as depicted in figure 4.2. Four of the puzzle pieces are related to enhancing individual self-efficacy and strengthening one's intention to change:

- promoting increased awareness and knowledge about a physically active lifestyle;
- enhancing motivation to become and remain physically active;
- teaching or enhancing the skills needed to establish and maintain the desired behavior; and
- enhancing readiness to change physical activity behavior.

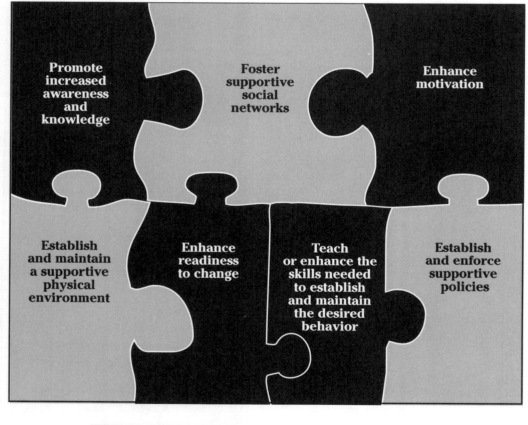

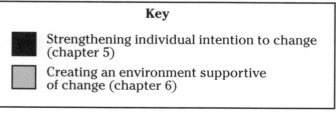

Figure 4.2   The intervention puzzle.

The remaining three puzzle pieces represent the environmental side of the equation:

- fostering social networks supportive of a physically active lifestyle;
- establishing and maintaining a physical environment supportive of an active lifestyle; and
- establishing and enforcing policies supportive of a physically active way of life.

Imagine, also, there are many ways to put the interchangeable pieces of the intervention puzzle together. Which pieces your program provides, the order in which you use them, and how you fit them together will depend on information revealed in your target audience profile (see pages 50–52 on profiling an audience) and assessment. The very process of *tailoring* an intervention is that of customizing a plan of action by matching program components to the needs and wants of the specific target population.

When completed, the picture created will look more like a one-of-a-kind tapestry than a traditional interlocking puzzle design. And because no two target population groups are identical, no two completed intervention puzzle designs will look entirely alike either, even if they are replicating exemplary intervention practices tested in similar communities. The principle of creating a unique intervention design is inherent in *tailoring* an intervention — identifying program components or pieces of the intervention puzzle that will best reach people where they currently are and move them successfully along the behavior change continuum.

By comparing where your target population is with where you want them to be, the priority areas for program planning will become clearer.

- Understanding what people already know about physical activity suggests to you gaps in their awareness of knowledge.

- Being aware of what people believe, perceive, or expect not only helps you point out misconceptions to be corrected but also gives you clues about people's attitudes and intentions to change.

- Recognizing what the target audience values most highly suggests to you what will motivate them to action.

- Clarifying what they are doing or not doing in regard to physical activity suggests what behaviors your program must reinforce or replace.

- Assessing what skills people lack suggests skill-building activities needed.

- Identifying who has an interest in being physically active identifies those most ready to change.

- Finding those who already live an active lifestyle provides you with potential role models, program leaders or program partners.

- Discovering physical and political environmental barriers suggests a place for program advocacy.

- Identifying those whose opinions matter most to the target population suggests secondary targets of intervention and a resource for social support.

In the following two chapters, we'll examine each piece of the puzzle separately. Chapter 5 will take you through the pieces of the puzzle related to individual approaches to behavior change, and chapter 6 will cover the environmental strategies that will help you help your population become more active.

Suggested Reading

For a list of organizations, agencies, and selected program materials for promoting physical activity, see:

Resource A, for general resources

Chapter 6, for environment-related resources

Chapter 9, for worksite-related resources

Chapter 10, for school-related resources

For more information about behavioral theories, read:

Baranowski T. Reciprocal determinism at the stages of behavior change: an integration of community, personal and behavioral perspectives. *International Quarterly of Community Health Education* 1989–90; 10(4):297–327.

Baranowski T. Beliefs as motivational influences at stages in behavior change. *International Quarterly of Community Health Education* 1992–93; 13(1):3–29.

Kanfer FH, Goldstein AP. *Helping People Change: A Textbook of Methods* (4th Edition). New York: Pergamon Press, 1991.

Maibach EW, Cotton D. Moving people to behavior change: a stages social cognitive approach to message design. In: Maibach EW, Parrott RL, editors. *Designing Health Messages: Approaches from Communication Theory and Public Health Practice.* Thousand Oaks, CA: Sage Publications, 1995.

Martin JP, Dubbert PM. Behavioral management strategies for improving health and fitness. *Journal of Cardiac Rehabilitation* 1984; 4:200–208.

O'Donnell MP, Harris JS, editors. *Health Promotion in the Workplace* (2nd Edition). New York: Delmar Publishers, 1994.

Winett R, King A, Altman D. *Health Psychology and Public Health.* New York: Pergamon Press, 1989.

> **For a valuable review of the literature regarding physical activity interventions, read:**

American Journal of Preventive Medicine. November 1998. 15(4): 255–440.
To obtain a copy of this special issue, contact the publisher, Elsevier Science, toll-free at 888-437-4636 or via fax 212-633-3913.

> **For more about the relationship between individual and environmental approaches, read:**

Brownson, RC, TL Schmid, AC King, AA Eyler, et al. Support for policy interventions to increase physical activity in rural Missouri. *Am J Health Promot* 1998; 12(4): 263–266.

Chapter 5 Strengthening Individual Intention to Change

A strong intention to carry out any given behavior implies a determined willingness to take action. What motivates that compelling desire to act may vary greatly from one individual to another, from one population to another. When you understand what the members of your target population perceive as compelling reasons to change their lifestyles or to engage in a specific behavior (i.e., to become regularly physically active), when you understand their level of mastery of skills necessary to adopt and maintain the desired behavior, and the absence or presence in their lives of social environmental constraints to change, you will have identified the information necessary to develop an effectively tailored intervention (Fishbein 1995; George Balch, personal communication, 1996).

Tailoring Your Intervention

As we discussed in chapter 3, according to Fishbein (1995), if the target audience *has not yet* formed a strong intention to change, your intervention plan may focus on strengthening their commitment by

- addressing gaps in knowledge,
- correcting misconceptions in their beliefs and outcome expectations,
- building self-efficacy,
- motivating the target audience by linking the desired behavior (e.g., regularly engaging in physical activities) to whatever it is they value highly, and
- creating supportive social norms.

If, however, the target audience *has* formed a strong intention to change, but they are not successfully acting upon that intention, your intervention plan may focus on identifying and minimizing barriers to being regularly active by

- improving the skills people need to adopt and successfully maintain the desired change (the physically active lifestyle),
- providing opportunities to practice new skills,
- increasing social support, and
- overcoming environmental constraints.

In this chapter, we will examine those pieces of the comprehensive intervention puzzle that comprise the individually-based strategies for behavior change:

- promoting increased awareness and knowledge of physical activity,
- enhancing motivation to change,
- teaching the skills needed to establish and maintain the behavior, and
- enhancing readiness to change.

A balanced approach to behavior change includes individual and environmental components: an intervention that focuses on one without the other will likely be unsuccessful in the long term.

You will learn why these strategies are effective, how you can put them into practice, and specific program ideas for getting your message out to your target population.

Promoting Increased Awareness and Knowledge of Physical Activity

Before people can make positive choices about their lifestyles—choices that will result in their maintaining regular physical activity—they must first become aware of their need for change. Your job is to capture the attention of members of your target audience long enough to make them *aware* that either a problem or opportunity exists that demands their attention. The idea of doing whatever it is you want them to do must grab their attention and convince them that your idea is better than others, or better than their current thinking on the subject.

If your message about a desirable action is going to compete for people's attention, it must stand out from the crowd. Every day people are bombarded with messages suggesting that they do something or buy something—whether good or bad for them. Why should members of your target audience buy what you are selling? How is your product, message, or service unique, new, or improved? Where is the excitement?

Perhaps the excitement is this: there is now convincing scientific evidence that men and women of all ages who at least moderately exert themselves in a wide variety of enjoyable physical activities at least 5 days a week can achieve significant health benefits and improve the quality of their lives (USDHHS 1996). To what extent are members of your target audience aware of this important news? To what extent are they aware of

- the benefits of engaging in regular, moderate physical activity (see chapter 1);
- the consequences of inactivity and what they might lose if they choose not to be regularly active (see chapter 1);
- what is meant by "a regularly physically active lifestyle," and which activities qualify as either moderate or vigorous intensity (see chapter 2);
- how to get started—taking that first step toward a more active lifestyle;
- how to overcome perceived barriers to physical activity; and
- resources in the community (e.g., exemplary worksite programs, walking clubs, other activity-oriented organizations) available to support people's efforts to be more physically active.

Because adult learners are individuals, with their own blend of characteristics, life experiences, levels of readiness to learn, as well as pace and style of learning, your educational programs or awareness-raising efforts need to be highly individualized—matched to the specific needs of the learners who are your target audience (Knowles 1984). Therefore, which of the above subjects you emphasize most will depend on the characteristics of the people you wish to reach.

Awareness strategies in health promotion have several purposes (Chapman 1994), such as

- communicating relevant information that facilitates the process of behavior change or reinforces existing behaviors by helping a person reevaluate his or her underlying values, perceptions, emotions, attitudes, or beliefs;

- empowering and enabling the individual to take some action, applying the information being conveyed to build self-efficacy and self-determination; and

- enabling the individual to gain practical access to information or services that can help to initiate or reinforce a specific desired behavior.

Understand the Process of Becoming Aware

Any time you present someone with an innovative idea, a new service, or a new product, you are demanding that a choice be made, either to reject the notion, or to consider it and decide whether it is personally relevant and therefore merits action. Whenever people must make a choice between alternatives, they need accurate and reliable *information,* conveyed simply and clearly.

Messages should be relevant to the audience, personally meaningful, and specific enough to set the stage for future action (Farquhar et al. 1984). Therefore, what information you provide about physical activity and how you provide it makes a difference in individuals' decision-making process (Rogers 1983). Educators describe this *learning* process—how adults move from awareness to knowledge—as follows (Bloom 1956; Kibler et al. 1974).

According to the principles of adult learning and instructional design, once they are *aware*, some people begin to respond by selectively paying attention, listening, or reading information about the new idea (Knowles 1984; Bloom 1956). As their interest in the subject grows, so does their *willingness to respond* to the point that they voluntarily and actively seek information on a given subject. By seeking appropriate information, people can weigh their options and reduce the uncertainty that often accompanies anything perceived as new.

Eventually, some people will have gathered enough data to earn a reputation among their peers as one who is *knowledgeable* on the subject of physical activity. Gradually, these learned people may demonstrate their mastery of knowledge by applying it to their own or to another's life. They will be able to analyze their options, weigh the pros and cons of the new idea, synthesize and reinforce their findings, and ultimately make judgments about suggested actions based on internal evidence or external criteria (Bloom 1956).

Recognize Life's Teachable Moments

Ordinarily, success in raising a population's awareness of an issue takes time and well-concerted efforts. However, emotion-laden circumstances, major life events, periods of life transition, or developmental milestones (e.g., marriage, the birth or adoption of a child, onset of a major illness, change in employment status, death of a loved one) may have a tremendous influence on people's behaviors, hastening their willingness and readiness to learn (Karoly 1985). (See also chapter 3, "Targeting Your Efforts.") Through recognizing the behavioral impact such events have on people's lives, program planners can take advantage of life's *teachable moments* by developing health promotion strategies appropriate to the needs of those experiencing life's transitions.

Time Your Message Strategically

When are members of your target audience most ready and willing to see or hear what it is you have to say? When and where might they be thinking about physical activity: in the morning as they listen to a weather and traffic report, in the closet as they decide what clothes to wear that day, over breakfast as they study the cereal box, during their commute to or from work, when they first come in the door at night? Communicators call it "the aperture"—that window of opportunity when people are in the most receptive frame of mind to see or hear your message, those moments throughout the day when the message is most strategically timed to foster the desired action.

Think About How You'll Convey the Message

The format of the message, the channels used to transmit it (i.e., whether by way of personal interaction versus one-way communication; or by television, radio, or the written word), and how potential receivers (your target audience) perceive and interpret the message all become very important variables when planning communication strategies. Mass media channels can be very effective when introducing new ideas, reinforcing old messages, attracting attention, increasing awareness, and when setting the public agenda. But mass media channels alone are unlikely to change attitudes, teach new skills, or create behavior change (USDHHS 1989).

Particularly when budgets are tight, your best alternative strategy might be to limit reliance upon the media and focus instead on environmental strategies, such as building bicycle lanes and sidewalks, converting vacant lots into community gardens, or opening school playing fields to community residents—all measures that may increase the likelihood that physical activity will be an accessible and enjoyable option for all members of your target audience.

Choose a Spokesperson Your Audience Relates To

If you choose a spokesperson to share information with your target audience, is this spokesperson reputable, trustworthy, convincing, and well accepted by members of your target population? Celebrity spokespersons are not always the best choice. In fact, people are often highly influenced by listening to and observing others who are most like themselves (Rogers 1983). The more your targeted audience can respect, relate to, or identify with the messenger, the more likely they are to accept the message.

Likewise, if a sponsor is indicated in the message, is that sponsor perceived by the target audience as a credible and trustworthy source of information? If your agency or organization is listed or mentioned, does your reputation convey the attributes that resonate most positively with those you are trying to reach? If not, consider partnering with the most credible source in town, co-sponsoring messages together, so that people will link your name with theirs (see chapter 8, "Working With Partners").

Link the Message to Your Audience's Values

The more compatible your message is with the prevailing values and social norms of your target audience, the more rapidly your target audience is likely to act on it. If you are not sure what values are most important to your audience, then ask them. What do they claim are the top priorities in their lives? What do they hold most dear—their family, their personal faith, their health, or their financial security?

Your messages will be motivating to your audience when linked to the values they have expressed. For example, if your audience values health, your message should emphasize the health-related benefits of physical activity. If your audience values time spent with family members, you might extol the benefits of shared activities as a means of creating memorable times together as a family.

Be Specific

Tell people precisely what it is you want them to do. For example, call a certain number; or find a walking partner and set a regular time to walk together; turn off the television and use that time to play actively with the children; or enroll today in a program offered at the worksite. To be most successful, your message should be relevant to your audience, personally meaningful to them, and specific enough to set the stage for future if not immediate action (Farquhar et al. 1984).

Speak Your Audience's Language

If you were conveying a message to someone from a foreign nation, the need to communicate in a language the individual understood would be obvious. But isn't it also obvious that words and phrases commonly used in scientific recommendations and terms such as *moderate-intensity, physical activity,* or *regularly active* might be misunderstood or foreign to many Americans?

For example, when the Centers for Disease Control and Prevention (CDC) presented the text of one scientific recommendation for increased physical activity, "Every American adult should accumulate 30 minutes or more of at least moderate physical activity on most, preferably all, days of the week" (Pate et al. 1995a), to 136 adults in focus groups throughout the country, participants raised numerous questions and offered several interpretations of every word and phrase in the recommendation (CDC 1995).

- *Every. . .* "you mean infants, children, and the elderly too?"
- *American . . .* "you mean it's only good for Americans?"
- *Adult . . .* "why not include children?"
- *Should . . .* "no one's going to tell me what I should do!" or "How do they know what's good for *me*?" And so forth.

Some participants believed that "accumulate 30 minutes or more" could be achieved by doing 5 minutes of activity each day for 6 days. Some interpreted "moderate-intensity" to mean "activities in the range of moderate to intense." And some participants thought the phrase "most days of the week" meant 3 or 4 days of the workweek, because "weekends don't count," while others translated it as "4 days a week—only slightly more than one-half week."

While most participants took issue with the words themselves, many also doubted that any health benefits could be derived from the recommended

amount of physical activity. Participants expressed the sentiment, "I already do that, and I'm not healthy." It only reinforces the fact that scientific messages are rarely consumer-ready messages. They must be translated into terms that are meaningful to the intended audience.

Realize Opportunities Are All Around

Help people become aware of the many daily opportunities they might have to be physically active, whether it is in helping them to discover a beautiful walking trail, obtain a current schedule of neighborhood dance and exercise classes, or become more aware of benefits derived from small daily decisions like taking the stairs versus the elevator. Whether people realize it or not, everyone has opportunity to be active. (See Resources I and J for ideas.)

Consider partnering with others to compile a directory of relevant programs and services in your community, create a map of natural trails for pedestrians or bicycles, or map the distance within local shopping malls, nearby neighborhoods, or along scenic byways. You can then provide the information using diverse formats and channels most likely to reach your target audience—for example, inserted in the Sunday paper, enclosed in weekly salary envelopes, posted on signs and billboards, or accessed via an Internet home page.

Don't Stop at Awareness and Knowledge

Too often program planners make the mistake of stopping here—at the awareness level. They provide information, yet fail to follow through with interventions that address skill-building, social support networks, or the surrounding environment. Move on to these other pieces of the intervention puzzle and give your specific audience the support they need in these areas.

Ideas for Action in Community

Promote Increased Awareness and Knowledge of Physical Activity

- Conduct highly visible events or activities to capture the attention of your target audience.
- Recruit local celebrities or public officials as chairpersons of promotional events.
- Work with the media to gain visibility for your messages.
  - —Invite newspaper reporters to visible or newsworthy events.
  - —Work with reporters in writing feature stories for National Fitness Month (May), National Recreation and Parks Month (July), or anytime during the year. See Resource G for a list of other "national days," opportunities for promoting physical activity.
  - —Write weekly newspaper columns on physical activity.
  - —Provide timely news releases or newspaper articles.
  - —Provide newspaper inserts or paid advertisements.
  - —Participate as a guest on radio or television talk shows.
  - —Inform local radio, television, or cable networks about newsworthy events.
  - —Offer to be the physical activity expert that local radio, television, or cable stations call when they want an editorial comment or expert opinion.
  - —Purchase radio, television, or cable advertising time or provide timely public service announcements.
  - —Invite radio shows to do remote broadcasting at special events.
- Display key messages and your logo in storefront windows, on community bulletin boards, on billboard signs, and as banners across the main street or at major community locations.
- Sponsor poster contests, and award prizes and incentives to as many people as you are able. Winners and their circles of influence will remember that you exist.
- Distribute written materials to local stores, post offices, and businesses and encourage them to post them on windows or bulletin boards. These materials can be flyers, memos, newsletters, inserts, brochures, or grocery bag stuffers.
- Insert notices about upcoming events in church bulletins or newsletters.
- Use logos on a variety of promotional items, such as flags, buttons, T-shirts, hats, refrigerator magnets, drink sippers, and tote bags.
- Design bumper stickers with physical activity and health promotion messages.

- Work with local grocers to have your message or logo printed on grocery bags. For large grocery store chains, the lead time may be as much as 2 years.
- Conduct physical activity fairs in public places, such as parks, shopping malls, and community centers, or at highly visible community events.
- Tap into the means by which your audience obtains information. Where do they look? Whom do they ask? How do they hear? Whom would they most believe? Put the message in the format most accepted by the audience you want to reach.
- Make creative use of educational media, such as educational television, films, videocassettes, audiocassettes, and interactive computer programs.
- Make health videos available at video stores and libraries.
- Make the most current information on health promotion or physical activity available to your target audience, and let people know where they can obtain current and credible information. For example, donate health promotion references or public education materials to your city or county library by enlisting the help of community partners who can help defray costs, and make the presentation a real event—invite the press!
- Set up a 24-hour telephone physical activity information line with tape-recorded messages.
- To make greatest use of word-of-mouth and informal networks, train people to serve as informal sources of information for their neighbors, friends, and peers.
- Conduct targeted informational campaigns and sessions through
  —lunch-n-learn or community lectures,
  —workshops, seminars, or adult education classes,
  —youth group programs,
  —one-on-one counseling or instruction,
  —guest talk show appearances on television and radio, and
  —columns or featured articles in the newspaper.
- Give informative presentations to worksites, schools, and community organizations, such as Rotary Clubs, Business and Professional Women, or the American Association of Retired Persons.
- Include health and physical activity tips in general publications.
- Ask utility companies, banks, physicians, and others to place promotional and educational information in their monthly billings. Ask to place promotional and educational materials in waiting rooms of hospitals and health maintenance organizations, private physicians' offices, clinics, mental health centers, and senior citizen centers.

Enhancing Motivation to Change

Motivational factors compel action or accelerate movement toward a certain behavior, or repel action and drive people away from engaging in it. Therefore, to design a successful program, you will want to build into your plans strategies that will influence people's motivation to change in a positive direction!

Motivation, itself, may be determined by any number of variables, including a person's perceptions, expectations, values, beliefs, emotions, attitudes, life experiences, feelings of self-efficacy, influences of others, role models, as well as the strength of their intentions or "readiness" to change. Individuals are thought to be positively motivated when they believe that by performing the desired behavior, they will experience positive outcomes or will at least prevent negative ones (Fishbein et al. 1992).

Finally, once individuals are motivated to try a new behavior, whether or not they ever try it again depends on additional influences, such as rewards and incentives, punishments and disincentives, feedback, guided practice, social support—ultimately, a great many more variables that are deeply interrelated.

Understand Your Audience's Perceptions and Expectations About Physical Activity

As knowledge and awareness about physical activity grows, individuals must decide whether this "new idea" (or this old idea perceived as new), has value and worth or is personally meaningful and relevant to them. If the answer is yes, then this newfound knowledge will affect their *beliefs* about physical activity. New ideas may replace old ones, and what people believe to be true may be strengthened, weakened, altered, or replaced based upon new information.

People's perceptions (how they see or the extent to which they understand an idea) and their expectations (what they anticipate as the result or outcome of some action) have great influence upon what they believe to be true. Consequently, the more positive a person's perceptions and outcome expectations related to physical activity (or of any idea or suggested action) and the more likely that person believes physical activity is a good thing, then the more likely he or she will consider change.

Because adopting any new behavior (or simply modifying an existing one) involves both losses and gains, for people to commit to an idea and become motivated to change, they must believe that the benefits of being physically active will eventually outweigh the personal costs, and that changing will produce desirable results. The more benefits people perceive will result from being physically active (whether those benefits are short-term or long-term; social, psychological, or physical), the more likely they are to make a strong personal commitment to being active.

Likewise, to the extent that people believe that being sedentary has serious consequences and feel vulnerable or susceptible to those consequences, they will be motivated to change (Rosenstock et al. 1988). Take, for example, the situation in which persons are motivated to make significant changes in their lifestyles following news of a life-threatening diagnosis affecting them or their loved ones. By acknowledging the behavioral impact that major life events and periods of life transition have on people's lives, program planners may respond with health promotion strategies that take advantage of these "teachable moments." (See page 63 on targeting by life stage.)

Ideas for Action in the Community

Increase Personal Motivation for Adopting a Physically Active Lifestyle

- Help members of your target audience see how your message relates to their lives by

  —personalizing health and fitness messages;

  —recommending they set personal goals for individual achievement;

  —disseminating self-assessment questionnaires (such as the Physical Activity Readiness Questionnaire [PAR-Q] in chapter 2, page 34);

  —hosting health and fitness fairs that include exercise testing to demonstrate that each person needs more physical activity;

  —establishing self-help methods for people to monitor their own progress (e.g., logs or diaries); and

  —encouraging small, incremental changes (the "start with 10 minutes" concept).

- Disseminate messages that link physical activity to values or issues that motivate your target audience (e.g., family, respect for the environment, health, or self-esteem).

- Choose a spokesperson that the target audience trusts, respects, believes, or can identify with. Identify role models, preferably from within the community or target audience, of the desired behaviors. Recruit local celebrities, sports figures, business leaders, or public officials to endorse your program and be role models or spokespersons.

- Invite famous personalities, athletes, people who have overcome major obstacles, or authors to give motivational speeches, give book signings, or promote a special event.

- Appeal to the public's competitive spirit with contests, prizes, incentives, publicity, recognition, awards, and fun promotional items. Establish competitive programs between individuals, neighborhoods, churches, organizations, or businesses. Incentives might include discounts for recreational facilities, fitness club memberships, sports or exercise equipment, or apparel; a free lunch, book, T-shirt, or pair of walking shoes; public recognition, community awards, ceremonies, trophies, plaques, or special privileges; free promotional items; discount coupons; or a free day at a health facility.

- Work with health care providers to encourage them to advise their patients to increase their levels of physical activity and to take advantage of the many community resources you can identify.

- Help people to visualize success—to visualize a happy, healthy, and active lifestyle.

- Build a "you can do it" attitude into your life so that others will believe that they also can be successful. Strive to increase people's self-efficacy.

In theory, a key to successful program planning is to identify the anticipated outcomes of performing the desired behavior. Translated into practical terms, this means: What do members of the target population believe will happen if they do what it is you'd like them to do?

As a program planner, if you are successful in determining people's expectations and perceptions about physical activity, you will be able to develop educational strategies that address them. You may want to ask members of your target population: What do you believe will happen, or expect will happen, if you become regularly physically active? People may express their beliefs by responding to an open-ended question such as this, or by designating a series of statements as either true or false; they either believe the statement to be true or they don't; they either agree or disagree. The top 5 to 10 most frequently mentioned perceptions and expectations are the most salient beliefs held by your population. Are their beliefs about physical activity accurate and realistic? What new information do you need to provide so that negative or counterproductive beliefs may be addressed while accurate beliefs are reinforced?

Beliefs that result in a strengthened *intention* to change or take action (e.g., becoming increasingly more likely to become physically active) perhaps depend most critically on two major variables: (1) a person's attitude, and (2) the social influences on a person by others whose opinions matter most to the individual considering behavior change (a characteristic known as subjective norm).

Positive Attitudes

Attitudes reflect personal feelings based on a continuum of how favorably or unfavorably a person perceives an idea or an action to be. As a program planner, it is important that you understand whether members of your target audience have a positive attitude toward physical activity and to what extent they are convinced that being physically active is a desirable pursuit. The more favorably members of your target population view the consequences or benefits of being physically active, the more favorable will be their attitude toward adopting a physically active lifestyle. And the more favorable their attitude, the greater the likelihood they will take some action.

Using terminology that is both relevant and meaningful to your target audience, you might assess people's attitudes by asking them to respond to a series of items or questions rating the statements on a rising scale of 1 to 10 (Ajzen and Fishbein 1980). The continuum might include any descriptions you want to explore, including very pleasant to very unpleasant, helpful versus harmful, enjoyable versus not enjoyable, easy versus difficult, wise versus unwise, safe versus dangerous, or likely versus unlikely. Certainly, there are numerous ways to assess people's attitudes. Doing so will help you link your messages and interventions to some of the underlying factors that motivate your target audience to action.

Find Out What Your Audience's Peers Say and Do

Who cares what others think? You do. And so do the people who compose your target population. Positive and negative social influences are complex, so you must consider not only the opinions of others, but also the target audience's vulnerability to those opinions. People have a tendency to respond to what they believe others want them to do (social influence), or to what they believe that others like them are actually doing (social norms).

The concept of *subjective norms* brings these social influences into a new perspective. A person's subjective norm includes the opinions of those who are most important and most influential in his or her life (whether they are peers, family members, friends, coworkers, physicians, or community leaders). And most importantly, subjective norms include the individual's *perception* of what others think.

If an individual believes that others would approve of her being physically active or changing her lifestyle in some way, then she is far more likely to make those changes. A classic example is peer pressure during adolescence. Even if personal beliefs, attitudes, and personal values motivate someone to take action in one direction, she has tremendous obstacles to overcome if her strongest peer influences are motivating her to move in a different direction.

Therefore, to more fully understand why a person does or does not engage in a desired behavior such as regular physical activity, it becomes necessary to identify the important and influential people in the lives of members of your target audience. What social pressures are motivating your population to perform or not perform? Who are the people who would approve or disapprove if members of your target population became more active?

Perhaps approving and supportive individuals can assist you if you include them directly or indirectly in your intervention. Perhaps disapproving others are likely secondary targets for intervention or represent social barriers requiring creative strategies to overcome their negative influence.

Use Emotional Motivators Cautiously

Feelings and emotions play a role in motivation and intention to change. Behavior change can occur *as a result* of situations that are highly charged with emotion (celebrations or sorrows), or the changing itself might *bring about* the emotional response. Some people may need to experience strong feelings to re-evaluate their lives. And raising concerns about specific behaviors may be needed to motivate people to make a decision regarding the behaviors that now concern them (Prochaska et al. 1992).

Some program planners craft messages that will evoke strong emotions—for example, messages that raise concern or fear over the consequences of inactivity. But fear is motivating only when the message or situation has aroused no more than moderate levels of fear and the person feels some sense of control over the outcome—he or she knows what to do to reduce the fear. Either inadequate concern (apathy) or excessive fear are emotions that tend to paralyze individuals and may do more to suppress the performance of healthy behavior. Clearly, overly anxious persons need to be calmed and the uncon-cerned need to become concerned in order to facilitate behavior change (Baranowski 1989–90). However, interventions that provide training in prob-lem solving and stress management, or that include opportunities to practice skills in emotionally arousing situations, are more likely to succeed in changing behavior in these situations.

Offer Incentives and Rewards

As every parent and teacher knows, behavior responds to rewarding and punishing consequences. People might be willing at last to try something new, but whether or not they ever try it again has a great deal to do with the rewards or reinforcements they experience as a result of their early attempts to change.

When something is new, both tangible incentives and rewards (such as colorful T-shirts or prizes) and intangible rewards (such as setting a new milestone for "personal best," or a sense of accomplishment) may be motivat-ing in initiating physical activity. Because rewards are subjective and personal, you should match the nature of the reward to the unique characteristics of your target audience so that the rewards are valued by those they are intended to influence.

Incentives and rewards help people to feel better about themselves (intrinsic value) and work best to entice people to initiate a new action. Extrinsic or tangible rewards may be less effective for people trying to sustain long-term change (Glanz et al. 1997). If extrinsic rewards are given too frequently over an extended period of time, people may find them no longer motivating.

Promoting physical activity may require efforts to maximize the rewards while minimizing perceived negative effects of being active (e.g., pain, injury, competing for the time needed for other obligations, or perceptions of activity as boring). People also need information and regular feedback about their performance in order to learn how to regulate their behavior with little outside assistance.

Encourage Commitment

As people become accepting of a new idea, they gradually become willing to identify themselves with it, and may eventually *commit* themselves to the new idea. Commitment involves a personal pledge to engage in physical activity, even in the face of uncertain outcomes and potential failure.

The very act of making a commitment (especially if done publicly) greatly increases the likelihood that the individual will carry out the intended behavior. Those who have progressed in their acceptance of an idea to the extent that they are now committed to it (e.g., they are committed to the merits of a physically active lifestyle) may then demonstrate their conviction by trying to convince others of the idea's worth (Kibler et al. 1974).

Teaching the Skills Needed to Establish and Maintain the Behavior

You cannot expect people to carry out your recommendations to be more physically active unless they know what to do and how to do it. Precisely what does someone need to do if they wish to be regularly physically active? What skills are required to achieve the active lifestyle?

Move Beyond the Barriers

Begin by evaluating what people in your targeted population perceive as barriers to being physically active. What is it that keeps them from being active on a regular basis? (See also "Barriers to Being Active Quiz" on pages 100–101.) What do they believe would help them achieve success? From this assessment, you can determine what competencies and skills they may require to overcome obstacles and move beyond their barriers.

Teach people how to maintain their commitment to increased physical activity in spite of obstacles, such as illness, family emergencies, inclement weather, vacations, and holidays. Learning to overcome the inevitable obstacles is an essential ingredient in successful behavior change. Programs can build in opportunities for people to visualize how to handle a situation, practice their response to the situation, role-play, or develop self-reminders so they are better equipped to handle difficult situations. In this way, physical activity promotion programs help people avoid the discouragement that can result when the intended course of action cannot be pursued. For additional suggestions on overcoming barriers to being active, see pages 71–72.

Encourage Small Steps to Success

At first, set small goals that people can easily achieve. Learning may be enhanced by segmenting difficult skills into smaller components. Each component can be learned separately, then one component added at a time until the more complex skill is mastered. Physical activities begun at an easy pace for a short duration may advance into more intense, more frequent, or longer sessions.

For example, if a person can fit in a 10-minute walk today, perhaps next week she will be able to walk for 15 minutes. Or, if she starts out slowly, she can increase her pace until she can walk briskly with relative ease. As confidence grows, the 5-minute segments grow into 15- or 30-minute chunks of time, and the activities that started out at an easy pace may advance into more intense or frequent episodes.

Barriers to Being Active Quiz

Directions: Listed below are reasons that people give to describe why they do not get as much physical activity as they think they should. Please read each statement and indicate how likely you are to say each of the following statements:

How likely are you to say?	Very likely	Somewhat likely	Somewhat unlikely	Very unlikely
1. My day is so busy now, I just don't think I can make the time to include physical activity in my regular schedule.	3	2	1	0
2. None of my family members or friends like to do anything active, so I don't have a chance to exercise.	3	2	1	0
3. I'm just too tired after work to get any exercise.	3	2	1	0
4. I've been thinking about getting more exercise, but I just can't seem to get started.	3	2	1	0
5. I'm getting older so exercise can be risky.	3	2	1	0
6. I don't get enough exercise because I have never learned the skills for any sport.	3	2	1	0
7. I don't have access to jogging trails, swimming pools, bike paths, etc.	3	2	1	0
8. Physical activity takes too much time away from other commitments—like work, family, etc.	3	2	1	0
9. I'm embarrassed about how I will look when I exercise with others.	3	2	1	0
10. I don't get enough sleep as it is. I just couldn't get up early or stay up late to get some exercise.	3	2	1	0
11. It's easier for me to find excuses not to exercise than to go out and do something.	3	2	1	0
12. I know of too many people who have hurt themselves by overdoing it with exercise.	3	2	1	0
13. I really can't see learning a new sport at my age.	3	2	1	0
14. It's just too expensive. You have to take a class or join a club or buy the right equipment.	3	2	1	0
15. My free times during the day are too short to include exercise.	3	2	1	0
16. My usual social activities with family or friends do not include physical activity.	3	2	1	0

How likely are you to say?	Very likely	Somewhat likely	Somewhat unlikely	Very unlikely
17. I'm too tired during the week and I need the weekend to catch up on my rest.	3	2	1	0
18. I want to get more exercise, but I just can't seem to make myself stick to anything.	3	2	1	0
19. I'm afraid I might injure myself or have a heart attack.	3	2	1	0
20. I'm not good enough at any physical activity to make it fun.	3	2	1	0
21. If we had exercise facilities and showers at work, then I would be more likely to exercise.	3	2	1	0

Follow these instructions to score yourself:

- Enter the circled number in the spaces provided, putting the number for statement 1 on line 1, statement 2 on line 2, and so on.
- Add the three scores on each line. Your barriers to physical activity fall into one or more of seven categories: lack of time, social influences, lack of energy, lack of will power, fear of injury, lack of skill, and lack of resources. A score of 5 or above in any category shows that this is an important barrier for you to overcome.

____ + ____ + ____ = _____
  1   8   15   Lack of time

____ + ____ + ____ = _____
  2   9   16   Social influence

____ + ____ + ____ = _____
  3   10   17   Lack of energy

____ + ____ + ____ = _____
  4   11   18   Lack of willpower

____ + ____ + ____ = _____
  5   12   19   Fear of injury

____ + ____ + ____ = _____
  6   13   20   Lack of skill

____ + ____ + ____ = _____
  7   14   21   Lack of resources

Change need not take place all at once. During the early phases of skill development, success is facilitated by *guided practice*, in which an instructor guides the learner, with timely and appropriate feedback, in the proper way of carrying out an activity. By rewarding each correct step, the instructor actually "shapes" the desired behavior (Parcel and Baranowski 1981).

Build into your program design numerous opportunities for people to experience success in their attempts to reach their goals. There is nothing like a feeling of success to motivate a person to achieve more!

Give People Opportunities to Sample New Behaviors

Help people try on the idea of being physically active by sampling new behaviors and skills with real "hands-on" experiences. As with the strategies used by major marketing firms, you can provide "miniature samples" and "taste tests" of new products and services by offering brief exposures to a variety of physical activities.

Consider sponsoring seasonal campaigns and special events with meaningful incentives that will entice target population members to try something new. Events should emphasize fun. Examples include

- a step aerobics class where hundreds of people can participate at once,
- a free family pass for a visit to the community pool,
- a free family night at the ice rink, an afternoon community-wide walk on a nature trail, or
- a free paddle-boat or tandem bicycle rental in the park.

Such sampling may convince people that adopting a more physically active lifestyle can be fun and enjoyable.

Model the Desired Behavior

A basic premise of *modeling* is that people of all ages can gain a great deal of information by observing the actions of others and seeing the consequences of those actions played out in other's lives (Wallston 1994; Bandura 1986). Identify people who can serve as effective role models for an active lifestyle. An effective role model is someone with whom the target audience can identify.

People may prefer to model those who are like themselves—their friends, relatives, neighbors, and peers—rather than celebrities and athletes. These are people whom they perceive as credible and trustworthy, and who have demonstrated successfully that regular physical activity can be maintained even in the busiest daily schedules.

To be effective, the lessons to be learned or the skills to be demonstrated must be clearly observable. For example, people can observe experts demonstrating a new skill, watch actors or puppeteers conveying a message through a skit, listen to storytellers reciting a lesson-filled story, or overhear friends sharing how being physically active has made a difference in their lives.

Observations need not be limited to in-person interactions. With the growing popularity of advanced technologies, your program could take advantage of a variety of media, such as television, video, satellite broadcasts, interactive CD ROM, and computer-generated animation. You have numerous creative channels from which to choose.

Provide Opportunities for Safe, Guided Practice

Learning a new skill and becoming proficient in it often requires more than simple observation. Learning can be enhanced by *guided practice* as one imitates someone who demonstrates a skill step by step, as one practices under the expert guidance of someone who does it well, as one engages in simple trial and error, or as one experiences repeated successes until a new skill is mastered (Kibler et al. 1974).

As a program planner, you can provide safe settings in which people have the opportunity to practice being physically active for short periods of time. For example, people learning how to drive a car often try at first in an empty parking lot and in the presence of someone who knows how to drive. They practice their driving skills before venturing onto the interstate highway. The same principle holds true for learning physical activity-related skills.

People need to practice in a safe environment—a setting free from unnecessary physical and psychological harm (e.g., embarrassment, teasing, or criticism). Your program can find or create those places where people know it is okay to be imperfect or to look silly as they practice newly acquired skills and make early attempts to incorporate regular physical activity into their lives.

Encourage Self-Reporting and Self-Discovery

Various forms of record keeping and *self-monitoring* may be useful techniques in building self-control as people learn to track their personal progress toward their goals (Bandura 1986). To enhance the process of self-discovery, you might encourage people to become aware of potential as well as missed opportunities to engage in a desired behavior by keeping a daily activity diary or by writing in a personal journal. In it they might note the times of day most conducive to being active; keep track of the people and the community resources that best support their intention to change; and describe their personal progress in setting priorities, achieving personal goals, and in overcoming daily obstacles to changed behavior.

Build in Cues for Action

Consider teaching people how to restructure their personal environments in ways that reinforce their intention to carry out a desired action—the concept of *stimulus control*. Help them to purposefully build into their daily schedules tangible reminders to be active (e.g., keep a pair of comfortable shoes by the door, in the car, or at the office as a reminder to take a walk) while minimizing temptations that may deter them from successful behavior change (e.g., keep the television remote control out of site).

Contract for Success

As you teach people how to get started, consider using a behavioral contract in which people are asked to specify in writing their goals and precisely what they plan to do in order to achieve them. This may be an effective technique to use with individuals who need a little more structure in developing a personal plan of action (Parcel and Baranowski 1981). Include a realistic time frame and have people describe how they will reward themselves along the way.

Contracting is a potent educational tool in adult education because it lends itself easily to the educational needs most characteristic of adult learners. For example, contracting (Knowles 1984)

- allows individuals or small groups of adults to tailor-make their own learning plans, bringing together people who have a wide range of backgrounds, education, experience, interests, motivations, and abilities;
- gives the learner a sense of ownership of the objectives he or she will pursue;
- makes optimal use of a wide variety of resources so that different learners can go to different resources to learn the same things;
- provides each learner with a visible structure for systemizing his or her learning; and
- provides a systematic procedure for involving the learner responsibly in evaluating the learning outcomes.

Enhance Self-Efficacy

How confident are members of your target audience in their ability to incorporate physical activity into their daily lives? Do they believe they can do it? *Self-efficacy* is a person's belief that he or she has mastered the skills necessary to engage successfully in a new behavior (Abrams et al. 1986). This perceived confidence to act is one of the most powerful predictors of behavior change (Wallston 1994). People who rate highly in self-efficacy may be more willing to take risks, more confident in their ability to try something new, more likely to persist until they succeed, and more likely to resist episodes of relapse (Bandura 1986).

If people intend to be more physically active, yet lack the essential self-efficacy to carry out their intentions, they will have difficulty getting started and will be more easily discouraged whenever they run into obstacles. In order to strengthen their self-efficacy, these individuals require adequate training in the essential skills needed to engage in a regularly active lifestyle, with opportunity for guided practice and constructive feedback until they can perform those skills confidently on their own, with increasingly less dependence on factors outside of themselves, such as motivating rewards or incentives, the expertise of an instructor, various forms of social support or financial support, certain characteristics of the physical environment, drug therapies if used, or even sheer luck. If members of your population attribute their successful ability to change behavior on the basis of one of these external factors, they will be highly vulnerable to relapse once their perceived supports are removed (Abrams et al. 1986). If physical activity promotion efforts fail to build self-efficacy within individuals desiring to change, the new behaviors may last only as long as the program exerts its external pressures.

Ideas for Action in the Community

Teach or Enhance Skills Needed to Establish and Maintain a Physically Active Lifestyle

- Identify the skills that people need to make a change in their physical activity levels, then plan programs to teach those skills—for example,
  - —increasing physical activity routinely throughout the day;
  - —starting a walking or jogging program;
  - —selecting the right shoes, clothing, or equipment;
  - —using exercise or sports equipment properly and safely;
  - —stretching, warm-up, and cool-down techniques;
  - —exercising while sitting in a chair, standing, or watching television;
  - —avoiding the risks of injury from exercise;
  - —taking lessons of any kind (e.g., swimming, sailing, golf, or tennis); or
  - —maintaining physical activity and preventing relapse to a sedentary lifestyle.
- For groups of various ages or levels of experience, work with physical education instructors, physical therapists, or exercise physiologists to design appropriate and quality instructional programs.
- Enhance the skills of gatekeepers who can successfully reach members of the target audience. Instruct physicians on effective techniques of assessment and counseling for physical activity.
- Develop or make available self-instructional materials, such as videotaped instruction, cassette tape instruction, computer-based instruction, how-to guides, manuals, and kits.
- Develop a community resource list so that people will know where to find courses or opportunities to develop skills.
- Provide formal and informal activity-oriented instructional programs, such as workshops, classes, seminars, demonstrations, lessons, and lectures.
- Provide individual assessment and counseling or personal trainers for a fee or as an incentive.
- Sponsor "meet the expert" events so community members can learn directly from those who have mastered various skills.
- Conduct demonstrations or small-group classes with active involvement by participants.
- Provide opportunities to try the desired behavior for just 1 day or for one event, such as
  - —community walking events;
  - —using stairs instead of elevators for 1 day or 1 week;
  - —bicycle-to-work day or other bicycling events;
  - —periodic fun runs, such as the turkey trot (Thanksgiving), reindeer run (Christmas), and bunny hop (Easter);
  - —lunchtime walking groups at local businesses, schools, or shopping malls; and
  - —trial memberships and guest passes to use recreational facilities.
- Reward each effort appropriately, praise success, and provide constructive feedback.

Enhancing Readiness to Change

One of the more challenging pieces of the intervention puzzle is to tailor your intervention based on your population's readiness to change based on the Stages of Change Model (Prochaska et al. 1992). If your population is in the Contemplation stage, for example, you'll want to focus on specific messages that are likely to help them progress to the Preparation stage. You don't want to waste your time on activities or messages that are more appropriate for someone who's at a different stage.

What motivates individuals to make progress along the continuum of behavior change differs considerably according to the person's stage of change—that is, their degree of readiness and intention to change. Because needs and motivations vary from one stage to another, program strategies that match the individual to a variety of stage-specific messages and activities may be most effective in achieving behavior change (Marcus et al. 1994). Your challenge is to help people progress from one stage in the continuum to the next, rather than from one end of the continuum to the other. The following sections describe common characteristics of people in each stage, and what your intervention can do to encourage progress to the next stage.

> Recent studies have suggested that helping people progress through just one stage can double the chances of successful action in the near future.
>
> *C. DiClemente et al., 1991*

Questions to Assess Stage of Change

NOTE: Questions target both moderate and vigorous physical activity, by interchanging the terms in survey items.

If a person does not currently participate in physical activity, ask:

"Do you intend to increase your participation in moderate (vigorous) physical activity in the next six months?"

If answer is "no," they are in Precontemplation.

If answer is "yes," they are in the Contemplation stage.

If a person currently participates in physical activity, ask:

"Do you engage in regular moderate physical activity?"

If the answer is "no," that person is in the Preparation stage.

If answer is "yes," that person is in either the Action stage or the Maintenance stage.

Common Characteristics of People in Precontemplation

People in this stage have no serious intention to change behavior in the forseeable future, and certainly not within the next 6 months.

They really do not want to change to become physically active. They may resist suggestions that they could benefit from a more active lifestyle; they may deny that their activity level is less than optimal. Precontemplators may be unaware of the problem or risk associated with their behavior (inactivity) or deny that the consequences of being sedentary are relevant to them. People in this stage may be unaware of the many benefits of the desirable behavior (being regularly physically active); consequently they minimize the importance of a regularly active lifestyle. Their reasons *not to change* (to become regularly physically active) outnumber or outweigh their reasons *to change*. Precontemplators may feel discouraged about their ability to change (low self-efficacy). Perhaps they have tried and failed in the past and have become demoralized, no longer believing that they are capable of changing. Or, they may have become disillusioned by having attempted too great or too rapid a behavior change at some time in the past.

THE CHANGE CONTINUUM

How to Encourage Progress from Precontemplation Toward Contemplation

- Provide accurate information and convincing or compelling evidence. Help them to see and appreciate the benefits of the desired behavior, by emphasizing the benefits of physical activity rather than dwelling on the risks of chronic inactivity. Increase awareness of what they might miss if they choose *not to be active.*

- Emphasize the short-term benefits of being active (e.g., feeling invigorated, sleeping better, reducing stress, feeling better about oneself), how being active today can have relatively immediate effects.

- Link benefits of a physically active lifestyle to people's highest priorities and values in life (e.g., relationship with family, personal faith, health, or happiness). (For more on life priority exercises, see White and Maloney 1990.)

- Explore possible misconceptions about being regularly active and assist people in identifying ways to overcome them. For example, if someone is afraid of injury, point out that the risk of injury is low and unlikely if someone starts out slowly and gradually builds in intensity.

- Assess how sedentary people see themselves. Can they visualize themselves as active people? Is that image a positive one? Bolster their self-esteem with unconditional positive feedback at first and then with more selective and helpful feedback as self-esteem improves.

- Help them understand how their current behavior affects them personally and others in their lives—that is, how and why a physically active and healthy lifestyle is relevant to them. For example, sedentary parents model an unhealthy lifestyle to their children.

Common Characteristics of People in Contemplation

People in the Contemplation stage are thinking about becoming more physically active within the next 6 months but have not yet committed to taking action.

They are considering overcoming a problem or making a change from an old way of life to a new, but there is still considerable ambivalence.

They might know what to do but are not quite ready to take the first step. They may be substituting thinking for action ("Someday, I'll change").

They are still stuck in "decisional balance" (weighing the pros and cons). Perhaps for them the reasons not to change still outweigh the reasons to change. Perhaps their rule of thumb is "When in doubt, don't change" (a rule that until now may have served them well).

For them, the barriers to being regularly active outweigh what they perceive to be the benefits of an active lifestyle. Perhaps a barrier to being active, such as time or energy, seems too difficult to overcome.

THE CHANGE CONTINUUM

How to Encourage Progress from Contemplation Toward Preparation

- Help them to specifically identify their barriers to change. Determine what is standing in their way (e.g., know-how, time, money, convenience, access, or attitude). Explore alternatives. Do they have misconceptions about physical activity that may be hindering action?

- Help them weigh the pros and cons of a physically active lifestyle. Focus on the costs of changing— the effort, the energy, and the things they must give up to overcome a sedentary lifestyle. Ask them what would motivate them to overcome their perceived barriers.

- Assess their levels of self-efficacy on being physically active. How confident are they in incorporating regular activity into their daily lives? Do they believe that they can do what you ask them to do? Provide motivating messages to build self-confidence.

- Cultivate the most basic skills needed to achieve a physically active lifestyle. The skills might be as simple as selecting appropriate shoes or clothing.

- Explore a variety of activities available to each person. Identify a short menu of such activities, including past activities that were enjoyable, activities that have never been tried before but sound interesting, activities that could be done with family members and friends, and solitary activities.

- Help them to set small, specific goals such as "I will walk the dog for 10 minutes every day" rather than "I will be more active each day." Goals can be slowly increased each week. Be realistic. Help build into the goals a small reward for achievement.

- Emphasize that by starting small and progressing slowly they can be successful. Assist them in identifying ways in which activity can be built into their daily routines (e.g., taking the stairs at work).

Characteristics of People in Preparation

People in this stage are ready to begin participating in physical activity, or they may currently exercise but not regularly.

They may have a plan and may know what they need to do, yet they may be uncertain or anxious about the outcomes of their actions.

They may show small signs of progress. Perhaps they have taken some action in the recent past that had mixed or inconsistent results.

They may be acting on their desire to change and make short-term attempts at the desired behavior.

Their activities may be sporadic and less than a total of 30 minutes per day of moderate physical activity or 20 minutes of vigorous physical activity 3 or more days per week. For example, they joined an aerobics dance class but failed to attend the recommended number of times each week or dropped out after a few sessions. Or they walk on the weekends but need a nudge to achieve consistent activity over the course of the week.

THE CHANGE CONTINUUM

How to Encourage Progress from Preparation Toward Action

- Help develop a plan for regular activity, and emphasize small, specific, and realistic goals. By helping people to achieve small successes, you will improve their levels of self-efficacy.
- Show them how much fun physical activity can be.
- Reinforce attempts to become more active. Emphasize that any activity is healthier than no activity at all.
- Teach methods of self-monitoring, such as keeping a log or diary, to increase awareness of current behavior patterns or to keep track of progress.
- Help them focus attention on goals accomplished rather than on failures. Encourage use of self-rewards and analysis of failures to develop appropriate coping techniques.
- Discuss barriers to regular activity and elicit ways to overcome those barriers.
- Give anticipatory guidance. Emphasize that progress is gradual and has occasional setbacks. Help them to identify situations likely to lead to lapses, and develop an action plan of at least three alternative responses. Occasionally missing an exercise time is inevitable. The key is in helping them think through how they will handle it (perhaps by modifying defeatist or negative thoughts, promptly rescheduling the missed event, or allowing themselves a certain number of missed exercise times each month).
- Encourage them to make use of social support networks, such as walking clubs or friends or co-workers who exercise during lunch breaks.
- Reinforce the basic skills needed to change behavior (e.g., planning ahead or rewarding behavior). To be successful, what do they need to know how to do?
- Encourage them to make a commitment to change, perhaps by signing a contract promising to make the desired change. Have them share their decision with another person to confirm that they have decided to act.
- Help them restructure their daily environment to avoid problematic behaviors and increase the probability of acting on desired ones. For example, keep comfortable walking shoes at the office or in the car, have a bag for the gym packed and ready to go, post motivating messages on the mirror, keep a walking buddy's phone number by the phone, or keep the dog's leash by the door.

Characteristics of People in Action

People in this stage are active but have been active for less than 6 months. They have modified their behavior or environment to overcome their barriers and change their lifestyles.

They are now physically active and are accumulating 30 minutes of moderate physical activity daily or participating in at least 20 minutes of vigorous physical activity at least 3 times per week.

During this phase, they are particularly at risk of reverting to old patterns of behavior.

THE CHANGE CONTINUUM

How to Encourage Progress from Action Toward Maintenance

- Provide positive, direct, and appropriate feedback. Nothing builds self-confidence and self-efficacy like being successful.

- Help them develop long-range goals for physical activity (e.g., "I would like to participate in next year's five-mile fun walk") and short-term goals that will facilitate achievement of the long-range goals (e.g., "I will be able to walk three miles by December").

- Explore and develop a menu of activities that will reduce risk of injury and boredom. Encourage them to sample a variety of activities and to practice being active in different places and situations.

- Help them maintain buddy systems.

- Inform them that people building healthy lifestyle habits often become discouraged when they fail to meet their goals, especially when the behavior is fairly new. Help them to anticipate lapses and accept them as a normal part of the change process. A lapse does not mean failure.

- Identify episodes when they had brief lapses and explore underlying reasons. Anticipate and prepare for these same events if they are likely to recur (e.g., normal demands of work and family, occasional illness, bad weather, or out-of-town visitors).

- Watch for times when temporary lapses lead to loss of confidence, discouragement, or giving up.

- Remind them to build in rewards to maintain motivation. These can be intangible, such as achieving goals or developing self-regulatory skills, or tangible, such as a new pair of walking shoes.

- Encourage them to restructure their daily environments to increase the likelihood that they will continue their efforts. For example, keep comfortable walking shoes at the office or in the car, arrange for babysitting on aerobics class nights, or take 15 minutes each morning to walk.

Characteristics of People in Maintenance

People in this stage have successfully sustained the desired behavior for more than 6 months. They may have experienced periods of time when lapses occurred, but they were successful in reestablishing the desired behavior.

THE CHANGE CONTINUUM

How to Encourage Continuation of a Desired Behavior

- Help ensure that they set realistic goals to reduce risk of injury.
- Provide a supportive environment or a boost of support from time to time. Make use of naturally occurring groups for support (e.g., friends, coworkers, neighbors, or family members).
- Give positive reinforcement and direct, positive feedback. Help them recognize and appreciate their higher self-confidence. Reinforce their sense of personal responsibility for having successfully made changes. The more people can attribute success to their own decisions and actions, the better.
- Encourage them to build variety into the physically active lifestyle. Keep making it fun; try new or different twists to an old theme. Engage successful people to serve as role models, and arrange for them to help others with similar situations (buddy systems). Being a role model may bring intrinsic rewards (the good feelings one experiences from helping others) and extrinsic rewards (e.g., honoraria for speaking engagements, appreciation awards, or public recognition) and will reinforce their motivation to persist with their active lifestyles.

Adapted from Marcus et al. 1992a and 1992b; Prochaska et al. 1992; and Cotton and Jarvis 1993.

Helping People Who May Be in Relapse

Relapse management skills become important to people regardless of the stage they are in. In fact, about one-half of the people who undertake an exercise program drop out during the first 3 to 6 months (Carmody et al.1980; Dishman 1988), and so repeat an earlier stage of change.

Those who remain committed to implementing the desired lifestyle change may, at times, take a break from their regular activities, perhaps during illness or injury, inclement weather, conflicting family needs, or any simple interruption to daily routine. If they are unsuccessful in reestablishing their activities in a reasonable time, and you question them about their level of activity within the past 6 months, you might determine them to be in the Precontemplation, Contemplation, or Preparation stage.

But knowing that an individual had once been in the Action or Maintenance stage might help you to customize your messages or services even more precisely. Suddenly, this individual has relevant past experiences from which to draw new lessons. How did he or she overcome barriers to being active and maintain active lifestyles before? What has worked for him or her in the past? What was not helpful? What has caused this current relapse and how can you help them to prevent its recurrence?

Although relapse itself is not a stage, knowledge of it does provide helpful information to the program planner. Consider, then, asking each person who is not now active: "Was there ever a time in the recent past when you were regularly active for at least 3 months?" Certainly, you would interpret someone's fond memories of being active during his college years differently depending on whether the person is a young man in his 20s or a middle-aged man in his 40s. Regardless of age, however, if a person responds affirmatively to such a question, there is a possibility that he or she is in relapse.

Read More About It

Relapse Prevention

Brownell KD, Stunkard AJ, Albaum JM. Evaluation and modification of exercise patterns in the natural environment. *American Journal of Psychiatry* 1980; 137:1540–1545.

Dishman RK. Increasing and maintaining exercise and physical activity. *Behavior Therapy* 1991; 22:345–378.

Marcus BH, Stanton AL. Evaluation of relapse prevention and reinforcement interventions to promote exercise adherence in sedentary females. *Research Quarterly for Exercise and Sport* 1993; 64:447–452.

Marlatt GA, George WH. Relapse prevention and the maintenance of optimal health. In: Shumaker SA, Schron EB, Ockene JK, Parker CT, Probstfield JL, Wolle JM, editors. *The Handbook of Health Behavior Change.* New York: Springer Publishing Co., 1990:44–63.

Examples of Stage-Matched Interventions

Project PACE

The Physician-Based Assessment and Counseling for Exercise Project (Project PACE) was developed by researchers and clinicians at San Diego State University, with support from the Centers for Disease Control and Prevention, and the Association of Teachers of Preventive Medicine. Project PACE materials inform physicians and other health professionals about the benefits of physical activity and how to respond to patients' questions about physical activity. The materials enable physicians to evaluate patients' health status and readiness to become more active (using an assessment form that can be completed by the patient in the waiting room in 1–2 minutes) and provide physicians standardized forms and guidelines to help them counsel patients regarding their activity levels. Patient counseling can be done in 1–5 minutes using the PACE forms.

The objective of the Project PACE patient counseling protocol is to assess individuals' current physical activity habits, to determine their readiness to change according to the Stages of Change model (using only the Precontemplation, Contemplation, and Action stages), and to move them to the next stage. Although Project PACE focuses on individual patient behavior change, the organizational structure of a health care setting (e.g., making sure patients are provided PACE forms and that the forms are included with the patients' charts) and the personnel (administrative personnel, physicians, support staff, nurses, nurse practitioners, physician assistants, and other health professionals) need to be supportive of physical activity counseling for patients if counseling is to be successful. Such support will be necessary whether PACE is used in a large setting such as a managed health care organization or in a physician's private office. See the Suggested Reading list at the end of this chapter for more resources related to Project PACE.

A Sample Worksite Study

In one worksite study, an intervention was designed to increase the initiation, adoption, and maintenance of physical activity among employees. Employees were randomly assigned to either a stage-matched self-help intervention group or a standard self-help intervention group. Both interventions consisted only of printed materials. After 3 months, significantly more employees in the stage-matched group had increased their physical activity level and had advanced to the next stage of change. The employees in the standard group, however, displayed no stage change or regression to earlier stages (Marcus et al. 1998).

A Sample Comprehensive Program

In one Rhode Island community with a population of about 72,000 people, 610 residents enrolled in a 6-week intervention program designed to encourage participation in physical activity among those in the Contemplation (39% of residents), Preparation (37% of residents), and Action (24% of residents) stages.

The campaign reached people through worksites, area schools, organizations, and local media. The participants in the intervention received written materials matched to their individual stage of change. The intervention included materials designed to encourage participants to initiate or increase physical activity, a resource manual describing activity options in the community, and information about weekly "fun walks" and "activity nights."

After 6 weeks, 62% of participants in the Contemplation stage and 61% in the Preparation stage had become significantly more active. Among those who were already in the Action stage at baseline, fewer than 10% relapsed to an earlier stage of change (Marcus et al. 1992a).

While some researchers point to problems in this study's research design (for example, there was no control group), the intervention might yet be effective in motivating other program designers to consider a stage-based approach.

Suggested Reading

For a list of organizations, agencies, and selected program materials for promoting physical activity, see:

Resource A, for general resources

Chapter 6, for environment-related resources

Chapter 9, for worksite-related resources

Chapter 10, for school-related resources

For more information about conducting successful awareness campaigns, read:

Backer TE, Rogers EM, Sopory P. *Designing Health Communication Campaigns: What Works.* Newbury Park, CA: Sage Publications, 1992.

Backer TE, Rogers EM. *Organizational Aspects of Health Communication Campaigns.* Newbury Park, CA: Sage Publications, 1993.

Maibach E, Parrott RL. *Designing Health Messages: Approaches from Communication Theory and Public Health Practice.* Thousand Oaks, CA: Sage Publications, 1995.

Rice RE, Atkin CK, editors. *Public Communication Campaigns* (2nd Edition). Newbury Park, CA: Sage Publications, 1989.

Salmon CT, editor. *Information Campaigns: Balancing Social Values and Social Change.* Newbury Park, CA: Sage Publications, 1989.

For more information about Project PACE, and the physician's role in behavior change, read:

Long B, Calfas K, Wooten W, Sharpe D, Patrick K, Sallis J. *Project PACE Physician Manual: Physician-Based Assessment and Counseling.* Atlanta: Centers for Disease Control and Prevention, 1992.

Patrick K, Sallis JF, Long B, Calfas KJ, Wooten W, Heath G, Pratt M. A new tool for encouraging activity: Project PACE. *The Physician and Sportsmedicine* 1994; 22(11):45–52.

Wechsler H, Levine S, Idelson RK, et al. The physician's role in health promotion: a survey of primary care practitioners. *New England Journal of Medicine* 1983; 308:97–100.

For cost and ordering information, contact:

Project PACE
San Diego State University
Student Health Service
5500 Campanile Drive
San Diego, CA 92182-4701
Phone: 619-594-5949
Fax: 619-594-5613

For a valuable review of the literature regarding physical activity interventions, read:

American Journal of Preventive Medicine. November 1998. 15(4): 255–440.
To obtain a copy of this special issue, contact the publisher, Elsevier Science, toll-free at 888-437-4636 or via fax 212-633-3913.

Dishman RK, Oldenburg B, O'Neal H, Shephard RJ. Worksite Physical Activity Interventions. *American Journal of Preventive Medicine* November 1998; 15(4): 344–361.

King AC, Rejeski WJ, Buchner DM. Physical Activity Interventions Targeting Older Adults: A Critical Review and Recommendations. *American Journal of Preventive Medicine* November 1988; 15(4): 316–333.

For more information on implementing the Stages of Change model, read:

Chapman LS. The Role of Incentives in Health Promotion. *Art of Health Promotion* (newsletter) 2 no. 3 (July/August 1998): 1–4.

Prochaska JO, DiClemente CC, Norcross JC. In Search of How People Change: Applications to Addictive Behaviors. *American Psychologist* 1992; 47(9):1102–1114.

Prochaska JO, Norcross JC, DiClemente CC. *Changing for Good.* New York: William Morrow and Company, 1994.

Chapter 6 Creating a Supportive Environment

Now that you've learned about how to implement the pieces of the intervention puzzle that are related to the individual, it's time to focus on what you can do to your target population's environment to help promote a more physically active lifestyle.

The *environment* refers to all of the objective structural factors, external to the individual, that both positively and negatively influence a person's behavior (Baranowski et al. 1997). *Environmental interventions* contribute to behavior change by advocating and implementing measures that will make it easier for people to engage in the desirable behaviors, whether they are aware of it or not, while making it more difficult to engage in competing and less desirable behaviors.

> People seek five things in an environment. In a private conversation with a highly accomplished airlines marketing director, I learned the secret five things all people seek from a service, event, or place they use or visit. These are: Security, Convenience, Efficiency, Comfort, and Welcome. The omission of any one of these five factors leads the customer to somebody else's hotel, airline, theme park, street, or transit. . . . [A]nd these five factors can be achieved to the advantage of alert and competitive businesses or towns.
>
> *Dan Burden, March 1997*
> Walkable Communities: A Search for Quality

To be *supportive,* the environment must provide certain material, human, and political resources—factors that can effectively promote and protect the adoption, implementation, and maintenance of the desired behavior in a given population. In physical activity promotion, a supportive environment would be one in which members of the target population could freely achieve and maintain a physically active lifestyle. It would include

- a social network in which people are supportive of one another's efforts to be physically active;
- a variety of favorable and safe physical conditions, such as climate, natural topography, or human-made land-use design; as well as abundant opportunities to be physically active; and
- a political infrastructure where policies and legal incentives exist to support a person's desire to achieve and maintain a physically active lifestyle, while removing or altering real or perceived social, physical, and political barriers to being active.

Deciding which environmental resources and characteristics are most supportive, relevant, and appropriate depends on several things: on the nature of the desired behavior itself, characteristics of the targeted population members who require support, and the specific situation in which a desired action must take place. This chapter will cover three strategies you can use to develop the environmental aspects of the intervention puzzle:

- fostering supportive social networks,
- establishing a supportive physical environment, and
- establishing and enforcing supportive policies.

 ## Fostering Supportive Social Networks

In Roger's Diffusion of Innovation theory (1983), social networks and interpersonal channels are considered more important than mass media in influencing behavior-change or adoption decisions. In fact, innovations do not even seem to "take off" until social networks have become activated—until people are actively talking about the innovative idea, program, or product (Rogers 1983).

Using a *social network* approach to building a supportive environment, a program planner must consider all of the linkages that exist among people—the complex web of social interactions affecting members of the targeted population. This approach focuses on more than one relationship at a time and considers how change to any one relationship affects other relationships in the social network. Each relationship in the social network can vary in its type and intensity, and tends to serve a function that may or may not lend social support.

Recognize the Need for Social Support

The influence that one person has on another cannot be overemphasized. Having supportive others in one's life, available to talk, share feelings, ask questions, or receive honest feedback, is critical to initiating and maintaining the process of behavior change. Therefore, program planners must consider the social influences, positive as well as negative, surrounding the individual who is trying to change. Learning itself is greatly enhanced by interaction with others who share ideas and common life experiences (Knowles 1984).

To qualify as socially supportive, an interpersonal relationship or transaction must provide some form of assistance, perhaps in the form of tangible aid and service; timely and appropriate information; constructive criticism, feedback, suggestions, or advice; or as genuine expressions of openness, caring, empathy, trust, and love (Heaney and Israel 1997).

Unsupportive relationships are those characterized by distrust, criticism, domination, disagreement, harassment, or abuse. Of the many types of relationships that exist between individuals, relationships that are emotionally supportive are most consistently associated with good health and well-being (Heaney and Israel 1997; House 1987).

Who provides social support has a great effect on the type, amount, skillfulness, and effectiveness of the support given. Therefore, *who* provides social support is such a critical factor that it is ultimately more important than *what* help is given or *when* it is given (Heaney and Israel 1997). Support is most

successfully shared among individuals who are socially similar, who have shared common life experiences, who have coped with similar stressors and situations, and who tend to have similar personal attributes, such as beliefs, educational level, or other common traits (Rogers 1983).

Perhaps these characteristics enhance not only the support provider's empathy, but also the appropriateness of the help given, for the assistance is more likely to be consistent with the needs and values of the recipient. And the recipient's perceptions of the helper may be more positive, as one who is empathetic and understanding, someone with whom they can identify, someone whose opinions they can trust.

When the social support is given also determines to some extent the effectiveness of the interaction. The social support needs of the recipient will greatly vary according to the individual's chronological age, developmental age, life stage, and level of readiness and intention, or stage of change (Heaney and Israel 1997).

Whenever people are undergoing periods of transition in their lives, in addition to the emotionally close ties they require for optimal mental health,

Ideas for Action in the Community

Foster Supportive Social Networks

- Encourage people to find support for their decision to be physically active from coworkers, family, friends, neighbors, or significant others.
- Set up teams, buddy systems, or adopt-an-exercise partner programs for increased accountability.
- Encourage personal contracts or pledges between close friends or family members.
- Establish small group classes or support groups for special sites, target audiences, or the community at large.
- Make use of team or group contests and team sports or events.
- Involve spouses, family members, and significant others in programs whenever possible.
- Set up hot lines or help lines for additional information and support.
- Form or support local walking and sports clubs. Neighborhoods could form walking clubs for their residents (possibly reducing crime with increased resident visibility).
- Develop community resource lists so that people will know where to find physical activity-related clubs, organizations, or events.
- Conduct family- or peer-oriented events, instruction, or programs.
- Work with local health professionals to improve their physical activity assessment skills, and help them be more supportive of their patients who are trying to increase their physical activity level.
- Provide specialized programs for people who have similar concerns, such as physical disabilities, multiple risk factors for chronic disease, or age-specific characteristics.
- Build community-based or site-based coalitions or health planning task forces to plan and carry out health promotion activities for their groups.

Social Network Intervention Strategies

Strengthen existing social network linkages

- Train network members in skills to improve their provision of social support across diverse situations.
- Train members of the targeted population in skills needed to mobilize and maintain social networks.
- Train or counsel significant social groups (e.g., marriage and family counseling, team building, peer group counseling).

Develop new social network linkages

- On the individual level, introduce people to each other.
- Create new linkages to people who can provide specialized roles, such as teaching, counseling, modeling, or mentoring.
- Encourage people to be accountable to others; develop partnerships and buddy systems.
- Coordinate self-help and support groups, interactive computer technologies such as chat rooms, listserves, interactive Internet sites.
- On the organizational or community level, introduce organizations to each other. Foster partnership development, encourage coalition building, bring together organizations whose social networks overlap to address the needs of common target audiences or common goals.

Enhance network linkages by endorsing the specialized roles of particular members, "lay advisors," or other indigenous natural helpers

- Identify exemplary network members who might serve as role models of desired behaviors.
- Identify natural leaders who are capable of positively influencing and supporting others in the social network.
- Identify individuals who are natural helpers in the community, individuals to whom others naturally turn for advice or assistance
- Train and equip natural leaders and helpers with knowledge and skills needed to foster behavior change in the community, such as teaching them health topics and community problem-solving strategies.
- Compensate network members who take on specialized roles and responsibilities by providing appropriate rewards and recognition.

Strive to mitigate the potentially harmful or unsupportive interactions within social networks

- Consider restructuring the social, physical, or political environments to lessen the intensity or frequency of the deleterious social interactions (e.g., administering disciplinary action, requesting a transfer, moving away, changing schools, changing careers, adding police protection).
- Replace harmful network linkages with new or enhanced and intensely positive linkages to counterbalance negative effects with positive ones.
- Train or counsel individual members to build self-esteem and self-efficacy for the desired behaviors.

Adapted from Heaney and Israel 1997.

they benefit most from having reliable social networks that are large and widely scattered (diffuse). These less intense social ties tend to be adaptable, and may therefore be best suited for the purpose of facilitating change by providing the social outreach and supportive information most needed during transitional periods (Israel 1982; Heaney and Israel 1997).

Program planners should include target audience participation in assessing existing and potential social network characteristics and significant social influences. What were the target population's answers when you asked, "Who would support you, and who would oppose you if you were to become more physically active? How important are each of these individuals in your life?" (Ajzen and Fishbein 1980). Whom did they identify among their friends, relatives, neighbors, or acquaintances, peers, classmates, teachers, colleagues, coworkers, supervisors, employees, or health professionals? These people are critical to your intervention plans, for they represent the sources of social influence and the contributors to the social norms that will greatly determine whether members of the targeted population will be motivated to change.

Filling in the Gaps

Once you have identified gaps or potential problems in the social support network, you can respond to the need for supportive relationships by creating opportunities for people to interact in positive and meaningful ways, perhaps through confidential counseling and help lines, skill-building and training sessions, open discussion groups, playful competitions, team-building experiences, supportive buddy systems, or interactive computer technologies.

You may also enhance group, organizational, and community linkages by establishing creative partnerships (for more information on partnerships, see chapter 7), expanding opportunities for direct and indirect communication, fostering competition and recognition through awards; by building databases and information clearinghouses; as well as by using a variety of other high-technology interactive opportunities. Chapters 9 and 10 provide additional suggestions on developing supportive social networks within worksites and schools, respectively.

 ## Establishing a Supportive Physical Environment

The physical surroundings describe everything from the quality of the air people breathe to the quantity and quality of the activity-related resources available at home, at school, at work, and throughout the community. A physical environment should provide ample opportunities to be physically active.

Learning theorists seem to agree that the richness and accessibility of resources, both material and human, are critical to effective learning and are therefore critical to adopting and maintaining desired behavior change (Knowles 1984). Resources should have the following characteristics:

- **Available.** Do resources exist?
- **Accessible.** Can people obtain them or reach them with relative ease? To what extent is access barrier free? Are the resources available *when* they are needed; *where* they are needed?

- **Affordable.** What are the perceived or actual costs (e.g., financial, emotional) of access?

- **Acceptable.** Do people perceive the resource favorably? Do its benefits outweigh costs?

- **Appropriate.** Are resources commensurate with need—in the quantity needed; of the quality needed; for the purpose intended?

By assessing the target population's daily physical environments, a program planner considers the extent to which environmental characteristics will either positively or negatively influence the population's attainment of desired behavioral goals. Intervention strategies may include making the following efforts within the surrounding areas or throughout the community in which members of the targeted population work, worship, live, and play:

- Identifying potential resources
- Eliminating, modifying, or mitigating negative environmental influences
- Establishing, maintaining, or advocating for positive environmental influences

As you plan strategies to enrich the physical environment with increased opportunities to be physically active, do not be surprised if you start looking at your community from an entirely new perspective. Perhaps for the first time, you may find yourself

- noticing whether neighborhoods have sidewalks with appropriate pedestrian buffers,
- searching busy intersections for safe pedestrian crosswalks,
- measuring the shoulders on highways for potential bicycle pathways,
- testing the quality of soil on vacant city lots for potential use as a community garden,
- entering office buildings to determine how inviting their stairwells are,
- surveying businesses in the community to determine which have exercise facilities on site, or
- looking at the school grounds at dusk to see if timed lights are working effectively on the playing fields.

In times past, a neighborhood was a place where everyone knew most of their neighbors, where it was easy to walk to a friend's house, to the store for a few essential items, to the bus stop or even around the block for an evening stroll. Sadly, they just don't build 'em like that anymore. . . . In fact, it is almost impossible to walk directly to a friend's house, the store, the bus stop, or the park (if there is a park) in today's suburban neighborhood. By eliminating the direct connections between neighbors, shops, and home, these development patterns have also effectively eliminated public life and the very feel of a neighborhood. Maybe that's why people aren't apt to talk about their "neighborhood"; instead, they talk about their "development" or, even worse, their "subdivision."

Pedestrian Federation of America, 1995

Your list of program goals may now include promoting a shift from motorized transportation to pedestrian modes of travel (e.g., walking, bicycling), converting unutilized and underutilized spaces (e.g., empty hotel swimming pools, vacant school playing fields, or closed shopping malls) into community-wide resources for physical activity, or linking local worksites to health clubs that can provide showers and bicycle storage spaces for company employees.

From an environmental intervention perspective, community design and land use become critical factors in physical activity promotion, for they affect when and how people travel, particularly their mode of transportation (either motorized, mass transit, or pedestrian). To grasp their effects, imagine if you can the pre-1950s way of life, when people could do their errands by walking to the post office or to the corner store, and when children were free to ride their bicycles to school or to visit a friend. Now, in many areas, as cities expand and scenic rural byways diminish at an alarming rate, and as the fear of potential crimes affects nearly everyone's life, we are faced with the evidence that walking and biking have become unpleasant or even dangerous experiences:

- Data from the 1996 Behavioral Risk Factor Surveillance System in selected states revealed that physical inactivity increases as perceived neighborhood declined (MMWR 1999).

- In 1995, 46% of children in grades 7 through 12 made at least one change in daily routine because of concerns about personal safety, crime, and violence in their communities (Harris 1995).

The U.S. Department of Transportation (NHTSA 1999) reports these statistics:

- In 1997, 5,307 pedestrians were killed and another 77,000 pedestrians were injured in traffic-related crashes in the United States, representing 13% of all traffic fatalities and 2% of all people injured in traffic-related crashes that year.

- Most pedestrian fatalities in 1997 occurred in urban areas (70%), at nonintersection locations (79%), in normal weather conditions (89%), and at night (62%).

- More than one-fourth (29%) of all children between the ages of 5 and 9 years who were killed in traffic-related crashes were pedestrians. Pedestrian children under the age of 16 accounted for one-fifth (20%) of all traffic fatalities under age 16 and 7% of all traffic injuries under age 16.

- Older pedestrians (ages 70+) accounted for 17% of all pedestrian fatalities and 3% of all pedestrian injuries. The death rate for this age group was 3.76 per 100,000 population—higher than for any other age group.

- In 1997, 813 bicyclists *(pedalcyclists)* were killed and an additional 58,000 injured in traffic-related crashes in the United States, representing 2% of all traffic fatalities and 2% of all people injured in traffic-related crashes during that year.

- Almost one-third (30%) of the pedalcyclists killed in traffic-related crashes in 1997 were youth between the ages of 5 and 15 years.

If urban sprawl and suburban development land-use patterns and a society built for the convenience of the automobile have discouraged walking as a normal mode of transportation, what factors would encourage use of nonmotorized transportation and creation of a walkable community, including high accessibility for people on foot or in wheelchairs?

A pedestrian-friendly environment includes the presence of well-maintained and continuous sidewalks, wide sidewalks, ramped curbs, safe and easy street crossings, a level terrain (preferable, though not essential), well-lighted streets, a grid-patterned street design, high street connectivity, a buffer between pedestrians and motorized vehicles (i.e., trees, shrubs, streetside parked cars, green space), low traffic pattern, minimal building setbacks, cleanliness (absence of graffiti), and land-use patterns—the physical layout of a region—characterized as mixed-use and high-unit density (USEPA 1998 Pedestrian Federation of America 1995).

Making Your Community More Walkable

Problem areas in your community	What you and your family can do immediately	What you and your community can do with more time
Not enough room to walk safely: • Sidewalks or paths started and stopped • Sidewalks broken or cracked • Sidewalks blocked • No sidewalks, paths, or shoulder • Too much traffic	• Pick another route for now. • Tell local transportation engineers or public works department about specific problems.	• Speak up at board or development meetings. • Write or petition the city for walkways. • Gather neighborhood signatures. • Make media aware of the problem.
Not easy to cross streets: • Road too wide • Traffic signals made you wait too long or did not give you enough time to cross • Crosswalks or traffic signals needed • View of traffic blocked by parked cars, trees, or plants • Needed curb ramps • Curb ramps needed repair	• Pick another route for now. • Share problems with local transportation engineers or public works department. • Trim your trees and bushes that block the street, and ask neighbors to do the same. • Leave nice notes on problem cars, asking owners not to park there.	• Push for crosswalks, signals, or parking changes at city meetings. • Give report identifying parked cars that are safety hazards to transportation engineers. • Report illegally parked cars to the police. • Request that public works department trims trees and plants. • Make media aware of the problem.
Drivers do not behave well: • Back out without looking • Do not yield • Turn cars into walkers • Drive too fast • Speed up to make traffic lights or drive through red lights	• Pick another route for now. • Set an example: slow down and be considerate of walkers. • Encourage your neighbors to do the same. • Report unsafe driving to police.	• Organize neighborhood speed watch program. • Petition for more enforcement. • Ask city planners and traffic engineers for traffic calming ideas.

(continued)

Making Your Community More Walkable *(continued)*

Problem areas in your community	What you and your family can do immediately	What you and your community can do with more time
Everyone needs to know and follow these safety rules: • Cross at crosswalks or where you can see and be seen • Stop and look left, right, left, before crossing • Walk on sidewalks (or on shoulders if there are no sidewalks) facing traffic • Cross with the light	• Educate yourself and your family about safe walking. • Organize parents in your community to walk children to school.	• Encourage schools to teach pedestrian safety. • Help schools start Safe Routes to School programs. • Encourage corporate support for flexible schedules so parents can walk children to school.
Your walk was unpleasant: • Needs grass, flowers, trees • Scary dogs • Suspicious activity • Not well lit • Dirty, littered	• Pick another route for now. • Ask neighbors to keep dogs leashed or fenced. • Report scary dogs to animal control department. • Report suspicious activity to police. • Report lighting needs to the city. • Take a walk with a trash bag. • Plant trees, flowers, and bushes in your yard.	• Request increased police enforcement • Start a crime-watch program in your neighborhood. • Organize a community clean-up day. • Sponsor a tree planting day. • Sponsor a neighborhood beautification day.
Health Check—You could not go as far as you wanted: • You were tired • You were short of breath • You had sore feet or muscles	• Start with short walks and work up to 30 minutes of walking on most days • Invite a friend or child along • Replace some driving trips with walking trips	• Get media to do a story about the health benefits of walking. • Call parks and recreation departments about community walks. • Encourage corporate support for employee walking programs.

Adapted from U.S. Department of Transportation, Walkability Checklist. DOT HS 808 619. September 1997. May be reproduced.

Understanding Environmental Terms

Here's a warning for the novice environmental interventionist: If you are seriously interested in getting involved in physical environmental change, the following definitions and partners might prove to be valuable.

- **Density**

  Density refers to the compactness of development. Common measures of density include population per acre or square mile, dwelling units (DU) per acre, and square feet per acre (for commercial, retail, and industrial uses).

- **Land use mixing**

  The mix of land uses refers to the juxtaposition of land classifications (such as residential, office, commercial, and industrial) for a particular site or area.

- **Pedestrian/bicycle environment (urban design factors)**

  Urban design factors affect the "friendliness" of an area to different modes of transportation. Factors include amenities (e.g., the presence of footpaths and public bicycle racks), accessibility (such as the directness of sidewalks and bike paths relative to roads and the quality of the terrain), safety (lighting, security, and protection from on-road vehicles), and aesthetics of routes and the areas surrounding trip origins and destinations.

- **Street network design**

  Street network design refers to roadway patterns and connectivity. Traditional urban "grid" patterns involve a dense grid of interconnected streets. Hierarchical street patterns, common in suburban areas, consist of a few major arteries, collectors, and sets of small, disconnected local roads (e.g., dead ends and cul-de-sacs).

- **Transit-oriented development (TOD), neotraditional development, and traditional neighborhood development**

  These development patterns promote transit and pedestrian activity over vehicle travel through their design, configuration, and mix of uses. Transit-oriented developments are typically designed to include a mix of land uses within a quarter-mile walking distance of a transit stop and/or core commercial area. Neotraditional and traditional neighborhood development emphasize pedestrian accessibility and the orientation of houses toward narrower, tree-lined, gridded or integrated streets. These communities often include gridded street patterns and design elements, such as wide sidewalks and building orientation toward the street, that encourage pedestrian and bicycle travel.

- **Typical suburban development or planned unit development**

  Typical suburban development is characterized by low densities, separation of land uses, and design so that most trips must be made by automobile. Suburban-style development usually includes hierarchical streets (a network of few arteries, collectors, and cul-de-sacs), wide streets, off-street surface parking lots, deep setbacks, commercial establishments centered on highway strips and malls, and single-use parcels. Many of these design characteristics became widespread in the 1970s in an effort to reduce through traffic on residential streets and to take advantage of inexpensive land prices at the urban periphery.

From USEPA 1998

Making Your Community Bicycle-Friendly

In *Bicycling* magazine's "First Major Study of the U.S. Bicycle Market, Phase II" (1991), when individuals who had purchased a bicycle in the previous year were asked "Why do you cycle?" the most common answers were: fast recreation, family togetherness, and an interest in weekend touring. When asked "What would make consumers ride more often?" they answered: companionship, safer places to ride, and safer places to park their bicycles. According to a report submitted to the Federal Highway Administration in 1992, safety and finding safer places to ride is the key issue that would encourage more people to ride for recreation and for health (U.S. DOT 1992).

To encourage bicycling, a community needs safe places to ride, such as bicycle lanes along all major streets and highways, multi-use trails for recreation and transportation that include bicycle access, and courteous motorists; highway signage that clearly points the way to various places and how far away those places are; bicycle parking at all major destinations; as well as consideration of a bicyclist's needs reflected in zoning laws, road design standards, and regional transportation plans.

Consider the city of Seattle, Washington, which consistently ranks among *Bicycling* magazine's annual list of Most Bicycle-Friendly Cities in America (Williams 1993). Through the persistent efforts of active citizen's groups and a variety of bicycle-related committees and organizations, Seattle has developed an extensive trail network for off-road riding and safer on-road conditions, such as bicycle lanes, filled potholes, rubberized railroad crossings, and improved road signs.

In Davis, California, car commuting is discouraged, while bicycling to work, to school, and around college campuses is so popular that a bicycle is prominently featured in the city's logo. And in Portland, Oregon, famous for its bicycle-friendly

environment and over 185 miles of bike lanes and off-road pathways, a mass transportation bus and commuter train system comes equipped with bicycle racks. Once in town, bicycling commuters can drop off their bicycles at local shops who advertise "valet parking," or they may join a program to securely store their bicycles and to take showers at downtown health clubs before heading off to work. Through the success of an organized statewide effort, Oregon had made tremendous strides in elevating the bicycle from a child's toy or dusty piece of weekend sports equipment to a prominent role in providing for the transportation and recreation needs of everyday life (Sharp 1998).

Ideas for Action in the Community

Establish and Maintain a Supportive Physical Environment

- Establish safe, well-lighted walking, jogging, and bicycle paths or convert abandoned railroad right-of-ways to walking or jogging paths. Build biking paths a safe distance from roadways. Promote safety campaigns for people using such paths and for drivers who are unaccustomed to sharing the road with bicyclists.

- Provide areas to secure bicycles near workplaces, shopping areas, and other public or private buildings.

- Convert downtown centers into pedestrian malls. Arrange for shopping malls or school gymnasiums to open early for walkers.

- Secure access to and adequate lighting for outdoor playing fields, university or school track fields, parks, tennis court facilities, and other community resource areas to allow evening use by community residents.

- Make public stairwells accessible, ventilated, well-lighted, safe, and clean. Post signs clearly pointing out stairways.

- To increase the safety of all program participants, establish police precincts at inner-city community recreation facilities and security escort services from program locations to parking lots or garages.

- Develop parks or playgrounds in vacant lots or accessible rooftops, or convert surplus public lands (e.g., closed military bases) into park and recreation facilities.

- Establish playgrounds for children and adults. Develop walking paths in and around children's playgrounds to foster activity among the adults accompanying the children.

- Provide transportation, child-care services, or other services that overcome barriers to participation. Advocate for inclusion of major community exercise or athletic facilities on public transportation routes.

- Map out neighborhood walking paths, and install distance mile markers along trails, beaches, neighborhood, and city blocks to help people judge distances. Inform physicians so they can encourage patients to walk to so many markers each day. Also inform real estate agents: markers could be selling points in some communities.

- Combine physical activity and environmental projects, such as cleaning up beaches, along park trails, or along roads.

- Build fitness and walking paths convenient to all community residents. Work with local businesses to build fitness courses on their properties for use by employees as well as the whole community.

Establishing and Enforcing Supportive Policies

> Life still demands the best we can give. Leisure must not mean physical inactivity and idleness. Instead we must recognize it as an opportunity to strengthen and refresh ourselves for our roles as creative and productive citizens.
>
> *Lyndon B. Johnson*

The political environment embraces all of the laws, rules, regulations, guidelines, or policies that govern how people shall live within a specified area or jurisdiction. Using policies to affect environmental change to make physical activity possible, safer, and easier is a critical component of physical activity promotion. Following are examples of policy-level environmental program strategies:

- Establishing and enforcing bicycle helmet laws
- Initiating employer incentives such as physical activity or exercise breaks during the workday
- Enforcing pedestrian right-of-way laws
- Passing ordinances requiring
  —that public housing projects include recreational facilities,
  —that new subdivisions include sidewalks,
  —that schools open their facilities to community members during after-school hours, or
  —that mass transit buses make provisions for transporting a rider's bicycle.

Communities that have implemented many of these interventions have shown significant improvements in physical activity and fitness levels among their citizens (Linegar 1991).

Chapters 9 and 10 will provide specific ideas for action appropriate to the worksite and school settings, respectively.

 ## Spotlight on TEA-21

The Transportation Equity Act for the 21st Century (TEA-21) reauthorizes the landmark 1991 Intermodal Surface Transportation Efficiency Act (ISTEA), providing authorization and funding to transform America's transportation priorities from their origins in the 1950s era of highway building programs into new, innovative, and flexible opportunities responsive to the needs of the states and communities in the 21st century. For detailed information on the provisions, strengths, and weaknesses of this legislation, visit the following websites:

- The TEA-21 home page and information site maintained by the Federal Highway Administration, U.S. Department of Transportation: **http://www.fhwa.dot.gov/tea21.** Particularly helpful are the detailed fact sheets available through this site.

- A TEA-21 information and current commentary site maintained by the Surface Transportation Policy Project: **http://www.tea21.org.** To learn more, request their helpful user's guide.

Surface Transportation Policy Project. *TEA-21 User's Guide: Making the Most of the New Transportation Bill*, Washington, DC: STPP, 1998.

Ideas for Action in the Community

Establish and Enforce Policies, Laws, and Regulations Supportive of a Physically Active Lifestyle

- Work with Department of Transportation TEA 21 Coordinators to identify potential and approved projects throughout the state.
- Use tax revenues to pay for pedestrian-friendly modifications.
- Change traffic signals and crosswalk signage.
- Establish urban growth boundaries.
- Establish traffic calming measures such as lower speed limits, stop lights, new standards for road design, narrowed street access, street surface alternatives, and so on.
- Address existing highway safety laws to protect pedestrians.
- Modify parking regulations and impose ceilings on the number of spaces developed.
- Modify parking regulations to minimize the number of parking spaces required for businesses and new construction.
- Convince influential community, business, and political leaders of the need for environments supportive of a physically active lifestyle among citizens of all ages.
- Establish a community steering committee for physical activity promotion, and guide the authorities on matters related to health promotion.
- Be certain that all public lands and facilities are covered adequately by insurance or worker's compensation.
- Partner with professionals who can assess issues such as the appropriateness of liability legislation in relation to public fitness and recreation areas or in relation to specific components of your physical activity promotion program.
- Advocate that a portion of highway and transportation funds be set aside to construct bicycle paths or footpaths, and to promote walking and bicycling.
- Advocate that zoning regulations permit development of recreational areas, sidewalks, and bicycle trails in new communities and business parks. Include zoning for park and recreation areas in urban renewal projects. Advocate for reclamation of urban or suburban wastelands.
- Pass ordinances stipulating the type of street lighting necessary to improve safety along streets, along paths, and in parking garages.
- Work with persons who establish building construction codes to ensure that stairwells are accessible, well-lighted, and visible near elevators; that sidewalks are available; that bicycle "parking" spots are created; and so on.
- To promote pedestrian and bicycle traffic, advocate a ban on vehicular traffic in certain areas.
- Advocate that community developers construct sidewalks and playgrounds in their neighborhoods.
- Establish and enforce safety regulations or laws (e.g., bicycle helmet use regulations), conduct safety workshops for parents and children, and provide incentives for complying with safety regulations.

(continued)

(continued)

- Develop a consensus statement among community partners that can be used to promote policies, regulations, or laws supportive of increased physical activity throughout the community.

- Work with the business community to support worksite policies promoting "exercise flextime," which grants all employees a portion of the scheduled workday (i.e., up to 30 minutes per day) for an exercise-related activity, such as jogging, walking, or participation in a worksite aerobics class.

- Consider financial incentives or disincentives (affecting taxes, salaries, insurance premiums, and rebates) for physical activity promotion. For example, provide sales tax incentives or rebates on the purchase of a bicycle if the customer uses the bicycle to commute to work.

- Establish a Governor's or Mayor's Council on Physical Activity and Health.

- Work to establish a governor's, mayor's, or corporate report on the state of physical activity among members of its jurisdiction.

- Obtain formal recognition of exemplary programs and program participants.

- Develop a consortium of community sites to share exercise facilities.

- Establish "Adopt-a-Highway" or "Adopt-a-Beach" programs to encourage local groups to increase their physical activity level while beautifying the environment.

Planning for Special Populations

For more information about cultural diversity, read:

Gonzalez VM, Gonzalez JT, Freeman V, et al. *Health Promotion in Diverse Cultural Communities*. Stanford, CA: Stanford Center for Research in Disease Prevention, Health Promotion Resource Center, 1991. This publication lists organizations serving diverse cultural communities, contains suggestions for training in cultural sensitivity and awareness, and provides additional references and program tips of particular value to those working with intercultural groups. Order by contacting:

Health Promotion Resource Center
1000 Welch Road
Palo Alto, CA 94304-1885
Phone: 650-723-0003

Locke DC. *Increasing Multicultural Understanding: A Comprehensive Model*. Newbury Park, CA: Sage Publications, 1992.

Ramirez S. *Health Promotion for All: Strategies for Reaching Diverse Populations at the Workplace*. Omaha, NE: Wellness Councils of America, 1994. Call 402-572-3590 to order.

Randall-David E. *Strategies for Working with Culturally Diverse Communities and Clients*. Washington, DC: Association for the Care of Children's Health, 1989.

For more resources related to persons with disabilities, see:

Resource E: Selected Organizations and Agencies Concerned With Persons With Disabilities

Resource F: Americans With Disabilities Act

To learn more about physical activity promotion among older adults, read:

American Association of Retired Persons. *Pep Up Your Life: A Fitness Book for Mid-Life and Older Persons*. Washington, DC: American Association of Retired Persons, 1995.

Amundsen LR, DeVahl JM, Ellingham CT. Evaluation of a group exercise program for elderly women. *Physical Therapy* 1989; 69(6):475–483.

Benson L, Nelson EC, Napps SE, et al. Evaluation of the Staying Healthy After Fifty Education Program: impact on course participants. *Health Education Quarterly* 1989; 16(4):485–508.

DiGilio DA. *Activating Ideas: Promoting Physical Activity Among Older Adults*. Washington, DC: American Association of Retired Persons, 1995. For a free single copy of this publication, contact AARP Fulfillment at 601 E Street, NW, Washington, DC 20049 and ask for stock #D-15566.

Dychtwald K, editor. *Wellness and Health Promotion for the Elderly*. Rockville, MD: Aspen Publications, 1986.

Flatten K, Wilhite B, Reyes-Watson E. *Exercise Activities for the Elderly*. New York: Springer Publishing Co., 1988.

Garnet ED. *Movement Is Life: A Holistic Approach to Exercise for Older Adults*. Princeton, NJ: Princeton Book Co., 1982.

Heath GW. Exercise programming for the older adult. In: *Resource Manual for Guidelines for Exercise Testing and Prescription.* Philadelphia: Lea & Febiger, 1988.

Howze EH, Smith M, DiGilio DA. Factors affecting the adoption of exercise behavior among sedentary older adults. *Health Education Research* 1989; 4(2):173–180.

Lewis CB, Campanelli LC. *Health Promotion and Exercise for Older Adults.* Rockville, MD: Aspen Publications, 1990.

Nelson ME. *Spring into Action Exercise and Nutrition Programs.* Boston: Tufts University, 1987.

Simmons JJ, Nelson EC, Roberts E, et al. A health promotion program: Staying Healthy after Fifty. *Health Education Quarterly* 1989; 16(4):461–472.

Simmons JJ, Salisbury ZT, Kane-Williams E, et al. Interorganizational collaboration and dissemination of health promotion for older Americans. *Health Education Quarterly* 1989; 16(4):529–550.

Smith EL, Gilligan C. Physical activity prescription for the older adult. *Physician and Sportsmedicine* 1983; 6(6):443–450, 464.

U.S. Department of Transportation Federal Highway Administration. 1994. *A Compendium of Available Bicycle and Pedestrian Trip Generation Data in the United States: A Supplement to the National Bicycling and Walking Study.* Chapel Hill, NC: University of North Carolina, Highway Safety Research Center, (October).

U.S. Department of Transportation Federal Highway Administration. 1994. *Final Report: The National Bicycling and Walking Study. Transportation Choices for a Changing America.* FHWA-PD-94-023. Washington, DC.

Warner-Reitz A, Grothe C. *Healthy Lifestyle for Seniors: An Interdisciplinary Approach to Healthy Aging.* New York: Meals for Millions/Freedom from Hunger Foundation, 1981.

To learn more about physical activity for overweight people, take advantage of these resources:

National Heart, Lung, and Blood Institute. (1998) Clinical Guidelines on the Identification, Evaluation, and Treatment of Overweight and Obesity in Adults. Bethesda, MD: National Institutes of Health; National Heart, Lung, and Blood Institute. NIH Publication No. 98-4083.

National Heart, Lung, and Blood Institute. *Strategy Development Workshop for Public Education on Weight and Obesity: September 24-25, 1992 Summary Report.* Bethesda, MD: U.S. Department of Health and Human Services, Public Health Service, National Institutes of Health, 1995. NIH Publication No. 95-3314.

Contact the Weight Control Information Network (WIN) sponsored by the National Institute of Diabetes and Digestive and Kidney Diseases (NIDDK)

7910 Woodmont Avenue, Suite 300
Bethesda, MD 20814-3015
Phone: 301-951-1120
Fax: 301-951-1107

In addition to research and communication projects, WIN staff support the work of the National Task Force on Prevention and Treatment of Obesity.

Subscribe to *The Weight Control Digest*, which is published bimonthly by the American Health Publishing Company and distributed by the LEARN Education Center. Address inquiries to *The Weight Control Digest*

P.O. Box 35328
Dallas, TX 75235-0328
Phone: 214-637-7700

To learn more about promoting physical activity among pregnant and postpartum women, read:

American College of Obstetricians and Gynecologists. *Exercise During Pregnancy and the Postpartum Period.* Washington, DC: American College of Obstetricians and Gynecologists, 1994. Technical Bulletin No. 189. For a copy, telephone the Public Education Department at 202-638-5577 x2528.

White J. Exercising for two: what's safe for the active pregnant woman? *Physician and Sportsmedicine* 1992; 20(5):179–186.

To learn more about promoting physical activity among American Indians, take advantage of these resources:

For *How To Run a Weight-Loss Program*, contact

Zuni Wellness Center
P.O. Box 308
Zuni, NM 87327

For *H.E.L.P.: Holiday Eating Learning Program and Team Weight-Loss Competition, The Human Race: Zuni Fitness Challenge*, or *100-Mile Club*, contact the Zuni Diabetes Project, Zuni PHS Indian Hospital, Zuni, NM 87327. The last can also be obtained from

Indian Health Service Diabetes Program
2401 12th Street, NW
Room 211-North
Albuquerque, NM 87102
Phone: 505-766-3980

For *Promoting Healthy Traditions Workbook: A Guide to the Healthy People 2000 Campaign*, contact:

American Indian Health Care Association
245 East 6th Street, Suite 499
St. Paul, MN 55101

For additional information about these and other physical activity-related programs among American Indians, contact:

Director of the Indian Health Service Diabetes Program
2401 12th Street, NW
Room 211-North
Albuquerque, NM 87102
Phone: 505-766-3980

For a valuable review of the literature regarding physical activity interventions, read:

American Journal of Preventive Medicine. November 1998. 15(4): 255–440.
To obtain a copy of this special issue, contact the publisher, Elsevier Science, toll-free at 888-437-4636 or via fax 212-633-3913.

Key Environmental Resources

Making the environment more friendly to a physically active lifestyle won't be easy. And you won't be able to do it alone. The organizations in the following list may have a stake in improving environmental factors in your community so that your target population can enjoy a more supportive environment in which to get active and stay active.

The Active Living and Environment Program

Visit this website to find out more about Canada's effort to enhance the environment and encourage outdoor physical activity:

http://www.goforgreen.ca

American Planning Association

For information about community and environmental planning, contact:

American Planning Association
122 S. Michigan Avenue
Suite 1600
Chicago, IL 60603
Phone: 312-431-9100
Website: **http://www.planning.org**

Bicycle Federation of America

For information about pedestrian and bicycle-related issues, and great resourse kits such as *The Bicycle Advocate's Action Kit,* contact:

Bicycle Federation of America
1506 21st Street, NW
Suite 200
Washington, DC 20036
Phone: 202-463-6622
Fax: 202-463-6625
Website: **http://www.bikefed.org**

For more information about pedestrian and pedalcyclist safety, contact the U.S. Department of Transportation, National Highway Traffic Safety Administration at the following address:

USDOT/NHTSA
National Center for Statistics and Analysis
NRD-31
400 Seventh Street, SW
Washington, DC 20590
Phone: 202-366-4198
Website: **http://www.nhtsa.dot.gov/people/ncsa**

Center for Livable Communities

Call the Center for Livable Communities or see its website for information about land use and transportation planning in your community, including a listing of publications, newsletters, and videos available.

> Center for Livable Communities
> Toll-free: 800-290-8202
> Website: **http://www.lgc.org**

Congress for the New Urbanism

For information about reforming America's urban growth patterns, contact:

> Congress for the New Urbanism
> The Hearst Building
> 5 Third Street, Suite 500A
> San Francisco, CA 94103
> Phone: 415-495-2255
> Fax: 415-495-1731
> Website: **http://www.cnu.org**

Federal Highway Administration

For more information about street design and traffic calming, contact:

> Federal Highway Administration
> Pedestrian and Bicycle Safety Research Program
> HSR-20
> 6300 Georgetown Pike
> McLean, VA 22101
> Website: **http://www.tfhrc.gov**

Florida Sustainable Communities Center

Visit this website to learn more about the effort to make Florida communities cleaner, healthier, and more efficient in their use of land and other natural resources:

> **http://sustainable.state.fl.us**

Healthy Communities Program

Call the phone number below or visit the Healthy Communities website to learn more about its effort to improve communities around the world.

> Healthy Communities Program
> Phone: 303-571-4343
> Website: **http://www.ncl.org**

Highways and Local Roadways

Visit this website for a list of pedestrian and bicycle-related publications:

> **http://www.wsdot.wa.gov/hlrd/Pedestrian-Pages/PedBicPubAvail.htm**

Institute of Transportation Engineers

To learn more about creating safe and efficient surface transportation in your community, contact:

Institute of Transportation Engineers
525 School Street, SW, Suite 410
Washington, DC 20024
Phone: 202-554-8050
Fax: 202-863-5486
Website: **http://www.ite.org**

National Arbor Day Foundation

To find out more about how to make your community safer and more attractive, contact:

National Arbor Day Foundation
100 Arbor Avenue
Nebraska City, NE 68410
Phone: 402-474-5655
Website: **http://www.arborday.org**

National Bicycle and Pedestrian Clearinghouse

For more information about street design and traffic calming, contact:

National Bicycle and Pedestrian Clearinghouse
Campaign to Make America Walkable
1506 21st Street, NW
Suite 200
Washington, DC 20036
Toll-free: 800-760-NBPC
Website: **http://www.bikefed.org**

National Crime Prevention Council

To find out more about how to make your community safer and more attractive, contact:

National Crime Prevention Council
1700 K Street, NW
Second Floor
Washington, DC 20006-3817
Phone: 202-466-6272
Website: **http://www.ncpc.org**

National Highway Traffic Safety Administration

Visit this website for more information about vehicle and pedestrian safety:

http://www.nhtsa.gov

National Park Service Trails

Visit this website to learn more about American walking, bicycling, horseback riding, snowmobiling, mountain biking, backpacking, cross-country skiing, jogging, canoeing, and historical trails:

http://www.nps.gov

National SAFE KIDS Campaign

To find out more about pedestrian safety, contact:

National SAFE KIDS Campaign
1301 Pennsylvania Avenue, NW
Suite 1000
Washington, DC 20004-1707
Phone: 202-662-0600
Website: **http://www.safekids.org**

Partnership for a Walkable America

For more information about making your neighborhood safer for pedestrians, more attractive, and more accessible, contact:

Partnership for a Walkable America
National Safety Council
1121 Spring Lake Drive
Itasca, IL 60143-3201
Phone: 630-285-1121
Website: **http://www.nsc.org**

Pedestrian Federation of America

To order copies of *Walk Tall: A Citizen's Guide to Walkable Communities,* send $2 per copy to:

Pedestrian Federation of America
1506 21st Street, NW
Suite 200
Washington, DC 20036

Prevention Magazine's Walking Club

To find out more about pedestrian safety, contact:

Prevention Magazine's Walking Club
33 East Minor Street
Emmaus, PA 18098

Rails-to-Trails Conservancy

Visit this website for more information about converting former rail lines and connecting corridors into public trails:

http://www.railtrails.org

Safest Route to School Program

To find out more about this program, contact your local AAA Club and ask for publications #3201, #3212, #3213, and #3320.

The Seaside Coolum Neighborhood

To learn more about this walkable community in Australia, including the urban, architectural, and landscape regulations that have worked to make it an attractive, efficient, and healthy place to live, visit this website:

http://www.townofseaside.com.au

Surface Transportation Policy Project

Visit this website for more information about street design and traffic calming:

http://www.transact.org

Transportation for Livable Communities

To learn more about traffic calming and street design, visit this website:

http://www.tlcnetwork.org

Urban Land Institute

For more information about responsible land use and enhancing the environment, visit this website:

http://www.uli.org

U.S. Access Board

For more information about creating accessible sidewalks, contact:

U.S. Access Board
1331 F Street, NW
Suite 1000
Washington, DC 20004-1111
Toll-free: 800-872-2253
800-993-2822 (TTY)
Website: **http://www.access-board.gov**

Walk a Child to School Program

To find out more about pedestrian safety, contact:

Walk a Child to School Program
Walking Magazine
45 Bromfield St., 8th Floor
Boston, MA 02108
Toll-free: 800-266-3312

World Health Organization (WHO) Healthy Cities Program

For more information about improving quality of life through improved environmental, social, and economic conditions, visit this website:

http://www.who.int/peh/hlthcit

Suggested Reading

For a list of organizations, agencies, and selected program materials for promoting physical activity, see:

Resource A, for general resources

Chapter 9, for worksite-related resources

Chapter 10, for school-related resources

To learn more about creating people-friendly environments, read:

Bicycle Advocate's Action Kit. Washington, DC: The Bicycle Federation of America, 1993.

Blumenauer E. *Reclaiming Our Streets: Traffic Solutions, Safer Streets, More Livable Neighborhoods. A Community Action Plan.* Portland, OR: City of Portland, Bureau of Traffic Management, Department of Public Works, Reclaiming Our Streets Task Force, 1993.

Calthorpe P. *The Next American Metropolis: Ecology, Community, and the American Dream.* Princeton Architectural Press, 1993.

Conservation Law Foundation. *City Routes, City Rights: Building Livable Neighborhoods and Environmental Justice by Fixing Transportation.* Boston, MA: Conservation Law Foundation, June 1998.

Corbett J, Velasquez J. The Ahwahnee principles: toward more livable communities. *Western City* September 1994. A summary of the principles is also available at the following website:

http://www.lgc.org/clc/ahwan.html

Corbett J, Zykofsky P. *Building Livable Communities: A Policymaker's Guide to Transit-Oriented Development.* Sacramento, California: The Center for Livable Communities, Local Government Commission. August 1996.

The Center for Livable Communities' e-mail address is **lgc@den.davis.ca.us**

Ewing R. *Pedestrian- and Transit-Friendly Design.* Ft. Lauderdale, FL: Joint Center for Environmental and Urban Problems, Florida Atlantic University/Florida International University, 1996.

Lyman, F. Twelve gates to the city: A dozen ways to build strong, livable, and sustainable urban areas. *Sierra* May 1997; 82(3) 28–35.

Moore JA, Johnson JM. *State Transportation Policy Initiative: Transportation, Land-Use, and Sustainability.* Tampa, FL: Florida Center for Community Design and Research and the Center for Urban Transportation Research, University of South Florida, 1994. The report is also available at the following website:

http://www.arch.usf.edu/flctr/projects/tlushtml/default.htm

Neighborhoods reborn. *Consumer Reports.* May 1996; 61(5): 24–30.

Parkwood Research Associates. *Pathways for People II: Americans' Attitudes Toward Walking, Bicycling and Running in Their Communities.* Summary Report. Emmaus, PA: Rodale Press, May, 1995.

Pedestrian Federation of America. *Walk Tall: A Citizen's Guide to Walkable Communities.* Emmaus, PA: Rodale Press, 1995.

http://www.bikefed.org

Surface Transportation Policy Project. *Mean Streets: Pedestrian Safety and Reform of the Nation's Transportation Law.* Washington, DC: Environmental Working Group, April 1997.

Surface Transportation Policy Project's e-mail address is **stpp@transact.org**

The Environmental Working Group's e-mail address is **info@ewg.org** or visit its website at **www.ewg.org**

U.S. Department of Transportation. Federal Highway Administration.1994. *The National Bicycling and Walking Study: Transportation Choices for a Changing America.* Publication no. FHWA-PD-94-023. Washington, DC.

For more information about promoting physical activity among inner-city or disadvantaged youth, read:

California Healthy Cities Project. *Promoting Healthy Youth: Strategies for Recreation and Community Services Partnerships.* Sacramento, CA: California Healthy Cities Project, 1994.

California Healthy Cities Project. *Taking Back Our Communities: Strategies for Violence Prevention.* Sacramento, CA: California Healthy Cities Project, 1994. For more information about the California Healthy Cities Project or for copies of their publications, contact

California Healthy Cities Project
P.O. Box 942732
Mail Station 675
Sacramento, CA 93434-7320
Phone: 916-327-7017

To learn more about the role of the environment in behavior change, read:

Sallis JF, Bauman A, Pratt M. Environmental and policy interventions to promote physical activity. *American Journal of Preventive Medicine* November 1998; 15(4): 379–397.

Stokols D. Establishing and maintaining healthy environments: toward a social ecology of health promotion. *American Psychologist.* January 1992; 47(1): 6–22.

To learn more about the influence of crime and environmental factors on youth's lifestyles, read:

Teens, Crime, and the Community. *Between Hope and Fear: Teens Speak Out on Crime and the Community.* Washington, DC: Street Law Inc. and the National Crime Prevention Council, which summarizes a 1995 nationwide poll conducted by Louis Harris Associates, Inc. with 2000 junior and senior high school students. For more information about the survey or the nationwide Teens, Crime, and Community Program, contact:

Street Law, Inc.
918 16th Street, NW
Suite 602
Washington, DC 20006-2902
Websites: **http://www.streetlaw.org**
         http://nationaltcc.org

Part III

Strategies for Planning and Implementing Your Intervention

Now that you've learned about the scientific and behavioral aspects of physical activity promotion, it's time to put all your new knowledge to use. Part III will focus on helping you with the nuts and bolts of planning and implementing a successful promotion program.

Before you begin any planning at all, you need to have your program objectives in mind: What do you want to accomplish and how will you know when you have achieved it? Chapter 7 will show you how setting objectives will not only help your program get off to a good start, but will also give you the tools to evaluate the effectiveness of your efforts along the way.

Bringing about lasting behavior change in your community, worksite, or school, often takes more resources than any one organization may have. And odds are you won't be able to provide all of those resources by yourself. That's where the concept of partnering comes into play. Chapter 8 will help you know where to look in your community for partners who will complement your program goals effectively, ultimately helping your target population on its way to lifetime physical activity.

The ideas and advice presented in this publication all have one overarching goal in mind: helping people learn about, begin, and maintain a more physically active lifestyle. The tips you've picked up in this book apply to any target group within any setting: family, community, school, or worksite. But chapters 9 and 10 go even further by providing you with even more resources and ideas geared specifically for worksites and schools. Each chapter includes a comprehensive list of resources that will give you program ideas and places to look for help, including the names and addresses of dozens of agencies and organizations with an interest in promoting physical activity in the workplace and in school settings.

Chapter 7 Setting Objectives and Measuring Success

After you have gathered information about your target audience and have completed your audience profile, you are in the best position to custom design an effective physical activity promotion program for them.

As you venture into program implementation, you will want timely feedback on how well your tailored program is working. A well-designed and well-executed evaluation plan can provide the information you need at every decision point. For example, your organization may need information on which to base tough decisions about resource allocations. Your partners will be interested in knowing whether the partnership has been effective in achieving both their personal organizational goals and your joint programmatic goals. Meanwhile, your sponsors will wonder if their investment has been worthwhile and whether they should continue supporting your program. And your colleagues will be interested in learning about your experiences.

Program planning is more than a "to do" list, and evaluation planning is more than administering "before" and "after" questionnaires. Evaluation involves continually asking meaningful questions, gathering information, summarizing responses, reporting information, and using your findings to fine-tune your delivery of messages and services. If you carefully select and track appropriate progress indicators from the very start of your program, you will have the information you need to measure the program's success.

If, at its conclusion, your intervention has been responsive to the identified health-relevant needs of your target population and your evaluation honestly portrays what you have learned, it will have been successful. The steps of program and evaluation planning covered in this chapter are: defining your expectations, deciding what aspects of your program to evaluate, selecting your evaluation measures, collecting and analyzing program data, and reporting your results.

> It's the set of the sail and not the gale that determines the way you go.
>
> *Jim Rohn, 1993*
> The Art of
> Exceptional Living

Begin with the end in mind. Begin every endeavor, project, initiative, task or undertaking by asking: "Why are we doing this? What results do we want? Whose needs (customer, suppliers, employees, etc.) are we trying to fill? What are their needs? What principles and values will guide our behavior? Developing a mission statement that reflects the answers to these questions can be a powerful process for developing committed unity around any objective, task or project.

Stephen R. Covey, 1993
The Seven Habits of Highly Effective People

Defining Your Expectations

Your vision statement as well as your written goals, objectives, and time line of activities serve as your navigational chart as the intervention unfolds. Throughout the intervention, you will be able to refer to the charted plan of action to see whether you are staying on course. Occasionally you may discover that a midcourse change in plans will help you arrive at your destination more effectively. By taking the time before the journey begins to put your plan in writing and by keeping your eyes focused on your goals, you are far more likely to stay true to strategy and arrive at your goals.

Questions to Consider as You Determine Your Expectations

- What is your goal or vision? What do you hope to accomplish?
- Who is your target population? How would you portray their characteristics and lifestyle?
- What does your target population need and want?
- What current target population attitudes or behaviors are you trying to change? What action do you want your target population to take as a direct result of your intervention?
- When and where are members of your target population most open to your message or call to action? What channels might reach your population effectively?
- Which components of change will your intervention address (i.e., awareness, knowledge, motivation, readiness, self-efficacy, social support, or environmental support)?
- What specifically do you propose to do? What are your objectives?
- When will the proposed activities take place? What is your timetable?
- Who needs to be involved in carrying out the plan? What resources are required? With whom can you partner?
- What resistance might you encounter? From whom? How can you involve potential resisters in planning and implementation?
- To what extent do stakeholders, gatekeepers, and intermediaries support your plans?
- How will you know if you have achieved your objectives? What will "success" look like?
- What would be the consequences of doing nothing at all?

Developing Your Program Goals and Objectives

Developing goals and objectives and effective evaluations go hand in hand. Well-written objectives easily translate into measures that help you document the process, immediate impact, and eventual outcome of your program. Goals are general, broad statements that describe the overall improvement you hope to achieve in your site, community, or target population. If achieved, the goal would solve a problem or fulfill a purpose. In health promotion, goals are generally structured to improve the health status or quality of life of a particular target population. The following are examples of goals:

If you clearly define your destination and accurately chart your course, you will be able to compare where you are with where you want to be.

- Improve the overall cardiovascular health of the target population by reducing the proportion of members who report a sedentary lifestyle.
- Enhance the quality of life of citizens of ABC County by increasing the proportion of adults in the community who engage in regular moderate- or vigorous-intensity physical activities.

Read More About It

Bloom's Taxonomy

In 1956, educational psychologist Benjamin Bloom and a group of colleagues developed a classification of levels of intellectual behavior important to a particular type of behavior change: the learning process. Known as "Bloom's Taxonomy," the classification includes three overlapping domains:

1. the cognitive domain, which deals with behaviors dealing with increased awareness and knowledge;
2. the affective domain, which deals with behaviors pertaining to feelings and emotions; and
3. the psychomotor domain, which deals with behaviors focusing on the development of motor skills.

Using Bloom's Taxonomy can help you develop learning objectives tailored specifically to your target population's needs and readiness within each of the three domains. For more information about Bloom's Taxonomy, consult these resources:

Ames EE, Trucano LA, Wan JC, Harris MH. *Designing school health curricula: Planning for good health.* Dubuque, IA: William C. Brown, 1992.
Or see this website:
http://www.auburn.edu/academic/education/eflt/bt.html

Objectives, on the other hand, are action-oriented statements that reflect your expectations for the development and delivery of an intervention, its costs, and intended effects. Objectives should be written in specific, measurable, achievable, and time-limited terms. See page 149 for sample objectives that include all five elements of an objective. Well-written behavioral and instructional objectives include these five elements (Kibler et al. 1974):

1. **Who** is to perform the desired behavior; how many will be affected or will participate
2. **What** it is you want them to do; the **actual behavior** or action to be demonstrated or performed
3. The **result or product** which you can observe, or the deliverable that tells you the objective has been mastered
4. The **relevant conditions** or circumstances under which the behavior is to be performed, or the product is to be demonstrated
5. The **standard** that will be used to evaluate the success of the performance or product

Objectives can vary in their scope and intent. The most common objectives are those that relate to how you expect the program to be delivered or intervention to be carried out *(process objectives)*, and those that relate to the intended effects of the intervention—whether immediate or short-term *(impact objectives)*, or long-term *(outcome objectives)*. Process objectives are the smaller day-to-day objectives that describe the actions needed to accomplish the broader impact objectives. Outcome or impact objectives may have numerous process objectives that need to take place to bring about the desired result.

Sample Objectives

- By September 1 (*when*), at least 40% (*how many*) of the students in the ABC County School District (*who*) will be participating (*what*) in daily (*to what extent*) school physical education programs (*where*).

- By December 31 (*when*), reduce to 20% or less (*how many*) the proportion of employees in the XYZ Corporation (*who*) who report engaging in no leisure-time physical activity (*what*) when asked in a company-wide interview survey (*specific conditions*).

- Within six months of the conclusion of the "Step Ahead" campaign (*when*), at least 25% (*how many*) of participants age 18 or older (*who*) in the Contemplation or Preparation stage for physical activity (*specific conditions*) at the beginning of the campaign will have progressed to the next stage of change (*what*).

- By September 30 (*when*), at least 40% (*how many*) of the population of ABC County age 18 or older (*who*) will state that they engage in 30 minutes or more of at least moderate-intensity physical activities on 5 or more days of the week (*what*) when asked in a random-sample community-wide telephone survey (*specific conditions*).

Using National Objectives and Model Standards as Guides in Program Planning

As you and your partners write your objectives, you may find it helpful to review the national physical activity goals and objectives developed by the Public Health Service in *Healthy People 2000: National Health Promotion and Disease Prevention Objectives* (1991). One chapter is devoted to physical activity and fitness, and another discusses educational and community-based programs. (For a list of national objectives pertinent to physical activity promotion, see page xxi in the introduction). To complement this document, the American Public Health Association published *Healthy Communities 2000. Model Standards: Guidelines for Community Attainment of the Year 2000 National Health Objectives* (1991), which serves as a template for people who want to translate the national objectives into community-based action plans. The *Healthy Communities 2000* template appears in Resource H. The specific objectives within the template can be adapted to suit your community's needs by filling in the blanks with goals that are appropriate for your target population. Revised physical activity and fitness objectives are currently under development for the year 2010. To view the latest version, please visit this website: **http://web.health.gov/healthypeople/**.

The national objectives and model standards are, perhaps, least relevant for programs targeting special populations, particularly minorities and the elderly (Green and Kreuter 1991). Nevertheless, they provide guidelines for those working to improve the health and well-being of communities. Your own program helps your community contribute to these national goals and objectives.

Writing Your Program Plan

A sample program plan for promoting physical activity is shown on page 151. Note how it lists a goal, ties the goal to a specific outcome objective, lists an impact objective, and then outlines the specific process objectives that will need to take place to make the impact objective happen. The plan specifies a

Sample Program Plan to Promote Physical Activity in Sedentary County, USA

Goal: A majority of residents of Sedentary County will engage in a physically active lifestyle.

Outcome objective: By the year 2010, increase to at least 30% the proportion of people aged 18 and older who engage regularly, preferably daily, in sustained physical activity for at least 30 minutes per day.

Impact objective: By the year 2008, increase by 10% the proportion of adults aged 18 and older who regularly walk, run, or bicycle for at least 30 minutes per day on 5 or more days of the week as evidenced by annual community-wide behavioral risk factor surveys.

Partners in this objective: Sedentary County Departments of Health, Transportation, and Parks and Recreation; Sedentary County Board of Commissioners; Mayor's Council on Physical Fitness and Sports; American Association of Retired Persons; State Intermodal Surface Transportation Efficiency Act (ISTEA) Coordinator; the ABC Real Estate Agency; and the Citaspel Corporation Wellness Task Force.

Process objective	Target date	Lead person	Measures of success
Establish neighborhood walking clubs in the three largest communities in the county	Sept 30, 2000	Tom Walker	Real estate agents agreement completed Neighborhoods identified Meetings with home owners' associations Number of walking clubs established Number of members within each walking club Neighboring Partners contest plans completed Sponsors identified Contest launched
Convert at least three miles of unused railroad beds to walking and bicycling trails throughout the county	Sept 30, 2004	Betty Ties	Department of Transportation and County Commission secures ISTEA funding Walking trail plans approved Community sponsors identified; number of sponsors Miles of railroad beds cleared Number of community organizations recruited to help develop trails Names of community organizations and contact information recorded
Identify walking programs currently available in Sedentary County and contiguous counties	Sept 30, 2002	Fred Foot	Meet with partners to identify all existing walking programs in the county Plan developed to promote identified walking programs Promotional materials designed and focus group tested Materials revised and disseminated; copies placed in scrapbook

151

target date, a contact person, and measures of success for each process objective. Writing down your plan in this manner, with input from your partners, will help keep your program on track from beginning to end.

Deciding What Aspects of Your Program to Evaluate

The keys to successful evaluation planning are to decide what questions you will need to answer, what information will help you answer them, and how you will obtain and interpret that information.

It's important to determine how effectively your intervention is delivered (process), what the short-term and intermediate effects are (impact), and what the long-term effects might be (outcome). Let's take a closer look at these three aspects of program evaluation.

Process Evaluation

Process evaluation can help you understand the internal dynamics of a program and identify areas for improvement while there is still time to make corrections to the program plan. Keeping track of what is happening in your program allows you to

- review your progress,
- make sure that program activities are being implemented as planned,
- compare what you want to happen and what is really happening,
- identify what strategies are or are not working,
- list obstacles, barriers, or problem areas and make needed changes,
- redirect and energize your plan of action,
- understand which program components work best and which need revision, and
- help others replicate your program.

Although process evaluation can tell you whether everything is going according to your plan, it cannot tell you whether the plan will bring about the results you hope to achieve. The following list describes measurement tools you might use to document the process.

- Count the number of programs or activities provided; count how often programs or activities are provided. Implement "head counting" techniques through attendance logs:
    —Number of people invited to participate
    —Number or percentage of people participating at start of program
    —Number or percentage of people participating at end of program
    —Percentage growth (or decline) in participation over time
    —Description of people who participate, by age, race, gender, and site
    —Number or percentage who do not participate
    —Differences observed between participants and nonparticipants
- Track messages disseminated through television, radio, or written media:
    —Number of messages or articles released
    —Number of times message was played or publicized

—Estimated or actual number of people reached with each type of message

—Copies of audio, and video, of radio or television coverage

—Scrapbook of relevant materials, news clippings, and photos

- Develop registration forms that ask for key demographic or psychographic information.
- Keep staff and volunteer records and time logs to get qualitative feedback.
- Get information through interviews or open-ended questionnaires.
- Track public records of important meetings and proceedings.
- Review activity logs or diaries of participants and staff.
- Keep progress checklists.
- Routinely record successes and lessons learned (e.g., what you would do again, what you would do differently, and what makes an activity successful or unsuccessful).
- Conduct formal or informal focus groups with participants to learn which factors contribute to the success or failure of your activities.
- Visit sites to see firsthand what changes are taking place.
- Document involvement of decision makers.
- Write activity reports quarterly and annually.

Questions to Consider During Process Evaluation

- What are we doing (i.e., to address awareness, knowledge, motivation, skills, social support, physical environments, or policies)?
- When?
- Where?
- Are we delivering the program as it was planned? If not, how has it varied and why?
- Who is doing it? Who is helping?
- Are partnerships working effectively?
- Is anyone or anything working against us?
- Whom are we reaching with our messages and program components? How many are we reaching?
- Who is participating in our activities? How many are participating?
- Do we appear to be reaching those we most wanted to reach?
- How are we doing?
- What seems to be working? What factors are contributing most to success?
- What is not working very well and why not?
- Are we on track with time and resources? Are we on schedule—why or why not? Are we using funds effectively—why or why not?
- Should we be doing anything differently from now on? Do we need to revise our expectations as detailed in our objectives?

Impact Evaluation

Impact evaluation systematically gathers information required to answer questions about the short- and medium-term effects of your intervention. The information gathered in an impact evaluation is also compared to impact objectives to determine the extent of discrepancy that exists between the short- and medium-term effects you expect and those you observe through the evaluation process.

Impact evaluation measures variables such as changes in knowledge, attitudes, beliefs, behaviors, skills, stage of change, resources, social support systems, policies, and the environment. In short, impact evaluation looks at the more immediate effects a program has on the participants, the organization, or the community at large.

Following are methods for measuring the short-term and intermediate effects of your physical activity promotion program.

- Conduct "before" and "after" testing of knowledge, attitudes, beliefs, skills, or fitness levels through surveys, questionnaires, or skills review.
- Assess the health status of participants before and after the intervention (e.g., changes in health indicators, risk factors, physical or psychological well-being, activities of daily living, and quality of life) through surveys, interviews, observations, or case studies.
- Conduct surveys to assess changes in sources and levels of social support.
- Review records to determine whether practices and policies have changed.
- Analyze changes and trends in absenteeism rate.
- Analyze health care costs of employees.
- Conduct follow-up surveys or interviews on consumer satisfaction with your program.
- Make follow-up observations (e.g., after 6 months and 1 year) through site visits.
- Conduct case studies at the organizational or community level.

Outcome Evaluation

Outcome evaluation systematically gathers information required to answer questions about the long-term effects of your intervention. The information gathered in an outcome evaluation is compared to outcome objectives to determine the extent of discrepancy that exists between the long-term effects you expect and those you observe through the evaluation process.

In short, outcome evaluation can help you assess the long-term effects of your intervention and the extent to which you have achieved your goals. It measures changes in health status; quality of life; and the prevalence of risk factors for disability, morbidity, or mortality. Long-term outcome measures may be too expensive and impractical to assess within the time and resource constraints of most community-based programs. Also, it may be difficult to determine whether your program was responsible for or contributed significantly to outcomes that may not be evident until many years after your program was completed. Therefore, it may be best to concentrate your evaluation planning on process and impact measures. Pages 155–156 can be used to evaluate long-term effects (outcome) of your physical activity promotion program.

Questions to Consider During Impact and Outcome Evaluation

- What did we accomplish? Did we achieve our objectives? Why or why not?

- Did the participants move forward at least one stage in the behavior change continuum? What percentage of the group progressed through one or more stages of change (e.g., from the Contemplation stage to the Action stage)? What percentage maintained physical activity for at least 6 months?

- Was there a change in physical activity knowledge, attitudes, beliefs, skills, or behaviors among participants? If so, how much? If not, why not?

- Are people more physically active as a result of what we did?

  —Number of people who started a physical activity program

  —Number or percentage who completed the program

  —Number or percentage who had increased their activity levels by the end of the program, 6 months later, and 1 year later

  —Number or percentage of people who changed their behaviors or lifestyle in some way, or their intention to do so

- What can we learn about those who dropped out?

- What is different as a result of our actions?

  —In the people: what happened in the lives of those who participated and those who did not

  —In the environment: the place or the facilities

  —In the curricula, procedures, and policies

  —In how we link with the community

  —In our relationships with other organizations or our partners

- Have more policies or environmental interventions (e.g., walking trails, exercise facilities, and physical activity policies in schools) been established?

- Are people healthier as a result of what we did? Have they modified their risk factors for disease and disability?

- How expensive was the program compared with other physical activity interventions? How effective was the program compared with other programs?

- What did we learn as a result? What went right? What went wrong? What would we do differently next time?

Selecting Your Evaluation Measures

By evaluating your intervention, you will be in a better position to learn from your experiences and share those experiences with others. Your evaluation measures—those indicators you will count or track over time—were either suggested or clearly defined by the goals and objectives specified in your program plan.

For example, if one of your objectives was to convert at least three miles of unused railroad beds into walking and bicycling trails, you will want to describe how you achieved that objective. You could record when the project began and ended, its cost, how many miles of track were converted, and whether the new trails are being used. You would also want to know what community residents think about the trails and their impression of the promotional program.

Examples of Community-Level Measures of Physical Activity

Awareness, knowledge, and skill-building measures

- Prevalence (numbers and rates) of physical activity and sedentary behaviors among adults and youth or by members of a specific target population
- For grades kindergarten (K) through 12, percentage of time in physical education classes spent on lifetime activities
- Qualifications of instructors or teachers of physical education or exercise classes, and percentage of those who are certified by a reputable organization or who are college graduates with a degree in physical education
- Percentage of health care providers who routinely advise patients to be active
- Availability of physical activity-related educational and motivational materials in worksites, community libraries, video stores, and other targeted locations
- Number and placement of physical activity promotion messages on billboards, bulletin boards, and other public places
- Number of media reports (television, radio, or print) promoting physical activity or specific message components

Social and environmental measures

- Number of physical activity events in the community per year
- Presence and extent of special physical activity-related incentives in the community, such as free bicycles for public use, extensive mass transit systems, sections of town closed to vehicular traffic, or presence of sidewalks
- Percentage or miles of walking trails, bike lanes, or sidewalks per capita
- Observation of use (whether trails or lanes are being used)
- Number of physical activity facilities per capita
- Availability of all physical activity facilities to community members
- Acres of parks or recreational space (per total community acres or per capita)
- Census of use of physical activity facilities (worksite, community, etc.)
- Membership in physical activity-related organizations (YMCA, YWCA, health clubs, walking clubs, etc.)
- Number of worksites that sponsor teams, jogging groups, mall walking, etc.
- Number of worksites that allow staff to participate in physical activity during work hours
- Presence or absence of formal worksite policies that support physical activity (such as flextime or longer breaks and lunches)
- Tracking of targeted items (such as sales or rental of sports equipment and videos)

Policy measures

- Transportation and highway funds designated for nonvehicular transports
- Zoning or rezoning requirements to include sidewalks, walking trails, or bike paths
- Total amount or percentage of state or local budget per capita devoted to physical activity and recreation
- Presence or absence of policies promoting inclusion of recreation facilities in new construction, remodeling, and restoration projects
- Evidence that the local zoning board considers health-related quality of life in its decisions
- Regulations allowing and accommodating bicycles on mass transit systems
- State or local policy to include physical activity in school curricula for grades K–12
- Extent to which school curricula for grades K–12 include lifetime activity skills; comparisons by schools, districts, or other jurisdictions
- Health insurance reimbursement for physical activity-related services and counseling

Adapted from Fawcett et al. 1995.

Gathering the opinions of those who do and do not use the trail system can help you even more in determining what follow-up messages and activities are needed to improve or maintain the project's success. When planning any level of intervention, you'll want to consider some of the evaluation measures of physical activity listed on page 156.

Questions to Consider When Selecting Your Evaluation Measures

- What will you count or track?
- What will you document, save, clip, or record?
- What factors or measure will you compare before, during, and after the intervention?

Deciding what to count, track, save, and document is determined by the information needs of your organization or community group and other stakeholders (e.g., decision makers, program administrators, participants, and sponsors). Various stakeholders have different interests. For example, public officials may expect feedback on activities they perceive to be costly

or that require many resources, participants may be most interested in the immediate benefits to their health or quality of life, and researchers may want to know which activities were most effective in reaching a particular target population. Balancing the information needs of these groups is part of the art of evaluation.

As you determine what data you will measure and collect, consider the following:

- The relative importance of each question you wish to answer as it relates to your program goals.
- The cost (in time and resources) required to answer each question describing your program and what you have accomplished.
- The relevance of the information in addressing the concerns and questions of your stakeholders. By planning ahead to answer stakeholders' concerns and by letting them know what evaluation questions will be used before the program begins, you will make your results more meaningful to the people whose opinions are important to the continuation of your program.

Collecting and Analyzing Program Data

Once you have decided what objectives you will evaluate and how you will evaluate your progress, you must collect and analyze relevant data from the moment your program planning begins. Timing is an important component to a successful evaluation plan. If you try to gather impact data too quickly, not enough time may have elapsed to see any results; if you wait too long after your program ends, however, you may not be able to determine whether your findings are the result of your program. For ongoing programs, you may want to collect data at several times, such as at the beginning of the program (baseline), then periodically (e.g., every 6 months), and after the program ends. Examine early findings so that you can fine-tune your evaluation methods as well as your program plans if necessary.

Questions to Consider When Collecting and Analyzing Program Data

- Where will you obtain feedback or information to help you critique your program?
- How will you gather it? Who will help you in gathering it?
- How will you store it?
- How will you analyze it? Who can help you?

Obtaining the Data You Need

You will need to identify the questions you'll need to ask, where and how you can obtain the data to answer those questions, and what techniques you will use to record the data (e.g., paper-and-pencil test, face-to-face interview, telephone interview, or recording data from existing records).

You may want to conduct personal interviews with program participants (e.g., asking what was most helpful in bringing about changes in physical-activity levels) or gather your information more indirectly (e.g., estimating the number of people using walking trails at certain times of the day). Together these methods can indicate both the qualitative and quantitative changes occurring in community-wide physical-activity practices. The following list includes techniques for data collection you can use to evaluate program process and its effects.

- Questionnaires or surveys
- Physical measures (e.g., body weight or blood pressure)
- Self-reported inventories and diaries
- Structured or semistructured interviews
- Skills testing
- Focus groups
- Role playing
- Scenarios
- Document review
- Case studies
- Direct observation
- Site visits
- Policy evaluations
- Monitoring of media coverage

Although data collection should be closely monitored, it should not become burdensome. To make evaluations easier and more efficient, try collecting information in ways that minimize the time and resources required. For example, use existing data sources whenever possible and collect only the information you are most likely to use. Also, design data collection forms that both your project staff and the participants completing the forms will find easy to use. Try out the forms on a few people before using them with a larger audience.

Planning Data Storage

When planning your evaluation approach, decide how and where to keep the information you collect. Information accumulates rapidly! Will you enter the facts and figures into a computerized data file, or will you tally them by hand? Your method does not have to be fancy; it simply has to work for you. For example, if your program is very small, filing participant cards in a shoe box may be all you need. For larger programs, computerized information storage, sorting, and reporting may work best. Regardless of the size of your program, you may want to consider contracting with someone to handle the data for you or partnering with someone who has that expertise.

Planning Data Analysis

Before you start gathering information, decide how you will interpret, analyze, and use the data. Then, while your program is in progress, your evaluation data can provide valuable feedback for making midcourse adjustments. Never wait until the end of a program to begin looking at the data you have collected. Nothing is more frustrating than finding out that you cannot answer questions describing your program because you gathered information in the wrong way or because you collected lots of data you cannot use and not enough of the information you really need.

Deciding Who Will Manage the Evaluation Data

Choose someone who will manage and be responsible for carrying out the evaluation. The data manager should keep track of specified tasks, timelines for each task (including start and end dates), and the person or people responsible for each task. For example, your manager may want to assign someone primary responsibility for handling and storing the data, ensuring confidentiality of the data, and checking its accuracy within reasonable limits. This plan will help clarify roles and keep track of the evaluation process itself.

You and your data manager may want to develop a written protocol to clarify how information will flow. Having written procedures will help ensure some consistency in handling routine problems as they arise, such as what to do if the data are incomplete or incorrect.

It's important to decide early who will be responsible for data entry, how record keeping will be done, how you'll collect information, and how you'll report your results.

Reporting Your Results

You need to decide how your program data, accomplishments, and lessons learned will be shared with others. You can present results as quarterly reports, executive summaries, internal reports, interim reports, or final reports. Channels may include health newsletters, press releases, press conferences, town meetings, newspaper articles, letters to the editor, appearances on radio talk shows, in-person communications, and presentations at conferences and to individual organizations. Also consider whether you will report your findings in writing or orally—both have important uses and can be highly effective.

Questions to Consider When Reporting Your Results

- With whom will you share your results?
- What aspects of your intervention will you share with whom?
- How can you describe your intervention and communicate your results appropriately and meaningfully to others (i.e., partners, other professionals, constituents, or the media)?
- When will you share your results?

A well-written evaluation report is an excellent way to share data with interested parties. You may want to develop more than one version of the report to distribute to different audiences. Make your findings work for your program. For example, provide stakeholders information that will help you defend the program and keep it going. Your results might prove valuable in convincing citizens, politicians, or decision makers about the need for policy changes or resource allocations within the community.

Shorter, more direct, and simpler evaluation reports are more likely to be used. Confidentiality, sensitivity, and objectivity are paramount. You might include the following components:

- A summary or abstract
- The purpose of the intervention
- The evaluation questions you were trying to answer
- A description of the intervention
- Methods of evaluation used
- Data analysis
- Findings and conclusions
- Key tables, graphs, and figures

An overriding consideration when deciding how to provide feedback are the information feedback preferences of stakeholders. That is, do they prefer oral or written reports? When you meet with your stakeholders to determine what questions they want answered by the evaluation, you should also ask them how often and in what format they want the information fed back to them. To wait until the evaluation is completed to present an all-encompassing report ignores the fact that stakeholders could be making decisions about your program on a day-to-day basis.

Suggested Reading

For a list of organizations, agencies, and selected program materials for promoting physical activity, see:

Resource A, for general resources

Chapter 6, for environment-related resources

Chapter 9, for worksite-related resources

Chapter 10, for school-related resources

To learn more about writing measurable objectives, read:

Fodor JT, Dalis GT, Giarratano SC. Formulating goals and objectives for health instruction. In: *Health Instruction: Theory and Application* (5th Edition). Malvern, PA: Williams & Wilkins, 1995.

Green LW. Human behavior and community health education. In: Green LW, editor. *Community Health* (6th Edition). St. Louis: Times Mirror/Mosby, 1990.

Mager RF. *Preparing Instructional Objectives* (Rev. 2nd Edition). Belmont, CA: Pitman Learning, 1984.

To learn more about program evaluation, read:

Green LW, Lewis FM. *Measurement and Evaluation in Health Education and Health Promotion.* Palo Alto, CA: Mayfield Publishing Company, 1986.

Green LW, Kreuter MW. *Health Promotion Planning: An Educational and Environmental Approach.* Mountain View, CA: Mayfield Publishing Company, 1991. See particularly chapter 7.

Herman JL, editor. *Program Evaluation Kit.* Newbury Park, CA: Sage Publications, 1987. This nine-volume kit takes the reader step-by-step through the entire evaluation process from program design to presentation. The easy-to-follow format includes tips, practice exercises, data collection forms, flowcharts, graphs, and measurement instruments.

King AC, Jeffery RW, Fridinger F, et al. Environmental and policy approaches to cardiovascular and disease prevention through physical activity: issues and opportunities. *Health Education Quarterly* 1995; 22(4):499–511.

U.S. Department of Health and Human Services. *Program Evaluation Handbook: Physical Activity.* Washington, DC: U.S. Department of Health and Human Services, 1988.

Windsor RA, Baranowski T, Clark N, et al. *Evaluations of Health Promotion, Health Education, and Disease Prevention Programs.* (2nd Edition). Palo Alto, CA: Mayfield Publishing Company, 1994.

Chapter 8 Working With Partners

Creating awareness and providing a range of services far-reaching enough to affect a community often requires more resources than one organization has to offer. But no matter where you are, how isolated you may feel, or how ambitious your goals, you do not have to face your challenges by yourself: partners can help you succeed. Partnerships are people working with people to accomplish greater things together than either could have accomplished alone. That is, partnerships create synergy. Your plans to promote physical activity and to foster lifestyle change may achieve greater success when diverse segments of the community become involved in your efforts.

Understanding How Partnerships Work

When spiderwebs unite, they can tie up a lion.

Old Ethiopian proverb

A partnership is any cooperative effort between individuals, groups, agencies, businesses, or municipalities to accomplish a goal. It can take many forms. For some efforts, the partnership may be formed just long enough to achieve a specific task. For other efforts, the partnership endures to focus on long-term or broader goals (Ames et al. 1992). Partnerships between individuals or agencies can vary in their level of cooperation, ranging from minimal involvement to the mutual sharing of all phases of program planning and implementation (see the list on page 165). Partnerships may also vary in their operational structure and formality, as shown in the box on page 166. Partners can help you in a variety of ways. They can

- direct more resources (both people and funding) toward promoting physical activity;
- broaden community support and strengthen the community's trust in your program;
- share forces of leaders, gatekeepers, and other influential people (and thereby increase your power base);
- share the knowledge, expertise (e.g., training capability), or credibility needed to bridge gaps in your overall program;
- provide increased access to the media to improve the public's awareness of physical activity issues—that is, increase visibility for your message;
- eliminate duplication of effort;
- reach more people within your target population in greater numbers and with greater effectiveness; and
- help achieve a bigger impact.

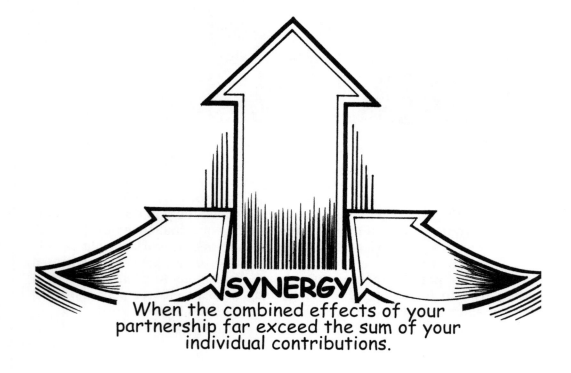

SYNERGY
When the combined effects of your partnership far exceed the sum of your individual contributions.

Levels of Involvement Among Partners

Networking or communication links

You and your partners share information for mutual benefit. Although minimally involved with each other, you keep one another aware of resources or events that may prove valuable later.

Attendance

Some people may become involved simply by attending your program, supporting you on the day of an event, or participating in your classes. They can be helpful in spreading the news of its characteristics or success.

Publicity

Some partners may serve as channels or intermediaries in helping you to spread the word. They might lend their mailing lists or include a notice in their regular mailings to their constituents. Perhaps they have access to media channels to help you disseminate your message.

Coordination

While maintaining your autonomy, you and your partners exchange information; schedule or alter activities to be mutually beneficial; and work together to achieve a common purpose. The partnership adds strength to your activities and may avoid duplication in effort. It involves a certain degree of trust and overlap in responsibilities.

Cooperation

You and your partners exchange information; schedule or alter activities to be mutually beneficial; and share resources (e.g., knowledge, expertise, people, time, influence, access, funds, or physical property) to achieve a common purpose. Whether volunteers, colleagues, or acquaintances, these partners are a valuable asset.

Endorsement

Some organizations may publicly acknowledge their support by endorsing your program with their logo or stamp of approval. An endorsement may broaden your program's appeal or legitimize your program to a greater extent than you would have been capable of alone.

Cosponsorship

Partners may share even more of their resources throughout segments of your planning or program efforts. Those partners deserve recognition and may share the visibility your program achieves.

Collaboration

You and your partners are together from beginning to the end, sharing information, altering your schedules and activities, sharing resources, as well as the risks, responsibilities, and rewards. You are helping each other become better at what you do best. Individuals from each of your organizations or settings meet regularly to plan and carry out specific objectives. Although you may lose your autonomy, you could gain a great deal more from the close relationship.

Source: American Heart Association, Georgia Affiliate, 1991; University of Georgia, 1991; and Arthur T. Himmelman, 1996, *Collaboration for a Change: Definitions, Models, Roles, and a Guide to the Collaborative Process.*

Kinds of Partnerships

Advisory council   A group of individuals selected to provide suggestions and guidance to organizations or programs.

Alliance   Semiofficial grouping of organizations connected by a common cause.

Coalition   Varied organizations and groups united around salient issues or common interests or problems, addressing their goals through cooperation, advocacy, capacity building, social change, or community action. Coalitions frequently start out without a formalized structure, yet as the organizations work together developing plans and blending resources, they generate the united structure (i.e., bylaws, committees, funding, staffing, and plans) sufficient to accomplish their common goal. Over time, goals characteristic of coalitions have evolved from specific, short-term and activity-centered to global, longer-term, and somewhat diffuse (CDC 1997). Although member organizations are autonomous, free to enter or leave the group, commitment among those who assume leadership is necessary to achieve a coalition's success.

Collaborative   The most organized and structured form of partnership, a collaborative is, as its name implies, an interagency group working in collaboration to accomplish a shared vision. The term collaborative has been used to describe a coalition; yet a collaborative relationship implies that goals are more clearly defined and narrowly focused on a common issue. If the collaborative is successful, a new identity emerges; organizations form a long-term and durable relationship. Together, collaborating partners set defined criteria for membership in the group, clearly state the roles and responsibilities of membership, and join together in the process of planning and measuring progress toward a desired outcome.

Commission   A group appointed by official bodies. It usually consists of citizens rather than organizations or agencies.

Consortium   A formal relationship among professional individuals or organizations who are linked by similarities in the services they provide or in the audiences they reach (HRSA 1998). The relationships between and among consortium members is generally more structured than a network or alliance, but less so than found in a coalition or collaborative.

Network   Spontaneous and often loosely knit communication links between individuals or organizations as a means of maintaining contact or keeping informed. Network structures are less formal and hierarchical than most other forms of partnerships and are therefore best suited to short-term goals and immediate action.

Task force   A group of individuals who want to accomplish a specific series of activities, most often at the request of some other, overseeing body.

Source: Van Hulzen 1992; Bracht 1990.

PARTNERSHIP IN ACTION
The "Laurens Falls for Fitness" Campaign

In Laurens, South Carolina, the "Laurens Falls for Fitness" campaign won a Secretary's Community Health Promotion Award from the U.S. Department of Health and Human Services for involving nearly 500 people in a 6-week public awareness campaign to promote physical activity. The campaign's planning committee included representatives from local colleges, the district health department, the county parks and recreation department, local schools and their staff, local golf clubs, the YMCA, and the local government.

For more information about other physical activity programs, search the CHID (see page 241 in resource A) or contact your state health department's physical activity contact person.

Finding a Partner That Complements Your Organization

Before you develop your list of potential partners, inventory your organization's strengths. What do you have to offer in accomplishing the goals you have set forth for your program? Do you have the necessary resources, personnel, funding, programmatic expertise, visibility, or credibility?

After you have identified your strengths, identify gaps that partners could fill. Contrast your goals and objectives—all that you hope to accomplish—with your weaknesses. Where are the gaps? What do you need to complement your strengths? If you need personnel, for example, look for partners who can bring volunteers or staff into the relationship. If you lack access to certain subgroups of the community, identify potential partners who already have access to them. A list of potential partners from a variety of community sectors is provided on pages 169–172, but don't stop here! You may think of many others.

Partners may come from a number of likely and unlikely sources. They may be individuals or organizations that

• share a vision nearly identical to your own. Although their target populations may differ slightly from your own, they share your desire to promote physical activity.

• have gone before you with similar missions or goals. At some time in the past whether they had conducted community-wide programs or had promoted physical activity and the benefits of a healthy lifestyle, their history of experiences provide valuable lessons for your own program efforts.

• share at least one common element with your program. Perhaps these partners have goals very different from your own, but you share a common target audience or at least one common objective. For example, an intercultural task force devoted to stopping urban violence may work with you to establish after-school physical activity programs for inner-city youth.

- are instrumental in reaching your target audience. They may
    —currently be reaching your target population with successful programs or services;
    —be gatekeepers to your target population, people you must work with or work through to gain access to members of your target population;
    —be intermediary organizations that may serve as effective channels for distributing program messages, materials, or services to members of your target population; or
    —have influence or have earned the respect and admiration of your target population, or be representatives and members themselves.

- have access to staff, volunteers, facilities, equipment, materials, funding, or other resources that will aid in your efforts to promote your message or service.

- have the expertise, knowledge, authority, or influence to help you accomplish your goals.

- are stakeholders—they have something to gain or to lose, or they are directly influenced by actions you take in your efforts to promote physical activity.

Once you have identified potential partners, involve them as early as possible in program planning so that they will have a stake in the outcomes. However, be careful not to compromise your strengths. Avoid partnering with those who might have questionable intentions or distract the public's attention away from your intended goals. If you doubt whether a partnership is right for you, ask some of your constituents for their opinion. You may occasionally find that certain partnerships are unwise. Pages 169–172 list many potential partnering organizations in these community sectors: government, health, education, transportation, business, media, recreation, religious, and voluntary or service.

Potential Partners in Promoting Physical Activity

 Government sector

National, state, and local elected officials

Representatives of federal, state, county, or city government

Regional or local planning commissions

State or county department of health or mental health

State or county cooperative extension service

State or county department of education

State or county department of transportation (TEA 21 program); bicycle and pedestrian coordinators

State or county department of parks and recreation

Governor's or mayor's council on physical fitness and sports

Local council on physical fitness and sports or wellness

State department of natural resources

State department of tourism

Public utility companies

Area agencies on aging

Law enforcement agencies

State, county, or local crime prevention task forces

Emergency rescue agencies (e.g., medical and fire)

Libraries

Public housing communities

State, county zoning board

Healthy Cities Program, Healthy Communities Program, and Healthier Communities Program (each has a strong government component)

 Health sector

Wellness councils or coalitions

Planned Approach to Community Health (PATCH) program coalitions

State and local health departments

State and local health and fitness coalitions

Hospitals, health maintenance organizations, or clinics

Private practicing physicians

Physical and occupational therapists

Cardiovascular rehabilitation centers

Professional medical associations and auxiliaries

Emergency medical teams

Mental health centers or crisis intervention centers

Insurance companies

(continued)

(continued)

Health and fitness organizations, such as local chapters of

- the American College of Sports Medicine,
- the National Association of Sport and Physical Education, and
- the American Association of Health, Physical Education, Recreation and Dance.

National and state health education associations, such as

- the Association for the Advancement of Health Education,
- the Society of Public Health Educators, and
- the American Public Health Association, Health Education Section.

National and state nursing and medical associations, such as

- the American Nurses' Association,
- the American Association of Occupational Health Nurses,
- the American Medical Association,
- the National Medical Association,
- the American Academy of Family Physicians,
- the American College of Occupational Medicine, and
- the American College of Preventive Medicine.

Education sector

State and local departments of education

Universities and colleges

Technical schools

Public elementary, middle, and high schools

Private elementary, middle, and high schools

School boards

Day care centers, preschool programs, and after-school programs

Special education programs

Parent-teacher associations

School wellness captains

State and local chapters of professional teachers' and administrators' associations, such as

- the National Education Association,
- the American Federation of Teachers,
- the National Association of Elementary School Principals,
- the National Association of Secondary School Principals, and
- the American Association of School Administrators.

 Transportation and environmental development sector

Environmental Protection Agency (EPA)

National Park Service

State and local department of transportation officials; bicycle and pedestrian coordinators (TEA 21 program)

National and state highway traffic and safety officials

City and regional planning commissions; urban planners

Colleges and institutes of city and regional or urban planning and research

Colleges and schools of architecture, civil engineering, landscape design, and social ecology

Colleges and schools of law and criminal justice

Professional associations and environmental advocacy groups such as

- American Planning Association
- American Institute of Architects
- Urban Land Institute
- Congress for the New Urbanism
- Citizen Planner Institute
- Institute of Transportation Engineers
- Partnership for a Walkable America
- Bicycle Federation of America
- Rails-to-Trails Conservancy
- Insurance Institute for Highway Safety
- Surface Transportation Policy Project
- International Federation of Pedestrians
- Pedestrian Federation of America
- National Coalition for Promoting Physical Activity
- Go for Green (Canada)

Healthy Communities project staff

Sierra Club; private walking, hiking, bicycling, and other sporting organizations

Private nature, garden, and other outdoor conservation organizations

County commissioners regulating zoning laws

 Business sector

Chamber of commerce

Business coalitions and labor organizations

Large businesses and industries

Small businesses and industries

Real estate agencies

Worksite wellness coordinators

Shopping mall managers

Fitness clubs and health spas

Athletic or sporting goods industries

Professional sports teams

 Media and communication sector

Television stations (cable and public)

Radio station managers

Newspaper editors (daily and weekly; state and local), especially health section editors

Newsletter editors

Electronic mail and Internet consultants

Professional journal editors

Health and fitness publication editors

Public relations and marketing professionals or consultants

(continued)

 Recreation sector

National, state, or local parks

Local park and recreation departments

Young Men's and Women's Christian Associations (YMCA and YWCA)

Young Men's and Women's Hebrew Associations (YMHA and YWHA)

Senior centers

Community centers

Walking, hiking, or running clubs

Community team sports clubs (e.g., softball, soccer, basketball, volleyball, football, and ice hockey) for youth, adults, or special populations

Outdoor sporting clubs of any kind, such as hiking, walking, bicycling, skiing, tennis, golf, orienteering, and sailing

Special Olympics or Wheel Chair Sports, Inc.

Sports governing bodies and state athletic associations

State Games Associations (e.g., Senior Games and Corporate Games)

 Religious sector

Clergy and ministerial associations or councils

Churches and synagogues

Women's groups and men's groups

Youth groups

Church-owned recreation facilities, camps, etc.

 Voluntary or service organization sector

American Heart Association

American Red Cross

National Arthritis Foundation

American Lung Association

American Diabetes Association

Special public or private foundations

Neighborhood or homeowner associations

Girl Scouts of America, Boy Scouts of America, Boys' and Girls' clubs, 4-H clubs, and other youth organizations

American Association of Retired Persons, elder hostels, and other predominantly seniors' organizations

Rotary, Lions, Kiwanis, Jaycees, and other service organizations

League of Women Voters, Junior League, and other predominantly women's organizations

Graduate students in schools of public health, medical students, physical therapy students, and education students (particularly physical education or health education)

College fraternities and sororities

Local physicians, sports figures, and celebrities

Spouses of local physicians; hospital auxiliaries

Spouses of state governors

Maintaining a Successful Partnership

Working with partners is time-consuming. You must identify potential partners, convince them to work with you, gain internal approvals, and possibly undergo training—all even before you can plan your program. Partnering may also require significant alterations in your program, since every organization has different priorities and perspectives and may want to make program changes to accommodate their needs.

For a partnership to be successful, the relationship formed must benefit all parties involved, so that each partner achieves some sense of gain or worth from having been involved in the effort. Confusion and misunderstanding can be minimized if early in the process you clearly define your goals in a language common to all parties involved (i.e., free of jargon or vague terminology); reach agreement on the role each partner will play; involve competent individuals, whether staff or volunteer, who represent each partner; build a relationship upon mutual respect, recognizing and appreciating each partner's organizational identity and contribution; develop trust and cooperation so that you feel comfortable sharing leadership; and communicate regularly to exchange information, to address concerns or problems that arise, and to report on progress within each area of responsibility.

Define Your Goals

For your intervention to be successful, it's important that you and your partners know from the outset what it is that you are hoping to accomplish. If program goals are unclear, it's easy for your efforts to deviate from the intended course. Likewise, if you have goals that are different from your partner's goals, it's better to talk through differences and come to some agreement at the beginning to avoid competing efforts, misunderstandings, or disappointment later. The time it takes to become familiar with your partner's needs and intentions, listening openly to their desires, is time well invested and is a necessary step in creating a shared understanding of the entire task.

Embrace Differences

A common challenge to collaborating among partners is resolving differences and finding ways to meet a variety of needs while making progress toward a shared vision. Encountering differences of opinion is common to all interrelationships. And, styles of conducting collaborative work may differ by social class, ethnicity, cultural orientation, education, training, profession, geography, age, gender, and past experiences. Expect, invite, and work with these differences, for successful collaborative work transcends them in order to achieve a common purpose (ACS 1996). The key to success is in handling conflict constructively and fairly, and to the extent possible, channeling differences of opinion into creating useful solutions.

Define Each Partner's Role and Responsibilities

Success also depends on how specifically each organization defines and understands its role in the partnership and in accomplishing the tasks at hand. In spite of personal differences, successful collaborators understand that the task and the goal transcends personal issues. The partnership exists because the partners believe they each have something of value to contribute and they need each other to get the job done (ACS 1996). By agreeing on roles and responsibilities early in the relationship, and by giving partners flexibility to match responsibilities to their needs, interests, and resources, the working relationships established will be healthier in the long run.

PARTNERSHIP IN ACTION

Wellness Activities in Colorado

In Colorado, the Foothills Parks and Recreation District along with the Jefferson County Department of Health and Environment planned a broad spectrum of creative wellness activities. For example, with funding from the Jefferson County Commissioner's Office, they purchased and outfitted a 34-foot bus. This "mobile wellness classroom" delivered disease prevention, health promotion, and physical activity programs throughout the community and to schools, worksites, and outlying neighborhoods.

The Fort Morgan Parks and Recreation Department in Colorado joined forces with a local cemetery administrator to allow walking programs on the grounds of the memorial park, with a local motel owner to provide water aerobics classes in his underused swimming pool, and with the staff of a 240-acre wildlife preserve (formerly a dump site and wasteland) to develop walking trails and a variety of educational and recreational opportunities for community members.

The Colorado Wray Parks and Recreation Department (with a staff of two) linked with local schools, the Future Homemakers of America Clubs, and the local Area Agency on Aging to develop intergenerational programs such as older adults walking with elementary school-age children.

Barriers to Effective Partnerships

Working with other organizations can be challenging. Be aware of the types of problems you might encounter so that you can avoid them or at least handle them when they arise.

- Historical or ideological differences
- Institutional ideologies that discourage collaboration or partnering
- Competition for resources
- Lack of leadership and no clear direction
- Domination by one organization or individual
- Perceived or actual loss of ownership and control by one of the partners
- Inadequate participation by important groups
- Unrealistic expectations about partners' roles, responsibilities, or time commitments
- Working together poses too great a burden on time or resources
- Disagreements among partners regarding values, vision, goals, or actions
- Inability or unwillingness to negotiate or compromise on important issues

Develop Trust and Cooperation

Trust and cooperation are also crucial to developing cohesive and effective partnerships. Take time to foster trust and credibility among individuals and organizational representatives through open, regular communication and team-building.

Trust includes sharing leadership by rotating such tasks as hosting meetings and organizing events. Sharing leadership helps all partners feel ownership in the project. One partner may lose a feeling of ownership and control when another partner changes the time schedule, the activities, or even the message, or takes full credit for the program (National Cancer Institute 1989); so it's important to share the leadership and keep communication lines open.

PARTNERSHIP IN ACTION

Youth-Related Crime Intervention in Arizona

In Phoenix, Arizona, partnership among agencies in the public sector—the departments of housing and urban development, law enforcement, and parks and recreation—resulted in a program addressing youth-related crime in one economically disadvantaged area. These agencies provided a variety of summer recreational activities and strong social support for youth in a housing project. Police calls from the community decreased by 35% when the physical activity programs were in effect.

For more information about other physical activity programs, search the CHID (see page 241 in resource A) or contact your state health department physical activity subject specialist.

You might also identify specific individuals within each organization who can lead various activities, and help them obtain what they need to implement their part of the program—be it funding, training, information, or tools. Consider providing partners with new local, regional, and national contacts that would be valuable for their ongoing activities. Whenever possible, give partners permission to personalize and adapt program materials to fit their needs.

Communicate Regularly

Effective communication is more than sending the occasional e-mail or memo, leaving a message, or even holding regular meetings. It is ensuring that all parties comprehend each other's point of view, even if they do not speak the same language. It might seem obvious that you should keep in touch with partners as your program progresses, but frequent communication is important for many reasons.

Periodically review program objectives to be certain that each partner is accomplishing what you had intended and according to the time frame you had established together in your work plan. Develop written reports summarizing everyone's progress to date. (For more information about documenting the milestones of your success, read chapter 7.)

Strive for Early Successes

Achieving a clear success early in the partnership is a first test of strength to the relationship. Those early victories may carry you through harder times, so choose your first tasks carefully. Don't take on more than you can handle, more than you have a realistic chance of affecting. An early task should be neither too trivial nor too difficult, yet significant enough to be both challenging and achievable (ACS 1996).

Acknowledge Each Partner's Contributions

It is important that each partner's distinct organizational identity and contribution to the project be recognized and appreciated. Be generous with praise. Providing moral support, frequent thanks, and other rewards such as letters or certificates of appreciation to those who worked to accomplish a goal are an important element of maintaining a successful relationship. Be generous, as well, in recognizing your partners' contributions to the task— share the visibility, the credit, and the glory. Whether project staff are paid or volunteer, respecting the needs of everyone is a courtesy that will yield its own rewards.

Suggested Reading

For a list of organizations, agencies, and selected program materials for promoting physical activity, see:

Resource A, for general resources

Chapter 6, for environment-related resources

Chapter 9, for worksite-related resources

Chapter 10, for school-related resources

For more information about media advocacy, read:

Wallack L, Dorfman L, Jernigan D, Themba M. *Media Advocacy and Public Health: Power for Prevention.* Newbury Park, CA: Sage Publications, 1993.

For more information about partnerships in promoting physical activity, read:

Butterfoss FD, Goodman R, Wandersman A. Community coalitions for prevention and health promotion. *Health Education Research* 1993; 8(3): 315–330.

Fridinger F, Provence S. Promoting partnerships for physical activity. *Parks and Recreation* 1994; 29(10):52–57.

National Cancer Institute. *Sowing Seeds in the Mountains: Community-Based Coalitions for Cancer Prevention and Control.* Couto R, Simpson N, Harris G, eds. Washington, DC: National Institutes of Health, 1994.

Wandersman A, Goodman R, Butterfoss F. Understanding coalitions and how they operate: an "open systems" organizational framework. In: *Community Organizing & Community Building for Health* edited by M. Minkler. NJ: Rutgers University Press, 1997: 261–277.

To learn more about the collaborative process, read:

American Cancer Society. 1+1=3, *A Collaboration Guidebook.* August 1996. For more information or to obtain a copy of this publication, contact:

Laura Greiner
Director of Collaborative Relations
American Cancer Society—National Home Office
1599 Clifton Road, NE
Atlanta, GA 30329
E-mail: **Lgreiner@cancer.org**

Himmelman A. *Collaboration for a Change: Definitions, Models, Roles, and a Guide to the Collaborative Process.* Minneapolis, MN: Arthur T. Himmelman Consulting Group; May 1996.

Mattessich P, Monsey B. *Collaboration: What Makes It Work — A Review of Research Literature on Factors Influencing Successful Collaboration.* St. Paul, MN: Amherst H. Wilder Foundation, 1992.

Winer M, Ray K. *Collaboration Handbook: Creating, Sustaining, and Enjoying the Journey.* St. Paul, MN: Amherst H. Wilder Foundation, 1994.

To learn more about building coalitions, read:

Bertcher HJ. *Group Participation Techniques for Leaders and Members* (2nd Edition). Newbury Park, CA: Sage Publications, 1994.

Brown CR. *The Art of Coalition Building: A Guide for Community Leaders*. New York: The American Jewish Committee, Institute of Human Relations, 1984.

Cox FM, Erlich JL, Rothman J, et al. *Strategies of Community Organization: A Book of Readings* (3rd Edition). Itasca, IL: Peacock Publishers, 1979.

Dluhy MJ. *Building Coalitions in the Human Services*. Newbury Park, CA: Sage Publications, 1990.

Health Promotion Resource Center, Stanford Center for Research in Disease Prevention. *How-To Guides on Community Health Promotion: Building and Maintaining Effective Coalitions (Guide #12)*. Palo Alto, CA: Stanford University School of Medicine in Cooperation with The Henry J. Kaiser Family Foundation, 1990.

Larson CE, LaFasto FMJ. *Team Work: What Must Go Right/What Can Go Wrong*. Newbury Park, CA: Sage Publications, 1989.

Minnesota Department of Health. *Community Health Promotion Kit*. Minneapolis, MN: Minnesota Department of Health, Division of Health Promotion and Education, 1989.

For more information about collaboration and effective group process, read:

Benard B. Working together: principles of effective collaboration. *Prevention Forum* 1989; 10(1):4–9.

Breckon DJ, Harvey JR, Lancaster RB. *Working With Groups in Leadership Roles in Community: Setting, Roles, and Skills for the 21st Century* (3rd Edition). Gaithersburg, MD: Aspen Publishers, 1994.

Cadwell, K. Growing a Breastfeeding Friendly Community. Sandwich, MA: Karin Cadwell 1996.

Centers for Disease Control and Prevention. *Reaching Women for Mammography Screenings: Successful Strategies of National Breast and Cervical Cancer Early Detection Program (NBCCEDP) Grantees*. Atlanta: U.S. Department of Health and Human Services, Centers for Disease Control and Prevention, 1997.

Gray B. *Collaborating: Finding Common Ground for Multiparty Problems*. San Francisco, CA: Jossey-Bass Publishers, 1989.

Tjosvold D. *Facilitating*. New York: Praeger, 1990.

Tjosvold D. *Learning to Manage Conflict: Getting People to Work Together Productively*. New York: Lexington Books/Macmillan, 1993.

Wheelan SA. Identifying and managing group processes. In: *Facilitating Training Groups: A Guide to Leadership and Verbal Intervention Skills*. New York: Praeger, 1990:13–27.

To learn more about the role of media advocacy in health promotion, read:

Atkin C, Wallack L, editors. *Mass Communication and Public Health: Complexities and Conflicts*. Newbury Park, CA: Sage Publications, 1990.

"How-To" Guides on Community Health Promotion are available from:

Health Promotion Resource Center
Stanford Center for Research in Disease Prevention
1000 Welch Road
Palo Alto, CA 94304-1885
Phone: 650-723-0003

Office of Cancer Communications. *Making Health Communication Programs Work: A Planner's Guide.* U.S. Department of Health and Human Services, National Institutes of Health, National Cancer Institute, 1989. NIH Publication No. 89-1493.

Office of Disease Prevention and Health Promotion. *Mass Media and Health: Opportunities for Improving the Nation's Health.* U.S. Department of Health and Human Services, Public Health Service, Office of Disease Prevention and Health Promotion, 1991.

To learn about promoting physical activity through religious organizations, read:

DePue JD, Wells BL, Lasater TM, et al. Volunteers as providers of heart health programs in churches: a report on implementation. *American Journal of Health Promotion* 1990; 4(5):361–366.

Eng E, Hatch J, Callan A. Institutionalizing social support through the church and into the community. *Health Education Quarterly* 1985; 12(1):81–92.

Hatch JW, Cunningham AC, Woods WW, et al. The Fitness Through Churches Project: description of a community-based cardiovascular health promotion intervention. *Hygiene* 1986; 5(3):9–12.

Interfaith Health Program, The Carter Center. *The Challenge of Faith and Health.* Atlanta: The Carter Center, 1994. For more information or to obtain a copy of this publication, contact:

The Carter Center
Public Information Department
One Copenhill
Atlanta, GA 30307

Lasater TM, Wells BL, Carleton RA, et al. The role of churches in disease prevention research studies. *Public Health Reports* 1986; 101(2):125–131.

Lasater TM, Carleton RA, Wells BL. Religious organizations and large-scale health related lifestyle change programs. *Journal of Health Education* 1991; 22(4):233–239.

Marty ME, editor. *Healthy People 2000: A Role for America's Religious Communities.* Chicago: Park Ridge Center, 1991. For more information or to obtain a copy of this publication, contact:

Park Ridge Center
211 E. Ontario
Suite 800
Chicago, IL 60611

National Heart, Lung, and Blood Institute. Ideas for religious organization programs. In: *With Every Beat of Your Heart: An Ideabook for Community Heart Health Programs.* Bethesda, MD: U.S. Department of Health and Human Services, Public Health Service, National Institutes of Health, 1987. NIH Publication No. 87-2641.

National Heart, Lung, and Blood Institute. *Churches as an Avenue to High Blood Pressure Control.* Bethesda, MD: U.S. Department of Health and Human Services, Public Health Service, National Institutes of Health, 1989. NIH Publication No. 89-2725.

For more information on organizing communities for environmental and behavioral change, visit:

The "Community Toolbox" at **http://ctb.lsi.ukans.edu.** The "toolbox" provides practical information and solutions to the most common problems experienced by people who are trying to build healthier, stronger communities. This website offers "one-stop shopping" and hundreds of practical "how-tos" for people interested in community health and development. The "Community Toolbox" connects people to personalized assistance to help them improve their community change efforts.

Chapter 9 Promoting Physical Activity in the Worksite

According to the U.S. Public Health Service, Department of Health and Human Services, between 110 and 115 million people go to work each day (USDHHS 1993, PHS 1995). By the year 2010, an estimated 141–153 million people will be in the labor force, spending at least one-third of their lives at their place of employment. Focusing physical activity promotion programs in the worksite, then, can be an effective way of spreading the message in your community.

By encouraging healthy behaviors, worksite programs can contribute much to the national effort to reduce preventable deaths, diseases, and disabilities. Employers can affect the health of their employees by establishing supportive policies and environments; providing recreation facilities; and offering health promotion education, targeted preventive services, and comprehensive health insurance.

181

Understanding Worksite Health Promotion Trends

Since the early 1980s, the U.S. Public Health Service has played an instrumental role in stimulating and coordinating projects to develop model worksite intervention programs, developing policies supportive of health promotion and disease prevention, and documenting examples of successful worksite programs in both the public and private sectors.

In 1985 and again in 1992, the Office of Disease Prevention and Health Promotion of the Public Health Service conducted a national survey to determine the degree to which the private sector was involved in health promotion activities (USDHHS 1993). The 1992 survey examined health promotion and disease prevention activities in 1,507 private worksites with at least 50 employees to assess the growth of worksite health promotion since the first survey in 1985 and to document progress toward achieving related year 2000 objectives (PHS 1991).

How each of us makes a living affects our economic status, social network, geographic location, family structure, political convictions, lifestyle, and personality. Thus the worksite, with its "captive audience," facilities, social support structure, convenience, and communication structure, can be an efficient and effective setting for significantly improving the health and well-being of individuals, their families, and perhaps even the community as a whole.

J. Michael McGinnis, 1995, Former Director
Office of Disease Prevention and Health Promotion
Public Health Service

The findings from the 1992 survey were remarkable: from 1985 to 1992, the percentage of worksites offering physical activity, exercise, or fitness-related programs and services to their employees increased substantially (USDHHS 1993). In fact, so many worksites had developed programs during this period that, by 1992, the year 2000 worksite objectives had already been exceeded (see the list on page 183).

Establishing an Employee Health Promotion Committee

If your challenge is to increase employees' exposure to targeted, stage-specific messages and to a variety of opportunities to be more physically active, you will need to recruit people to help you. Many worksite wellness programs have established an employee health promotion committee composed of representatives from major areas of the company and, when appropriate, representatives from external partnering organizations.

Consider recruiting people from sections in your organization that have responsibility for some aspect of employee health or well-being, such as occupational safety, human resources, employee assistance programs, the medical unit, the employee cafeteria, or employee unions. If your business is small, consider linking with other small businesses to form a health promotion council. The responsibilities of the employee council might include

- developing a plan for the physical activity program (starting small but thinking big),

- implementing and monitoring the plan,
- reporting regularly to decision makers on the status of the program,
- putting the costs and benefits of physical activity in monetary terms, and
- soliciting management's support.

The worksite wellness committee or council can use the year 2000 objectives as a guide in developing its own goals and objectives.

Once you have profiled your employee population, you are ready to select intervention strategies that will be motivating to them. As you review the many program ideas presented in this chapter, keep in mind the suggestions for successful intervention planning that were presented in chapters 1 through 6. For example, as in communities, worksite interventions should (Abrams 1991)

- be true to the science of physical activity,
- be based on sound behavioral science,
- include processes of change appropriate to each of the stages of change,

Healthy People 2000 Objectives Related to the Worksite

The goal of worksite physical activity promotion, as outlined in *Healthy People 2000: National Health Promotion and Disease Prevention Objectives* (PHS 1991) is to increase the proportion of worksites offering employer-sponsored physical activity and fitness programs as follows:

50–99 employees	20%
100–249 employees	35%
250–749 employees	50%
750+ employees	80%

Other objectives supporting worksite physical activity promotion include the following:

- Increase to at least 30% the proportion of people aged 6 and older who engage regularly, preferably daily, in light to moderate physical activity for at least 30 minutes per day.
- Increase to at least 20% the proportion of people aged 18 and older and to at least 75% the proportion of children and adolescents aged 6 through 17 who engage in vigorous physical activity that promotes the development and maintenance of cardiorespiratory fitness 3 or more days per week for 20 or more minutes per occasion.
- Reduce to no more than 15% the proportion of people aged 6 and older who engage in no leisure-time physical activity.
- Increase to at least 40% the proportion of people aged 6 and older who regularly perform physical activities that enhance and maintain muscular strength, muscular endurance, and flexibility.
- Increase to at least 50% the proportion of overweight people aged 12 and older who have adopted sound dietary practices combined with regular physical activity to attain an appropriate body weight.

Revised physical activity and fitness objectives are currently under development for the year 2010. To view the latest version, please visit this website: **http://web.health.gov/ healthypeople/**

PHS 1991

WORKSITE ACTIVITY IN THE SPOTLIGHT

Providing Opportunities to Practice Skills

"WALKTOBERFEST"

Based on the traditional German Oktoberfest, develop a fall walking promotion around this concept (sans the beer and bratwurst). Walking should be a mainstay of any health promotion program and needs regular highlighting. Some of these ideas can help keep your walking programs going.

Starting Points

- Use your walking club to organize a Walktoberfest or use the event to organize a walking club. Have your cafeteria participate by serving healthy German-style lunches. Serve nonalcoholic beer and hire a band to play traditional German folk tunes during the event.
- Develop an exercise journey with an Oktoberfest theme.
- Offer seminars or demonstrations on speedwalking or powerwalking.
- Organize a family Volksmarch in the European tradition. Designate planned and measured walking routes within easy reach of your worksite. Or involve local community recreation departments for a more expanded event.
- Conduct a litter cleanup while walking over your designated walking routes.
- Consider repeating or continuing some of these activities during the winter months at local shopping malls or other available facilities with a new theme of *Walking in a Winter Wonderland, Walking in an Indoor Wonderland,* or *Walking in a Winter Indoorland.*

Reprinted, by permission, from T. Glaros, 1997, *Health promotion ideas that work* (Champaign, IL: Human Kinetics), 47.

- involve all levels of social structure,
- blend individual and environmental approaches, and
- be consumer-driven (i.e., tailored to the specific needs, interests, and priorities of your target population).

Be sure to keep accurate notes and records of what you are learning and doing. Employers will want to know that the resources used to promote physical activity are being well spent. It is up to you to provide that convincing evidence (review the sections in chapter 7 on measuring and reporting your success).

Overcoming Barriers to Worksite Promotion

Though it reported that promotion programs had by 1992 already exceeded the year 2000 objectives, the 1992 Public Health Service survey also indicated that the most significant barriers to achieving even greater success were the cost of providing worksite health promotion, a general lack of management support, and a lack of employee interest as evidenced by low program participation rates (USDHHS 1993). Let's take a closer look at how these barriers affect the overall success of worksite health promotion initiatives.

Perceived Costs

In the early 1990s, the estimated annual cost to employers of worksite-based physical activity programs was $20 to $400 per employee, where-as the estimated rate of return was $513 per employee year in reduced health care costs and increased productivity (Bellingham and Isham 1990; CDC 1993). In addition to cost savings, worksite health promotion—and physical activity promotion in particular—can produce many benefits to employers, such as (IRSA 1992;

Shephard 1992; Pelletier 1993; The Wellness Councils of America, The Wellness Councils of Canada 1998).

- improved corporate image,
- improved community relations,
- selective recruitment of employees,
- improved job satisfaction,
- improved employee morale,
- reduced staff turnover,
- decreased cost of recruitment and retaining,
- increased quality and quantity of production,
- reduced absenteeism,
- reduced sick days and hours lost
- fewer on-the-job injuries,
- fewer disability days,
- reduced worker compensation claims,
- increased capability of employees to handle job stress,
- decreased level of conflict at work, and
- reduced health care costs.

Ideally, health promotion results in benefits for both the employee and the employer: the employee gains improved health and energy, and the company has more productive and satisfied employees and lower health care costs and absenteeism. Too often, however, businesses view health promotion as a luxury—an added cost of doing business—rather than as an integral part of employee development (Bellingham and Isham 1990).

Read More About It

Comprehensive Reviews of the Costs and Benefits of Health Promotion

Heaney C, Goetzel R. A review of health-related outcomes of multi-component worksite health promotion programs. American Journal of Health Promotion 11 (March/April 1997): 290–307.

Pelletier K. A review and analysis of the health and cost-effective outcome studies of comprehensive health promotion and disease prevention programs at the worksite: 1993–1995 update. *American Journal of Health Promotion* 10 (May/June 1996): 380–388.

Pelletier KR. Clinical and cost outcomes of multifactorial, cardiovascular risk management interventions in worksites: a comprehensive review and analysis. *J Occup Environ Med* 39 (Dec 1997): 1154–69.

Shephard RJ. Worksite fitness and exercise programs: a review of methodology and health impact. American Journal of Health Promotion 10 (July/August 1996): 436–452.

Wilson MG, Hofman PB, Hammock, A. A comprehensive review of the effects of worksite health promotion on health-related outcomes. *American Journal of Health Promotion* 10(6): 429–435 (July/August 1996).

Lack of Management Support

Throughout business and industry, too few managers are rewarded for supporting positive lifestyle behaviors among their employees or are held accountable for contributing to employee stress or to a poor working environment. Unless health promotion is built into the reward system for both managers and employees and unless both take responsibility for employees' health, progress in enhancing health promotion activities at the worksite will be slow.

Without management's support in establishing environmental and policy changes, employees are unlikely to maintain desired lifestyle changes (Bellingham and Isham 1990). Convincing management that physical activity promotion should be a top priority and is a good investment in human resources is not easy; yet it is necessary for a successful worksite health promotion program.

Low Employee Interest and Participation

It is not uncommon for program managers to recruit no more than 20% of employees to participate in worksite physical activity programs. Because of high dropout rates, over time good programs may retain no more than 10% of the employee population (Wanzel 1994). Yet, the 20% of the workforce who tend to join vigorous fitness programs are typically not the employees who contribute to high absenteeism rates or who drive up medical costs; generally, those who participate already adhere to a physically active lifestyle, have a good health status, and have a low absenteeism record (Sharratt and Cox 1988; Shephard 1992). It is the 80% or more of employees who ordinarily do not join health promotion programs who should cause employers most concern (Wanzel 1994).

WORKSITE ACTIVITY IN THE SPOTLIGHT

Promoting Increased Awareness

"SPRING TRAINING"

In many work settings, the spring months offer an excellent opportunity to reach employees at a number of levels. First, some have been sedentary all winter and get the urge to begin some form of fitness activity in the spring. Second, some athletes, while generally in good shape, are switching sports and need some sport-specific conditioning. And third, there are those potential participants whose only fitness activity is participation in community-sponsored sports leagues such as softball, tennis, or golf. These people are in notoriously poor physical condition and tend to suffer soft-tissue injuries as a result of their weekend athlete behaviors.

Starting Points

- Time your event to coincide with either major league baseball's opening of spring training, or that of a local college or university. Use a spring camp format.
- Prepare handouts with sport-specific stretching guides.
- Prepare customized sport-specific strength workouts for use in your fitness center or with participants' private clubs, or prepare customized sport-specific calisthenics-based workouts for employees who do not have access to equipment.
- Offer single- or multiple-session introductory seminars on any or all of these topics to guide participants through the process of getting in shape. Bring in local high school or college coaches to conduct fundamental skills sessions for golf, softball, walking, running, and biking.
- Host an athletic training session to discuss first aid and home treatment for common sports injuries.
- Consider offering some public service education for nonfitness-related activities such as fishing or gardening.

Reprinted, by permission, from T. Glaros, 1997, *Health promotion ideas that work* (Champaign, IL: Human Kinetics), 44.

If worksite physical activity promotion programs continue to "preach to the choir" (attracting only those persons who are already physically active and practicing healthy behaviors) and fail to reach sedentary employees, little will have been accomplished toward improving the health status of all employees. The number and magnitude of the benefits to employers of increased physical activity levels would be even greater than current statistics indicate if sedentary employees could be persuaded to regularly participate in worksite health promotion programs and to adopt a physically active lifestyle (Shephard 1992; Wanzel 1994).

Unfortunately, relatively few employees find messages which are directed to the "general employee population" appealing, or benefit from programs that focus on vigorous activities (e.g., high-impact aerobic dance classes, step aerobics, weight training, or jogging). Action-oriented messages and programs tend to appeal most to those already taking action.

Program messages and interventions that have been tailored to the employee's stage of readiness for exercise adoption may be more effective in reaching those who would benefit most from increased levels of physical activity (Marcus et al. 1998 and 1996)—those who are less than optimally active. Offering employees a variety of simple, low-cost programs and physical activities like those built into the normal day for each employee (e.g., walking breaks, taking the stairs, or bicycling to work) may prove to be both more effective and more cost-efficient in increasing physical activity among all employees (Shephard 1992) than offering standard exercise classes alone.

Changing the Workplace Environment

Although relatively few employees participate in and benefit directly from traditional worksite physical activity or health promotion programs, all employees may benefit indirectly if even the presence of such a program improves general perceptions and attitudes toward health and physical activity (Grosch et al. 1998; Leatt et al. 1988; Shephard 1992). If social norms were supportive of physical activity and employees perceived that "everyone is exercising," those least motivated could become motivated and move closer to action themselves.

For example, even though retention in worksite physical activity programs is poor, people who drop out are sometimes motivated to begin exercise programs elsewhere in the community (Leatt et al. 1988). Planners of comprehensive worksite programs should view the workplace as an integral member of a larger community in which the corporation, its managers, individual employees, and their families are linked to a wealth of community-based resources, programs, and services (Wanzel 1994).

The following pages list specific ideas for promoting physical activity in the workplace. The ideas are categorized by how they fit into several pieces of the intervention puzzle introduced in chapters 5 and 6.

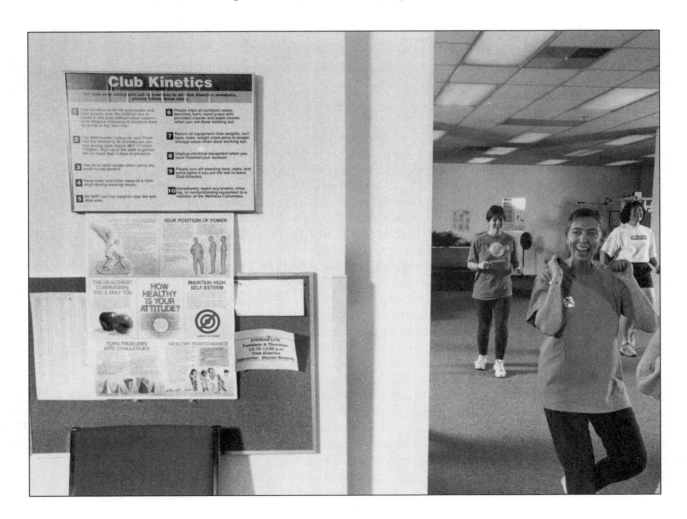

Ideas for the Worksite

Promote Increased Awareness of Physical Activity

- Kick off your program with a special event, such as a celebrity guest speaker, T-shirts for every employee, group pictures, or ribbon-cutting to a new on-site exercise facility. Make it highly visible.

- Place eye-catching information in prominent locations throughout the facility: at the front entrance, in reception areas, by the elevators or stairwells, on bulletin boards, at the coffee or snack machines, in the restrooms, or via electronic mail.

- Make the vehicle of your messages or information colorful, fun, and attention-getting. For example,

    —enlist the assistance of local celebrities, the chief executive officer or administrative officer, a favorite retiree, or a costumed character in delivering or disseminating materials to the employees;

    —use attractive displays, colorful banners and posters, payroll stuffers, balloons, bumper stickers, magnets, pens, water bottles, hats, and other promotional items; or

    —develop a program logo.

- Deliver some physical activity-related promotional item, such as walking shoes, to the president, chief executive officer, or the entire board of directors. You also might want to invite the press.

For more information on effective awareness strategies, see Chapman 1994.

Increase Knowledge About Physical Activity

- Tap into the means by which your audience obtains information. Where do they look? Whom do they ask? How do they hear about news? Whom would they most believe? Then put the message in the format most accepted by the audience you want to reach. How do they prefer to be informed?

- Expose people to your message. Set up informational displays in prominent places. Make information about physical activity readily available to all employees via newsletters, booklets, pamphlets and brochures, flyers, payroll stuffers, table tents, posters, bulletin boards, computer disks, electronic bulletin boards, cassette tapes, videos, self-assessment guides, and self-instructional kits.

- Establish a physical activity and health promotion library with good educational materials, books, literature, cassettes, videos, computer programs, and kits.

- Conduct a health and physical activity promotion fair that offers physical fitness assessments.

- Involve the employee health center and occupational health nurse.

- Set up a 24-hour telephone line with recorded messages. Make sure that employees are aware of this service. Change the messages frequently to keep employees interested and motivated to use the system weekly.

- Provide classes, workshops, and lunch-n-learns. Invite guest speakers and other resource people.

- Inform employees where they can go to obtain additional, credible information. Compile community resource lists.

- To make greatest use of word-of-mouth and informal networks, train people who serve as informal sources of information for their peers.

- Train team leaders, supervisors, and directors on the importance of physical activity promotion, and encourage them and their staff to participate in an active lifestyle.

(continued)

(continued)

Increase Personal Motivation for Adopting a Physically Active Lifestyle

- Assess employees' reasons for not engaging in regular physical activity.
- Help employees see how your messages relate to their lives by
    —personalizing messages;
    —recommending they set personal goals for individual achievement;
    —providing self-assessment questionnaires or exercise testing to individualize the need for increased physical activity; and
    —establishing methods for monitoring individual progress (e.g., logs, diaries, or wall charts on display).
- Disseminate motivational messages on the importance of physical activity. Who is giving the message? Is it someone that employees trust, respect, or believe? Place motivational reminders for physical activity in prominent locations.
- Select role models—people of all shapes and sizes who regularly incorporate physical activity into their lifestyles—from within the worksite setting.
- Involve top administrators and supervisors whenever possible. Recruit them as chairpersons of promotional events, such as a fun run or heart walk for National Employee Health and Fitness Day.
- Create a point system for making progress toward a physically active lifestyle. Make points redeemable for meaningful recognition or rewards, such as lunch with the chief executive officer or donated gifts from local sponsors.
- Help people visualize successful behavior change. Help them believe they can be successful by setting achievable goals and building a "you can do it" spirit.
- Make participation appealing. Reward initial participation with incentives such as contests or fun promotional items, and reward consistent participation with meaningful gifts, prizes, publicity, recognition, or privileges.
- For those who have a competitive spirit, establish competition among employee units or divisions, locations, or companies; incentives might include
    —corporate discounts for fitness club memberships, recreational facilities, sports or exercise equipment, or apparel;
    —a free lunch, book, T-shirt, or pair of walking shoes;
    —cash or time rewards for milestones in personal progress; or
    —public recognition, ceremonies, plaques, or special privileges.
- Take pictures of employees being physically active. Display poster-sized enlargements, along with signs encouraging other people to be physically active, at prominent locations.

For more ideas on incentives, see Chapman 1996.

Teach or Enhance Skills Needed to Have a Physically Active Lifestyle

- Identify the skills people need to make a change in their physical activity level, then plan programs to teach those skills. For example, the following might be taught:
    —Increasing physical activity routinely throughout the day
    —Starting a walking or jogging program
    —Selecting the right shoes, clothing, or equipment
    —Using exercise or sports equipment properly and safely

—Stretching, warm-up, and cool-down techniques

—Avoiding the risk of injury from exercise

—Lessons of any kind (e.g., swimming, sailing, golf, or tennis)

—Maintaining physical activity and preventing relapse to a sedentary lifestyle

- Teach skills that will help people overcome stumbling blocks and potential barriers to change.

- Provide instructional programs, such as classes, workshops, lunch-n-learns, seminars, demonstrations, lessons, and lectures, for both formal and informal activities. Whenever possible, train employees to lead educational sessions.

- Provide individual assessment and counseling or personal trainers.

Provide Opportunities to Practice New Skills and Behaviors in a Safe Setting

- Conduct demonstrations or small-group classes with active involvement by participants.

- Provide opportunities to try the desired behavior for just one day or for one event, such as

—walk to work day;

—use of the stairs, not the elevator, for one day or week;

—incentives for the number of flights walked in a given period;

—bicycle to work day;

—"stretch at your desk" breaks;

—fun runs; and

—lunch-time walking groups for a week.

- Rent a gymnasium, pool, or rollerblade or ice rink for an employee day or evening of fun and physical activity.

- Set the tone for a judgment-free environment, one that is free of ridicule and embarrassment. Convey that it is fine to be less than perfect in one's attempts toward change. Identify potential emotional barriers, then work to overcome them.

Foster Supportive Social Networks

- Encourage people to find support for their decision to change from coworkers, supervisors, family, and friends.

- Involve spouses, other family members, and significant others in programs whenever possible. Sponsor or provide activities that encourage family involvement.

- Set up teams or buddy systems to walk together.

- Encourage employees to contract with someone or to make a public pledge to change toward a more physically active lifestyle.

- Establish small-group classes or help sessions, such as walking clubs, aerobics classes, stair-climbing clubs, sports teams (e.g., softball, bowling, golf, volleyball, or tennis), and dance groups.

- Set up hot lines or help lines for additional information and support.

- Obtain the support of top and middle management for increased physical activity.

For more information on building a supportive social environment in the workplace, read Gottlieb and McLeroy 1994.

(continued)

(continued

Establish and Maintain a Physical Environment Supportive of a Physically Active Lifestyle

- Provide showers, locker rooms, and exercise facilities on site. Put full-length mirrors and accurate weight scales in employee rest rooms.
- Map walking paths with measured distances within the building, around the building, and in the surrounding community.
- Build a walking or jogging trail on worksite grounds. Make these trails available to employees and their families or to the community at large.
- Place signs showing the location of stairwells. Make sure the stairwells are easily accessible and well-lighted when new buildings are designed.
- Negotiate an arrangement for employees to use off-site exercise or recreation facilities that are convenient to the workplace.
- Hire qualified full-time or part-time staff to conduct health promotion or exercise programs.
- Connect business and residential areas with walking and bicycling paths.
- Provide areas where employees can keep bicycles secure.

Establish and Enforce Policies, Laws, and Regulations Supportive of a Physically Active Lifestyle

- Obtain management and union support for health promotion and physical activity promotion for employees.
- Ask the corporate president, chairman, or agency head to sign a policy or proclamation supporting physical activity among all employees. Obtain formal recognition of exemplary programs and program participants.
- Be sure that all employees have adequate insurance or worker's compensation coverage in case facility-related injuries occur.
- Establish work-related policies to allow employees flextime to exercise or attend health promotion programs during the workday.
- Establish personnel policies that emphasize health as an organizational goal.
- Establish an employee steering committee for worksite health promotion. This group would give recommendations to management on issues related to physical activity promotion.
- Allow specified stretch breaks during the workday. Use electronic mail to post reminders to stretch or take a short walk periodically.
- Work with insurance contractors to establish more favorable rates for employees who are physically active.
- Organize a consortium of companies to make shared arrangements for reduced rates at area exercise facilities if none are available at each specific site.

Key Resources for Worksite Promotion

The following organizations can help you establish worksite physical activity promotion plans.

American Heart Association (AHA)

The association produces numerous educational and promotional materials for use in worksites, including a comprehensive Heart At Work kit with a segment devoted to physical activity promotion. Most materials are free. In many states, AHA affiliates have active worksite committees that bring together local partners in worksite health promotion.

7272 Greenville Ave.
Dallas, TX 75231
Toll-free: 800-AHA-USA1
Website: **http://www.americanheart.org**

American Medical Athletic Association (AMAA)

AMAA is a nonprofit educational association formed to educate and motivate physicians (including private practice, hospital- or managed care-affiliated, and occupational health physicians) to disseminate information about aerobic exercise and nutrition to their patients or clients. Members receive a quarterly journal filled with the latest sports medicine information and have complete access to all of the member benefits of their parent organization, the American Running and Fitness Association.

American Medical Athletic Association
c/o American Running and Fitness Association
4405 East-West Highway
Suite 405
Bethesda, MD 20814
Phone: 301-913-9517
Toll-free: 800-776-ARFA
Website: **http://www.arfa.org**

American Running and Fitness Association (AR&FA)

AR&FA is a nonprofit, educational association dedicated to encouraging people to exercise and keep fit. Serving as a valuable resource to individuals, worksites, and community groups, AR&FA helps people begin or maintain an exercise program by providing motivation; referrals to sports medicine professionals; and information on diet, training, health, and injury prevention. Members receive a monthly newsletter filled with information on sports medicine, training, fitness, and nutrition research and are entitled to free written medical advice and personalized training schedules, medical referrals, access to AR&FA motivational challenge programs, the Running Shoe Database, discounts on sporting goods, publications, insurance, etc.

American Running and Fitness Association (AR&FA)
4405 East-West Highway
Suite 405
Bethesda, MD 20814
Phone: 301-913-9517
Toll-free: 800-776-ARFA
Website: **http://www.arfa.org**

Association for Worksite Health Promotion (AWHP)

Formerly known as the Association for Fitness in Business, this international organization for worksite health promotion serves a variety of interdisciplinary health and fitness professionals who conduct physical activity programs for employees. It was established to influence corporate decision makers in health promotion issues. It promotes employee health and fitness by publishing a number of statistical and educational materials, offering continuing education programs, and encouraging professional networking. Members receive a quarterly journal, membership directory, resource guides, and an annual buyers' guide.

Association for Worksite Health Promotion
60 Revere Drive
Suite 500
Northbrook, IL 60062
Phone: 847-480-9574
Fax: 847-480-9282
E-mail: **awhp@awhp.org**

National Association of Governor's Councils on Physical Fitness and Sports (NAGCPFS)

The NAGCPFS sponsors the National Employee Health and Fitness Day, which is celebrated each year on the third Wednesday in May. On this day, employers are encouraged to conduct noncompetitive fitness activities that allow everyone in their organizations to participate. Contact NAGCPFS for a registration packet and resource materials.

National Association of Governor's Councils on Physical Fitness and Sports
201 South Capitol Avenue
Suite 560
Indianapolis, IN 46225-1072
Phone: 317-237-5630
Website: **http://www.fitnesslink.com/Govcouncil/**

National Association for Public Worksite Health Promotion

This association is a national nonprofit organization serving people involved in health promotion programs for public employees at the city, county, state, or federal level or in state-supported colleges and universities. The association promotes communication and program idea exchange, publishes a quarterly newsletter, and sponsors an annual conference each year. Contact them for resource materials and other information.

The Council of State Governments
2760 Research Park Drive
P.O. Box 11910
Lexington, KY 40587-1910
Phone: 606-244-8000
Fax: 606-244-8001
E-mail: **info@csg.org**
Website: **http://www.csg.org**

National Fitness and Wellness Coalition

The National Recreation and Park Association's (NRPA) National Fitness and Wellness Coalition is a network group of national organizations and state recreation and park leaders interested in the comprehensive delivery of quality messages and programs in health, fitness, and nutrition. Representative of the "wellness spectrum," this coalition is coordinated by NRPA but is collectively focused on national issues and local implementation.

National Recreation and Park Association
22377 Belmont
Ridge Road
Ashburn, VA 20148
Phone: 703-858-0784

National Wellness Institute

The institute is a nonprofit resource center that provides new and innovative professional development programs, educational lifestyle assessments, and health promotion resources. Its membership division, The National Wellness Association, provides additional resources for members such as keeping them up to date on the latest developments in health and wellness promotion.

National Wellness Institute
P.O. Box 827
Stevens Point, WI 54481-0827
Phone: 715-342-2969
Website: **http://wellnessnwi.org**

Washington Business Group on Health

The Washington Business Group on Health is the nation's only coalition of major employers devoted to the analysis of national health policy and related worksite issues.

Washington Business Group on Health
777 North Capitol Street, NE
Suite 800
Washington, DC 20002
Phone: 202-408-9320
Website: **http://www.wbgh.com**

Wellness Councils of America (WELCOA)

WELCOA is a national nonprofit membership organization dedicated to promoting healthier lifestyles for all Americans, especially through health promotion activities at the workplace. WELCOA has a nationwide network of locally affiliated Wellness Councils and direct memberships serving thousands of organizations and their employees. Also, WELCOA acts as a national clearinghouse and information center on corporate health promotion for companies everywhere. WELCOA has set the standards for measuring the effectiveness of corporate health promotion programs; companies that meet the rigorous standards earn the coveted Well Workplace Award and are listed on WELCOA's roster of "America's Healthiest Companies."

Wellness Councils of America
Community Health Plaza
Suite 311
7101 Newport Avenue
Omaha, NE 68152-2175
Phone: 402-572-3590
Website: **http://www.welcoa.org**

Suggested Reading

For a list of organizations, agencies, and selected program materials for promoting physical activity, see:

Resource A, for general resources

Chapter 6, for environment-related resources

Chapter 10, for school-related resources

For more information about the benefits of worksite health promotion, read:

Collingwood TR. Fitness programs. In: O'Donnell MP, Harris JS, editors. *Health Promotion in the Workplace* (2nd Edition). Albany, NY: Delmar Publishers, 1994:240–270.

Heaney CA, Goldenhar LM, editors. *Health Education Quarterly* 1996; 23(2):133–255.

Kaman RL, Patton RW. Costs and benefits of an active versus an inactive society. In: Bouchard C, Shephard RJ, Stephens T, editors. *Physical Activity, Fitness, and Health: International Proceedings and Consensus Statement.* Champaign, IL: Human Kinetics, 1994:134–144.

Pelletier KR. A review and analysis of the health and cost-effective outcome studies of comprehensive health promotion and disease prevention programs at the worksite: 1991–1993 update. *American Journal of Health Promotion* 1993; 8(1):50–62.

Wellness Councils of America. *Healthy, Wealthy & Wise: Fundamentals of Workplace Health Promotion.* Omaha, NE: Wellness Councils of America, 1995. Note especially the chapter on the costs and benefits of wellness.

To learn more about employee wellness councils and advisory boards, read:

Sorensen G, Hsieh J, Hunt M, et al. Employee advisory boards as a vehicle for organizing worksite health promotion programs. *American Journal of Health Promotion* 1992; 6(6):443–450, 464.

Wellness Councils of America. *Healthy, Wealthy & Wise: Fundamentals of Workplace Health Promotion.* Omaha, NE: Wellness Councils of America, 1995. Note especially the chapter on organizing an employee wellness committee.

For more information about physical activity promotion at the worksite, review:

Chapman LS. *Proof Positive: Analysis of the Cost-Effectiveness of Wellness.* Seattle: Summex Corporation, 1996.

Summex Corporation
P.O. Box 55056
Seattle, WA 98155
Phone: 206-364-3448
Fax: 206-368-9719

DeJoy DM, Wilson MG. *Critical Issues in Worksite Health Promotion.* Boston: Allyn & Bacon, 1995. This book provides a valuable overview on the benefits and challenges of designing effective worksite health promotion programs.

Mayer JP, David JK, editors. *Worksite Health Promotion: Needs, Approaches, and Effectiveness: Annotated Bibliography.* Lansing, MI: Michigan Department of Public Health, 1991.

O'Donnell MP, Harris JS, editors. *Health Promotion in the Workplace* (2nd Edition). Albany, NY: Delmar Publishers, 1994.

U.S. Department of Health and Human Services. *1992 National Survey of Worksite Health Promotion Activities.* Washington, DC: U.S. Government Printing Office, 1993. For information about this survey, contact the National Technical Information Service at 703-487-4650 and follow the instructions given by their voice response system. A computer diskette of the full final report and technical appendix is available for about $152 (request PB93-500023), and a paper copy of the full final report and appendix is available for $49 (request PB93-100204). Additional copies of the brief summary report may be obtained from the U.S. Government Printing Office.

Wellness Councils of America. *Healthy, Wealthy & Wise: Fundamentals of Workplace Health Promotion.* Omaha, NE: Wellness Councils of America, 1995.

If you are new to worksite health promotion, start by reviewing these publications:

Action, the member newsletter of the Association of Worksite Health Promotion, can be obtained by writing to 60 Revere Drive, Suite 500, Northbrook, IL 60062, or telephoning 708-480-9574.

American Journal of Health Promotion is published bimonthly by:

American Journal of Health Promotion
1812 S. Rochester Road, Suite 200
Rochester Hills, MI 48307-3532
Phone: 810-650-9600

American Journal of Preventive Medicine, the official journal of the American College of Preventive Medicine, is published bimonthly by:

Oxford University Press
198 Madison Avenue
New York, NY 10016

Employee Health and Fitness Newsletter: The Executive Update on Health Improvement Programs is published by:

American Health Consultants
3525 Piedmont Road
Building 6, Suite 400
Atlanta, GA 30305
Phone: 404-262-7436
Toll-free: 800-688-2421

Health Education Quarterly is available with membership to:

Society of Public Health Educators
605 Third Avenue
New York, NY 10158

Journal of Occupational Medicine is published monthly by:

Lippincott Williams & Wilkins
227 East Washington Square
Philadelphia, PA 19106
Phone: 215-238-4200

Chapter 10 Promoting Physical Activity in the Schools

Childhood is the time to introduce a healthy and active lifestyle. Young people do not automatically develop the skills, knowledge, attitudes, and behaviors that lead to regular participation in physical activity. They must be taught, and that is where the concept of health-related physical education comes into play.

Without a doubt, schools have an influence on the lives of youth, their families, and the community at large. Therefore, school-based programs—health and physical education programs in particular—increase the likelihood that children and their families will commit to enjoyable, lifelong physical activity (Sallis and McKenzie 1991).

Schools and communities can create powerful, dynamic, and reciprocally beneficial partnerships. Physical activity promotion efforts targeting children and adults will be more effective if schools and other community groups are promoting the same message about the importance of maintaining a physically active lifestyle. Schools and universities should be proactive in establishing partnerships with the residents and institutions that make up the greater community. Likewise, community-based physical activity networks that unite community organizations, worksites, and health care institutions need to involve schools in their efforts for promoting physical activity.

All children should have the opportunity to learn to be physically competent and to gain health-related fitness through regular, developmentally appropriate physical activity.

Judith Young, PhD, 1996
Executive Director
National Association for Sport and Physical Education

You and your partners can undertake many activities to increase the level of physical activity in your schools and throughout your communities. We know that schools, through physical education programs, offer efficient ways of providing instruction in skill development. But schools can also play an important role in promoting the other pieces of the intervention puzzle that we discussed in chapters 5 and 6: creating awareness and knowledge about physical activity, creating a supportive social network, establishing and maintaining a supportive physical environment, enhancing motivation, and establishing and enforcing supportive policies. Pages 212–217 provide numerous ideas for activities to address these components of a successful physical activity promotion intervention, and pages 217–224 offer a list of resources that may help you get started with your school-based promotion program.

But first, this chapter will review what scientific research tells us about physical activity and young people, including current recommendations related to promoting physical activity among children and adolescents.

The Physically Educated Person

Has learned skills necessary to perform a variety of physical activities

- Moves using concepts of body awareness, space awareness, effort, and relationships
- Demonstrates competence in a variety of manipulative, locomotor, and nonlocomotor skills
- Demonstrates competence in combinations of manipulative, locomotor, and nonlocomotor skills, performed individually and with other persons
- Demonstrates competence in many different forms of physical activity
- Demonstrates proficiency in a few forms of physical activity
- Has learned how to learn new skills

Is physically fit

- Assesses, achieves, and maintains physical fitness
- Designs safe, personal fitness programs in accordance with principles of training and conditioning

Participates regularly in physical activity

- Participates in health enhancing physical activity at least 3 times a week
- Selects and regularly participates in lifetime physical activities

Knows the implications of and the benefits from involvement in physical activities

- Identifies the benefits, costs, and obligations associated with regular participation in physical activity
- Recognizes the risk and safety factors associated with regular participation in physical activity
- Applies concepts and principles to the development of motor skills
- Understands that wellness involves more than being physically fit
- Knows the rules, strategies, and appropriate behaviors for selected physical activities
- Recognizes that participation in physical activity can lead to multicultural and international understanding
- Understands that physical activity provides the opportunity for enjoyment, self-expression, and communication

Values physical activity and its contributions to a healthful lifestyle

- Appreciates the relationships with others that result from participation in physical activity
- Respects the role that regular physical activity plays in the pursuit of lifelong health and well-being
- Cherishes the feelings that result from regular participation in physical activity

Reprinted from *Moving Into the Future: National Standards for Physical Education* (1995) with permission from The National Association for Sport and Physical Education (NASPE),1900 Association Drive, Reston, VA 20191-1599.

How Inactive Are American Youth?

The benefits of regular physical activity for children and youth include improved aerobic endurance, improved muscular strength, enhanced skeletal health, and higher levels of physical fitness (Morrow and Freedson 1994; Bailey and Martin 1994). Active young people may also experience improvements in self-esteem, self-concept, depressive symptoms, and anxiety and stress (Calfas and Taylor 1994).

Among healthy young people, physical activity may favorably affect risk factors for cardiovascular disease, such as body mass index, blood lipid profiles, and resting blood pressure; it decreases blood pressure in adolescents with borderline hypertension, and it lowers levels of body fatness in obese children (USDHHS 1996; CDC 1997).

Although children and adolescents tend to be more physically active than adults, many young people do not engage in daily moderate physical activity or in vigorous physical activity at least 3 days per week. Support for the belief that today's youth are not getting enough physical activity is evidenced by the following research findings:

- Physical activity levels among both girls and boys tend to decline steadily during adolescence (USDHHS 1996).

- Many American high school students do not engage in regular physical activities that maintain or improve their cardiorespiratory fitness, strength, and flexibility. Results of the 1997 national school-based Youth Risk Behavior Surveillance (YRBS) system revealed that 63.8% of high school students reported being vigorously active for at least 20 minutes on 3 or more of the past 7 days. Only about half reported participating in stretching or strengthening exercises on 3 or more of the past 7 days (Kann et al. 1998).

- According to the 1997 YRBS, high school girls are less likely to be vigorously active than are high school boys (53.5% and 72.3%, respectively), African-American girls are less active than white girls (53.9% and 66.8%, respectively), and students in grades 11 and 12 are less active than students in grade 9 (60%, 57.5%, and 72.7%, respectively) (see figure 10.1) (Kann et al. 1998).

- Girls and boys perceive the benefits of physical activity very differently. For example, boys more often cite competition and girls more often cite weight management as their reasons for engaging in physical activity (Tappe et al. 1990; Kelder et al. 1995).

- Although nearly all children in the United States are enrolled in physical education in elementary school, not all receive instruction of sufficient quantity and quality for fitness and motor skill development (Ross and Pate 1987; McKenzie et al. 1993).

- The 1997 YRBS indicated that 48.8% of high school students were enrolled in a physical education class and that physical education enrollment was less likely among students in grades 11 and 12 than among students in grade 9 (39.3%, 36.1%, and 69.2%, respectively) (Kann et al. 1998).

- Students who do participate in physical education classes spend large amounts of class time being inactive (Silverman 1991; Simons-Morton 1994).

- Youth who have physical disabilities often receive little or no encouragement to be physically active. Often, schools are not equipped to handle their special needs and so exempt these students from participating in physical

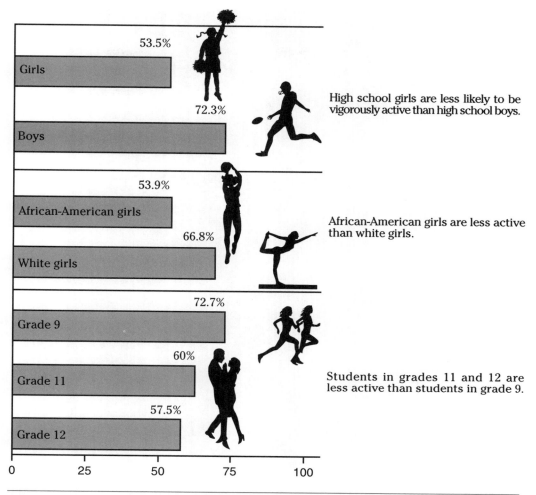

Figure 10.1   American youth are not as physically active as they need to be to enjoy the health benefits of physical activity.
Data from YRBS 1997 (Kann et al. 1998)

education (Brown and Gordon 1987; Bedini 1990). Physical education is required or recommended for students with special needs in 79.2% of states and 84.0% of school districts. Many schools (58.3% of middle or junior high schools and 58.7% of senior high schools) exempt students with a physical disability from a required physical education class (Pate et al. 1995).

In addition, many existing programs that do promote youth physical education may not be as effective as desired:

• Many elementary school physical education classes are taught by nonspecialists who have limited training in physical education. Only 17.4% of states require that elementary physical education teachers have specialized teacher certification in physical education (Pate et al. 1995).

• Only 65.2% of states that require schools to offer health education also require instruction specifically in physical activity and fitness. Some schools choose to include this instruction even though it is not mandated. In 1994, 77.6% of schools offering health education included the topic of physical activity and fitness in their curricula (Collins et al. 1995).

• Most middle or junior high schools (89.1%) and senior high schools (88.5%) allow students to be exempted or excused from physical education courses. At one of five schools, students may be exempted from physical education if they participate in interscholastic sports or other school activities such as band, chorus, or cheerleading or because their parents wrote a letter requesting exemption (Pate et al. 1995).

• The activities most commonly included in physical education courses are competitive team sports rather than activities that people could enjoy over a lifetime (Pate et al. 1995).

• Only 26.0% of states require a course in lifetime physical activity in senior high school (Pate et al. 1995).

Physical Activity Recommendations and Objectives for Young People

Daily physical education from kindergarten through 12th grade is recommended not only as a national health objective for the year 2000, but also by the National Association for Sport and Physical Education (NASPE 1995) and by the American Heart Association (AHA 1995). As you begin to develop goals and objectives for your school-based physical activity promotion program, you may find it helpful to review the specific physical activity recommendations and objectives developed for young people by several national and international organizations.

Overall, the K–12 program should build progressively toward the ultimate goal: producing members of society who take lifelong personal responsibility for engaging in health-related physical activity not only because they know it's good for the body and why, but also because they know how intrinsically rewarding it is to move in ways they enjoy.

AAHPERD, *Physical Education for Lifelong Fitness*, 1999

In 1991, the Public Health Service released its *Healthy People 2000: National Health Promotion and Disease Prevention Objectives,* which includes several objectives specifically related to schools or youth (see page 206). You might adapt these goals based on the specific needs of your school population. If your students already meet these objectives, you can raise the bar and aim for greater physical activity participation. Or, if your students haven't been physically active at all, you might adapt your goals so they are more easily within your students' reach.

In 1997, CDC developed a set of 10 guidelines aimed specifically at helping school and community programs promote lifelong physical activity among young people. Pages 207–209 outline these 10 guidelines (in boldface) as well as specific strategies (the bulleted items) for implementing each guideline. Don't be intimidated by the long list of recommendations. You shouldn't expect to be able to do everything at once. Start out slowly and conquer the areas where you're able to immediately make a difference. Once you enjoy some success and get your students (and your school administration) excited about physical activity, you can move on to the tougher recommendations on the list.

Depending on the ages of the young people you are trying to reach, you may want to also review NASPE's guidelines developed especially for elementary school-age children or the international guidelines developed for adolescents (page 210). If you—and the young people in your school—need to know where to start, the guidelines and objectives appearing in this book may serve as just the starting point you are looking for to help you assess the needs, resources, and abilities of the school community you are hoping to reach with your program.

Healthy People 2000 Objectives Related to Schools

The school or youth-related goals outlined in *Healthy People 2000: National Health Promotion and Disease Prevention Objectives* (PHS 1991) include the following:

School-Related Goals

- Increase to at least 50% the proportion of children and adolescents in 1st through 12th grade who participate in daily school physical education.
- Increase to at least 50% the proportion of school physical education class time that students spend being physically active, preferably engaged in lifetime physical activities.

Youth-Related Goals

- Increase to at least 30% the proportion of people aged 6 and older who engage regularly, preferably daily, in light to moderate physical activity for at least 30 minutes per day.
- Increase to at least 20% the proportion of people aged 18 and older and to at least 75% the proportion of children and adolescents aged 6 through 17 who engage in vigorous physical activity that promotes the development and maintenance of cardiorespiratory fitness 3 or more days per week for 20 or more minutes per occasion.
- Reduce to no more than 15% the proportion of people aged 6 and older who engage in no leisure-time physical activity.
- Increase to at least 40% the proportion of people aged 6 and older who regularly perform physical activities that enhance and maintain muscular strength, muscular endurance, and flexibility.
- Increase to at least 50% the proportion of overweight people aged 12 and older who have adopted sound dietary practices combined with regular physical activity to attain an appropriate body weight.

Revised physical activity and fitness objectives are currently under development for the year 2010. To view the latest version, please visit this website: **http://web.health.gov/ healthypeople/.**

PHS 1991

SCHOOL PROGRAM IN THE SPOTLIGHT

"Fitness Fever"

About the Program: Fitness Fever aims to excite Minnesota children and their families about physical activity and good nutrition through education, ready-to-use ideas, and, most important, FUN. According to its website, Fitness Fever "has the highest participation rate of any school health promotion program in Minnesota" (**http://www/fitnessfever.com/adults/** October 20, 1998).

The school component of Fitness Fever is free to registered schools and provides classroom teachers, physical educators, and food service coordinators with all the materials and ideas they need to transform the month of February into a fun and fit environment. Fitness Fever also has community and workplace components that focus on exciting the rest of Minnesota about physical activity and good nutrition.

Program Partners: Fitness Fever was developed in 1995 by Blue Cross and Blue Shield of Minnesota; Minnesota Department of Health; Minnesota Department of Children, Families, and Learning; and Minnesota Service Cooperatives. To learn more, visit the Fitness Fever website: **http:// www.fitnessfever.com.**

CDC's Guidelines for School and Community Programs to Promote Lifelong Physical Activity Among Young People

1. Policy

Establish policies that promote enjoyable, lifelong physical activity among young people.

- Require comprehensive, daily physical education for students in kindergarten through grade 12.
- Require comprehensive health education for students in kindergarten through grade 12.
- Require that adequate resources, including budget and facilities, be committed for physical activity instruction and programs.
- Require the hiring of physical education specialists to teach physical education in kindergarten through grade 12, elementary school teachers trained to teach health education, health education specialists to teach health education in middle and senior high schools, and qualified people to direct school and community physical activity programs and to coach young people in sports and recreation programs.
- Require that physical education instruction and programs meet the needs and interests of all students.

2. Environment

Provide physical and social environments that encourage and enable safe and enjoyable physical activity.

- Provide access to safe spaces and facilities for physical activity in the school and the community.
- Establish and enforce measures to prevent physical activity-related injuries and illnesses.
- Provide time within the school day for unstructured physical activity.
- Discourage the use or withholding of physical activity as punishment.
- Provide health promotion programs for school faculty and staff.

3. Physical Education

Implement physical education curricula and instruction that emphasize enjoyable participation in physical activity and that help students develop the knowledge, attitudes, motor skills, behavioral skills, and confidence needed to adopt and maintain physically active lifestyles.

- Provide planned and sequential physical education curricula from kindergarten through grade 12 that promote enjoyable, lifelong physical activity.
- Use physical education curricula consistent with the national standards for physical education.
- Use active learning strategies and emphasize enjoyable participation in physical education class.
- Develop students' knowledge of and positive attitudes toward physical activity.
- Develop students' mastery of and confidence in motor and behavioral skills for participating in physical activity.
- Provide a substantial percentage of each student's recommended weekly amount of physical activity in physical education classes.
- Promote participation in enjoyable physical activity in the school, community, and home.

(continued)

207

4. Health Education

Implement health education curricula and instruction that help students develop the knowledge, attitudes, behavioral skills, and confidence needed to adopt and maintain physically active lifestyles.

- Provide planned and sequential health education curricula from kindergarten through grade 12 that promote lifelong participation in physical activity.
- Use health education curricula consistent with the national standards for health education.
- Promote collaboration among physical education, health education, and classroom teachers as well as teachers in related disciplines who plan and implement physical activity instruction.
- Use active learning strategies to emphasize enjoyable participation in physical activity in the school, community, and home.
- Develop students' knowledge of and positive attitudes toward healthy behaviors, particularly physical activity.
- Develop students' mastery of and confidence in the behavioral skills needed to adopt and maintain a healthy lifestyle that includes regular physical activity.

5. Extracurricular Activities

Provide extracurricular physical activity programs that meet the needs and interests of all students.

- Provide a diversity of developmentally appropriate competitive and noncompetitive physical activity programs for all students.
- Link students to community physical activity programs, and use community resources to support extracurricular physical activity programs.

6. Parental Involvement

Include parents and guardians in physical activity instruction and in extracurricular and community physical activity programs, and encourage them to support their children's participation in enjoyable physical activities.

- Encourage parents to advocate for quality physical activity instruction and programs for their children.
- Encourage parents to support their children's participation in appropriate, enjoyable physical activities.
- Encourage parents to be physically active role models and to plan and participate in family activities that include physical activity.

7. Personnel Training

Provide training for education, coaching, recreation, health care, and other school and community personnel that imparts the knowledge and skills needed to effectively promote enjoyable, lifelong physical activity among young people.

- Train teachers to deliver physical education that provides a substantial percentage of each student's recommended weekly amount of physical activity.
- Train teachers to use active learning strategies needed to develop students' knowledge about, attitudes toward, skills in, and confidence in engaging in physical activity.
- Train school and community personnel how to create psycho-social environments that enable young people to enjoy physical activity instruction and programs.
- Train school and community personnel how to involve partners and the community in physical activity instruction and programs.
- Train volunteers who coach sports and recreation programs for young people.

8. Health Services

Assess physical activity patterns among young people, counsel them about physical activity, refer them to appropriate programs, and advocate for physical activity instruction and programs for them.

- Regularly assess the physical activity patterns of young people, reinforce physical activity among active young people, counsel inactive young people about physical activity, and refer young people to appropriate physical activity programs.
- Advocate for school and community physical activity instruction and programs that meet the needs of young people.

9. Community Programs

Provide a range of developmentally appropriate community sports and recreation programs that are attractive to all young people.

- Provide a diversity of developmentally appropriate community sports and recreation programs for all young people.
- Provide access to community sports and recreation programs for young people.

10. Evaluation

Regularly evaluate school and community physical activity instruction, programs, and facilities.

- Evaluate the implementation and quality of physical activity policies, curricula, instruction, programs, and personnel training.
- Measure students' attainment of physical activity knowledge, achievement of motor and behavioral skills, and adoption of healthy behaviors.

CDC's *Guidelines for School and Community Programs to Promote Lifelong Physical Activity Among Young People* can be reproduced and adapted without permission. Copies of the guidelines can be downloaded from the Internet at **http://www.cdc.gov**. (On the CDC home page, click on *MMWR*, select *Recommendations and Reports,* and then select March 7, 1997.) Print copies are available from: CDC, Division of Adolescent and School Health, ATTN: Resource Room, 4770 Buford Highway, Mailstop K-32, Atlanta, GA 30341-3742; phone: 888-CDC-4NRG.

SCHOOL PROGRAM IN THE SPOTLIGHT

"Physical Dimensions"

About the Program: Physical Dimensions is an integrated health and physical education program designed to give teens the "knowledge and skills needed to engage in a physically active, healthy lifestyle throughout life" (Program Adds New Dimensions to School Health. *Health Issues* October 1997, 5(3)).

The curriculum focuses on three dimensions of a healthy lifestyle: health-related fitness, lifetime physical activity, and health/wellness concepts and skills. After an initial orientation, students receive 3 weeks of instruction in each of the three dimensions every 9 weeks. Upon successful completion of Physical Dimensions, students receive the High School PhD, a certificate of achievement that offers congratulations and encouragement and helps reinforce the importance of a healthy lifestyle.

Program Partners: Physical Dimensions was created by the Kansas High School Physical Activity and Health/Wellness Curriculum and is funded in part by the Kansas Health Foundation. For more information about Physical Dimensions, contact project director Bobbie Harris at Wichita State University, 1845 Fairmount, Wichita, KS 67260-0016, 316-978-5957, or curriculum coordinator Kathy Ermler at Emporia State University, Emporia, KS 66801, 316-341-5945.

NASPE's Physical Activity Guidelines for Children

- Elementary school-age children should accumulate *at least 30 to 60 minutes* of age and developmentally appropriate physical activity from a variety of physical activities on all, or most days of the week.

- An accumulation of *more than 60 minutes, and up to several hours per day,* of age and developmentally appropriate activity *is encouraged* for elementary school-age children.

- Some of the child's activity each day should be in periods lasting 10 to 15 minutes or more and include moderate to vigorous activity. This activity will typically be intermittent in nature involving alternating moderate to vigorous activity with *brief periods* of rest and recovery.

- *Extended periods of inactivity are inappropriate* for children.

- *A variety of physical activities selected from the Physical Activity Pyramid is recommended* for elementary school children.

Reprinted from *Physical Activity for Children: A Statement of Guidelines* (1998) with permission from The National Association for Sport and Physical Education (NASPE), 1900 Association Drive, Reston, VA 20191-1599.

International Physical Activity Guidelines for Adolescents

In 1993, the International Consensus Conference on Physical Activity Guidelines for Adolescents convened in San Diego, California, to establish two main guidelines relating to physical activity among adolescents (Sallis and Patrick 1994):

Guideline 1:   All adolescents should be physically active daily, or nearly every day, as part of play, games, sports, work, transportation, recreation, physical education, or planned exercise, in the context of family, school, and community activities.

Guideline 2:   Adolescents should engage in 3 or more sessions per week of activities that last 20 minutes or more at a time, and that require moderate to vigorous levels of exertion.

Ideas for Action in the Schools

As you review the many school physical activity promotion ideas and resources presented in this chapter, keep in mind major points discussed in previous chapters:

A safe environment is one in which the risk of injury or illness is minimized.

✔ Your program will need to consist of strategies and actions tailored to the specific needs, interests, readiness stages, and priorities of your target audience. When working with youth, carefully assess the barriers to regular physical activity or quality playtime. For example, does the child have a safe environment in which to play? Does he or she have playgrounds or facilities (e.g., bicycling trails, swimming pools, basketball and tennis courts, parks and open spaces for recreation) available? Is the child given adequate and appropriate time in which to play? Does the child have positive role models and parental or peer support to be regularly active? How do cost, transportation, or other safety factors influence activity levels? The quiz on pages 100–101 in chapter 5 has been used successfully with adults and with youth in grades 9–12 (Jim Sallis, personal communication, 1997).

✔ Use enjoyable physical education and physical activity experiences that actively involve students in learning (e.g., brainstorming, cooperative group process, simulation, and situational analysis), which may help to foster positive attitudes toward, as well as active participation in, physical activity programs and a physically active lifestyle (CDC 1997).

✔ Match the skill level of the participants with challenges that will encourage skill development and fun, and with games and program elements not based exclusively on winning.

✔ Treat the school as a member of the community, and promote an environment in which school administrators, faculty, staff, students, and their families can readily participate in some form of physical activity in or out of school. By emphasizing healthy play and having fun, your activities will help others to value the benefits of a lifelong involvement in regular physical activity.

✔ Review the International Physical Activity Guidelines for Adolescents on page 210, NASPE's *Physical Activity for Children* guidelines on page 210, and the physical activity recommendations for adults discussed in chapter 2 of this publication. Keep young people, parents, faculty, and administrators informed of the benefits of a lifetime of physical activity.

✔ Read the CDC *Guidelines for School and Community Programs to Promote Lifelong Physical Activity Among Young People* (CDC 1997) for further information about, and recommendations for, programs targeting young people. A summary of those guidelines appears on pages 207–209 of this chapter.

✔ Be sure to keep accurate notes and records of what you are doing and learning. Others will be eager to learn from your experiences, and administrators will need to know that their investment of resources into physical activity promotion has had desirable results.

Ideas for Schools

Promote Increased Awareness and Knowledge of a Physically Active Lifestyle

- Create awareness of the importance of physical activity by using a variety of communication avenues:

  —Include health, physical activity, and fitness tips in school publications, and post information and educational flyers on school bulletin boards.

  —Develop class, school, and district proclamations promoting physical activity.

  —Have students write letters to local and state officials urging their support of health, nutrition, and physical education programs.

  —Provide students or health education, physical education, and nutrition service staff as guest speakers on local radio and television talk shows.

  —Each morning, have a student present a health, nutrition, or physical activity fact or tip over the school's intercom or instructional television system.

  —Have students compose advertisements, jingles, or spot announcements promoting health, nutrition, and physical activity and broadcast them over the school's intercom or instructional television system or submit them to local radio and television stations, newspapers, and magazines.

- Incorporate the theme of physical activity throughout the curriculum. For example, in English essays, debates, dramatic skits, math problems, or art.

- Use camera-ready graphics and logos related to physical activity on classroom handouts, newsletters to parents and the community, the school cafeteria menu, and other school publications.

- Hold school-wide events promoting physical activity concepts:

  —Conduct a poster, essay, or skit contest.

  —Hold a school health, physical activity, or fitness fair and invite the health department, hospital, blood bank, and voluntary and other health organizations to provide health screening, exhibits, and demonstrations.

  —Invite health, physical activity, and fitness experts and athletes from the community to give presentations at assemblies or in classes.

- Sponsor or participate in a jump rope, running, or dance marathon in the community. For example, contact your local division of the American Heart Association for details on its "Healthy Choice American Heart Walk" event (see resource G on page 314).

- Encourage student councils, school newspapers, school clubs, athletic teams, and other peer-led groups to adopt promoting physical activity as a project.

- Administer health risk appraisals to faculty and parents to increase health awareness.

- Inform local newspapers, radio stations, and television stations of special school-related activities being conducted to promote physical activity. Invite members of the community to participate.

- Plan a statewide physical activity festival for physical education teachers and their students. Focus on noncompetitive activities.
- Create classroom activities that promote physical activity concepts:
  —Plan field trips to health, nutrition, and physical activity facilities in the community, or give students homework assignments to visit and report on such facilities (e.g., health food stores, weight-loss clinics, health spas or fitness centers, hospitals, health departments, parks and recreation departments, and voluntary health agencies).
  —Give students homework assignments related to health, nutrition, and physical activity that require parental involvement.
  —Give essay, research, debate, speech, and reading assignments dealing with health and physical activity.
  —Invite health, nutrition, and physical activity experts in the community to talk to classes. Such experts might include physicians, nurses, and dietitians who can describe the effects of poor health decisions.
  —Show films and other audiovisuals available on health and physical activity, then discuss how to promote good health. Check the school or district media center for available materials.
  —Have students write letters to health and physical activity agencies and request information on specific topics of interest.
  —Study health, nutrition, and fitness fads and fallacies.
  —Set up an anonymous question box for students to ask questions on health, physical activity, and fitness. Have students research answers or invite experts to respond.
- Conduct surveys to determine which school or community activities are considered most beneficial in promoting healthier lifestyles.
- Set up displays in school auditoriums, hallways, media centers, cafeterias, and classrooms as well as in supermarkets, shopping malls, athletic clubs, and community and recreation centers. These displays can be of
  —physical activity posters obtained from voluntary health associations; county or state health departments; insurance companies; professional organizations such as the American Alliance for Health, Physical Education, Recreation and Dance; nutrition groups; and other public and private agencies;
  —photographs and slides portraying healthy living, physical activity, and lifetime sports;
  —newspaper articles featuring district and school health and physical education programs and activities; and
  —student-made posters, pictures, and murals.
- Have students write and present a play or puppet show about how good physical activity and health habits are important.
- Design games emphasizing health, nutrition, and physical activity.
- Have students write to an Olympic or Special Olympic athlete or to one of the winners of the Healthy American Fitness Leader Award to learn of that person's struggles and accomplishments.

(continued)

(continued)

Increase Motivation for Increased Physical Activity

- Emphasize the pleasure and fun involved in being physically active.

- Assess reasons for not engaging in regular physical activity.

- Address ways of overcoming the most common barriers to a physically active lifestyle or to a regular playtime.

- Invite to the school or promote as role models school athletes, professional athletes, people who excel in lifestyle activities (such as racewalking, golf, or karate), and people who are successfully making changes in their lifestyles. Invite youth who have organized safe play activities for younger children, young people who tried a new outdoor adventure, or a handicapped person who competes in wheelchair racing. Try to include role models that reflect the diversity of the students according to gender, racial or ethnic background, and level of physical fitness.

- Provide multicultural experiences (e.g., Native American traditions or ethnic dances) to foster awareness and appreciation of differences associated with sex, race, ethnicity, culture, and physical disability.

- Allow students to role-play and model experiences that will build self-confidence and enhance self-efficacy.

- Develop fun and meaningful rewards, recognition, and incentives for those who achieve a higher standard of physical activity in their lifestyle.

- Reward students who try by providing incentives to participate in certain events.

- Enter students in contests to win athletic and fitness equipment for the school.

Teach or Enhance Skills Needed for Lifelong Physical Activity

- In physical education classes, place greater emphasis on activities that can be enjoyed over a lifetime. Consider offering electives such as aerobic dance classes, step aerobics, stretching or weight-training classes, racewalking, golf, tennis, cross-country skiing, or swimming.

- Ask medical agencies to give or loan to the school for demonstrations medical equipment no longer in use (e.g., devices for measuring pulmonary function and blood pressure) to help students learn self-monitoring skills and to reinforce the link between physical activities and health.

- Develop mastery of motor skills and perceptions of physical competence that support a wide range of developmentally appropriate physical activity options. For example, teach how to walk, run, or play individual sports; how to stretch or warm up; or muscle strengthening activities.

- Throughout the health or physical education curriculum, place greater emphasis on the physical, social, and mental benefits of physical activity and the development of personal skills needed to adopt, maintain, and support physically active lifestyles—skills such as self-assessment, goal setting, self-monitoring and self-regulation, decision making, identifying and overcoming barriers, self-reinforcement, communication, and advocacy skills.

- Incorporate into the physical education curriculum more time for all students to be physically active. Modify traditional games to allow all students to participate. Experiment with innovative ways to keep the students actively involved and in motion.

- Provide teachers, coaches, administrators, and other school-related personnel pre-service and in-service training in promoting enjoyable, lifelong physical activity among youths. A number of national guidelines are available for persons planning the training sessions.

Provide Opportunities to Practice New Skills and Behaviors in a Safe Setting

- Provide opportunities for the students and faculty to be more physically active or to try a new activity for one day or one event:
  - —Sponsor periodic fun walks or runs, such as the turkey trot (Thanksgiving), reindeer run (Christmas), and bunny hop (Easter).
  - —Have students set a schoolwide walking or jogging goal for a specified time (e.g., the equivalent of crossing the state or country).
  - —Have daily exercise, relaxation, or stress-reduction breaks conducted over the school's intercom or instructional television system.
  - —Hold new games festivals or field day events.
- Provide opportunities throughout the day for unstructured physical activity, not only within physical education classes, but also during recess, homeroom periods, and immediately before and after school.
- Explore options so that all children can participate and all can feel like winners—not just those who are more athletically gifted. Create awards or some form of recognition for reasons other than physical prowess, such as most improved, best attitude, or best team worker. Try to provide an environment free of ridicule or embarrassment (this can be challenging in a peer-oriented environment).
- Coordinate a bicycle tour, hike, or outdoor adventure day.
- Sponsor a 24-hour walk, run, bike, in-line skating, or dance fund raiser.
- Promote the idea that family time can be active time by conducting family-oriented physical activity nights or weekend events.

Foster Supportive Social Networks

- Build a coalition with individuals and organizations committed to improved health and physical activity for youth and families. Cosponsor events for greater community visibility and impact.
- Establish before- or after-school recreational clubs for students who enjoy similar activities, such as walking or hiking, aerobics, tennis, strength training, swimming, or golf. Emphasize having fun, developing camaraderie, and improving personal skills.
- Solicit parental involvement. Consider offering classes or fun events that the whole family could join, such as family aerobic dance, family volleyball, or family gym nights. Solicit faculty involvement.
- Have students develop buddy systems, small groups, or teams to help develop commitment to skills and values that foster regular physical activity or playtime.
- Help youth find opportunities in the community to join physical activity-related clubs or organizations, such as hiking clubs, racewalking groups, bicycling clubs, or cross-country and downhill skiing clubs.

(continued)

(continued)

Establish and Maintain a Physical Environment Supportive of Physical Activity

- Establish well-equipped playing fields and a physical activity center on the school grounds that are for supervised use by students, staff, families, and the community. If possible, provide participants access to clean and safe showers and locker rooms.

- Establish physical activity trails and walking, jogging, or bicycling paths on school grounds for use by students, staff, and the community.

- Work to ensure that schools and nearby residential areas are connected by walking or bicycling paths.

- Establish safe areas to secure bicycles.

- Install lights in outdoor fields for evening use by all community residents.

- Ensure that outdoor or indoor facilities are safe or that they minimize the potential for injury due to negligence, poorly maintained equipment, or unsanitary conditions.

- Make school physical activity facilities and playing fields available during the summer to establish a supervised summer playground for community use.

Establish and Enforce Administrative Guidelines and Policies Supportive of Physical Activity

- Discourage faculty from using or withholding physical activity as student punishment.

- Mandate daily physical education in grades K–12.

- Mandate health education in grades K–12.

- Establish physical education and health education requirements for graduation.

- Use the national physical education standards (NASPE 1995) to develop physical education curricula and assessment strategies.

- Use national health education standards (Joint Committee on National Health Education Standards 1995) to develop health education curricula to foster the development of goal setting, decision making, communications, and advocacy skills that students need to adopt, maintain, and support physically active lifestyles.

- Incorporate physical activity throughout the school curriculum.

- Emphasize lifetime activities in physical education and not just team sports.

- Allocate funds to increase the number of certified physical educators at each school, build additional facilities to handle increased physical education time, and purchase equipment.

- Establish an employee steering committee to address health in the school environment.

- Obtain administrative and union support for health promotion and specifically for physical activity promotion efforts.

- Obtain formal recognition of exemplary programs and program participants.

- Obtain funding for physical activity and exercise facilities for new schools as well as renovations for older schools.
- Organize coalitions or task forces of state teacher associations, other educational associations, the parent-teacher association, school boards, and so on, to address physical activity issues, advocate for change, and obtain resources.
- Partner with private industry in Adopt-a-School programs to increase resources for specific projects related to physical activity promotion.
- Establish minimum and optimum standards for lifetime physical activity skills training for students.
- Coordinate physical activity instruction between physical education and health education.
- Provide screenings, physical activity assessment, and counseling to students and their parents as a part of school entrance, preparation for participating in sports, and periodic physical examinations.

Key Resources for School-Based Promotion

Resources to help you in promoting safe and enjoyable physical activity are available from a number of sources, including government agencies, professional organizations, and voluntary organizations. For example, at the state and community levels, materials and technical assistance might be available from

- state and local departments of health,
- state departments of education and local school districts,
- state departments of transportation (bicycle and pedestrian programs),
- state and local departments of parks and recreation,
- governor's councils on physical fitness and sports,
- state chapters of national professional organizations, such as the American Association for Health, Physical Education, Recreation and Dance (AAHPERD); the National Association for Sport and Physical Education (NASPE); and the American School Health Association (ASHA),
- state affiliates or divisions of voluntary organizations, such as the American Heart Association (AHA) and the American Cancer Society (ACS), and
- associations that serve youth (e.g., Boys and Girls Clubs, Young Men's and Young Women's Christian Associations, Boy Scouts, and Girl Scouts).

The following list of resources is not intended to be inclusive but rather to provide examples of materials that have been developed to support school-based physical activity programs, although all of the resources listed may not be currently available. Inclusion of materials in this list does not imply endorsement by CDC.

Theory Resources

NASPE's Quality Physical Education Package

Appropriate Practices for High School Physical Education (1998)

Appropriate Practices for Middle School Physical Education (1995)

Developmentally Appropriate Physical Education Practices for Children (1992)

Developmentally Appropriate Practice in Movement Programs for Young Children, Ages 3–5 (1995)

Including Students with Disabilities in Regular Physical Education (1995)

Looking at Physical Education from a Developmental Perspective (1994)

Moving into the Future: National Standard for Physical Education (1995)

Physical Activity for Children: A Statement of Guidelines (1998)

Physical Education Program Improvement and Self-Study Guide—High School (1998)

Physical Education Program Improvement and Self Study Guide—Middle School (1998)

Program Guidelines and Appraisal Checklist for Elementary School Physical Education (1994)

National Association for Sport and Physical Education
1900 Association Drive
Reston, VA 20191-1599
Toll-free: 800-213-7193 ext. 410
To order: 800-321-0789
Website: **http://wwwaahperd.org/naspe/naspe.html**

Activity and Program Resources

American Fitness Alliance (AFA) Youth Fitness Resource Center

Human Kinetics, the American Alliance for Health, Physical Education, Recreation and Dance, and The Cooper Institute for Aerobic Research have joined forces to form a partnership to promote physical activity among youth. The major objective of the AFA is to improve young people's fitness and health by promoting physical activity and other healthy behaviors. The AFA seeks to achieve this objective by being a national resource center for fitness- and activity-related products and services and by creating new programs to promote physical activity and fitness throughout life.

AFA products available in 1999:

* *The New Physical Best,* offering a Health-Fitness Specialist Certification
* *FITNESSGRAM 6.0,* with updated tests and powerful new software
* *FitSmart,* the first national youth fitness knowledge test
* *Fitness Challenge,* a new national fitness test for youths with disabilities

For more information about AFA products and services, contact:

Human Kinetics
P.O. Box 5076
1607 N. Market Street
Champaign, IL 61825-5076
Toll-free: 800-747-4457
Fax: 217-351-2674
Website: **http://www.americanfitness.net** or **http://www.humankinetics.com**

American Heart Association Schoolsite Programs

HeartPower! is a supplemental language-arts based program that motivates children to learn how to keep their hearts healthy for a lifetime. *HeartPower!* kits are available for children in prekindergarten through grade 8. There are four key lessons in the kits: nutrition, physical activity, living tobacco-free, and how the heart works. The *HeartPower!* kits expand instructional options for teachers, making it easier and more fun to teach about heart health in today's curriculum.

Jump Rope For Heart (JRFH) and Hoops For Heart (HFH) are school-based American Heart Association (AHA) fund-raising events that promote the activities of jumping rope and basketball while raising community awareness of the AHA. The money raised from JRFH and HFH funds lifesaving research and educational programs like *HeartPower!* They also teach students the benefits of physical activity, how to keep the heart healthy, and that they can help save lives right in their own community.

American Heart Association
National Center
7272 Greenville Avenue
Dallas, TX 75231-4596
Phone: 214-373-6300
Toll-free: 800-AHA-USA1
Website: **http://www.americanheart.org**

The Child and Adolescent Trial for Cardiovascular Health (CATCH)

CATCH is a nationally tested program that helps teach elementary school students healthy habits to prevent heart disease. This intervention project, funded by the National Heart, Lung, and Blood Institute (NHLBI) from 1986 to 1994, was the largest school-based health promotion study ever done, involving more than 5,000 ethnically diverse students in grades 3–5 in nearly 100 schools in four states. The program consisted of cafeteria, physical activity, classroom, and family components.

NHLBI Information Center
P.O. Box 30105
Bethesda, MD 20824-0105
Fax: 301-251-1223
E-mail: **NHLBIIC@dgsys.com**
Website: **http://www.nhlbi.nih.gov**

Energy²Burn

Created by the American Council on Exercise (ACE) in cooperation with the National Fitness Leaders Association, Energy²Burn (previously known as "Fun to Be Fit") is a unique fitness program designed for elementary school children. By volunteering in local elementary schools, certified ACE instructors serve as role models who teach children how to maintain physically fit lifestyles.

American Council on Exercise
5820 Oberlin Drive, Suite 102
San Diego, CA 92121-3787
Phone: 619-535-8227
Fax: 619-535-1778
Website: **http://www.acefitness.org**

Every Child a Winner With Physical Education

This program has been implemented successfully in grades prekindergarten through 6 since 1974. It uses the concepts of space awareness, body awareness, qualities of movement, and relationships as the basis for child-designed games, gymnastics, and dance. Competition is handled developmentally and appropriately in child-originated games. The problem-solving method is used, as children are encouraged to reach their personal potential. Winning is achieved as each child does his or her best. This program is designed for all children regardless of their physical or mental abilities.

Every Child a Winner Program
Educational Excellence, Inc.
P.O. Box 141
Ocilla, GA 31774
912-468-7098

Exercise Across America Motivational Challenge Program

Students choose a state or states to exercise across and an aerobic sport. They receive recognition, a special certificate, and a patch for taking the challenge. Several levels of assistance to teachers are available.

American Running and Fitness Association
4405 East-West Highway, Suite 405
Bethesda, MD 20814
Phone: 301-913-9517
Toll-free: 800-776-ARFA
Website: **http://www.arfa.org**

First Choice

First Choice is a physical fitness program developed for teaching at-risk youth about physical activity as an alternative for lifestyles such as gang activity, violence, and substance abuse.

First Choice
c/o Fitness Intervention Technologies
2505 Canyon Creek
Richardson, TX 75080
Phone: 214-231-8866

Growing Healthy

This comprehensive health education program is designed to foster student competencies to make decisions enhancing their health and lives. Growing Healthy includes a planned sequential curriculum for children of all abilities in grades K–6, a variety of teaching methods, a teacher-training program, and strategies for eliciting community support for school health education. Through group and individual activities, children learn about themselves by learning about their bodies. The curriculum has been developed to enhance other school subjects such as reading, writing, math, science, and creative arts.

National Center for Health Education
Director, School-Based Programs
72 Spring Street, Suite 208
New York, NY 10012
Phone: 212-334-9470
Website: **http://www.nche.org**

Physical Activity Ideas for Action

Ideas for Action (elementary and secondary school) is a cooperative project of The President's Council on Physical Fitness and Sports, the National Association for Sport and Physical Education (NASPE), and the Sporting Goods Manufacturers Association (SGMA). These books provide teachers with "kid-tested," developmentally appropriate physical activities, supplemental programs, and additional resources.

Human Kinetics
P.O. Box 5076
1607 N. Market Street
Champaign, IL 61825-5076
Toll-free: 800-747-4457
Website: **http://www.humankinetics.com**

Olympic Curriculum Guide

The structured curriculum guide is for use in primary and secondary grades. It encourages children to use the spirit and meaning of the Olympic movement to enrich their lives and to develop their bodies through sports and fitness.

Griffin Publishing
544 W. Colorado St.
Glendale, CA 91204
Toll-free: 800-472-9741
Website: **http://www.griffinpublishing.com**

Physical Management Program

This program was developed to give overweight students in grades 10–12 the knowledge and opportunity to interrupt the cycle of obesity and inactivity that prevents a fully healthy and effective lifestyle. The curriculum includes behavior change, physical conditioning, nutrition, education, and building self-image.

Project Director
Physical Management Project
3513 Prestwick Rd.
Billings, MT 59101
Phone: 406-252-4822

Play Leadership Training

The Professional Play Leaders Association is dedicated to developing positive, enriching relationships with today's sophisticated children through play. Their *Play Leadership Training* includes practical leader strategies, proactive guidance, and relational skills based on the national bestseller *How to Play with Kids* and the companion video, *Essentials of Play Leadership*. Seminar costs depend on length and type of training.

Professional Play Leaders Association-USA
P.O. Box 161713
Austin, TX 78716
Toll-free: 800-359-7331

Play Up a Sweat

This dynamic physical fitness program promotes noncompetitive play and movement as it teaches kids to have fun, build self-esteem, and enjoy a physically active lifestyle.

Pam Staver
1022 Fairway Valley Drive
Woodstock, GA 30189
Phone: 770-516-1628
Fax: 770-516-1625
To order: 800-222-7774

President's Challenge

The President's Challenge is a physical fitness testing program for youth ages 6–17, including students with special needs. The test battery consists of five required components of physical fitness. Awards are based on three levels of physical fitness, and include T-shirts, emblems, certificates, decals, pins, and magnets.

President's Council on Physical Fitness and Sports
HHH Building, Room 738H
200 Independence Ave., SW
Washington, DC 20201
Phone: 202-690-9000

Project ACES (All Children Exercise Simultaneously)

The first Wednesday in May (10 AM local time), approximately 20 million school children participate in physical activity for 15 minutes. Project ACES aims to educate children and the general public about the importance of fitness.

Youth Fitness Coalition, Inc.
P.O. Box 6452
Jersey City, NJ 07306-0452
Phone: 201-433-8993

Project Adventure

This is a program designed to help students increase self-confidence, develop leadership, enhance decision making, learn to respect differences, discover the power of group cooperation, and learn to view obstacles as opportunities for growth. The principal activities are noncompetitive games, group problem-solving initiatives, and ropes course events.

Project Adventure
P.O. Box 100
Hamilton, MA 01936
Phone: 978-468-7981
Fax: 978-468-7605
E-mail: **info@pa.org**
Website: **http://www.pa.org**

Skate-in-School Program

Developed by the National Association of Sport and Physical Education in cooperation with Rollerblade, Inc., the Skate-in-School Program is designed to help physical education and recreational programs provide safe, educationally sound and affordable in-line skating opportunities. It comes with a complete curriculum.

National Association of Sport and Physical Education (NASPE)
1900 Association Drive
Reston, VA 20191-1599
Toll-free: 800-213-7193 ext. 410
Website: **http://www.aahperd.org/naspe/naspe.html**
Rollerblade, Inc.
Toll-free: 888-758-4386

Sports, Play, and Active Recreation for Kids (SPARK)

SPARK is a controlled trial of a school-based physical activity promotion intervention for elementary students. (To read more about it, see the Suggested Reading at the end of this chapter.)

SPARK Physical Education
6363 Alvarado Court, Suite 250
San Diego State University
San Diego, CA 92120
Phone: 619-594-4815
Fax: 619-594-4570

Start Smart Sports Development Program

This motor skill development program for children 3 years of age and older focuses on fundamental skills such as throwing, kicking, striking, and catching. The program is offered in two levels: junior (ages 3–5) and senior (ages 6 up)

National Alliance for Youth Sports
2050 Vista Parkway
West Palm Beach, FL 33411
Phone: 561-684-1141
Toll-free: 800-729-2057
Fax: 561-684-2546
Website: **http://www.nays.org**

Journals

Journal of Physical Education, Recreation and Dance (JOPERD)

The journal of the American Alliance for Health, Physical Education, Recreation and Dance (AAHPERD).

American Alliance of Health, Physical Education, Recreation and Dance (AAHPERD)
1900 Association Drive
Reston, VA 20191-1599
Toll-free: 800-213-7193, ext. 451
Website: **http://www.aahperd.org**

Strategies

Practical and applied articles about physical activity, physical education, and sports. Many articles are collaborations between K–12 and university-based educators.

AAHPERD/NAGWS/NASPE
1900 Association Drive
Reston, VA 20191-1599
Toll-free: 800-213-7193 ext. 451
Website: **http://www.aahperd.org**

Teaching Elementary Physical Education (TEPE)

Practical and applied articles based on research and best practices.

Human Kinetics
P.O. Box 5076
1607 N. Market Street
Champaign, IL 61825-5076
Toll-free: 800-747-4457
Website: **http://www.humankinetics.com**

Newsletters

The Great Activities Newsletter

Quick tips, activities, and resources for K–12 physical educators.

The Great Activities Publishing Company
P.O. Box 51158
Durham, NC 27717-1158
Toll-free: 800-927-0682

Physical Activity Today

A user-friendly newsletter summarizing physical activity, sports, and recreation research as it applies to real-life settings.

AAHPERD Research Consortium
1900 Association Drive
Reston, VA 20191-1599
Toll-free: 800-213-7193 ext. 480
Website: **http://www.aahperd.org/naspe/naspe.html**

The Right Moves

Designed to help elementary school physical educators teach children about the importance of an active lifestyle and healthy diet. Includes tips, facts, resources, activities, and applications related to fitness, motor skills, integration, and nutrition. Sponsored by NASPE and Hershey Foods Corporation.

National Association of Sport and Physical Education
1900 Association Drive
Reston, VA 20191-1599
Toll-free: 800-213-7193 ext. 410
Website: **http://www.aahperd.org/naspe/naspe.html**

Suggested Reading

For a list of organizations, agencies, and selected program materials for promoting physical activity, see:

Resource A, for general resources

Chapter 6, for environment-related resources

Chapter 9, for worksite-related resources

For more information about promoting physical activity among inner-city or disadvantaged youth, read:

California Healthy Cities Project. *Promoting Healthy Youth: Strategies for Recreation and Community Services Partnerships.* Sacramento, CA: California Healthy Cities Project, 1994.

California Healthy Cities Project. *Taking Back Our Communities: Strategies for Violence Prevention.* Sacramento, CA: California Healthy Cities Project, 1994. For more information about the California Healthy Cities Project or for copies of their publications, contact

California Healthy Cities Project
P.O. Box 942732
Mail Station 675
Sacramento, CA 93434-7320
Phone: 916-327-7017

Compton B, Hughes J, Smith JC. *Adolescents in Need: An Approach for Helping Rural At-Risk Youth.* Chapel Hill, NC: Community Pediatrics Division and the Center for Early Adolescence of the University of North Carolina at Chapel Hill School of Medicine, 1990. For more information and a listing of all publications, contact:

Center for Early Adolescence
University of North Carolina at Chapel Hill
Suite 211, Carr Mill Mall
Carrboro, NC 27510

DeMaio B, Zakrzewski B. Meeting the fitness needs of the inner city. *Parks and Recreation* 1993; 28(5):32–37.

For more information about assessing the child's physical activity level, read:

Sallis JF. Self-report measures of children's physical activity. *Journal of School Health* 1991; 61(5):215–219.

Sallis JF, Condon SA, Goggin KJ, Roby JJ, Kolody B, Alcaraz JE. The development of self-administered physical activity surveys for 4th grade students. *Research Quarterly for Exercise and Sport* 1993; 64(1):25–31.

For more information related to the Child and Adolescent Trial for Cardiovascular Health (CATCH), see:

Luepker RV, Perry CL, McKinlay SM, et al. Outcomes of a field trial to improve children's dietary patterns and physical activity: The Child and Adolescent Trial for Cardiovascular Health. *Journal of the American Medical Association* 1996; 275(10):768–776.

Resnicow K, Robinson T, Frank E, editors. The Multicenter Child and Adolescent Trial for Cardiovascular Health (CATCH): promoting cardiovascular health through schools. *Preventive Medicine* July/August 1996; 25(4):377–495. For additional information and to order copies of the CATCH Physical Education Curriculum or Heart Health Curriculum, contact:

NHLBI Information Center
P.O. Box 30105
Bethesda, Maryland 20824-0105
Fax: 301-251-1223

For more information about Sports, Play, and Active Recreation for Kids (SPARK), see:

McKenzie TL, Sallis JF, Faucette N, et al. Effects of a curriculum and inservice program on the quantity and quality of elementary physical education classes. *Research Quarterly for Exercise and Sport* 1993; 64(2):178–187.

Sallis JF, McKenzie TL, Alcaraz JE, et al. Effects of a two-year health-related physical education program on physical activity and fitness in elementary school students: SPARK. *American Journal of Public Health* 1997 (in press).

For more about physical activity promotion research targeting children and adolescents, read:

Chapter 6 of USDHHS. *Physical Activity and Health: A Report of the Surgeon General.* 1996:234–259.

National Association for Sport and Physical Education. Definition: the physically educated person. *Moving Into the Future. National Physical Education Standards: A Guide to Content and Assessment.* St. Louis: Mosby. 1995.

National Association for Sport and Physical Education. *Outcomes of Quality Physical Education Programs.* Reston, VA: National Association for Sport and Physical Education. 1992.

Stone EJ, McKenzie TL, Welk GJ, Booth ML. Effects of physical activity interventions in youth: review and Synthesis. *American Journal of Preventive Medicine* (November) 1998; 15(4): 298–315.

To learn more about nationally developed health education and physical education standards, read:

Joint Committees on National Health Education Standards. *National Health Education Standard: Achieving Health Literacy. An Investment in the Future.* Atlanta: American Cancer Society, 1995.

This document delineates seven voluntary national standards for school health education from kindergarten through 12th grade. These standards describe what children and adolescents should know and be able to do as a result of quality school health education. This document also indentifies action needed to support the implementation of quality health education programs.

National Association for Sport and Physical Education. *Moving into the Future. National Physical Education Standards: A Guide to Content and Assessment.* St. Louis: Mosby, 1995.

Voluntary national standards for school physical education from kindergarten through 12th grade. This document identifies seven standards that describe what students should know and be able to do as a result of quality physical education.

To read about standards for professional development, see:

Joint Committees of the Association for the Advancement of Health Education and the American School Health Association. Health instruction responsibilities and competencies for elementary (K–6) classroom teachers. *Journal of Health Education* 1992; 23(6):352–354.

National Association for Sport and Physical Education (NASPE). *Quality Sports, Quality Coaches: National Standards for Athletic Coaches*. Reston, VA: Kendall/Hunt Publishing Company, 1995.

National Association for Sport and Physical Education (NASPE). *National Standards for Beginning Physical Education Teachers*. Reston, VA: National Association for Sport and Physical Education, 1995.

National Task Force on the Preparation and Practice of Health Educators. *A Guide for the Development of Competency-based Curricula for Entry Level Health Educators*. New York: National Task Force for the Preparation and Practice of Health Educators, 1983.

For more information about fitness education for youth, read:

Cheung L, Richmond JB, editors. *Child Health, Nutrition, and Physical Activity*. Champaign, IL: Human Kinetics, 1995.

Pate R. *Health and Fitness Through Physical Education*. Champaign, IL: Human Kinetics, 1994.

Virgilio S. *Fitness Education for Children: A Team Approach*. Champaign, IL: Human Kinetics, 1997.

For current recommendations on promoting physical activity among youth, read:

Active Youth: Ideas for Implementing CDC Physical Activity Promotion Guidelines. Champaign, IL: Human Kinetics, 1998.

Centers for Disease Control and Prevention. Guidelines for school and community programs to promote lifelong physical activity among young people. *Morbidity and Mortality Weekly Report* 1997; 46(No. RR-6):1–37.

Or visit CDC's home page at **www.cdc.gov.** You may order a copy of this publication by calling 888-CDC-4NRG (or 888-232-4674).

For more information about policy-level interventions in schools:

Policy Guide. The National Association of State Boards of Education (NASBE) is developing a practical, "how-to" guide to help state education agencies and local school districts establish policies related to physical activity, nutrition, and tobacco in the context of a coordinated school health program. The guide will suggest specific policy language based on the guidelines, present policy options, showcase exemplary policies, highlight relevant laws, offer practical suggestions for implementation, and identify key resources. It will be similar in structure to NASBE's HIV/AIDS policy guide, *Someone At School Has AIDS*. The policy guide is scheduled for publication in late 1998. NASBE also has developed a state policy database and provides state-level technical assistance in policy development and implementation.

Jennifer Chomicky
NASBE
Phone: 703-684-4000
E-Mail: **jchomicky@nsba.org**

Policy Database and Technical Assistance Service. The National School Boards Association (NSBA) has developed a database of school district policies and information resources related to physical activity, nutrition, and tobacco. This technical assistance service, which is based on NSBA's existing HIV/AIDS Education and School Health Resource Database, features a telephone help line and materials clearinghouse that provides policy makers and other access to sample school district policies, up-to-date information on policy topics, consultation on specific policy issues, and referrals to other experts. NSBA is also developing education and training sessions to increase awareness of guidelines policy recommendations and motivate action.

Jennifer Chomicky
NSBA
Phone: 703-838-6169
E-mail: **jchomicky@nsba.org**

For more information about the Guidelines for Adolescent Preventive Services (GAPS), contact:

The Department of Adolescent Health
American Medical Association
515 North State Street
Chicago, IL 60610

When you write, ask for a copy of the *Guidelines for Adolescent Preventive Services, Recommendations Monograph*, ISBN: 0-89970-749-1.

For more information about encouraging lifetime fitness, read:

Collingwood, TR, Sunderlin J, and Kohl HW, III. The use of a staff training model for implementing fitness programming to prevent substance abuse with at-risk youth. *American Journal of Health Promotion* September/October 1994; 9(1).

Corbin, CB. The fitness curriculum—climbing the stairway to lifetime fitness. In: Pate R, Hohn R, editors. *Health and Fitness Through Physical Education*. Champaign, IL: Human Kinetics, 1994.

Corbin CB, Pangrazzi RP. *Physical Activity for Children: A Statement of Guidelines*. Reston, VA: National Association for Sport and Physical Education.

Kolbe LJ, Kann L, Collins JL, Small ML, Pateman BC, Warren CW. School health policies and programs study: a summary report. *Journal of School Health* October 1995; 65(8).

Sallis JF, Patrick K. Physical activity guidelines for adolescents: consensus statement. *Pediatric Exercise Science* 1994; 6:302–314.

Part IV

Resources for Action

Now that you have read about the scientific basis for physical activity promotion in part I, behavior change strategies for physical activity promotion in part II, and the basics of planning and implementing a physical activity intervention in part III, it's time for you to learn about more resources that can help you help your target population get moving—and stay moving.

Resource A gives you information about organizations and programs across the country that are involved with some aspect of physical activity promotion. No matter who your target population is, or what they need, you're sure to find something in resource A that will help your intervention efforts.

Resource B gives you the At-A-Glance summary of the 1996 Surgeon General's report on physical activity and health as well as other related sources.

Resources C and D give you a sample target audience profile and sample focus group results from CDC physical activity initiatives. These resources will be especially helpful for those of you new to the social marketing approach to promotion.

Resources E and F provide you with important information to help you create interventions that support the needs of people with disabilities. Resource E provides contact information for a number of organizations and agencies concerned with people with disabilities and resource F summarizes the Americans With Disabilities Act (ADA).

Resource G is a listing of national days or months related to health and physical activity. By planning your physical activity promotion events around these popular times of the year, you'll likely gain more exposure for your message and have more reason to develop new partnerships with others interested in doing the same.

Resource H lists the Healthy Communities 2000 objectives, which you can use as a model as you create your own program goals and objectives for your target population.

Resource I reprints the CDC's "Ready. Set. It's Everywhere You Go" Campaign handbook—valuable information about using social marketing concepts working with the media, and developing physical activity promotion programs in your community.

And finally, resource J provides you with examples of creative physical activity promotion efforts in several states across the country. We hope you'll find these ideas inspiring and helpful as you work on your own promotion activities.

Resource A

Organizations and Selected Materials for Promoting Physical Activity

The following list of organizations and sample educational materials was compiled by the Centers for Disease Control and Prevention (CDC) and is not intended to be inclusive of all physical activity promotion organizations nor of materials currently available or under development. Inclusion of materials in this list should not be construed as CDC endorsement. This list is intended merely as a helpful sampling of known materials or programs pertinent to physical activity promotion and serves as a guide to the types of educational materials developed by organizations involved in physical activity promotion. Organizations listed may discontinue or revise materials from time to time; so all of the items listed may not be readily available, nor offered at the cost cited. All additions or corrections should be brought to the attention of:

The Division of Nutrition and Physical Activity
National Center for Chronic Disease Prevention and Health Promotion
Centers for Disease Control and Prevention
4770 Buford Highway, NE, Mail Stop K-46
Atlanta, GA 30341-3724
Phone: 770-488-5820
E-mail: **ccdinfo@cdc.gov**

For additional ideas on programs and materials, search the Combined Health Information Database (CHID). See page 241 for information about CHID.

American Association for Active Lifestyles and Fitness (AAALF)

American Association for Active Lifestyles and Fitness
1900 Association Drive
Reston, VA 20191-1599
Phone: 800-213-7193
Fax: 703-476-9527
Website: **http://www.aahperd.org/aaalf/aaalf.html**
E-mail: **AAALF@aahperd.org**

The American Association for Active Lifestyles and Fitness (AAALF) is one of six national associations of the American Alliance for Health, Physical Education, Recreation and Dance (AAHPERD). Its membership consists of professionals who promote active lifestyles by conducting programs, training future practitioners in higher education, and producing research. Members have particular expertise in addressing the needs of traditionally underrepresented groups, such as people with disabilities, aging adults, and ethnic minorities. As a resource, AAALF provides information on program and practitioner standards for senior fitness, adapted physical education and adapted aquatics, facility construction, performance evaluation, legal issues, and risk management in physical activity and fitness testing.

American Association of Retired Persons (AARP)

AARP Fulfillment Section
601 E Street, NW
Washington, DC 20049
Phone: 202-434-2277
Website: **http://www.aarp.org**

Activating Ideas: Promoting Physical Activity Among Older Adults
This program idea and resource book was written by the American Association of Retired Persons for community professionals interested in promoting physical activity among older adults. Published in 1995. Stock #D-15566

American Cancer Society's "Generation Fit"

Generation Fit, produced by the American Cancer Society, is an enrichment program designed for youth aged 11 to 18. It contains five health-related, community service learning projects that provide young people with the opportunity to take action on issues related to nutrition or physical activity in their schools and communities. These activities include improving the quality of school lunches, promoting healthy eating or physical activity to peers, working on community hunger issues, and increasing access to physical activity resources.

Generation Fit is designed for use by youth group leaders and educators. It is appropriate for a variety of settings where youth have the opportunity to work in teams, including the classroom, after-school programs, and youth clubs. Generation Fit is one part of a comprehensive approach to health promotion that can build personal and social skills, while addressing policy and environment issues. Generation Fit will be available in the fall of 1999.

American Cancer Society
1599 Clifton Rd NE
Atlanta, GA 30329
Toll-free: 800-ACS-2345
Website: **http://www.cancer.org**

American College of Sports Medicine (ACSM)

To receive an ACSM General Information Brochure, send your request and a self-addressed, business-sized envelope with two first-class stamps to the address shown. In addition, ACSM's extensive list of publications can be downloaded from the Internet.

American College of Sports Medicine
P.O. Box 1440
Indianapolis, Indiana 46206-1440
Phone: 317-637-9200
Fax: 317-634-7817
Website: **http://www.acsm.org/sportsmed**

ACSM, headquartered in Indianapolis, Indiana, is the largest, most respected sports medicine and exercise science organization in the world, with more than 17,000 members in almost 70 countries. ACSM's mission is to promote and integrate scientific research, education, and practical applications of sports medicine and exercise science to maintain and enhance physical performance, fitness, health, and quality of life. Working in a wide range of medical specialties, allied health professions, and scientific disciplines, ACSM members are committed to the diagnosis, treatment, and prevention of sports-related injuries and the advancement of the science of exercise.

ACSM certification has become a universally recognized mark of excellence (the "Gold Standard"), with an array of certification publications that help bridge the gap between science and practice; call the ACSM Certification Resource Center at 800-486-5643. Of particular interest is the new *ACSM's Health & Fitness Journal*, which is profiled below.

- Brochures from ACSM

Single copies of these brochures are available free of charge by sending a self-addressed, stamped, business-size envelope to the address listed above. Bulk quantities of each brochure are available (10 brochures for $1). Checks can be sent to the address listed above. Brochure bulk orders of $15 or more can be ordered with a credit card by calling ACSM Public Information at 317-637-9200.

Eating Smart, Even When You're Pressed for Time

Exercise Your Way to Lower Blood Pressure

Fitting Fitness in, Even When You're Pressed for Time

Female Athlete Triad: Amenorrhea, Eating Disorders, and Osteoporosis

Play It Safe: A Guide to Preventing Sports-Related Injuries in Young Athletes

ACSM Health/Fitness Facility Consumer Selection Guide

Fit Over 40

Exercise Lite

Nutrition, Training, and Injury Prevention Guidelines: A Guide for Soccer Players

Nutrition and Sports Performance: A Guide for Physically Active Young People

What Is an Exercise Physiologist?

Sports Medicine Umbrella

Stay Cool to Perform Best

- Slide Presentations from ACSM
    "Introduction to *Healthy People 2000*" ($25)
    "Guidelines for Exercise Training for Healthy Adults" ($25)
    "Female Athlete Triad" ($40)

- Position Paper Lay Summaries from ACSM
    Achieving and Maintaining Physical Fitness in Healthy Adults
    Alcohol in Sports
    Anabolic Steroids in Athletes
    Proper and Improper Weight Loss Programs
    Youth Fitness

- *ACSM's Directory of Graduate Programs in Sports Medicine and Exercise Science*

Annual Directory lists more than 200 colleges and universities offering graduate programs. Schools are listed geographically, with contact information provided, but no ranking is offered.

- *ACSM's Directory of Undergraduate Programs in Sports Medicine and Exercise Science*

Available September 1997. Directory will list colleges and universities throughout the country offering undergraduate programs, with contact information provided, but no ranking of schools.

- *ACSM's Essentials of Sports Medicine*

Discusses the fundamentals of primary care sports medicine, consistent with the subject matter covered in the CAQ. Presents the basic science of sports medicine, medical problems of athletes, sport-specific problems, and anatomical skeletal problems of athletes—all in outline format, allowing for rapid review of material. (ISBN: 0-8151-0157-0)

- *ACSM's Exercise Management for Persons with Chronic Diseases and Disabilities*

Reference for clinical exercise personnel, health lab personnel, personal trainers, and others who work with individuals with disabilities, chronic diseases, or multiple conditions. Text for adapted physical activity and health fitness leadership courses. (ISBN: 0-87322-798-0)

- *ACSM Fitness Book*

Easy-to-read, easy-to-understand advice on how to start an exercise program. (ISBN: 0-88011-460-6)

- *ACSM's Guidelines for Exercise Testing and Prescription* (5th Edition)

Written by ACSM experts, it sets the standards for rehabilitative and preventive exercise and includes knowledge, skills, and abilities (KSAs) underlying each ACSM Certification. (ISBN: 0-683-00023-3)

- *ACSM's Guidelines for the Team Physician* (Five-tape video series)

Series consists of five 20-minute tapes with each tape written and presented by some of the most renowned sports medicine authorities in the essential area of work for the team physician.

- *ACSM's Handbook for the Team Physician*

The definitive handbook for all physicians who treat activity-related, exercise, and athletic injuries. Provides indispensable information on a range of problems that could occur before, during, and after competition, including recognition, assessment techniques, treatment, referral, principles of rehabilitation, and return to play. (ISBN: 0-683-00028-4)

- *ACSM's Health & Fitness Journal*

This bimonthly publication responds to the information needs of fitness instructors, personal trainers, exercise leaders, program managers, and other front-line and fitness professionals. Includes material from the latest exercise science and nutrition research, components of ACSM certification workshops, current topics of interest for the fitness industry, and continuing education credit opportunities.

- *ACSM's Health & Fitness Facility Standards and Guidelines*

Provides those in the health and fitness facility industry with essential guidelines and criteria for establishing and maintaining a safe and proper facility. (ISBN: 0-87322-375-6)

- *ACSM's Resource Manual for Guidelines for Exercise Testing and Prescription* (2nd Edition)

Addresses more than 90% of the behavioral objectives associated with exercise testing and prescription. Publication is a must for ACSM certification candidates and noncandidates alike. (ISBN: 0-8121-1589-9)

- *ACSM's Sports Medicine Review*

A review of primary care sports medicine through the use of board-type questions and answers that are of the same type found in the CAQ in sports medicine. The answers serve as a review of the entire field, with emphasis given to those areas most difficult for physicians to master. (ISBN: 0-8151-0392-1)

- *Cardiac Comeback* Video Series

Three-part series, created to guide low-risk cardiac patients through a progressive home conditioning and education program.

- *Exercise and Sport Sciences Reviews (ESSR)*

Annual hardcover series that reviews current research concerning behavioral, biochemical, biomechanical, clinical, physiological, and rehabilitation topics involving exercise science.

- *Medicine & Science in Sports & Exercise (MSSE)*

ACSM's official monthly journal, featuring original investigations, clinical studies, and comprehensive reviews on current topics in sports medicine and exercise science. (ISSN: 0195-9131)

- *Starting an Exercise Program* Video

Created for use in physicians' offices, this video encourages sedentary viewers to reap the benefits of regular exercise by providing practical guidelines for beginning an exercise program and tips on incorporating exercise into daily routines.

- *Year Book of Sports Medicine*

Nationally recognized editors annually select the best, most relevant journal articles of the year from a survey of more than 950 journals nationwide. The articles are professionally abstracted and followed by clinically relevant commentary by the editors.

American Council on Exercise (ACE)

American Council on Exercise
5820 Oberlin Drive, Suite 102
San Diego, CA 92121-3787
Phone: 619-535-8227
Fax: 619-535-1778
Website: **http://www.acefitness.org**

Established in 1985, ACE is a nonprofit, educational organization committed to enriching quality of life through safe and effective physical activity. It is the largest nonprofit fitness certifying organization in the world.

- *ACE Fit Facts*

One-page information sheets on more than 70 health and fitness topics.

- *ACE FitnessMatters*

ACE FitnessMatters is a bimonthly publication that brings the latest health and fitness news to its readers. A one-year subscription is one of the benefits of ACE's public membership program "Friends of ACE."

- ACE Certification Programs

ACE currently offers certification programs for group fitness instructors, personal trainers, and lifestyle and weight management consultants. ACE certification exams are offered in February, May, August, and November across the United States, at select international locations, and in conjunction with many fitness conventions. For a free exam information brochure, call 800-825-3636.

- Energy²Burn

A unique fitness program designed for elementary school children. By volunteering in local elementary schools, certified ACE instructors serve as role models to other teachers on how to implement the Energy²Burn program.

- Toll-Free Hotlines

Each of the following information services can be reached at 800-825-3636:

  Consumer Fitness Hotline
  Certification Information
  Certified Professional Services Hotline
  Fitness Professional Referral Hotline

American Heart Association

American Heart Association
National Center
7272 Greenville Avenue
Dallas, TX 75231-4596
Phone: 214-373-6300
Website: **http://www.americanheart.org**

Contact your local AHA affiliate directly for a complete listing of materials currently available by simply dialing 800-AHA-USA1.

- *American Heart Walk*

An annual walking event that takes place in the early fall. The event focuses on the importance of exercise as part of a heart-healthy lifestyle, while raising funds for the AHA. The primary emphasis of the American Heart Walk is fundraising; however, it provides an excellent opportunity for physical activity promotion. A comprehensive coordinator's kit is available.

- *The American Heart Association's Statement on Exercise* (revised 1996)

A statement on the benefits and recommendations for physical activity programs for all Americans.

- *AHA Prevention Conference III. Behavior Change and Compliance: Keys to Improving Cardiovascular Health.*

Summary of a workshop held on January 15, 1993, in Monterey, California.

- *Exercise Standards*

Provides revised standards and guidelines for adult exercise testing and training in the laboratory setting. Highly technical and recommended for professional use only. (1980, 1995)

- *Clinical Competence in Exercise Testing*

A statement for physicians from the American College of Physicians (ACA), the American College of Cardiology (ACC), and AHA. Produced by the ACA/ACC/AHA Task Force on Clinical Privileges in Cardiology. Reprint of November 1990.

- *Guidelines for Clinical Exercise Testing Laboratories* (1995)

A statement for health care professionals from the AHA Committee on Exercise and Cardiac Rehabilitation.

- *Guidelines for Exercise Testing* (1997)

A joint statement from the AHA and the ACC, which includes recommendations for men, women, children, and the elderly.

- *Exercise and Your Heart: A Guide to Physical Activity*

Jointly published with the National Heart, Lung and Blood Institute, this booklet presents basic information to help individuals adopt a sensible exercise program as one way of keeping a healthy heart. The booklet includes practical guidelines for starting and sticking with a personal exercise program. (1990, 1993)

- Other public education materials include the following:

    "E" is for Exercise

    Exercise and Your Heart

    Just Move!

    Walking for a Healthy Heart

    Walking . . .The Natural Way to Fun and Fitness

    About Your Heart and Exercise

    Fitting Fitness in—Even When You Are Pressed for Time

Also look for physical activity components of other AHA programs designed for the worksite, healthsite, schoolsite, or community settings, such as the following:

- *Heart at Work* for the worksite
- *Active Partnership* patient recovery kit including numerous materials and a video series covering cardiac event topics, including exercise, stress management, nutrition, smoking cessation, understanding coronary heart disease, and risk-factor control.
- *Heart Power!* supplemental classroom materials for prekindergarten through the 8th grade
- *Jump Rope For Heart*, a jump rope special event for grades 1–6.
- *Hoops For Heart*, a basketball special event for middle schools.
- *HeartRide*, a bicycling special event.
- *Heart Challenge*, an exercise-oriented special event.
- *Search Your Heart*, a church-based heart health program targeting African Americans.
- *Answers by Heart,* 53 patient-education fact sheets on conditions, treatment, tests, lifestyle change, risk reduction, and other topics.

Also look for AHA books and tapes, available in bookstores everywhere or directly from the publisher listed.

- *AHA's The Healthy Heart Walking Book*

Presents the benefits and how-to's of a walking program in simple, motivational language. It also offers charts for tracking progress and a wide range of walking plans based on fitness level, lifestyle, and health goals. Published in 1995 by Macmillan USA. 800-428-5331.

- *AHA's The Healthy Heart Walking Tape*

Narrated by Rita Moreno. Has two 30-minute walking workouts, one for beginners and one for intermediate walkers. Published in 1996 by Simon & Schuster Audio. 800-223-2336.

- *AHA Fitting in Fitness*

Includes charts and hundreds of easy tips to help transform even the most sedentary person into a fitness enthusiast. Published in 1997 by Times Books, a division of Random House. 800-793-2665.

- *AHA's Your Heart: An Owner's Manual*

Covers care, maintenance, and troubleshooting for the heart, with hundreds of ideas on nutrition, exercise, stress reduction, and spotting problems. Published in 1995 by Prentice Hall Career & Personal Development. 800-947-7700.

- *AHA/ACS Living Well, Staying Well* (with the American Cancer Society)

Can help the reader maximize health and minimize the risk of heart disease and cancer. Published in 1996 by Times Books, a division of Random House. 800-793-2665.

- AHA stroke products that focus on exercise include the following:
    Stroke Connection Magazine
    What You Should Know About Stroke
    Stroke Survivor's Workout Video

Boys and Girls Clubs of America

Boys and Girls Clubs of America
1230 West Peachtree Street, NW
Atlanta, GA 30309
Phone: 404-815-5700
Toll-free: 800-854-CLUB
Fax: 404-815-5757

Boys and Girls Clubs of America comprises a national network of more than 2,000 neighborhood-based facilities annually serving some 2.8 million young people, primarily from disadvantaged circumstances. Known as "The Positive Place for Kids," the Clubs provide guidance-oriented character development programs on a daily basis for children 6–18 years old, conducted by a full-time trained professional staff. Key Boys and Girls Club programs emphasize educational achievement, career exploration, drug and alcohol avoidance, health and fitness, gang and violence prevention, cultural enrichment, leadership development, and community service.

Centers for Disease Control and Prevention (CDC), Division of Nutrition and Physical Activity

Centers for Disease Control and Prevention (CDC)
National Center for Chronic Disease Prevention and Health Promotion
Division of Nutrition and Physical Activity
Mail Stop K-46
4770 Buford Highway, NE
Atlanta, GA 30341-3717
Phone: 770-488-5820
Website: **http://www.cdc.gov/nccdphp/dnpa**
E-mail: **ccdinfo@cdc.gov**
Toll-free, 24-hour faxed information line: 1-888-CDC-4NRG or 1-888-232-4674

The Centers for Disease Control and Prevention (CDC), Division of Nutrition and Physical Activity pursues a public health approach to the prevention and management of physical inactivity and poor dietary practices across the life span by conducting surveillance, epidemiologic and behavioral research, applied social marketing and consumer research, intervention research and design, training and education, health promotion and leadership, policy and environmental change, health communication, and partnership development. For a description of selected publications, research, and program areas, visit our website.

Physical Activity and Health: A Report of the Surgeon General

Released in 1996, this landmark document was written in collaboration with the President's Council on Physical Fitness and Sports. To obtain an electronic or printed copy of the full report, the executive summary, the At-A-Glance, and related fact sheets, see resource B, or visit the website **http://www.cdc.gov/nccdphp/sgr/sgr.htm**.

Postgraduate courses in physical activity intervention development and research

- **Physical Activity and Public Health: A Postgraduate Course on Research Directions & Strategies**   Sponsored by the University of South Carolina (USC)Prevention Center and the Centers for Disease Control and Prevention, this eight-day course is directed at postdoctoral personnel and is designed to develop research competencies related to physical activity and public health. Topics include grant-writing skills; research funding opportunities; measurement of physical activity; design of epidemiologic studies; dose-response issues; individual and community interventions; critical research needs on physical activity in women, minorities, and youth; and numerous special topics. Instructional techniques include lectures, small group discussions, individual meetings with faculty, and individual grant writing projects. The faculty consists of a panel of leading researchers on physical activity and public health.

- **Physical Activity and Public Health: A Practitioner's Course on Community Interventions**   Sponsored by the University of South Carolina (USC) Prevention Center and the Centers for Disease Control and Prevention, this five-day course is for practitioners who are involved in or are interested in beginning community-based policy and environmental initiatives to promote physical activity. Topics include epidemiology; community and personal interventions; evaluations; and partnership development. Special sessions include research roundtables, resource updates, and a field trip to a nearby walkable community. The course provides one-on-one and small-group interaction with leading researchers and professional peers.

These postgraduate courses are held each year during the month of September at the beautiful Sea Pines Conference Resort, Hilton Head Island, South Carolina. For more information, check the websites for either the CDC Division of Nutrition and Physical Activity at **http://www.cdc.gov/nccdphp/dnpa** under training opportunities, or the University of South Carolina, School of Public Health, Prevention Research Center at or contact: Russ Pate, Exercise Science Department, USC School of Public Health, Phone: 803-777-9132; Fax: 803-777-8422.

Centers for Disease Control and Prevention (CDC), Division of Adolescent and School Health

Centers for Disease Control and Prevention (CDC)
National Center for Chronic Disease Prevention and Health Promotion
Division of Adolescent and School Health
Mail Stop K-32
4770 Buford Highway, NE
Atlanta, GA 30341-3717
Phone: 770-488-3168
Website: **http://www.cdc.gov/nccdphp/dash**
E-mail: **ccdinfo@cdc.gov**

The Centers for Disease Control and Prevention (CDC), Division of Adolescent and School Health works to prevent the most serious health risks among children, adolescents, and young adults. The Division collaborates with other federal agencies, national nongovernmental organizations, and state and local departments of education, health, and social services to plan and implement four interrelated strategies. These strategies include (a) identifying and monitoring critical health related events and interventions designed to influence those events, (b) synthesizing and applying research to increase the effectiveness of interventions, (c) enabling relevant constituents to plan and implement effective interventions, and (d)evaluating the impact of interventions over time. For a description of selected publications, research, and program areas, visit our website.

Guidelines for School and Community Programs to Promote Lifelong Physical Activity Among Young People

Released in 1997, these guidelines identify strategies most likely to be effective in helping young people adopt and maintain a physically active lifestyle. The guidelines were developed by CDC staff in collaboration with experts from other federal agencies, state agencies, universities, voluntary organizations, and professional associations. To obtain an electronic or printed copy of the full report, the At-A-Glance, and related fact sheets, visit the website: **http:// www.cdc.gov/nccdphp/dash/physact.htm.** See also pages 207–209; 278–279; and 287–290 of this book.

Youth Risk Behavior Surveillance System (YRBSS)

The YRBSS monitors physical activity and five other categories of priority health-risk behaviors that contribute to the leading causes of mortality, morbidity, and social problems among youth and adults in the United States. The system includes national, state, and local school-based surveys of representative samples of 9th through 12th grade students that are conducted biennially using a self-administered questionnaire. For information about the YRBSS or to see YRBSS data, visit the website: **http://www.cdc.gov/nccdphp/dash/yrbs/ov.htm**.

The Combined Health Information Database (CHID): Chronic Disease Prevention File (CDP File)

The **Combined Health Information Database (CHID)** is a federally-produced computerized bibliographic database of health information and health promotion resources. Current CHID producers are the Centers for Disease Control and Prevention (CDC), the National Institutes of Health, the Office of Disease Prevention and Health Promotion, and the Health Resources and Services Administration. At present, CHID has 18 subfiles with more than 100,000 abstracted items that focus on chronic disease prevention and health promotion. Several of the subfiles contain information on physical activity and exercise. These items include bibliographic citations and abstracts for journal articles, books, book chapters, manuals, reports, teaching guides, and other published and unpublished materials. CHID is available for on-line searching through the internet at **http://CHID.nih.gov.**

The **CDP File**, developed by the Editorial and Technical Information Services Branch of the National Center for Chronic Disease Prevention and Health Promotion, CDC, is a CD-ROM containing the following searchable databases with abundant information about health promotion and disease prevention programs and resources:

- Health Promotion and Education Database
- Cancer Prevention and Control Database
- Prenatal Smoking Cessation Database
- Epilepsy Education and Prevention Activities Database
- Combined Database incorporating the above 5 databases
- Smoking and Health Database
- Chronic Disease Prevention Directory Database, which includes the names and addresses of people and organizations who are key contacts in health promotion and disease prevention

- State Profile Database, linking all aspects of the CDP File with state-specific program descriptions and key contact information
- NCCDPHP Publications Database

The **Health Promotion and Education Database (HPED)**, available on CDP file and a subfile of CHID, contains abstracts of journal articles, monographs, proceedings, reports, curricular materials, and unpublished documents describing ongoing health promotion programs and intervention activities. Of this database's approximately 10,000 records, over 5,500 focus on physical activity and exercise.

If you are a health or community professional working to promote health and prevent chronic diseases, the CDP File can be a powerful tool for you. The database facilitates information sharing among program directors and others working to promote health and provides sources and availability information for the resources it describes to help users obtain materials directly.

Updated quarterly, CDP File is available from the Superintendent of Documents, Government Printing Office, Washington, DC 20402, 202-512-1800, for an annual subscription fee of about $96 (Stock #717-145-00000-3). Updates are then sent automatically to subscribers.

For more information on CHID or CDP File, contact:

Technical Information and Editorial Services Branch
National Center for Chronic Disease Prevention and Health Promotion
Centers for Disease Control and Prevention
4770 Buford Highway, NE
Mail Stop K-13
Atlanta, GA 30341-3717
Phone: 770-488-5080
Email: **ccdinfo@cdc.gov**

The Cooper Institute for Aerobics Research

Cooper Institute for Aerobics Research
12330 Preston Road
Dallas, TX 75230
Tel: 972-341-3200
Toll-free: 800-635-7050
Website: **http://www.cooperinst.org**

The Cooper Institute for Aerobics Research was established in 1970 to promote understanding of the relationship between living habits and health, to provide leadership in enhancing the physical and emotional well-being of individuals, and to promote participation in aerobic activity. This nonprofit research center also conducts studies to determine the methods and skills needed to facilitate changes in lifestyles. Among its publications are the following:

- *The Walking Handbook*

An easy-to-read manual written by Susan Johnson, EdD, to help people start and maintain a safe and effective walking program. *The Walking Handbook* is appropriate for use with walking classes or clubs, colleges, school programs, and health clubs; by physicians; or by any individual interested in a walking program. Cost is $7.95 each, plus $4 shipping. Discounts are available on bulk orders; businesses or programs have the option of putting their logo on the front cover.

- *Living with Exercise; Improving Your Health Through Moderate Physical Activity*

A practical book by Steven N. Blair designed for the individual who has considered starting a personal exercise program. Its step-by-step and often humorous approach guides readers into realistic ways of fitting moderate-intensity activities into their daily lives. This book is available for $18.95.

- *Personal Energy Plan (PEP)*

A self-directed 12-week worksite intervention kit initially developed and piloted in 1997 by the Centers for Disease Control and Prevention. Based on social marketing principles and the Stages of Change model, the intervention targets employees at their stage of readiness for healthy eating (encouraging 5 or more fruits and vegetables a day and limiting fat) and moderate physical activity (recommending 30 minutes or more on most days of the week) and seeks to assist persons in making progress along the change continuum.

Human Kinetics

- Academic Books

The foundation of the Human Kinetics publishing program is its academic and professional books. The mission of this division is the publishing of quality resources about all aspects of the physical activity field for physical educators, sports and exercise scientists, sports medicine specialists, fitness instructors, sports management professionals, aquatics specialists, and other professionals in the physical activity field.

Our Academic Books Division offers the most comprehensive list of scholarly and professional books in the physical activity field—over 300 titles in print.

- American Sport Education Program

Human Kinetics pioneered coaching education with the launching of the American Sport Education Program in 1976. The first coaching course was offered in 1981. Today, we provide the most widely used and respected educational courses and resources in the country. They are designed not only for coaches but for sports administrators and parents. Our staff coordinates the 40 national faculty and more than 2,000 instructors who teach our courses across America.

Nearly 300 groups are using the American Sport Education Program, including the National Federation of State High School Associations, the National Recreation and Park Association, the YMCA of the USA, USA Baseball, Pop Warner Football, U.S. Tennis Association, and Special Olympics (various chapters).

- Distance Education

Human Kinetics has created the Distance Education Division to fulfill the need among professionals for ongoing education of professionals in the physical activity field. The focus of this new division is self-study programs, certification preparation, workshops, and distance learning courses that will supply professionals with flexible opportunities for continuing education.

The first self-study program for continuing education credits (CEUs) is the Professional Achievement Self-Study program (PASS). This program is a collaborative effort between the NATA Research and Education Foundation and Human Kinetics to offer a series of self-study courses developed specifically for athletic trainers.

- Journals

Our Journals Division provides up-to-date research and timely reviews on the sports and exercise sciences through over 20 journals. Our journals cover such fields as adapted physical education, biomechanics, dance, nutrition, pediatric exercise, elementary and secondary physical education, sports management, sociology, sports history, motor control, strength/conditioning, and aging. You'll find all our journals listed along with their tables of contents for the past and current year and subscription and order information.

- Software Division

The Software Division develops software products as well as online services through our website. Those services include InfoKinetics: event and association listings, links to other physical activity websites, journals, career information, and classified ads such as job listings.

- Trade Books

As the demand for fitness and sports information has increased, Human Kinetics has published to fill that need. Our Trade Books Division publishes for the consumer market—specifically for fitness enthusiasts, sports participants, and coaches. The division's strength has been its ability to present authoritative books in attractive packages. Our authors are experts—top coaches, athletes, teachers, and writers—who provide special insight into coaching, participating, or understanding their areas of sports and fitness.

With nearly 300 titles in print, our Trade Books Division is recognized as the authoritative source for sports and fitness information.

- YMCA Program Store

Since 1984, Human Kinetics has been the official publisher for the YMCA of the USA. We also distribute books, instructor manuals, and educational program accessories (such as emblems, certificates, videos, and software). Under the name of the YMCA Program Store, we distribute nearly 1,000 different items for YMCA programs in aquatics, fitness, camping, child care, and youth sports.

Human Kinetics
P.O. Box 5076
1607 N. Market St.
Champaign, IL 61825-5076
Toll-free: 800-747-4457
Fax: 217-351-2674
Website: **http://www.humankinetics.com**

National Association for Sport and Physical Education (NASPE) — An Association of the American Alliance for Health, Physical Education, Recreation and Dance

Ask for a complete catalog of AAHPERD Publications. To order materials call 800-321-0789.

National Association for Sport and Physical Education
1900 Association Drive
Reston, VA 20191
Phone: 703-476-3410
Fax: 703-476-8316
Website: **http://www.aahperd.org/naspe/naspe.html**

NASPE, an association of the American Alliance for Health, Physical Education, Recreation and Dance, is devoted exclusively to improving the total sports and physical education experience in America. The primary focus of this national association is on educating the American public about the importance of physical education for all children and youth. NASPE has been successful in facilitating the national consensus and development of standards for physical education, coaching, teacher education, exercise science, and sports management programs. Its membership consists of professionals who study human movement or deliver sports and physical activity programs, including teachers, coaches, physical education administrators, fitness specialists, researchers, and sports medicine professionals. Through its members, NASPE develops and supports quality sports and physical activity programs that promote healthy behaviors and individual well-being.

Among its many publications, NASPE produces the following:

- *Moving Into the Future: National Physical Education Standards: A Guide to Content and Assessment*

This explains the voluntary national standards for K–12 school physical education and tells you what students should know and be able to do. These seven standards are based on the definition of a physically educated person and the original 20 outcomes of quality physical education. (1995)

- *Quality Coaches, Quality Sports: National Standards for Athletic Coaches*

A five-level program consisting of 8 domains, 37 standards, and over 300 competencies. The standards provide a common basis for all organizations that certify, evaluate, and/or select coaches. (1995)

- *Sport Management Program Standards and Review Protocol*

All the information to prepare for sport management program review; standards at the undergraduate, master's, and doctoral levels; overview and timeliness for the program review; application forms and fee structures. (1994)

- *Basic Standards for Professional Preparation in Exercise Science*

Includes standards to help colleges and universities plan their programs to prepare students for careers in applied exercise science. (1995)

- *National Standards for Beginning Physical Education Teachers*

A delineation based on a national consensus of the profession for what beginning teachers of physical education should know and be able to do. This document serves as the basis for teacher certification and program development for preparation of physical education teachers. (1995)

- *The New Leadership Paradigm for Physical Education: What We Really Need to Lead*

This book provides important information for the leaders who will chart the course of physical education in this era of curriculum and educational reform. It acknowledges the current state of affairs and provides a practical approach to current leadership theories as applied to the many duties of a physical education leader. In addition, it takes into consideration the various individuals (e.g., state director, regional director, district director, high school, middle school, and elementary school teacher) who currently assume leadership roles in the profession. (1998)

- *Physical Education Program Improvement and Self-Study Guides*

For use by physical educators in developing and implementing programs. These documents provide the essential ingredients in curriculum, instruction, assessment, and the learning environment that will produce quality middle school and high school physical education programs and services for students. (1998)

- *Physical Education Program Guidelines and Appraisal Checklist for Elementary School*

Instruments for developing and evaluating physical education programs based on research, accepted practice, and federal legislation. Teachers, administrators, and parents can all use these great checklists. (1994)

- *Including Students With Disabilities in Regular Physical Education*

NASPE (COPEC) and AAALF (APAC) developed a position statement on including individuals with disabilities in physical education. This paper outlines the background and origins of the inclusion concept. This 20-page pamphlet includes citations from federal legislation and research supporting the value of including all students in common learning environments and situations. Suggestions are also included to facilitate effective inclusion of all students in physical education experiences. (1995)

- *Concepts of Physical Education: What Every Student Needs to Know*

This book is an important piece for next steps in implementing a quality education program based on the National Standards for Physical Education. It provides concepts and content related to each of the subdisciplines of physical activity and suggests ways to apply them to K–12 physical education. (1998)

- *Developing Strength in Children: A Comprehensive Guide*

Excellent, comprehensive information about strength training for children—this book deals directly with the controversy about the safety and effectiveness of resistance training for children. An excellent resource, this book outlines numerous program design models as well as sport-specific training programs. It provides creative ways to develop strength in children and keep them motivated even when budgets are too limited to purchase equipment. (1996)

- *Ideas III: Middle School Physical Activities for a Fit Generation*

This publication is packed full of practical and exciting instructional ideas. Master teachers from across the country have provided 31 activities that fall under the categories of fitness games, individual activities, team activities, rhythm and gymnastics, initiatives, and special events. (1996)

- *Principles of Safety in Physical Education and Sport* (2nd Edition)

Explores the safety factors that must be considered in teaching sports and physical activities. Checklists, outlines, and commentary by experts provide information needed to conduct the safest possible programs. (1994)

- *Echoes II: Influences in Elementary Physical Education*

A project of the NASPE Council on Physical Education for Children, this collection of significant writings since 1980—grouped in categories of perspectives, foundations, curriculum, pedagogy, teacher education and research—contains articles with historical significance, contemporary relevance and direction for the future. These stimulating, innovative, and useful physical education ideas for children will challenge professionals to rethink and revise programs. (1994)

- *Physical Activity for Elementary School*

This publication presents physical activity guidelines specifically designed to meet the developmental needs of children. For use by physical education teachers, classroom teachers, youth physical activity leaders, administrators, parents, physicians, and others dedicated to promoting physically active lifestyles among children. (1998)

- *Are Your Children Fit to Achieve?*

New advocacy pamphlet to reach parents with the importance of physical education and physical activity. Package of 50. (1998)

- *Shape of the Nation*

A national survey of state physical education requirements, this document provides an overview of state mandates, who is teaching physical education, and examples of special state needs and initiatives. (1998)

- *Motor Development: Research and Reviews,* Volume 1

This book assembles in one place a collection of motor development research studies and reviews. The book is in two parts, an original research section that includes investigations on contemporary problems in motor development, and a reviews section that contains synthesized articles on critical issues by leading scholars in motor development. The reviews section is especially valuable to graduate students and practitioners who are less familiar with the technical aspects of the subject matter. (1997)

National Coalition for Promoting Physical Activity (NCPPA)

National Coalition for Promoting Physical Activity
P.O. Box 1440
Indianapolis, IN 46206-1440
Phone: 317-637-0349
Fax: 317-634-7817
Website: **http://www.ncppa.org/ncppa**

The NCPPA began as a fledgling in 1995, the brainchild of three lead organizations: the American Alliance for Health, Physical Education, Recreation and Dance (AAHPERD); the American College of Sports Medicine (ACSM); and the American Heart Association (AHA). Over a two-year period, via a series of meetings and with legal counsel, and three additional lead organizations later—Association for Worksite Health Promotion (AWHP); the International Health, Racquet & Sportsclub Association (IHRSA); and the National Association of Governors' Councils on Physical Fitness and Sports (NAGCPFS)—the NCPPA has been established as a 501c(4) tax-exempt, social welfare corporation.

As of February 2, 1998, the NCPPA elected a Board of Directors and formed committees of volunteers to plan and implement the many projects of the Coalition. The committees are as follows: administration/finance, advocacy, communications, executive, membership/sponsorship, program, state coalitions.

The NCPPA represents a collaborative partnership among private, public, and industry organizations whose purpose is to inspire all Americans to lead a physically active lifestyle to enhance their health and quality of life. NCPPA believes all adults and children should participate in regular moderate or vigorous physical activity, with the minimal goal of Americans accumulating at least 30 minutes of moderate physical activity most, if not all, days of the week. Persons meeting that guideline may well derive additional health and fitness benefits by becoming more physically active or including more vigorous physical activity in a regular routine. The National Coalition also believes that optimal progress across the nation cannot be made without a program that communicates, educates, and advocates favorable policies and practices at the federal, state, and local levels.

The eight major initiatives of the NCPPA are grassroots efforts via formation of state coalitions; health communications campaign; political education and advocacy; behavior change campaign; information collections and distribution via an Information Resource Center; attention to the need for enhancement of existing programs; support of *Healthy People 2000* and *2010* initiatives; and encouragement of organizational outreach efforts.

NCPPA Mission Statement: To unite the strengths of public, private, and industry efforts into a collaborative partnership to inspire Americans to lead physically-active lifestyles to enhance their health and quality of life.

National Heart, Lung, and Blood Institute (NHLBI)

Unless otherwise noted, contact the NHLBI Information Center for single copies:

NHLBI Information Center
P.O. Box 30105
Bethesda, MD 20824-0105
Phone: 301-251-1222
Fax: 301-251-1223

National Heart, Lung, and Blood Institute
National Institutes of Health
Building 31, Room 4A-21
Bethesda, MD 20892
Phone: 301-251-1222
Fax: 301-251-1223
Website: **http://www.nhlbi.nih.gov/nhlbi/nhlbi.htm**

- *NIH Consensus Development Conference Statement on Physical Activity and Cardiovascular Health, December 18-20, 1995.*

This summary report reviews the scientific evidence linking physical activity and cardiovascular disease and provides recommendations for the public. A complete copy of the panel report is available by calling 800-NIH-OMAR (644-6627) or via the Internet at **http://text.nlm.nih.gov**.

- *Exercise and Your Heart: A Guide to Physical Activity*

This booklet provides up-to-date information on the effects of physical activity on the heart and offers practical guidelines for starting and staying on an exercise program. It notes the importance of moderate levels of physical activity to cardiovascular health. In addition, it describes the benefits and risks of exercise, how to reduce the chances of heart attack, myths about exercise, ways to avoid injuries, and two sample physical activity programs. Originally developed by the NHLBI, this revised guide was produced through the collaborative efforts of the American Heart Association and the NHLBI. (Revised 1993) ($1.50)

- *Check Your Physical Activity and Heart Disease I.Q.*

This 12-question true or false quiz addresses the relationship of physical activity to heart health. The quiz is presented in a reproducible format. (1995)

- *The Sports Guide: NHLBI Planning Guide for Cardiovascular Disease Risk Reduction Projects at Sporting Events*

A thorough guide to planning cardiovascular education and screening events in conjunction with sporting events, such as baseball games, tennis matches, and bowling or golf tournaments. Such events effectively target young and middle-aged adults, males, and minority populations who may not be served by existing health education programs. (1995) ($3.00)

- *Check Your Healthy Heart I.Q.*

This brochure uses a true or false format to educate readers about heart disease and how to reduce all of the different risk factors for heart disease. (1992) (single copy free)

- *Facts About Heart Disease and Women: Be Physically Active*

This two-page fact sheet provides information on the benefits of low- to moderate-intensity exercise in lowering the risk of heart disease among women. It offers practical suggestions on making opportunities for exercise throughout the day and outlines a plan for starting a personal walking program. (1994)

National Recreation and Park Association (NRPA)

National Recreation and Park Association
22377 Belmont Ridge Rd.
Ashburn, VA 20148
Phone: 703-858-0784
Fax: 703-858-0794
Website: **http://www.nrpa.org**
E-mail: **info@nrpa.org**

The NRPA is a national not-for-profit professional organization dedicated to promoting comprehensive resources for parks, recreation, and conservation. National projects focus on health and physical activity, youth in at-risk environments, and intergenerational opportunities. The educational and program materials produced by NRPA include the following:

- *July is National Recreation and Parks Month!*

Each February, NRPA makes available an affordable and reproducible kit of information for use in National Recreation and Parks Month (July of each year).

- *Recreation Professional's Resource Guide for Fitness and Wellness*

This valuable resource directory was developed as a joint project between NRPA and the American Running and Fitness Association (ARFA) for the National Fitness and Wellness Coalition. Formatted as a desk reference, this publication provides information and fact sheets, relevant statistics, toll-free fitness numbers, a calendar of health observances, plus the names and addresses of dozens of national sports or fitness groups, community resource groups, seminar ideas, and more. Published at least every 2 years with current information.

- National Youth Fun and Fitness Program

This 6-week initiative for children of all abilities, ages 6–12 years, is sponsored in conjunction with the President's Council on Physical Fitness and Sports. The fun-filled, curriculum-based program features six theme weeks of cardiovascular fitness, nutrition, muscular strength, substance abuse, family fitness, and lifetime fitness choices. A coordinator's kit offers unique ideas, program worksheets, and planning guides. In 1992, the Fun and Fitness Program will be expanded to new audiences: preschoolers, minorities in the urban setting, and year-round program resources.

• National Therapeutic Recreation Society Publications

Provides information on therapeutic recreation programming ideas, specifics of the Americans With Disabilities Act, and innovative resources for program development.

The Leisure and Aging section has many resources appropriate for physical activity promotion among older Americans, including *Leisure Site Guidelines for People Over 55.*

This practical book suggests what facilities are needed and how to develop them so that they will be suitable for use by people as they grow older. The book assumes that many people who are involved with the planning, design, or operation of a leisure facility know relatively little about the leisure interests, needs, and capabilities of older people.

• *Active Living/Healthy Lifestyles Promotion Kit*

Since 1995, NRPA has been involved in a national campaign to promote healthier active lifestyles among all Americans. The 1996 national launch of the public education project was successfully implemented in over 550 communities. The Promotion Kit is designed to help recreation and health promotion professionals design messages and programs encouraging adults to become more physically active through fun recreation experiences. The project will also help local park and recreation agencies serve as a catalyst in developing active and healthy communities.

President's Council on Physical Fitness and Sports (PCPFS)

President's Council on Physical Fitness and Sports
200 Independence Ave. SW
Hubert H. Humphrey Bldg. Room 738H
Washington, DC 20201-0004
Phone: 202-690-9000
E-mail: **cspain@osophs.dhhs.gov**

The PCPFS was established in 1956 through an executive order by President Dwight D. Eisenhower as part of a national campaign to help shape up America's younger generation. Today, the PCPFS serves as an advisory body to the president and to the U.S. secretary of health and human services on matters involving physical activity, fitness, and sports that enhance and improve health. Through programs and initiatives that reach millions of Americans each year, the President's Council encourages regular participation in sports and physical activities for people of all ages.

• The President's Challenge Physical Fitness Awards Program

An awards program that recognizes and motivates students aged 6–17 years in meeting challenging levels of fitness. Originated in 1966 and revised in 1975 and again in 1985, with options incorporated in 1997, the program measures cardiorespiratory and muscular endurance, muscular strength, flexibility, and agility. Students may win one of four awards:

1. The Presidential Physical Fitness Award, recognizing students who score at or above the 85th percentile on all five test items
2. The National Physical Fitness Award for those achieving a score at or above the 50th percentile
3. The Participant Physical Fitness Award for those whose scores fall below the 50th percentile on one or more of the five test items
4. The Health Fitness Award for students who maintain a healthy level of fitness

Each award has an emblem and certificate signed by the president commending the student on his or her level of fitness. Children with physical disabilities may qualify for all four. Programs associated with the President's Challenge include the Physical Fitness Demonstration Centers and the State Champion Award.

- Presidential Sports Award

An awards program that recognizes participation in a regular program of physical activity, exercise, and sports. Individuals 6 years of age and older may qualify for the award in one or more of 69 different sports and fitness activity categories. Specific requirements for each activity have been established for a four-month period. Upon meeting the qualifying standards, participants receive a personalized presidential certificate of achievement, a blazer emblem, and a congratulatory letter.

- National Physical Fitness and Sports Month

Each year since 1983, May has been designated as National Physical Fitness and Sports Month in a major promotional effort to help "Shape Up America." Agencies and organizations are encouraged to conduct special events throughout the month to call attention to local physical activity and fitness programs and services.

The President's Council produces numerous publications, which are available free of charge, including:

> *Kids in Action* (fitness for children ages 2–6)
>
> *Get Fit: A Handbook for Youth Ages 6–17*
>
> *The Presidential Sports Award*
>
> *One Step at a Time: An Introduction to Running*
>
> *The Physician's Rx: Exercise*
>
> *Pep Up Your Life*
>
> *Exercise and Weight Control*
>
> *Fitness Fundamentals: Guidelines for Personal Exercise Programs*
>
> *The Nolan Ryan Fitness Guide*

- *President's Council on Physical Fitness and Sports Research Digest*

A synopsis of the latest scientific knowledge on physical activity and fitness research findings presented in a manner that is usable and easy to understand. A valuable source of practical information for professionals in the field, including teachers, coaches, and physicians.

National Association of Governor's Councils on Physical Fitness and Sports

National Association of Governor's Councils on Physical Fitness and Sports
201 South Capitol Avenue, Suite 560
Indianapolis, IN 46225
Phone: 317-237-5630
Website: **http://www.fitnesslink.com/Govcouncil/**

The National Association of Governor's Councils on Physical Fitness and Sports was established in 1979 as a nonprofit organization. It currently represents more than 40 state and local affiliates of governor's councils throughout the United States. While each state council is a unique expression of the governor, legislature, and people of the state it represents, all governor's councils are committed to promoting fitness, health, and sports activities for persons of all ages and abilities.

The national association provides technical support and guidance in developing collaborative partnerships, implementing public awareness campaigns, disseminating creative approaches to fitness and healthy lifestyle concerns, drafting model legislation, and implementing physical activity promotion programs.

Stanford Center for Research in Disease Prevention

For a complete listing of educational materials available from the Health Promotion Resource Center, you may request their recent *Materials Catalog*.

Health Promotion Resource Center (HPRC)
Stanford Center for Research in Disease Prevention
730 Welch Road, Suite B
Palo Alto, CA 94304
Phone: 650-723-0003

The HPRC serves as the dissemination arm of the Stanford Center for Research in Disease Prevention (SCRDP), administered through the Stanford University School of Medicine. The HPRC supports SCRDP's educational mission by maximizing the public benefit of the materials developed for SCRDP's nonprofit, public service status. HPRC proceeds are used for product distribution, customization, revision, development, promotion, and licensing, and to further the mission of the SCRDP. The HPRC is governed by the SCRDP Management Committee and Dr. Wes Alles, director of the Stanford Health Improvement Program (HIP), who also directs the HPRC.

The HPRC produces a catalog of over one hundred health promotion materials, including "how-to" print and video materials for health promotion professionals, as well as materials in English and Spanish designed for the public. Print materials range from brochures and booklets to program guides. Content areas include general heart health, blood pressure, weight control, nutrition, smoking, exercise, injury prevention, alcohol and other drugs, youth, adolescent pregnancy, stress management, mental health, and aging. The HPRC also distributes products of research from other sources.

Most of HPRC's materials for the general public were developed for use in SCRDP's "Five City Project," a community-based study in heart disease prevention. With the close of that study in 1986, SCRDP revised materials for general use, and undertook the development of publications and videos to make the expertise of the Center available to others in the health promotion field. In cooperation with SCRDP scientists, the HPRC updates materials as appropriate. These materials can be used in a variety of settings: classrooms, worksites, community or statewide interventions; they can be used independently of any program or to supplement existing programs. Among SCRDP's most popular materials are the self-help kits, which have been used extensively by HMOs and worksites.

The HPRC has sold well over 1.3 million items to over 9,000 customers since its inception in 1986. HPRC customers include health departments, hospitals, worksites, and insurance organizations. Community health organizations, clinics, state and federal agencies, schools and universities also purchase its materials.

The HPRC responds to requests regarding the tailoring, copyright, and licensing of SCRDP materials. Additional services available through the HPRC include Information Center health promotion database searches, the Stanford HIP health risk assessment and counseling program, and health promotion consulting and training for community and worksite groups.

South Carolina Prevention Research Center

South Carolina Prevention Research Center
University of South Carolina, School of Public Health
Columbia, SC 29208
Phone: 803-777-4253
Director: Barbara E. Ainsworth, PhD, MPH
Project Theme: Promoting Health Through Physical Activity

- Listserv for Physical Activity Advocates

The Physical Activity and Public Health On-Line Network is a listserv advancing public health approaches to promoting physical activity. Members include a national network of public health practitioners, researchers, and interested others. A listserv is a forum for an electronic discussion. When a member of the listserv sends a message to the listserv, it is e-mailed to all members of the list, and any member can reply. The reply is also sent to the entire list. This is an excellent way to get advice from colleagues, to share successes, and to pass on new information. Archives of past discussions are available at the USC Prevention Research Center's website, **http://prevention.sph.sc.edu.**

To join the listserv, send an e-mail message to **LISTSERV@VM.SC.EDU.** Include the following command in the text of the message: SUB PHYS-ACT yourfirstname yourlastname. Do not include any other text in the message, including an electronic signature.

For more information or assistance, contact Regina Fields at e-mail address **RMFields@sph.sc.edu** or telephone number 803-777-4159.

- Electronic Newsletter About Physical Activity

The USC Prevention Research Center Notes is a monthly e-mail newsletter with current information about physical activity and public health. The newsletter includes:

- Brief updates of current journal articles
- Training opportunities—conferences, workshops
- Notices of new reports, materials, and resources
- Current policy issues
- Recommended websites
- Reminders of national health observances
- Updates from national organizations

To subscribe, e-mail Steven Saniti, **SJSaniti@sph.sc.edu**, with your name, title, and organizational affiliation. There is no subscription cost. Past issues are available at the USC Prevention Research Center's website, **http:// prevention.sph.sc.edu.**

National Senior Games Organization

National Senior Games Organization
3032 Old Forge Dr.
Baton Rouge, LA 70802
Phone: 504-379-7337
Fax: 504-379-7343
E-mail: **nsga@idsmail.com**

The NSGA is the national organization that sanctions and coordinates the efforts of senior games organizations across the country. The NSGA presently serves 50 member organizations and well over 250,000 constituents.

The NSGA also governs the National Senior Games—the Senior Olympics—held every two years. The 1999 National Senior Games will be held October 19–29, 1999, at *Disney's Wide World of Sports* complex in Orlando, Florida. The 2001 National Senior Games will be held in Baton Rouge, Louisiana. Plans for 2000 Winter National Senior Games are unfolding.

The NSGA was formerly known as the United States National Senior Sports Organization. NSGA moved its headquarters from St. Louis, Missouri, to Baton Rouge, Louisiana, in November 1997.

The NSGA is a not-for-profit organization that is dedicated to promoting healthy lifestyles for seniors through education, fitness, and sports. By fostering athletic competition, wellness and education programs, and research initiatives, the NSGA assists seniors in achieving value and quality in their lives.

Wellness Councils of America (WELCOA)

Wellness Councils of America
Community Health Plaza, Suite 311
7101 Newport Avenue
Omaha, NE 68152-2175
Phone: 402-572-3590

WELCOA is a national nonprofit membership organization dedicated to promoting healthier lifestyles for all Americans, especially through health promotion activities at the workplace. The organization has a nationwide network of locally affiliated Wellness Councils and direct memberships serving thousands of organizations and their employees. Also, WELCOA acts as a national clearinghouse and information center on corporate health promotion for companies everywhere. WELCOA has set the standards for measuring the effectiveness of corporate health promotion programs; companies that meet the rigorous standards earn the coveted Well Workplace Award and are listed on WELCOA's roster of "America's Healthiest Companies."

WELCOA publishes a number of corporate health promotion materials, including the following:

- *Healthy YOUniverse*

A monthly newsletter providing employees with the most up-to-date, practical information about health issues.

- *Just for You!*

A series of interactive brochures designed to provide employees with current health information on a variety of health topics.

- *Health Promotion Sourcebook for Small Business*

A text written and published by Wellness Councils of America, sponsored by Metropolitan Life. (1998)

- *Healthy, Wealthy & Wise: Fundamentals of Workplace Health Promotion* (3rd Edition)

A text published by Wellness Councils of America. (1993; updated in 1995)

- Health Trip

An incentive campaign designed to increase awareness about the benefits of regular physical activity and adopting other healthy lifestyle behaviors. Developed in support of the Centers for Disease Control and Prevention National Partnership Program. (1996)

- *The Healthy Workplace: Health Fairs for Your Wealthfare*

Written by Fern Carness and colleagues. A valuable resource for those planning health fair events in the workplace, or throughout the community. (1995)

- *Health Promotion for All: Strategies for Reaching Diverse Populations at the Workplace*

Written by Stephen Ramirez. (1994)

- *"What a Great Idea!" Box: Healthy Suggestions to Save Your Company Time and Money*

Produced by Judy Creiner, this idea kit devotes a section to physical activity and recreation. (1995)

- *This is Corporate Wellness and Its Bottom Line Benefits*

Free to those who request it, this brochure is a quick and easy-to-read summary of the best research results proving that wellness works.

YMCA–USA

For more information on Y programs, contact your local YMCA.

National Council of Young Men's Christian Associations of the United States of America
101 North Wacker Drive
Chicago, IL 60606
Phone: 312-977-0031
Fax: 312-977-9063
Website: **http://www.ymca.net/**

YMCAs collectively are the nation's largest community service organization, providing values-based programs that promote the healthy development of children and teens, support families, and strengthen communities. YMCAs are at the heart of community life in neighborhoods and towns across the nation. They work to meet the health and social service needs of 14.5 million men, women, and children. Nationwide, Ys help people develop values and behavior that are consistent with Christian principles: caring, honesty, respect, and responsibility. YMCAs are for men, women, and children of all faiths, races, abilities, ages, and incomes; no one is turned away for inability to pay. YMCAs' greatest strength is in the people they bring together.

Long known for their community-based health and fitness programs, YMCAs teach children to swim, offer exercise classes for people with disabilities, and lead adult aerobics. They also offer hundreds of other programs in response to community needs, including day camp for kids, child care (the Ys collectively are the nation's largest not-for-profit provider), teen clubs, environmental programs, substance abuse prevention, youth sports, family nights, job training, international exchange, and many more. YMCAs are at work in more than 130 countries around the world, serving more than 30 million people.

Resource B

Excerpts from *Physical Activity and Health: A Report of the Surgeon General*

On the following pages, you will find several resources that excerpt information from *Physical Activity and Health: A Report of the Surgeon General* (1996). The report can also be viewed at the following website: **http://www.cdc.gov/nccdphp/sgr/sgr.htm.** Please note that the information in this resource is published in its original form and any addresses or websites contained in these excerpts may not be up-to-date.

These resources provide good snapshots of current physical activity-related information that you can share with your target population, your program partners, or your coworkers.

Though not excerpted from the Surgeon General's Report, *Promoting Lifelong Physical Activity:* At-A-Glance 1997 (page 287) also deals with physical activity and may provide your target population with important information in an easy-to-digest format.

A Report of the Surgeon General

Physical Activity and Health

At-A-Glance
1996

A NEW VIEW OF PHYSICAL ACTIVITY

This report brings together, for the first time, what has been learned about physical activity and health from decades of research. Among its major findings:

- People who are usually inactive can improve their health and well-being by becoming even moderately active on a regular basis.
- Physical activity need not be strenuous to achieve health benefits.
- Greater health benefits can be achieved by increasing the amount (duration, frequency, or intensity) of physical activity.

THE BENEFITS OF REGULAR PHYSICAL ACTIVITY

Regular physical activity that is performed on most days of the week reduces the risk of developing or dying from some of the leading causes of illness and death in the United States. Regular physical activity improves health in the following ways:

- Reduces the risk of dying prematurely.
- Reduces the risk of dying from heart disease.
- Reduces the risk of developing diabetes.
- Reduces the risk of developing high blood pressure.
- Helps reduce blood pressure in people who already have high blood pressure.
- Reduces the risk of developing colon cancer.
- Reduces feelings of depression and anxiety.
- Helps control weight.
- Helps build and maintain healthy bones, muscles, and joints.
- Helps older adults become stronger and better able to move about without falling.
- Promotes psychological well-being.

A MAJOR PUBLIC HEALTH CONCERN

Given the numerous health benefits of physical activity, the hazards of being inactive are clear. Physical inactivity is a serious, nationwide problem. Its scope poses a public health challenge for reducing the national burden of unnecessary illness and premature death.

U.S. DEPARTMENT OF HEALTH AND HUMAN SERVICES
Centers for Disease Control and Prevention
National Center for Chronic Disease Prevention and Health Promotion
The President's Council on Physical Fitness and Sports

The Nation's Prevention Agency
Centers for Disease Control and Prevention

The President's Council on Physical Fitness and Sports

WHAT IS A MODERATE AMOUNT OF PHYSICAL ACTIVITY?

As the examples listed in the box show, a moderate amount of physical activity* can be achieved in a variety of ways. People can select activities that they enjoy and that fit into their daily lives. Because amount of activity is a function of duration, intensity, and frequency, the same amount of activity can be obtained in longer sessions of moderately intense activities (such as brisk walking) as in shorter sessions of more strenuous activities (such as running):[†]

EXAMPLES OF MODERATE AMOUNTS OF ACTIVITY

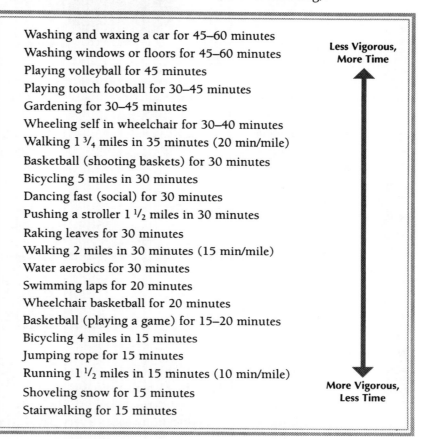

Washing and waxing a car for 45–60 minutes

Washing windows or floors for 45–60 minutes

Playing volleyball for 45 minutes

Playing touch football for 30–45 minutes

Gardening for 30–45 minutes

Wheeling self in wheelchair for 30–40 minutes

Walking 1 ¾ miles in 35 minutes (20 min/mile)

Basketball (shooting baskets) for 30 minutes

Bicycling 5 miles in 30 minutes

Dancing fast (social) for 30 minutes

Pushing a stroller 1 ½ miles in 30 minutes

Raking leaves for 30 minutes

Walking 2 miles in 30 minutes (15 min/mile)

Water aerobics for 30 minutes

Swimming laps for 20 minutes

Wheelchair basketball for 20 minutes

Basketball (playing a game) for 15–20 minutes

Bicycling 4 miles in 15 minutes

Jumping rope for 15 minutes

Running 1 ½ miles in 15 minutes (10 min/mile)

Shoveling snow for 15 minutes

Stairwalking for 15 minutes

Less Vigorous, More Time

More Vigorous, Less Time

*A moderate amount of physical activity is roughly equivalent to physical activity that uses approximately 150 Calories (kcal) of energy per day, or 1,000 Calories per week.

[†]Some activities can be performed at various intensities; the suggested durations correspond to expected intensity of effort.

PRECAUTIONS FOR A HEALTHY START

To avoid soreness and injury, individuals contemplating an increase in physical activity should start out slowly and gradually build up to the desired amount to give the body time to adjust. People with chronic health problems, such as heart disease, diabetes, or obesity, or who are at high risk for these problems should first consult a physician before beginning a new program of physical activity. Also, men over age 40 and women over age 50 who plan to begin a new *vigorous* physical activity program should consult a physician first to be sure they do not have heart disease or other health problems.

Adults

- More than 60 percent of adults do not achieve the recommended amount of regular physical activity. In fact, 25 percent of all adults are not active at all.
- Inactivity increases with age and is more common among women than men and among those with lower income and less education than among those with higher income or education.

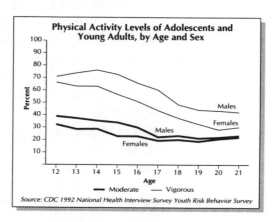

Adults

Regular Vigorous*

Both Regular Vigorous* and Regular Sustained†

Regular Sustained†

Inactive

Not Regularly Active

*Regular Vigorous–20 minutes 3 times per week of vigorous intensity
†Regular Sustained–30 minutes 5 times per week of any intensity
Source: CDC 1992 Behavioral Risk Factor Survey

Adolescents and Young Adults

- Nearly half of young people aged 12–21 are not vigorously active on a regular basis.
- Physical activity declines dramatically with age during adolescence.
- Female adolescents are much less physically active than male adolescents.

Physical Activity Levels of Adolescents and Young Adults, by Age and Sex

Percent / Age

Males / Females / Males / Females

— Moderate — Vigorous

Source: CDC 1992 National Health Interview Survey Youth Risk Behavior Survey

High School Students

- In high school, enrollment in daily physical education classes dropped from 42 percent in 1991 to 25 percent in 1995.
- Only 19 percent of all high school students are physically active for 20 minutes or more in physical education classes every day during the school week.

This report identifies promising ways to help people include more physical activity in their daily lives.

- Well-designed programs in schools to increase physical activity in physical education classes have been shown to be effective.
- Carefully planned counseling by health care providers and worksite activity programs can increase individuals' physical activity levels.
- Promising approaches being tried in some communities around the nation include opening school buildings and shopping malls for walking before or after regular hours, as well as building bicycle and walking paths separated from automobile traffic. Revising building codes to require accessible stairwells is another idea that has been suggested.

Older Adults

No one is too old to enjoy the benefits of regular physical activity. Of special interest to older adults is evidence that muscle-strengthening exercises can reduce the risk of falling and fracturing bones and can improve the ability to live independently.

Parents

Parents can help their children maintain a physically active lifestyle by providing encouragement and opportunities for physical activity. Family events can include opportunities for everyone in the family to be active.

Teenagers

Regular physical activity improves strength, builds lean muscle, and decreases body fat. It can build stronger bones to last a lifetime.

Dieters

Regular physical activity burns Calories and preserves lean muscle mass. It is a key component of any weight loss effort and is important for controlling weight.

People with High Blood Pressure

Regular physical activity helps lower blood pressure.

People Feeling Anxious, Depressed, or Moody

Regular physical activity improves mood, helps relieve depression, and increases feelings of well-being.

People with Arthritis

Regular physical activity can help control joint swelling and pain. Physical activity of the type and amount recommended for health has not been shown to cause arthritis.

People with Disabilities

Regular physical activity can help people with chronic, disabling conditions improve their stamina and muscle strength and can improve psychological well-being and quality of life by increasing the ability to perform activities of daily life.

For more information contact:

Centers for Disease Control and Prevention
National Center for Chronic Disease Prevention and Health Promotion
Division of Nutrition and Physical Activity, MS K-46
4770 Buford Highway, NE
Atlanta, Georgia 30341
1-888-CDC-4NRG or 1-888-232-4674 (Toll Free)
http://www.cdc.gov

The President's Council on Physical Fitness and Sports
Box SG
Suite 250
701 Pennsylvania Avenue, NW
Washington, DC 20004

Physical Activity and Health

A Report of the Surgeon General
Executive Summary

U.S. DEPARTMENT OF HEALTH AND HUMAN SERVICES
Centers for Disease Control and Prevention
National Center for Chronic Disease Prevention and Health Promotion
The President's Council on Physical Fitness and Sports

The Nation's Prevention Agency

Centers for Disease Control and Prevention

The President's
Council on
Physical Fitness
and Sports

Message from Donna E. Shalala
Secretary of Health and Human Services

The United States has led the world in understanding and promoting the benefits of physical activity. In the 1950s, we launched the first national effort to encourage young Americans to be physically active, with a strong emphasis on participation in team sports. In the 1970s, we embarked on a national effort to educate Americans about the cardiovascular benefits of vigorous activity, such as running and playing basketball. And in the 1980s and 1990s, we made breakthrough findings about the health benefits of moderate-intensity activities, such as walking, gardening, and dancing.

Now, with the publication of this first Surgeon General's report on physical activity and health, which I commissioned in 1994, we are poised to take another bold step forward. This landmark review of the research on physical activity and health—the most comprehensive ever—has the potential to catalyze a new physical activity and fitness movement in the United States. It is a work of real significance, on par with the Surgeon General's historic first report on smoking and health published in 1964.

This report is a passport to good health for all Americans. Its key finding is that people of all ages can improve the quality of their lives through a lifelong practice of moderate physical activity. You don't have to be training for the Boston Marathon to derive real health benefits from physical activity. A regular, preferably daily regimen of at least 30–45 minutes of brisk walking, bicycling, or even working around the house or yard will reduce your risks of developing coronary heart disease, hypertension, colon cancer, and diabetes. And if you're already doing that, you should consider picking up the pace: this report says that people who are already physically active will benefit even more by increasing the intensity or duration of their activity.

This watershed report comes not a moment too soon. We have found that 60 percent—well over half—of Americans are not regularly active. Worse yet, 25 percent of Americans are not active at all. For young people—the future of our country—physical activity declines dramatically during adolescence. These are dangerous trends. We need to turn them around quickly, for the health of our citizens and our country.

We will do so only with a massive national commitment—beginning now, on the eve of the Centennial Olympic Games, with a true fitness Dream Team drawing on the many forms of leadership that make up our great democratic society. Families need to weave physical activity into the fabric of their daily lives. Health professionals, in addition to being role models for healthy behaviors, need to encourage their patients to get out of their chairs and start fitness programs tailored to their individual needs. Businesses need to learn from what has worked in the past and promote worksite fitness, an easy option for workers. Community leaders need to reexamine whether enough resources have been devoted to the maintenance of parks, playgrounds, community centers, and physical education. Schools and universities need to reintroduce daily, quality physical activity as a key component of a comprehensive education. And the media and entertainment industries need to use their vast creative abilities to show all Americans that physical activity is healthful and fun—in other words, that it is attractive, maybe even glamorous!

We Americans always find the will to change when change is needed. I believe we can team up to create a new physical activity movement in this country. In doing so, we will save precious resources, precious futures, and precious lives. The time for action—and activity—is now.

Foreword

This first Surgeon General's report on physical activity is being released on the eve of the Centennial Olympic Games—the premiere event showcasing the world's greatest athletes. It is fitting that the games are being held in Atlanta, Georgia, home of the Centers for Disease Control and Prevention (CDC), the lead federal agency in preparing this report. The games' 100-year celebration also coincides with the CDC's landmark 50th year and with the 40th anniversary of the President's Council on Physical Fitness and Sports (PCPFS), the CDC's partner in developing this report. Because physical activity is a widely achievable means to a healthier life, this report directly supports the CDC's mission—to promote health and quality of life by preventing and controlling disease, injury, and disability. Also clear is the link to the PCPFS; originally established as part of a national campaign to help shape up America's younger generation, the Council continues today to promote physical activity, fitness, and sports for Americans of all ages.

The Olympic Games represent the summit of athletic achievement. The Paralympics, an international competition that will occur later this summer in Atlanta, represents the peak of athletic accomplishment for athletes with disabilities. Few of us will approach these levels of performance in our own physical endeavors. The good news in this report is that we do not have to scale Olympian heights to achieve significant health benefits. We can improve the quality of our lives through a lifelong practice of moderate amounts of regular physical activity of moderate or vigorous intensity. An active lifestyle is available to all.

Many Americans may be surprised at the extent and strength of the evidence linking physical activity to numerous health improvements. Most significantly, regular physical activity greatly reduces the risk of dying from coronary heart disease, the leading cause of death in the United States. Physical activity also reduces the risk of developing diabetes, hypertension, and colon cancer; enhances mental health; fosters healthy muscles, bones and joints; and helps maintain function and preserve independence in older adults.

The evidence about what helps people incorporate physical activity into their lives is less clear-cut. We do know that effective strategies and policies have taken place in settings as diverse as physical education classes in schools, health promotion programs at worksites, and one-on-one counseling by health care providers. However, more needs to be learned about what helps individuals change their physical activity habits and how changes in community environments, policies, and social norms might support that process.

Support is greatly needed if physical activity is to be increased in a society as technologically advanced as ours. Most Americans today are spared the burden of excessive physical labor. Indeed, few occupations today require significant physical activity, and most people use motorized transportation to get to work and to perform routine errands and tasks. Even leisure time is increasingly filled with sedentary behaviors, such as watching television, "surfing" the Internet, and playing video games.

Increasing physical activity is a formidable public health challenge that we must hasten to meet. The stakes are high, and the potential rewards are momentous: preventing premature death, unnecessary illness, and disability; controlling health care costs; and maintaining a high quality of life into old age.

David Satcher, M.D., Ph.D.
Director
Centers for Disease Control
and Prevention

Philip R. Lee, M.D.
Assistant Secretary
for Health

Florence Griffith Joyner
Tom McMillen
Co-Chairs
President's Council on
Physical Fitness and Sports

Preface

from the Surgeon General
U.S. Public Health Service

I am pleased to present the first report of the Surgeon General on physical activity and health. For more than a century, the Surgeon General of the Public Health Service has focused the nation's attention on important public health issues. Reports from Surgeons General on the adverse health consequences of smoking triggered nationwide efforts to prevent tobacco use. Reports on nutrition, violence, and HIV/AIDS—to name but a few—have heightened America's awareness of important public health issues and have spawned major public health initiatives. This new report, which is a comprehensive review of the available scientific evidence about the relationship between physical activity and health status, follows in this notable tradition.

Scientists and doctors have known for years that substantial benefits can be gained from regular physical activity. The expanding and strengthening evidence on the relationship between physical activity and health necessitates the focus this report brings to this important public health challenge. Although the science of physical activity is a complex and still-developing field, we have today strong evidence to indicate that regular physical activity will provide clear and substantial health gains. In this sense, the report is more than a summary of the science—it is a national call to action.

We must get serious about improving the health of the nation by affirming our commitment to healthy physical activity on all levels: personal, family, community, organizational, and national. Because physical activity is so directly related to preventing disease and premature death and to maintaining a high quality of life, we must accord it the same level of attention that we give other important public health practices that affect the entire nation. Physical activity thus joins the front ranks of essential health objectives, such as sound nutrition, the use of seat belts, and the prevention of adverse health effects of tobacco.

The time for this emphasis is both opportune and pressing. As this report makes clear, current levels of physical activity among Americans remain low, and we are losing ground in some areas. The good news in the report is that people can benefit from even moderate levels of physical activity. The public health implications of this good news are vast: the tremendous health gains that could be realized with even partial success at improving physical activity among the American people compel us to make a commitment and take action. With innovation, dedication, partnering, and a long-term plan, we should be able to improve the health and well-being of our people.

This report is not the final word. More work will need to be done so that we can determine the most effective ways to motivate all Americans to participate in a level of physical activity that can benefit their health and well-being. The challenge that lies ahead is formidable but worthwhile. I strongly encourage all Americans to join us in this effort.

Audrey F. Manley, M.D., M.P.H.
Surgeon General (Acting)

CHAPTER 1

INTRODUCTION, SUMMARY, AND CHAPTER CONCLUSIONS

Introduction

This is the first Surgeon General's report to address physical activity and health. The main message of this report is that Americans can substantially improve their health and quality of life by including moderate amounts of physical activity in their daily lives. Health benefits from physical activity are thus achievable for most Americans, including those who may dislike vigorous exercise and those who may have been previously discouraged by the difficulty of adhering to a program of vigorous exercise. For those who are already achieving regular moderate amounts of activity, additional benefits can be gained by further increases in activity level.

This report grew out of an emerging consensus among epidemiologists, experts in exercise science, and health professionals that physical activity need not be of vigorous intensity for it to improve health. Moreover, health benefits appear to be proportional to amount of activity; thus, every increase in activity adds some benefit. Emphasizing the amount rather than the intensity of physical activity offers more options for people to select from in incorporating physical activity into their daily lives. Thus, a moderate amount of activity can be obtained in a 30-minute brisk walk, 30 minutes of lawn mowing or raking leaves, a 15-minute run, or 45 minutes of playing volleyball, and these activities can be varied from day to day. It is hoped that this different emphasis on moderate amounts of activity, and the flexibility to vary activities according to personal preference and life circumstances, will encourage more people to make physical activity a regular and sustainable part of their lives.

The information in this report summarizes a diverse literature from the fields of epidemiology, exercise physiology, medicine, and the behavioral sciences. The report highlights what is known about physical activity and health, as well as what is being learned about promoting physical activity among adults and young people.

Development of the Report

In July 1994, the Office of the Surgeon General authorized the Centers for Disease Control and Prevention (CDC) to serve as lead agency for preparing the first Surgeon General's report on physical activity and health. The CDC was joined in this effort by the President's Council on Physical Fitness and Sports (PCPFS) as a collaborative partner representing the Office of the Surgeon General. Because of the wide interest in the health effects of physical activity, the report was planned collaboratively with representatives from the Office of the Surgeon General, the Office of Public Health and Science (Office of the Secretary), the Office of Disease Prevention (National Institutes of Health [NIH]), and the following institutes from the NIH: the National Heart, Lung, and Blood Institute; the National Institute of Child Health and Human Development; the National Institute of Diabetes and Digestive and Kidney Diseases; and the National Institute of Arthritis and Musculoskeletal and Skin Diseases. CDC's nonfederal partners—including the American Alliance for Health, Physical Education, Recreation, and Dance; the American College of Sports Medicine; and the American Heart Association—provided consultation throughout the development process.

The major purpose of this report is to summarize the existing literature on the role of physical activity in preventing disease and on the status of interventions to increase physical activity. Any report on a topic this broad must restrict its scope to keep its message clear. This report focuses on disease prevention and therefore does not include the considerable body of evidence on the benefits of physical activity for treatment or rehabilitation after disease has developed. This report concentrates on endurance-type physical activity (activity involving repeated use of large muscles, such as in walking or bicycling) because the health benefits of this type of activity have been extensively studied. The importance of resistance exercise (to increase muscle strength, such as by lifting weights) is increasingly being recognized as a means to preserve and enhance muscular strength and endurance and to prevent falls and improve mobility in the elderly. Some promising findings on resistance exercise are presented here, but a comprehensive review of resistance training is beyond the scope of this report. In addition, a review of the special concerns regarding physical activity for pregnant women and for people with disabilities is not undertaken here, although these important topics deserve more research and attention.

Finally, physical activity is only one of many everyday behaviors that affect health. In particular, nutritional habits are linked to some of the same aspects of health as physical activity, and the two may be related lifestyle characteristics. This report deals solely with physical activity; a Surgeon General's Report on Nutrition and Health was published in 1988.

Chapters 2 through 6 of this report address distinct areas of the current understanding of physical activity and health. Chapter 2 offers a historical perspective: after outlining the history of belief and knowledge about physical activity and health, the chapter reviews the evolution and content of physical activity recommendations. Chapter 3 describes the physiologic responses to physical activity—both the immediate effects of a single episode of activity and the long-term adaptations to a regular pattern of activity. The evidence that physical activity reduces the risk of cardiovascular and other diseases is presented in Chapter 4. Data on patterns and trends of physical activity in the U.S. population are the focus of Chapter 5. Lastly, Chapter 6 examines efforts to increase physical activity and reviews ideas currently being proposed for policy and environmental initiatives.

Major Conclusions

1. People of all ages, both male and female, benefit from regular physical activity.

2. Significant health benefits can be obtained by including a moderate amount of physical activity (e.g., 30 minutes of brisk walking or raking leaves, 15 minutes of running, or 45 minutes of playing volleyball) on most, if not all, days of the week. Through a modest increase in daily activity, most Americans can improve their health and quality of life.

3. Additional health benefits can be gained through greater amounts of physical activity. People who can maintain a regular regimen of activity that is of longer duration or of more vigorous intensity are likely to derive greater benefit.

4. Physical activity reduces the risk of premature mortality in general, and of coronary heart disease, hypertension, colon cancer, and diabetes mellitus in particular. Physical activity also improves mental health and is important for the health of muscles, bones, and joints.

5. More than 60 percent of American adults are not regularly physically active. In fact, 25 percent of all adults are not active at all.

6. Nearly half of American youths 12–21 years of age are not vigorously active on a regular basis. Moreover, physical activity declines dramatically during adolescence.

7. Daily enrollment in physical education classes has declined among high school students from 42 percent in 1991 to 25 percent in 1995.

8. Research on understanding and promoting physical activity is at an early stage, but some interventions to promote physical activity through schools, worksites, and health care settings have been evaluated and found to be successful.

Summary

The benefits of physical activity have been extolled throughout western history, but it was not until the second half of this century that scientific evidence supporting these beliefs began to accumulate. By the 1970s, enough information was available about the beneficial effects of vigorous exercise on cardiorespiratory fitness that the American College of Sports Medicine (ACSM), the American Heart Association (AHA), and other national organizations began issuing physical activity recommendations to the public. These recommendations generally focused on cardiorespiratory endurance and specified sustained periods of vigorous physical activity involving large muscle groups and lasting at least 20 minutes on 3 or more days per week. As understanding of the benefits of less vigorous activity grew, recommendations followed suit. During the past few years, the ACSM, the CDC, the AHA, the PCPFS, and the NIH have all recommended regular, moderate-intensity physical activity as an option for those who get little or no exercise. The *Healthy People 2000* goals for the nation's health have recognized the importance of physical activity and have included physical activity goals. The 1995 *Dietary Guidelines for Americans*, the basis of the federal government's nutrition-related programs, included physical activity guidance to maintain and improve weight—30 minutes or more of moderate-intensity physical activity on all, or most, days of the week.

Underpinning such recommendations is a growing understanding of how physical activity affects physiologic function. The body responds to physical activity in ways that have important positive effects on musculoskeletal, cardiovascular, respiratory, and endocrine systems. These changes are consistent with a number of health benefits, including a reduced risk of premature mortality and reduced risks of coronary heart disease, hypertension, colon cancer, and diabetes mellitus. Regular participation in physical activity also appears to reduce depression and anxiety, improve mood, and enhance ability to perform daily tasks throughout the life span.

The risks associated with physical activity must also be considered. The most common health problems that have been associated with physical activity are musculoskeletal injuries, which can occur with excessive amounts of activity or with suddenly beginning an activity for which the body is not conditioned. Much more serious associated health problems (i.e., myocardial infarction, sudden death) are also much rarer, occurring primarily among sedentary people with advanced atherosclerotic disease who engage in strenuous activity to which they are unaccustomed. Sedentary people, especially those with preexisting health conditions, who wish to increase their physical activity should therefore gradually build up to the desired level of activity. Even among people who are regularly active, the risk of myocardial infarction or sudden death is somewhat increased during physical exertion, but their overall risk of these outcomes is lower than that among people who are sedentary.

Research on physical activity continues to evolve. This report includes both well-established findings and newer research results that await replication and amplification. Interest has been developing in ways to differentiate between the various characteristics of physical activity that improve health. It remains to be determined how the interrelated characteristics of amount, intensity, duration, frequency, type, and pattern of physical activity are related to specific health or disease outcomes.

Attention has been drawn recently to findings from three studies showing that cardiorespiratory fitness gains are similar when physical activity occurs in several short sessions (e.g., 10 minutes) as when the same total amount and intensity of activity occurs in one longer session (e.g., 30 minutes). Although, strictly speaking, the health benefits of such intermittent activity have not yet been demonstrated, it is reasonable to expect them to be similar to those of continuous activity. Moreover, for people who are unable to set aside 30 minutes for physical activity, shorter episodes are clearly better than none. Indeed, one study has shown greater adherence to a walking program among those walking several times per day than among those walking once per day, when the total amount of walking time was kept the same. Accumulating physical activity over the course of the day has been included in recent recommendations from the CDC and ACSM, as well as from the NIH Consensus Development Conference on Physical Activity and Cardiovascular Health.

Despite common knowledge that exercise is healthful, more than 60 percent of American adults are not regularly active, and 25 percent of the adult population are not active at all. Moreover, although many people have enthusiastically embarked on vigorous exercise programs at one time or another, most do not sustain their participation. Clearly, the processes of developing and maintaining healthier habits are as important to study as the health effects of these habits.

The effort to understand how to promote more active lifestyles is of great importance to the health of this nation. Although the study of physical activity determinants and interventions is at an early stage, effective programs to increase physical activity have been carried out in a variety of settings, such as schools, physicians' offices, and worksites. Determining the most effective and cost-effective intervention approaches is a challenge for the future. Fortunately, the United States has skilled leadership and institutions to support efforts to encourage and assist Americans to become more physically active. Schools, community agencies, parks, recreational facilities, and health clubs are available in most communities and can be more effectively used in these efforts.

School-based interventions for youth are particularly promising, not only for their potential scope—almost all young people between the ages of 6 and 16 years attend school—but also for their potential impact. Nearly half of young people 12–21 years of age are not vigorously active; moreover, physical activity sharply declines during adolescence. Childhood and adolescence may thus be pivotal times for preventing sedentary behavior among adults by maintaining the habit of physical activity throughout the school years. School-based interventions have been shown to be successful in increasing physical activity levels. With evidence that success in this arena is possible, every effort should be made to encourage schools to require daily physical education in each grade and to promote physical activities that can be enjoyed throughout life.

Outside the school, physical activity programs and initiatives face the challenge of a highly technological society that makes it increasingly convenient to remain sedentary and that discourages physical activity in both obvious and subtle ways. To increase physical activity in the general population, it may be necessary to go beyond traditional efforts. This report highlights some concepts from community initiatives that are being implemented around the country. It is hoped that these examples will spark new public policies and programs in other places as well. Special efforts will also be required to meet the needs of special populations, such as people with disabilities, racial and ethnic minorities, people with low income, and the elderly. Much more information about these important groups will be necessary to develop a truly comprehensive national initiative for better health through physical activity. Challenges for the future include identifying key determinants of physically active lifestyles among the diverse populations that characterize the United States (including special populations, women, and young people) and using this information to design and disseminate effective programs.

Chapter Conclusions

Chapter 2: Historical Background and Evolution of Physical Activity Recommendations

1. Physical activity for better health and well-being has been an important theme throughout much of western history.

2. Public health recommendations have evolved from emphasizing vigorous activity for cardiorespiratory fitness to including the option of moderate levels of activity for numerous health benefits.

3. Recommendations from experts agree that for better health, physical activity should be performed regularly. The most recent recommendations advise people of all ages to include a minimum of 30 minutes of physical activity of moderate intensity (such as brisk walking) on most, if not all, days of the week. It is also acknowledged that for most people, greater health benefits can be obtained by engaging in physical activity of more vigorous intensity or of longer duration.

4. Experts advise previously sedentary people embarking on a physical activity program to start with short durations of moderate-intensity activity and gradually increase the duration or intensity until the goal is reached.

5. Experts advise consulting with a physician before beginning a new physical activity program for people with chronic diseases, such as cardiovascular disease and diabetes mellitus, or for those who are at high risk for these diseases. Experts also advise men over age 40 and women over age 50 to consult a physician before they begin a vigorous activity program.

6. Recent recommendations from experts also suggest that cardiorespiratory endurance activity should be supplemented with strength-developing exercises at least twice per week for adults, in order to improve musculoskeletal health, maintain independence in performing the activities of daily life, and reduce the risk of falling.

Chapter 3: Physiologic Responses and Long-Term Adaptations to Exercise

1. Physical activity has numerous beneficial physiologic effects. Most widely appreciated are its effects on the cardiovascular and musculoskeletal systems, but benefits on the functioning of metabolic, endocrine, and immune systems are also considerable.

2. Many of the beneficial effects of exercise training—from both endurance and resistance activities—diminish within 2 weeks if physical activity is substantially reduced, and effects disappear within 2 to 8 months if physical activity is not resumed.

3. People of all ages, both male and female, undergo beneficial physiologic adaptations to physical activity.

Chapter 4: The Effects of Physical Activity on Health and Disease

Overall Mortality

1. Higher levels of regular physical activity are associated with lower mortality rates for both older and younger adults.

2. Even those who are moderately active on a regular basis have lower mortality rates than those who are least active.

Cardiovascular Diseases

1. Regular physical activity or cardiorespiratory fitness decreases the risk of cardiovascular disease mortality in general and of coronary heart disease mortality in particular. Existing data are not conclusive regarding a relationship between physical activity and stroke.

2. The level of decreased risk of coronary heart disease attributable to regular physical activity is similar to that of other lifestyle factors, such as keeping free from cigarette smoking.

3. Regular physical activity prevents or delays the development of high blood pressure, and exercise reduces blood pressure in people with hypertension.

Cancer

1. Regular physical activity is associated with a decreased risk of colon cancer.

2. There is no association between physical activity and rectal cancer. Data are too sparse to draw conclusions regarding a relationship between physical activity and endometrial, ovarian, or testicular cancers.

3. Despite numerous studies on the subject, existing data are inconsistent regarding an association between physical activity and breast or prostate cancers.

Non–Insulin-Dependent Diabetes Mellitus

1.) Regular physical activity lowers the risk of developing non–insulin-dependent diabetes mellitus.

Osteoarthritis

1. Regular physical activity is necessary for maintaining normal muscle strength, joint structure, and joint function. In the range recommended for health, physical activity is not associated with joint damage or development of osteoarthritis and may be beneficial for many people with arthritis.

2. Competitive athletics may be associated with the development of osteoarthritis later in life, but sports-related injuries are the likely cause.

Osteoporosis

1. Weight-bearing physical activity is essential for normal skeletal development during childhood and adolescence and for achieving and maintaining peak bone mass in young adults.

2. It is unclear whether resistance- or endurance-type physical activity can reduce the accelerated rate of bone loss in postmenopausal women in the absence of estrogen replacement therapy.

Falling

1. There is promising evidence that strength training and other forms of exercise in older adults preserve the ability to maintain independent living status and reduce the risk of falling.

Obesity

1. Low levels of activity, resulting in fewer kilocalories used than consumed, contribute to the high prevalence of obesity in the United States.

2. Physical activity may favorably affect body fat distribution.

Mental Health

1. Physical activity appears to relieve symptoms of depression and anxiety and improve mood.

2. Regular physical activity may reduce the risk of developing depression, although further research is needed on this topic.

Health-Related Quality of Life

1. Physical activity appears to improve health-related quality of life by enhancing psychological well-being and by improving physical functioning in persons compromised by poor health.

Adverse Effects

1. Most musculoskeletal injuries related to physical activity are believed to be preventable by gradually working up to a desired level of activity and by avoiding excessive amounts of activity.

2. Serious cardiovascular events can occur with physical exertion, but the net effect of regular physical activity is a lower risk of mortality from cardiovascular disease.

Chapter 5: Patterns and Trends in Physical Activity

Adults

1. Approximately 15 percent of U.S. adults engage regularly (3 times a week for at least 20 minutes) in vigorous physical activity during leisure time.

2. Approximately 22 percent of adults engage regularly (5 times a week for at least 30 minutes) in sustained physical activity of any intensity during leisure time.

3. About 25 percent of adults report no physical activity at all in their leisure time.

4. Physical inactivity is more prevalent among women than men, among blacks and Hispanics than whites, among older than younger adults, and among the less affluent than the more affluent.

5. The most popular leisure-time physical activities among adults are walking and gardening or yard work.

Adolescents and Young Adults

1. Only about one-half of U.S. young people (ages 12–21 years) regularly participate in vigorous physical activity. One-fourth report no vigorous physical activity.

2. Approximately one-fourth of young people walk or bicycle (i.e., engage in light to moderate activity) nearly every day.

3. About 14 percent of young people report no recent vigorous or light-to-moderate physical activity. This indicator of inactivity is higher among females than males and among black females than white females.

4. Males are more likely than females to participate in vigorous physical activity, strengthening activities, and walking or bicycling.

5. Participation in all types of physical activity declines strikingly as age or grade in school increases.

6. Among high school students, enrollment in physical education remained unchanged during the first half of the 1990s. However, daily attendance in physical education declined from approximately 42 percent to 25 percent.

7. The percentage of high school students who were enrolled in physical education and who reported being physically active for at least 20 minutes in physical education classes declined from approximately 81 percent to 70 percent during the first half of this decade.

8. Only 19 percent of all high school students report being physically active for 20 minutes or more in daily physical education classes.

Chapter 6: Understanding and Promoting Physical Activity

1. Consistent influences on physical activity patterns among adults and young people include confidence in one's ability to engage in regular physical activity (e.g., self-efficacy), enjoyment of physical activity, support from others, positive beliefs concerning the benefits of physical activity, and lack of perceived barriers to being physically active.

2. For adults, some interventions have been successful in increasing physical activity in communities, worksites, and health care settings, and at home.

3. Interventions targeting physical education in elementary school can substantially increase the amount of time students spend being physically active in physical education class.

A Report of the Surgeon General

Physical Activity and Health

The Link Between Physical Activity and Morbidity and Mortality

HOW PHYSICAL ACTIVITY IMPACTS HEALTH

Regular physical activity that is performed on most days of the week reduces the risk of developing or dying from some of the leading causes of illness and death in the United States. Regular physical activity improves health in the following ways:

- Reduces the risk of dying prematurely.

- Reduces the risk of dying prematurely from heart disease.

- Reduces the risk of developing diabetes.

- Reduces the risk of developing high blood pressure.

- Helps reduce blood pressure in people who already have high blood pressure.

- Reduces the risk of developing colon cancer.

- Reduces feelings of depression and anxiety.

- Helps control weight.

- Helps build and maintain healthy bones, muscles, and joints.

- Helps older adults become stronger and better able to move about without falling.

- Promotes psychological well-being.

HEALTH BURDENS THAT COULD BE REDUCED THROUGH PHYSICAL ACTIVITY

Millions of Americans suffer from illnesses that can be prevented or improved through regular physical activity.

- 13.5 million people have coronary heart disease.

- 1.5 million people suffer from a heart attack in a given year.

- 8 million people have adult-onset (non-insulin–dependent) diabetes.

- 95,000 people are newly diagnosed with colon cancer each year.

- 250,000 people suffer from a hip fractures each year.

- 50 million people have high blood pressure.

- Over 60 million people (a third of the population) are overweight.

U.S. DEPARTMENT OF HEALTH AND HUMAN SERVICES
Centers for Disease Control and Prevention
National Center for Chronic Disease Prevention and Health Promotion
The President's Council on Physical Fitness and Sports

The Nation's Prevention Agency
CDC50
Centers for Disease Control and Prevention

The President's
Council on
Physical Fitness
and Sports

A Report of the Surgeon General

Physical Activity and Health

Adults

- Physical activity need not be strenuous to achieve health benefits.

- Men and women of all ages benefit from a moderate amount of daily physical activity. The same moderate amount of activity can be obtained in longer sessions of moderately intense activities (such as 30 minutes of brisk walking) as in shorter sessions of more strenuous activities (such as 15–20 minutes of jogging).

- Additional health benefits can be gained through greater amounts of physical activity. Adults who maintain a regular routine of physical activity that is of longer duration or of greater intensity are likely to derive greater benefit. However, because risk of injury also increases with greater amounts of activity, care should be taken to avoid excessive amounts.

- Previously sedentary people who begin physical activity programs should start with short sessions (5–10 minutes) of physical activity and gradually build up to the desired level of activity.

- Adults with chronic health problems, such as heart disease, diabetes, or obesity, or who are at high risk for these conditions should first consult a physician before beginning a new program of physical activity. Men over age 40 and women over age 50 who plan to begin a new program of *vigorous* activity should consult a physician to be sure they do not have heart disease or other health problems.

FACTS

- More than 60 percent of U.S. adults do not engage in the recommended amount of activity.

- Approximately 25 percent of U.S. adults are not active at all.

- Physical inactivity is more common among:
  - Women than men.
  - African American and Hispanic adults than whites.
  - Older than younger adults.
  - Less affluent than more affluent people.

- Social support from family and friends has been consistently and positively related to regular physical activity.

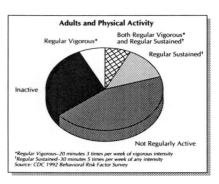

Adults and Physical Activity

Regular Vigorous*
Both Regular Vigorous* and Regular Sustained†
Regular Sustained†
Inactive
Not Regularly Active

*Regular Vigorous–20 minutes 3 times per week of vigorous intensity
†Regular Sustained–30 minutes 5 times per week of any intensity
Source: CDC 1992 Behavioral Risk Factor Survey

U.S. DEPARTMENT OF HEALTH AND HUMAN SERVICES
Centers for Disease Control and Prevention
National Center for Chronic Disease Prevention and Health Promotion
The President's Council on Physical Fitness and Sports

The Nation's Prevention Agency
CDC50
Centers for Disease Control and Prevention

The President's
Council on
Physical Fitness
and Sports

BENEFITS OF PHYSICAL ACTIVITY

- Reduces the risk of dying from coronary heart disease and of developing high blood pressure, colon cancer, and diabetes.
- Can help reduce blood pressure in some people with hypertension.
- Helps maintain healthy bones, muscles, and joints.
- Reduces symptoms of anxiety and depression and fosters improvements in mood and feelings of well-being.
- Helps control weight, develop lean muscle, and reduce body fat.

WHAT COMMUNITIES CAN DO

- Provide environmental inducements to physical activity, such as safe, accessible, and attractive trails for walking and bicycling, and sidewalks with curb cuts.
- Open schools for community recreation, form neighborhood watch groups to increase safety, and encourage malls and other indoor or protected locations to provide safe places for walking in any weather.
- Provide community-based programs to meet the needs of specific populations, such as racial and ethnic minority groups, women, older adults, persons with disabilities, and low-income groups.
- Encourage health care providers to talk routinely to their patients about incorporating physical activity into their lives.
- Encourage employers to provide supportive worksite environments and policies that offer opportunities for employees to incorporate moderate physical activity into their daily lives.

For more information contact:

Centers for Disease Control and Prevention
National Center for Chronic Disease Prevention and Health Promotion
Division of Nutrition and Physical Activity, MS K-46
4770 Buford Highway, NE
Atlanta, GA 30341-3724
1-888-CDC-4NRG or 1-888-232-4674 (Toll Free)
http://www.cdc.gov

The President's Council on Physical Fitness and Sports
Box SG
Suite 250
701 Pennsylvania Avenue, NW
Washington, DC 20004

A Report of the Surgeon General
Physical Activity and Health
Adolescents and Young Adults

KEY MESSAGES

- Adolescents and young adults, both male and female, benefit from physical activity.

- Physical activity need not be strenuous to be beneficial.

- Moderate amounts of daily physical activity are recommended for people of all ages. This amount can be obtained in longer sessions of moderately intense activities, such as brisk walking for 30 minutes, or in shorter sessions of more intense activities, such as jogging or playing basketball for 15–20 minutes.

- Greater amounts of physical activity are even more beneficial, up to a point. Excessive amounts of physical activity can lead to injuries, menstrual abnormalities, and bone weakening.

FACTS

- Nearly half of American youths aged 12–21 years are not vigorously active on a regular basis.

- About 14 percent of young people report no recent physical activity. Inactivity is more common among females (14%) than males (7%) and among black females (21%) than white females (12%).

- Participation in all types of physical activity declines strikingly as age or grade in school increases.

Physical Activity Levels of Adolescents and Young Adults, by Age and Sex

Source: CDC 1992 National Health Interview Survey/Youth Risk Behavior Survey

- Only 19 percent of all high school students are physically active for 20 minutes or more, five days a week, in physical education classes.

- Daily enrollment in physical education classes dropped from 42 percent to 25 percent among high school students between 1991 and 1995.

- Well designed school-based interventions directed at increasing physical activity in physical education classes have been shown to be effective.

- Social support from family and friends has been consistently and positively related to regular physical activity.

U.S. DEPARTMENT OF HEALTH AND HUMAN SERVICES
Centers for Disease Control and Prevention
National Center for Chronic Disease Prevention and Health Promotion
The President's Council on Physical Fitness and Sports

The Nation's Prevention Agency

Centers for Disease Control and Prevention

The President's Council on Physical Fitness and Sports

- Helps build and maintain healthy bones, muscles, and joints.
- Helps control weight, build lean muscle, and reduce fat.
- Prevents or delays the development of high blood pressure and helps reduce blood pressure in some adolescents with hypertension.

- Provide quality, preferably daily, K–12 physical education classes and hire physical education specialists to teach them.
- Create opportunities for physical activities that are enjoyable, that promote adolescents' and young adults' confidence in their ability to be physically active, and that involve friends, peers, and parents.
- Provide appropriate physically active role models for youths.
- Provide access to school buildings and community facilities that enable safe participation in physical activity.
- Provide a range of extracurricular programs in schools and community recreation centers to meet the needs and interests of specific adolescent and young adult populations, such as racial and ethnic minority groups, females, persons with disabilities, and low-income groups.
- Encourage health care providers to talk routinely to adolescents and young adults about the importance of incorporating physical activity into their lives.

For more information contact:

Centers for Disease Control and Prevention
National Center for Chronic Disease Prevention and Health Promotion
Division of Nutrition and Physical Activity, MS K-46
4770 Buford Highway, NE
Atlanta, GA 30341-3724
1-888-CDC-4NRG or 1-888-232-4674 (Toll Free)
http://www.cdc.gov

The President's Council on Physical Fitness and Sports
Box SG
Suite 250
701 Pennsylvania Avenue, NW
Washington, DC 20004

A Report of the Surgeon General

Physical Activity and Health

Older Adults

- Older adults, both male and female, can benefit from regular physical activity.

- Physical activity need not be strenuous to achieve health benefits.

- Older adults can obtain significant health benefits with a moderate amount of physical activity, preferably daily. A moderate amount of activity can be obtained in longer sessions of moderately intense activities (such as walking) or in shorter sessions of more vigorous activities (such as fast walking or stairwalking).

- Additional health benefits can be gained through greater amounts of physical activity, either by increasing the duration, intensity, or frequency. Because risk of injury increases at high levels of physical activity, care should be taken not to engage in excessive amounts of activity.

- Previously sedentary older adults who begin physical activity programs should start with short intervals of moderate physical activity (5–10 minutes) and gradually build up to the desired amount.

- Older adults should consult with a physician before beginning a new physical activity program.

- In addition to cardiorespiratory endurance (aerobic) activity, older adults can benefit from muscle-strengthening activities. Stronger muscles help reduce the risk of falling and improve the ability to perform the routine tasks of daily life.

- The loss of strength and stamina attributed to aging is in part caused by reduced physical activity.

- Inactivity increases with age. By age 75, about one in three men and one in two women engage in no physical activity.

- Among adults aged 65 years and older, walking and gardening or yard work are, by far, the most popular physical activities.

- Social support from family and friends has been consistently and positively related to regular physical activity.

U.S. DEPARTMENT OF HEALTH AND HUMAN SERVICES
Centers for Disease Control and Prevention
National Center for Chronic Disease Prevention and Health Promotion
The President's Council on Physical Fitness and Sports

- Helps maintain the ability to live independently and reduces the risk of falling and fracturing bones.
- Reduces the risk of dying from coronary heart disease and of developing high blood pressure, colon cancer, and diabetes.
- Can help reduce blood pressure in some people with hypertension.
- Helps people with chronic, disabling conditions improve their stamina and muscle strength.
- Reduces symptoms of anxiety and depression and fosters improvements in mood and feelings of well-being.
- Helps maintain healthy bones, muscles, and joints.
- Helps control joint swelling and pain associated with arthritis.

**WHAT COMMUNITIES
CAN DO**

- Provide community-based physical activity programs that offer aerobic, strengthening, and flexibility components specifically designed for older adults.
- Encourage malls and other indoor or protected locations to provide safe places for walking in any weather.
- Ensure that facilities for physical activity accommodate and encourage participation by older adults.
- Provide transportation for older adults to parks or facilities that provide physical activity programs.
- Encourage health care providers to talk routinely to their older adult patients about incorporating physical activity into their lives.
- Plan community activities that include opportunities for older adults to be physically active.

For more information contact:

Centers for Disease Control and Prevention
National Center for Chronic Disease Prevention and Health Promotion
Division of Nutrition and Physical Activity, MS K-46
4770 Buford Highway, NE
Atlanta, GA 30341-3724
1-888-CDC-4NRG or 1-888-232-4674 (Toll Free)
http://www.cdc.gov

The President's Council on Physical Fitness and Sports
Box SG
Suite 250
701 Pennsylvania Avenue, NW
Washington, DC 20004

Physical Activity and Health

Persons with Disabilities

KEY MESSAGES

- Physical activity need not be strenuous to achieve health benefits.
- Significant health benefits can be obtained with a moderate amount of physical activity, preferably daily. The same moderate amount of activity can be obtained in longer sessions of moderately intense activities (such as 30–40 minutes of wheeling oneself in a wheelchair) or in shorter sessions of more strenuous activities (such as 20 minutes of wheelchair basketball).
- Additional health benefits can be gained through greater amounts of physical activity. People who can maintain a regular routine of physical activity that is of longer duration or of greater intensity are likely to derive greater benefit.
- Previously sedentary people who begin physical activity programs should start with short intervals of physical activity (5–10 minutes) and gradually build up to the desired level of activity.
- People with disabilities should first consult a physician before beginning a program of physical activity to which they are unaccustomed.
- The emphasis on moderate amounts of physical activity makes it possible to vary activities to meet individual needs, preferences, and life circumstances.

FACTS

- People with disabilities are less likely to engage in regular moderate physical activity than people without disabilities, yet they have similar needs to promote their health and prevent unnecessary disease.
- Social support from family and friends has been consistently and positively related to regular physical activity.

BENEFITS OF PHYSICAL ACTIVITY

- Reduces the risk of dying from coronary heart disease and of developing high blood pressure, colon cancer, and diabetes.
- Can help people with chronic, disabling conditions improve their stamina and muscle strength.
- Reduces symptoms of anxiety and depression, improves mood, and promotes general feelings of well-being.
- Helps control joint swelling and pain associated with arthritis.
- Can help reduce blood pressure in some people with hypertension.

U.S. DEPARTMENT OF HEALTH AND HUMAN SERVICES
Centers for Disease Control and Prevention
National Center for Chronic Disease Prevention and Health Promotion
The President's Council on Physical Fitness and Sports

The Nation's Prevention Agency
CDC
Centers for Disease Control and Prevention

The President's
Council on
Physical Fitness
and Sports

- Provide community-based programs to meet the needs of persons with disabilities.

- Ensure that environments and facilities conducive to being physically active are available and accessible to people with disabilities, such as offering safe, accessible, and attractive trails for bicycling, walking, and wheelchair activities.

- Ensure that people with disabilities are involved at all stages of planning and implementing community physical activity programs.

- Provide quality, preferably daily, K–12 accessible physical education classes for children and youths with disabilities.

- Encourage health care providers to talk routinely to their patients with disabilities about incorporating physical activity into their lives.

For more information contact:

Centers for Disease Control and Prevention
National Center for Chronic Disease Prevention and Health Promotion
Division of Nutrition and Physical Activity, MS K-46
4770 Buford Highway, NE
Atlanta, GA 30341-3724
1-888-CDC-4NRG or 1-888-232-4674 (Toll Free)
http://www.cdc.gov

The President's Council on Physical Fitness and Sports
Box SG
Suite 250
701 Pennsylvania Avenue, NW
Washington, DC 20004

A Report of the Surgeon General

Physical Activity and Health

Women

- Physical activity need not be strenuous to achieve health benefits.

- Women of all ages benefit from a moderate amount of physical activity, preferably daily. The same moderate amount of activity can be obtained in longer sessions of moderately intense activities (such as 30 minutes of brisk walking) as in shorter sessions of more strenuous activities (such as 15–20 minutes of jogging).

- Additional health benefits can be gained through greater amounts of physical activity. Women who can maintain a regular routine of physical activity that is of longer duration or of greater intensity are likely to derive greater benefit. However, excessive amounts of activity should be avoided, because risk of injury increases with greater amounts of activity, as does the risk of menstrual abnormalities and bone weakening.

- Previously sedentary women who begin physical activity programs should start with short intervals (5–10 minutes) of physical activity and gradually build up to the desired level of activity.

- Women with chronic health problems, such as heart disease, diabetes, or obesity, or who are at high risk for these conditions should first consult a physician before beginning a new program of physical activity. Women over age 50 who plan to begin a new program of *vigorous* physical activity should first consult a physician to be sure they do not have heart disease or other health problems.

- The emphasis on moderate amounts of physical activity makes it possible to vary activities to meet individual needs, preferences, and life circumstances.

FACTS

- More than 60 percent of U.S. women do not engage in the recommended amount of physical activity.

- More than 25 percent of U.S. women are not active at all.

- Physical inactivity is more common among women than men.

- Social support from family and friends has been consistently and positively related to regular physical activity.

U.S. DEPARTMENT OF HEALTH AND HUMAN SERVICES
Centers for Disease Control and Prevention
National Center for Chronic Disease Prevention and Health Promotion
The President's Council on Physical Fitness and Sports

The Nation's Prevention Agency

CDC5Ｏ
Centers for Disease Control and Prevention

·The President's
Council on
Physical Fitness
and Sports

- Reduces the risk of dying from coronary heart disease and of developing high blood pressure, colon cancer, and diabetes.

- Helps maintain healthy bones, muscles, and joints.

- Helps control weight, build lean muscle, and reduce body fat.

- Helps control joint swelling and pain associated with arthritis.

- May enhance the effect of estrogen replacement therapy in decreasing bone loss after menopause.

- Reduces symptoms of anxiety and depression and fosters improvements in mood and feelings of well-being.

- Can help reduce blood pressure in some women with hypertension.

- Provide environmental inducements to physical activity, such as safe, accessible, and attractive trails for walking and bicycling, and sidewalks with curb cuts.

- Open schools for community recreation, form neighborhood watch groups to increase safety, and encourage malls and other indoor or protected locations to provide safe places for walking in any weather.

- Encourage employers to provide supportive worksite environments and policies that offer opportunities for employees to incorporate moderate physical activity into their daily lives.

- Provide community-based programs to meet the needs of older women, women with disabilities, women of racial and ethnic minority groups, and women with low incomes. Include child care arrangements to encourage the participation of women with children.

- Encourage health care providers to talk routinely to female patients about incorporating physical activity into their lives.

For more information contact:

Centers for Disease Control and Prevention
National Center for Chronic Disease Prevention and Health Promotion
Division of Nutrition and Physical Activity, MS K-46
4770 Buford Highway, NE
Atlanta, GA 30341-3724
1-888-CDC-4NRG or 1-888-232-4674 (Toll Free)
http://www.cdc.gov

The President's Council on Physical Fitness and Sports
Box SG
Suite 250
701 Pennsylvania Avenue, NW
Washington, DC 20004

Superintendent of Documents Publications Order Form

To fax your orders:
(202)512–2250

Order Processing Code
7895

☐ Yes, please send me _____ copies of the 1996 Surgeon General's Report on

Physical Activity and Health (S/N 017–023–00196–5) at $19 each.

The total cost of my order is $_____. (International customers please add 25%.) Prices include regular domestic postage and handling and are subject to change.

Please type or print

_____
(Company or personal name)

_____
(Additional address/attention line)

_____
(Street address)

_____
(City, state, ZIP Code)

_____
(Daytime phone including area code)

_____
(Purchase order number)

Please indicate method of payment

☐ Check payable to the Superintendent of Documents

☐ GPO Deposit Account ☐☐☐☐☐☐–☐

☐ VISA, Choice, or MasterCard Account

☐☐☐☐☐☐☐☐☐☐☐☐☐☐☐☐☐☐☐☐

☐☐☐☐ (Credit card expiration date)

_____
(Authorizing Signature)   7/96

*Thank you for
your order!*

Mail to: Superintendent of Documents, P.O. Box 371954, Pittsburgh, PA 15250–7954

286

Promoting Lifelong Physical Activity

At-A-Glance

Young people can build healthy bodies and establish healthy lifestyles by including physical activity in their daily lives. However, many young people are not physically active on a regular basis, and physical activity declines dramatically during adolescence. School and community programs can help young people get active and stay active.

BENEFITS OF PHYSICAL ACTIVITY

Regular physical activity in childhood and adolescence

- Improves strength and endurance.
- Helps build healthy bones and muscles.
- Helps control weight.
- Reduces anxiety and stress and increases self-esteem.
- May improve blood pressure and cholesterol levels.

In addition, young people say they like physical activity because it is fun; they do it with friends; and it helps them learn skills, stay in shape, and look better.

CONSEQUENCES OF PHYSICAL INACTIVITY

- The percentage of young people who are overweight has more than doubled in the past 30 years.

- Inactivity and poor diet cause at least 300,000 deaths a year in the United States. Only tobacco use causes more preventable deaths.

- Adults who are less active are at greater risk of dying of heart disease and developing diabetes, colon cancer, and high blood pressure.

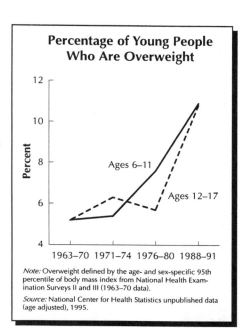

Percentage of Young People Who Are Overweight

Ages 6–11

Ages 12–17

Percent: 4, 6, 8, 10, 12

1963–70 1971–74 1976–80 1988–91

Note: Overweight defined by the age- and sex-specific 95th percentile of body mass index from National Health Examination Surveys II and III (1963–70 data).

Source: National Center for Health Statistics unpublished data (age adjusted), 1995.

U.S. DEPARTMENT OF HEALTH AND HUMAN SERVICES
Centers for Disease Control and Prevention
National Center for Chronic Disease Prevention and Health Promotion
March 1997

PHYSICAL ACTIVITY AMONG YOUNG PEOPLE

- Almost half of young people aged 12–21 and more than a third of high school students do not participate in vigorous physical activity on a regular basis.

- Seventy-two percent of 9th graders participate in vigorous physical activity on a regular basis, compared with only 55% of 12th graders.

- Daily participation in physical education classes by high school students dropped from 42% in 1991 to 25% in 1995.

- The time students spend being active in physical education classes is decreasing; among high school students enrolled in a physical education class, the percentage who were active for at least 20 minutes during an average class dropped from 81% in 1991 to 70% in 1995.

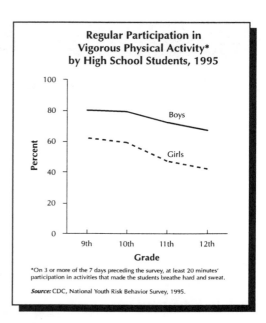

Regular Participation in Vigorous Physical Activity* by High School Students, 1995

*On 3 or more of the 7 days preceding the survey, at least 20 minutes' participation in activities that made the students breathe hard and sweat.

Source: CDC, National Youth Risk Behavior Survey, 1995.

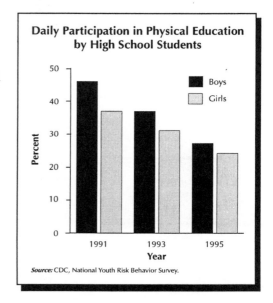

Daily Participation in Physical Education by High School Students

Source: CDC, National Youth Risk Behavior Survey.

How Much Physical Activity Do Young People Need?

Everyone can benefit from a moderate amount of physical activity on most, if not all, days of the week. Young people should select activities they enjoy that fit into their daily lives. Examples of moderate activity include

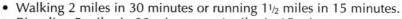

- Walking 2 miles in 30 minutes or running 1½ miles in 15 minutes.
- Bicycling 5 miles in 30 minutes or 4 miles in 15 minutes.
- Dancing fast for 30 minutes or jumping rope for 15 minutes.
- Playing basketball for 15–20 minutes or volleyball for 45 minutes.

Increasing the frequency, time, or intensity of physical activity can bring even more health benefits—up to a point. Too much physical activity can lead to injuries and other health problems.

CDC's Guidelines for School and Community Programs to Promote Lifelong Physical Activity Among Young People *were developed in collaboration with experts from other federal agencies, state agencies, universities, voluntary organizations, and professional associations. They are based on an extensive review of research and practice.*

KEY PRINCIPLES

The guidelines state that physical activity programs for young people are most likely to be effective when they

- Emphasize enjoyable participation in physical activities that are easily done throughout life.

- Offer a diverse range of noncompetitive and competitive activities appropriate for different ages and abilities.

- Give young people the skills and confidence they need to be physically active.

- Promote physical activity through all components of a coordinated school health program and develop links between school and community programs.

RECOMMENDATIONS

The guidelines include 10 recommendations for ensuring quality physical activity programs.

1 Policy

Establish policies that promote enjoyable, lifelong physical activity.

- Schools should require daily physical education and comprehensive health education (including lessons on physical activity) in grades K–12.

- Schools and community organizations should provide adequate funding, equipment, and supervision for programs that meet the needs and interests of all students.

2 Environment

Provide physical and social environments that encourage and enable young people to engage in safe and enjoyable physical activity.

- Provide access to safe spaces and facilities and implement measures to prevent activity-related injuries and illnesses.

- Provide school time, such as recess, for unstructured physical activity, such as jumping rope.

- Discourage the use or withholding of physical activity as punishment.

- Provide health promotion programs for school faculty and staff.

3 **Physical Education Curricula and Instruction**

Implement sequential physical education curricula and instruction in grades K–12 that

- Emphasize enjoyable participation in lifetime physical activities such as walking and dancing, not just competitive sports.
- Help students develop the knowledge, attitudes, and skills they need to adopt and maintain a physically active lifestyle.
- Follow the National Standards for Physical Education.
- Keep students active for most of class time.

4 **Health Education Curricula and Instruction**

Implement health education curricula that

- Feature active learning strategies and follow the National Health Education Standards.
- Help students develop the knowledge, attitudes, and skills they need to adopt and maintain a healthy lifestyle.

5 **Extracurricular Activities**

Provide extracurricular physical activity programs that offer diverse, developmentally appropriate activities—both noncompetitive and competitive—for all students.

6 **Family Involvement**

Encourage parents and guardians to support their children's participation in physical activity, to be physically active role models, and to include physical activity in family events.

7 **Training**

Provide training to enable teachers, coaches, recreation and health care staff, and other school and community personnel to promote enjoyable, lifelong physical activity to young people.

8 **Health Services**

Assess the physical activity patterns of young people, refer them to appropriate physical activity programs, and advocate for physical activity instruction and programs for young people.

9 **Community Programs**

Provide a range of developmentally appropriate community sports and recreation programs that are attractive to all young people.

10 **Evaluation**

Regularly evaluate physical activity instruction, programs, and facilities.

Resource C

Sample Target Audience Profile: The CDC's Target Audience for the "Ready. Set. It's Everywhere You Go" Physical Activity Campaign

CDC used DDB Needham's *Lifestyles Survey* and Porter Novelli's subset known as the *HealthStyles Survey*—including over 4,000 respondents who mirror the U.S. population as a whole, with over-sampling in low-income and monthly subgroups for the *HealthStyles* portion of the questionnaire.

Demographic Characteristics

73 million people (37.5% of Americans) between the ages of 18 and 45

The population skews toward youthfulness, with 43% of this target group under 35 years of age

41% are men

59% are women

75% White, 12% Black, 9% Hispanic

71% are married

2/3 have completed high school or some college

74% are employed

42% of annual household income is <$30,000

27% of annual household income is between $30,000 and $50,000

31% of annual household income is >$50,000

60% work outside the home

home ownership: 2/3 own a home

58% have children living at home

35% have children preschoolers (under the age of 5) living at home

Physical Characteristics

19.3% have been diagnosed with high blood cholesterol

17.5% have been diagnosed with high blood pressure

39.9% have not had a physical examination in the past year

Tend to be overweight

Geographic Characteristics

Nothing unique in that category—they're everywhere you go.

Psychographic Characteristics

In Contemplation or Preparation for Change, they want and intend to be regularly active.

More likely to be in Relapse. They can remember when they had been regularly active; a pattern of trying and failing to maintain an active lifestyle; often something happened to interrupt their routine (e.g., out-of-town guests, friend moved away, illness).

They tend not to enjoy exercise, but they are pleased with themselves when they do it.

They tend to think of "exercise" as something unpleasant, tedious, boring—a sweaty workout. It conjured up thoughts of torture, pain, and strenuous activity. Something done for exercise's sake.

They have a positive opinion of "physical activity," seeing it as something pleasant, enjoyable, fun, and a variety of activities you do with some other goal in mind (e.g., walking around the track is "exercise"; walking through the woods is "physical activity"). One focus group participant said: "dancing—who worries about calories and sweat when you're having fun."

They know or recognize the benefits of physical activity and they are already convinced that physical activity is important to health, a sense of well-being, and increased energy.

What they perceive as benefits to physical activity:

- Gives them more energy
- Feeling better and stronger
- Less stress
- Makes you more alert at work
- Helps with weight loss
- You feel better about yourself; self-esteem; body image
- Helps to prevent diseases that run in my family

But they are not as convinced that there is a health benefit to moderate-intensity physical activity; and they did not see fun and enjoyable activities, such as country dancing or riding a bicycle on a pretty day, in terms of their health benefits.

And they are pleased to learn that some of what they are already doing is moderate activity and that it indeed has benefits.

They tend to have low self-efficacy for being physically active; they lack confidence in their ability to maintain an active lifestyle.

Their perceived barriers to being active:

- Don't think they have time
- Hectic schedules
- Demanding family priorities; women were more likely to express feeling guilty if they took time for themselves—away from their families
- Juggling children's schedules; car pooling
- Long working hours
- Too tired when they got home
- It's too late when they get home
- Internal lack of motivation: "I'm too lazy"
- Don't like exercise
- Need to see quick results
- Prefer other sedentary pastimes (watching television or working at the computer)
- Embarrassment at health clubs
- The need for convenience
- Safety issues (particularly for women)

When asked what would help them to be more physically active, they said things like:

- internal motivation ("I know what to do, it's just doing it")
- making the physical activity experiences as manageable and as pleasant as possible
- support from family and friends (though support from a spouse did not count as highly as support from friends)
- convenience—convenient places to be active or to walk

Women were more likely than men to frame physical activity as "time just for me"; whereas men were more likely to view physical activity as something they already do as part of their jobs or as something they do in a team sport.

They are less likely to set goals for activity or to schedule time for more activity.

Many of their homes contain little-used exercise equipment; participants frequently joked about the dust or the laundry that had accumulated on their equipment.

They mentioned having memberships in exercise clubs or spas, but rarely going to use them.

Two-thirds are trying to lose weight; they want to stay thin or lose weight but they are less confident in their ability to do so.

They are not sensation-seeking types (e.g., mountain climbing, sky diving).

Less likely to say others would describe them as physically fit, athletic, rugged, a winner, sexy, and wealthy.

Three-quarters or more say others would describe them as interesting, friendly, mature, caring, fun, smart, sensitive, independent, easygoing, practical, honest, and content.

Regarding life priorities, when focus group participants were asked to rank 10 items as to their importance, the top 3 were:

1. being close to God,
2. being happy with my family, and
3. being healthy.

They were more likely than other groups to say: there are other things I care more about than my health.

Behavioral Characteristics

They enjoy eating rich, high-fat foods.

38% have been advised by a doctor to diet or change their eating habits; 63% would be willing to follow a doctor's advice.

More likely to say that they have had a moderate amount or a lot of stress in the past 2 weeks.

Media Habits

Newspaper
- 84% read the news section
- 66% read the advertising or supplement section
- 55% read the comics
- 51% read the lifestyle section

Weekly magazines
- 33% read *TV Guide*
- 12% read *People*
- 12% read *Newsweek*

Monthly magazines
- 27% read *Reader's Digest*
- 18% read *Family Circle*
- 16% read *Good Housekeeping*
- 15% read *Better Homes and Gardens; Women's Day; Parents Magazine*
- 12% read *National Geographic*

Noncable television
- 65% watch local news
- 59% watch prime-time movies
- 50% watch news interviews
- 42% watch evening network news
- 38% watch public television
- 30% watch morning network news; Monday night football; entertainment specials

Most popular shows include

- *Home Improvement, ER, Rescue 911, Unsolved Mysteries, Roseanne, Grace Under Fire, America's Funniest Videos, Seinfield, America's Most Wanted, Frasier, Mad About You, Coach, Married with Children, Matlock, Murphy Brown, Murder She Wrote*

Cable networks

- 60% watch USA Network
- 57% watch Discovery Network
- 54% watch WTBS
- 48% watch Arts and Entertainment Channel
- 43% watch Lifetime Network
- 42% watch the Weather Channel
- 40% watch CNN; ESPN

Radio format

- 38% country
- 35% soft rock
- 34% easy listening

Resource D

Healthy Eating and Physical Activity: Highlights from CDC's Focus Group Research With Adult Contemplators and Preparers, 1995

Focus Group Participant Description*

A total of 136 adults participated in 16 focus groups conducted in four cities (Atlanta, Kansas City, Baltimore, Los Angeles) during March and April, 1995. Participants were white and African-American adults, 29 to 54 years of age, who were in either Contemplation or Preparation stages of change for improving their eating habits and/or becoming more physically active. All participants qualified if their education level was between high school graduation and *some* graduate-level coursework—but no graduate-level degree completed. Separate groups were formed of white men, white women, African-American men, and African-American women. Also, separate groups were conducted with "healthy eating" Contemplators and Preparers, and with "physically active" Contemplators and Preparers. Mixed within the groups were participants who did and did not have children under the age of 18 years living in their households.

Top 3 Life Priorities

1. Being close to God
2. Being happy with my family
3. Being healthy

Although not considered as high a priority as the other two, having good health was more frequently cited than other items on the list. Participants commonly expressed that they had assigned an item top priority because they considered it to be a prerequisite for the others. Participants often cited as a priority things that they did not have. For example, for one man who was unemployed, having a good job was a very high priority. Another respondent who felt stressed by

*Nutrition and Physical Activity Communications Team (NuPACT), National Center for Chronic Disease Prevention and Health Promotion, Centers for Disease Control and Prevention. *Healthy Eating and Physical Activity: Focus Group Research with Contemplators and Preparers.* Atlanta, GA: Westat Corporation, July 1995.

the responsibilities of raising five children placed great importance on enjoying free time. Frequently, respondents who had experienced health problems placed greater emphasis on being healthy. Two items on the list—looking good and having a good love life—were most consistently absent from the groups' top three responses

Fitting Priorities into Daily Life

Groups said that the importance of true priorities is significant enough that they do manage to fit the priorities into their busy lives. Many stated that they might, for example, take time to pray before starting their day, or that they attend religious services each week. Similarly, family relationships are maintained by doing things such as calling siblings weekly, or specifically setting aside time to spend with their children. Efforts to stay or become healthy seemed less likely to translate into specific daily or weekly activities.

Participants commonly expressed their frustration at being too busy or not having enough time to meet life's demands. Virtually all participants, regardless of demographic and lifestyle differences, seemed to have this feeling of being busy and stressed. Many said that at the end of their workday they were simply too exhausted emotionally or physically to do much more.

Importance of Good Health

In general, good health was considered important in that it enables one to do the things one wants or needs to do in a hectic life. Some participants mentioned that good health had become more important to them as they got older. They cited maintaining good health as important to setting a good example for their children. Others mentioned that they now were concerned with living long enough and being healthy enough to enjoy their children and grandchildren.

Overarching Themes

Five overarching themes consistently emerged throughout the groups' discussions:

1. **Family as a priority**. Family was as important to those participants who had children as it was for those who did not. The members of one's household appeared to be a key influence on lifestyle decisions. "Being happy with my family" consistently ranked among the top three in the 10-item "Life Priorities" exercise completed by all participants.

2. **Life is busy and stressful.** Regardless of their life situation, participants shared a perception that life is busy and stressful. Virtually all participants complained about rushing through their days and expressed an acute need for convenience (e.g., fast and convenient food, gym nearby home). Lack of time was a chief complaint. Participants seemed to value the increased energy and stress relief benefit offered by physical activity.

3. **Life stages influence behavior.** Childrens' ages, more than the ages of parents/participants themselves, seemed to influence the "life stage" behavior and lifestyles. Parents of very young infants and toddlers spend considerable time in and near home, cooking and eating at home, and chasing after their children. Parents of children from elementary to early teen years devote considerable time to their children's activities (to the detriment of their own)— away from home, chauffeuring to and from events, sports practices, music lessons, and so forth. They tend to eat on the run, and spend unprecedented

amounts of time in their cars or vans. Once children reached their mid-to-late teen years, parents reported turning inward and having more time and energy to spend on themselves, individually or as a couple (e.g., taking up golf again, or preparing gourmet meals together). Some participants noted age-related changes to their own bodies (e.g., not being physically able to do the kinds of exercise they had once done), or health problems suffered by friends their own age (e.g., heart attacks, high blood pressure) as signals of their changing life stages and life priorities.

4. **Spiritual, mental, and physical health are connected.** "Being healthy" incorporated more than physical health for these participants. The mind, body, and spirit were all related to each other in describing total well-being and quality of life. For many, family troubles, stress, or lack of spiritual peace could contribute to a sense of poor health as easily as any physical ache or pain.

5. **Being healthy is desirable.** Participants valued good health, especially in how it enabled one to meet daily responsibilities, or to enjoy life's pleasures. Participants noted that physical activity and eating healthfully were deeply intertwined.

Common Themes Related to Physical Activity

For this research, "physical activity" refers to an active lifestyle. Participants were knowledgeable about several aspects of getting physical activity and exercise. They were aware of the health benefits (particularly of exercise), could recite the exercise "prescription" of 20–30 minutes of exercise, 3 days per week with heart rates within the target zone. They were able to identify numerous and varied types of exercise. The greatest barrier, they said, wasn't knowledge, but rather time and internal motivation. They were aware that they should exercise and many expressed feeling guilty that they did not do it regularly.

During their discussions, it was clear that participants tended to believe that their *busy* lifestyles were actually *physically active* lifestyles. Based on the examples they offered of what keeps them busy (e.g., chauffeuring children to and from activities, running errands), it was clear that most of those activities do not qualify as "physical activity," but are indicative of a busy lifestyle.

People frequently mentioned having tried and failed to sustain exercise as part of their lives. Often an injury, a change in daily routine, or a life event interrupted the regularity of exercising, and it was never resumed. Although safety issues were mentioned by some, lack of time and internal motivation seemed to be the most common barriers to exercise.

Differences Between "Physical Activity" and "Exercise"

When asked to differentiate between physical activity and exercise, participants consistently had more favorable attitudes toward physical activity than toward exercise. They tended to perceive "physical activity" as including enjoyable, fun activities such as taking a walk, playing with children, working in the garden, engaging in team sports. Physical activity included a range of in-motion activities, things you might even do sporadically, undertaken with a goal *other than* (or, for some, in addition to) good health, weight loss, or "getting exercise." You "do it for the enjoyment of it," and "you're not even aware that you're doing it." One participant described the difference as: "walking around a track is exercise; walking through the woods is physical activity." Physical activities, especially those things that participants do for pleasure and/or with friends and family, were thought to be pleasurable enough that the exertion was not considered uncomfortable. For example, one participant said, "Dancing—who worries about calories and sweat [when you're having] fun?"

On the other hand, participants perceived "exercise" as unpleasant, tedious, boring, uncomfortable, a sweaty workout. It conjured up thoughts of torture, pain, strenuous, rigid activity. "Something you don't ordinarily do." They spoke about exercise as something that requires setting aside a specific time for exertion, special clothes and shoes, a mindset, and going someplace (usually an inconvenient place) to do it. Then why did they do it? Exercise was most often done for the purpose of being healthy, feeling better, and losing weight. "You have to do it on a regular basis."

Physical activity was, in many cases, not considered by participants to offer enough exertion, nor done with enough regularity, to be considered "good for you." Participants closely associated physical activity with being generally active in life. It was considered by many to be what they *already* do, or an achievable extension of their normal activities. Many participants noted that unless physical activity "gets your heart rate up," it cannot possibly provide the same health benefits as activities they regard as "exercise."

Understanding of and Reaction to the Physical Activity Message

The scientific CDC/ACSM physical activity recommendation was presented to gauge participants' understanding and reaction to it. The statement was read:

> Every American adult should accumulate 30 minutes or more of moderate-intensity physical activity on most, preferably all, days of the week.

Responses ranged from the sense that the message is fairly sound to total confusion over its meaning. Many participants absolutely did not believe that any health benefits could be derived from the recommended amount of activity. However, once the moderator confirmed the statement's scientific validity, most participants tended to conclude that they were already getting, or could easily achieve, the recommended 30 minutes most days of the week. Many participants were intrigued and rather pleased to think that some of their everyday activities may have health benefits.

When asked to comment on the wording of the statement, participants found fault with every word to some extent. They found the statement confusing or troublesome. Often, participants expressed a general sense that the message lacked clarity. One man commented: "Boy, who wrote this? It sounds like a college exam"; while another said, "The people who said this . . . are they the same ones who came up with the food groups thing?"

Specific Problems With the Physical Activity Recommendations

First, there was consistent confusion about the meaning of "accumulate 30 minutes or more." It was not uncommon for participants to believe that one could meet that recommendation by getting 5 minutes of physical activity each day for 6 days (for a total 30 minutes over the week). There continued to be misinterpretation of which activities would qualify as "sustained physical activity"—even after a lengthy group discussion to clarify it—suggesting that adults who are merely exposed to the message could easily misinterpret it.

The term "moderate-intensity" was questioned, and at times interpreted as "moderate to intense" activity. Even the meaning of "most days" of the week was confusing to some. Several participants interpreted it as 3 days or 4 (because weekends don't count). One participant, echoed by others, mentioned that the vagueness of the term "most days" could offer some people an excuse for not getting physical activity on a given day. He recommended specifying the number of days.

Over the course of 16 focus groups, every word of the recommendation came into question at some point. *Every* . . . "you mean infants, children, and the elderly too?" *American* . . . "you mean it's only good for Americans?" *Adult* . . . "why not children . . . it has to start with the young!" *Should* . . . "no one's going to tell me I 'should' do something," or "How do they know what's good for *me*?" And so forth.

While most participants took issue with the words themselves, many also doubted that any health benefits could be derived from the recommended amount of physical activity. One man commented, "This says 'should' and not 'why.' Add the benefit." On several occasions, participants expressed the sentiment that, "I already do that, and I'm not healthy."

Barriers to Physical Activity

When participants were asked, "What keeps you from being physically active," the most compelling barriers to increasing levels of physical activity were time constraints and an internal lack of motivation or ability to consistently be more active. Others barriers mentioned were laziness, having tried and disliked it, physical and mental fatigue by the end of the day, the need to see quick results, the influence of others, other sedentary pastimes which they preferred (such as watching television or working at the computer), embarrassment at health clubs, the need for convenience, and safety (e.g., the perception that it is too dangerous for women to be outdoors in the evening).

Specifics Regarding "Time" as a Barrier to Action

Many cited their hectic schedules, family priorities, long working hours, "It's always something . . ."; or "I barely have time to do the things I *have* to do. There's never any time for the things I'd *like* to do." Many participants who had children in the home saw their children's busy after-school, evening, and weekend activities as a barrier. Parents spend their time carpooling and chauffeuring kids about, or sitting on the sidelines as their children make that home run or soccer goal.

For others . . . they were too tired. They described being too mentally and physically exhausted after work to think about more physical activity: "I run for the couch." "All I want to do is go to bed."

Specifics Regarding Motivation as a Barrier to Action

Focus-group participants were quick to say that they lacked the willpower or the right frame of mind. "I'm lazy." "I'm not motivated." They would point to themselves and describe something *within* that kept them from doing it. "YOU choose how you use the time you have." "It's a matter of priorities."

What Would Help People Become More Physically Active?

Some participants believed that knowing the many benefits achieved by the physical activity recommendation might be motivating. And while lack of knowledge or skills were sometimes mentioned, internal motivators were perceived as the *key* determinant for most. "The first step has to come from me," "*I* keep me from exercising," "I know what to do . . . it's just doing it." Motivators for beginning and maintaining physical activity included physiological reasons ("if my doctor told me," or "if my life were on the line"), as well as appearance reasons.

Perceived Benefits of Increased Physical Activity

- Feeling better, stronger.
- Having more energy, more stamina.
- Less stress.
- Makes you more alert at work.
- Helps with weight loss.
- You feel better about yourself; self-esteem, improved body image—a better profile, more self-confidence.
- Helps prevent the diseases that "run in my family."
- Physical activity, they believed, could contribute to increasing energy and brain power, or stamina to do the things you have to do in a busy day.

Specific Helps or Motivators to Action

Some practical suggestions offered by the participants included making the physical activity experience as manageable and as pleasant as possible.

- Find something that you enjoy, that is fun, and do it more often.
- Walk with a friend, a family member, or a "buddy."
- Delegate household chores and make time for yourself.
- Get into the mindset. "Separate yourself from [all of the] things you have to do once in a while."
- Support from family and friends seemed very important (though spouses didn't seem to count as highly as friends). One participant stated, "You just have to do it . . . to make the time." Some participants noted that it was important to have convenient places to exercise, or to walk, but those who reported having shopping mall walking programs or worksite facilities did not take advantage of them.

Women were more likely than men to mention exercise or physical activity as something they must do for themselves or "time just for *me*." Men were more likely to view physical activity as something that they already do as part of their jobs (walking up and down the stairs, up and down the hall, carrying computer equipment from office to office) or something they do as part of a team sport (pickup basketball or baseball).

The Skills and Knowledge Area—What Do People Need?

The barriers people face in their efforts to increase physical activity are substantially more related to motivation than to skills and knowledge factors. As a matter of fact, participants' knowledge of the exercise prescription and target heart rate appeared deeply ingrained.

Most people were in "Relapse"—there was a theme of trying and failing.

- Most had attempted to exercise regularly, but did not maintain that behavior. They used phrases like: "when I was being good," or "when I was in my exercise phase."
- Often something had happened to interrupt the routine, like an injury, a walking partner moved away, or unforeseen changes in their daily schedules, or their children's schedules.

- Many of their homes contained little-used exercise equipment, and participants frequently joked about the dust or the laundry that had accumulated on their equipment. They also mentioned having memberships in exercise clubs or spas, but rarely going to use them.

Participants did not tend to think of fun and enjoyable activities (such as country dancing or riding a bicycle on a pretty day) in terms of their health benefits. They needed to "redefine" exercise and physical activity in their minds. Examining the barriers they mentioned to being active indicates that some higher-order skills could be useful as well—tips that could facilitate behavior change and maintenance rather than education alone. (See chapter 4 for specific suggestions.) For example, improving time-management skills, practicing techniques for self-motivation, or learning effective ways to enlist family members' support may help address the barriers most frequently faced by the participants. Lower-level skills (e.g., proper stretching/warm-up techniques, or choosing the appropriate exercise) would *not* be among those needed by these very knowledgeable and experienced participants to increase their physical activity.

Convincing Others to Increase Physical Activity

When participants were asked to convince the other side of the table to incorporate more physical activity into their lives, participants came up with a wide variety of persuasive strategies, some related to positive benefits of physical activity, others related to the risks/dangers of *not* incorporating physical activity into their schedules. Men were more likely than were women to cite the risks (particularly health risks) of not being more active. Women were more likely to mention the benefits of being physically active as motivating (e.g., "Fun is *good* for you"; "Feel better about yourself").

Resource E

Selected Organizations and Agencies Concerned With Persons With Disabilities

American Athletic Association of the Deaf
3607 Washington Boulevard, Suite 4
Ogden, UT 84403-1737
Phone: 801-393-8710

Disabled Sports USA
(formerly known as National Handicapped Sports)
451 Hungerford Drive, Suite 100
Rockville, MD 20850
Phone: 301-217-0960
Website: **http://www.dsusa.org/dsusa**

Dwarf Athletic Association of America
418 Willow Way
Lewisville, TX 75067
Phone: 214-317-8299

International Paralympic Committee
Adenauerallee 212
5 3113 Bonn
Germany
Phone: 49-228-2097-200
Fax: 49-228-2097-209
Website: **http://info.lut.ac.uk/research/paad/ipc/ipc.html**

National Institute of Arthritis and Musculoskeletal and Skin Diseases
1 AMS Circle
Information Clearinghouse
Bethesda, MD 20892
Phone: 301-495-4484

National Council on Independent Living
2111 Wilson Blvd
Arlington, VA 22201
Phone: 703-525-3406

National Council on Disability
1331 F Street, NW
Washington, DC 20004-1107
Phone: 202-272-2004
Website: **http://www.ncd.gov**

National Multiple Sclerosis Society
733 3rd Avenue, 6th Floor
New York, NY 10017
Phone: 212-986-3240
Website: **http://www.nmss.org**

Paralyzed Veterans of America
801 18th Street, NW
Washington, DC 20006
Phone: 202-872-1300
Website: **http://www.pva.org**

Special Olympics International
1325 G Street, NW, Suite 500
Washington, DC 20005
Phone: 202-628-3630
Website: **http://www.specialolympics.org**

United States Association of Blind Athletes
33 North Institute
Colorado Springs, CO 80903
Phone: 719-630-0422
Website: **http://www.usaba.org**

United States Cerebral Palsy Athletic Association
1600 L Street, NW, Suite 700
Washington, DC 20036-5602
Website: **http://www.ucpa.org**

Wheelchair Sports USA
3595 E. Fountain Boulevard, Suite L-1
Colorado Springs, CO 80910
Phone: 719-574-1150
Website: **http://www.wsusa.org**

Resource F

Americans With Disabilities Act (ADA)

The Americans With Disabilities Act ensures that programs and services are equally accessible to individuals with and without disabilities, and therefore has implications to anyone planning and conducting physical activity programs. The areas addressed by the ADA include employment, public services, public accommodations, communications, and miscellaneous topics such as insurance coverage. An individual with a disability is defined as a person who:

- has a physical or mental impairment that substantially limits a "major life activity,"
- has a record of such an impairment, or
- is regarded as having such an impairment.

Examples of physical or mental impairments include, but are not limited to, diseases and conditions such as the following:

orthopedic, visual, speech, and hearing impairments

cerebral palsy

epilepsy

muscular dystrophy

multiple sclerosis

cancer

heart disease

diabetes

mental retardation

emotional illness

specific learning disabilities

HIV, whether or not symptomatic

tuberculosis

drug addiction

alcoholism

"Major life activities" include functions such as caring for oneself, performing manual tasks, walking, seeing, hearing, speaking, breathing, learning, and working. Of particular interest to planners of physical activity programs is Title II of the ADA, which covers state and local governments. Its provisions include the following:

State and local governments

- may not refuse to allow a person with a disability to participate in a service, program, or activity simply because the person has a disability;
- must provide programs and services in an integrated setting, unless separate or different measures are necessary to ensure equal opportunity;
- must eliminate unnecessary eligibility standards or rules that deny individuals with disabilities an equal opportunity to enjoy their services, programs, or activities unless "necessary" for the provisions of the service, program or activity;
- are prohibited from enforcing requirements that tend to screen out individuals with disabilities;
- are required to make reasonable modifications in policies, practices, and procedures that deny equal access to individuals with disabilities, unless a fundamental alteration in the program would result;
- must furnish auxiliary aids and services when necessary to ensure effective communication, unless an undue burden or fundamental alteration would result;
- may provide special benefits beyond those required by the regulation to individuals with disabilities;
- may not place special charges on individuals with disabilities to cover the cost of measures necessary to ensure nondiscriminatory treatment, such as making modifications required to provide program accessibility or providing qualified interpreters;
- shall operate their programs so that, when viewed in their entirety, they are readily accessible to and usable by individuals with disabilities.

Safety requirements that are necessary for the safe operation of the program in question, such as requirements for eligibility for drivers' licenses, may be imposed if they are based on actual risks and not on mere speculation, stereotypes, or generalizations about individuals with disabilities.

For more information on the Americans with Disabilities Act, contact:

The Disability Rights, Education and Defense Fund
2212 6th Street
Berkeley, CA 94710
Phone: 510-644-2555

Resource G

National Days or Months: Opportunities for Physical Activity Promotion

January

Healthy Weight Week
(January 17–23)

Healthy Weight Journal
402 South 14th Street
Hettinger, ND 58639
Phone: 701-567-2646
Fax: 701-567-2602
Website: **http://www.healthyweightnetwork.com**

February

American Heart Month

American Heart Association
7272 Greenville Ave.
Dallas, TX 75231
Toll-free: 800-AHA-USA1
Website: **http://www.americanheart.org**

National Girls and Women in Sports Day
(1st Thursday in February)

Women's Sports Foundation
Eisenhower Park
East Meadow, NY 11554
Toll-free: 800-227-3988
Website: **http://www.lifetimetv.com/WoSport**
E-mail: **wosport@aol.com**

National Cardiac Rehabilitation Week
(February 7–13)

American Association of Cardiovascular and Pulmonary Rehabilitation
7611 Elmwood Avenue, Suite 201
Middleton, WI 53562
Phone: 608-831-6989
Fax: 608-831-5122
Website: **http://www.aacvpr.org**

March

National Nutrition Month

American Dietetic Association
Phone: 312-899-0040
Toll-free: 800-877-1600
Website: **http://www.eatright.org**

American Red Cross Month

American Red Cross Public Affairs
National Headquarters
430 17th Street NW
Washington, DC 20006
Phone: 703-206-6000
Website: **http://www.redcross.org**

National Youth Sports Safety Month

National Youth Sports Safety Foundation, Inc.
333 Longwood Avenue, Suite 202
Boston, MA 02115
Phone: 617-277-1171
Fax: 617-277-2278
Website: **http://www.nyssf.org**

April

World Health Day
(April 7th)

American Association for World Health
1825 K Street NW, Suite 1208
Washington, DC 20006
Website: **http://www.aawhworldhealth.org**
E-mail: **aawhstaff@aol.com**

May

National Physical Fitness and Sports Month

President's Council on Physical Fitness and Sports
HHH Building, Room 738H
200 Independence Avenue SW
Washington, DC 20201
Phone: 202-690-9000
Fax: 202-690-5211

National Physical Education and Sports Week
(1st week in May)

American Alliance for Health, Physical Education, Recreation and Dance
(AAHPERD)
1900 Association Dr.
Reston, VA 20191
Phone: 703-476-3412
Website: **http://www.aahperd.org**

National Bike Month and National Bike-to-Work Day

League of American Bicyclists
190 W. Ostend St., Suite 120
Baltimore, MD 21230

National Bike Ride

Bicycle Institute of America
1818 R St. NW
Washington, DC 20009

Project ACES Day
(1st Wednesday in May)

Youth Fitness Coalition, Inc.
PO Box 6452
Jersey City, NJ 07306
Phone: 201-433-8993
Fax: 201-332-3060

National Running and Fitness Week
(2nd week in May)

American Running and Fitness Association
4405 East West Highway, Suite 405
Bethesda, MD 20814
Phone: 301-913-9517
Toll-free: 800-776-2732
Website: **http://www.arfa.org**
E-mail: **arfarun@aol.com**

National Playday for Health
(formerly known as National Employee Health and Fitness Day)
(3rd Wednesday in May)

National Association of Governor's Councils on Physical Fitness and Sports
621 E. Park Ave.
Indianapolis, IN 46225
Phone: 317-237-5630
Website: **http://www.fitnesslink.com/Govcouncil/**

National Senior Health and Fitness Day
(last Wednesday in May)

Mature Market Resource Center
P.O. Box 883
Libertyville, IL 60048-9922
Phone: 847-816-8660
Toll-free: 800-828-8225
Fax: 847-816-8662
Website: **http://www.fitnessday.com**
E-mail: **maturemkt@aol.com**

World Challenge Day
(last Wednesday in May)

Trim and Fitness International Sport For All Association (TAFISA)
Frankfort, Germany
Phone: 49 69 67 00 225
Fax: 49 69 67 87 801

Older Americans Month

Administration on Aging
Phone: 202-619-0641
Website: **http://www.aoa.dhhs.gov**
E-mail: **AoAInfo@ban-gate.aoa.dhhs.gov**

June

National Safety Month

American Society of Safety Engineers
1800 East Oakton
Des Plaines, IL 60018-2187
Phone: 847-699-2929
Website: **http://www.asse.org**

National Men's Health Week
(June 14–20)

National Men's Health Foundation
14 East Minor Street
Emmaus, PA 18098-0099
Phone: 610-967-8620
Fax: 610-967-8955
Website: **http://www.menshealth.com**

National Special Recreation Week
(for the physically challenged)
(June 27–July 4)

John Nesbitt, President
SRD International Center on Special Recreation
362 Koser Avenue
Iowa City, IA 52246-3038
Phone: 319-337-7578
E-mail: **john-nesbitt@uiowa.edu**

July

National Recreation and Park Month

National Recreation and Park Association
22377 Belmont Ridge Rd.
Ashburn, VA 20148
Phone: 703-858-0784
Website: **http://www.nrpa.org**

National Therapeutic Recreation Week
(July 11–17)

National Therapeutic Recreation Society
22377 Belmont Ridge Road
Ashburn, VA 20148
Phone: 703-858-0784
Fax: 703-858-0794
Website: **http://www.nrpa.org**

September

Family Health and Fitness Days USA
(last weekend in September)

Health Information Resource Center
621 E. Park Ave.
Libertyville, IL 60048
Toll-free: 800-828-8225
Fax: 847-816-8662
Website: **http://www.fitnessday.com**
E-mail: **hlthinfo@aol.com**

National Cholesterol Education Awareness Month

National Heart, Lung, and Blood Institute Information Center
P.O. Box 30105
Bethesda, MD 20824-0105
Phone: 301-251-1222
Fax: 301-251-1223
Website: **http://www.nhlbi.nih.gov/nhlbi/nhlbi.htm**

October

National Walk a Child to School Week
(First week in October)

Partnership for a Walkable America
1121 Spring Lake Drive
Itasca, IL 60143-3201
Toll-free: 800-621-7615, ext. 2383
Fax: 630-775-2185
Website: **http//www.nsc.org/walkable.htm**

World Walking Day
(3rd Sunday in October)

TAFISA (see May page 312)

Healthy Choice American Heart Walk Event

American Heart Association
7272 Greenville Ave.
Dallas, TX 75231
Toll-free: 800-AHA-USA1
Website: **http://www.americanheart.org**

Family Health Month

American Academy of Family Physicians
Phone: 816-333-9700
Toll-free: 800-274-2237
Website: **http://www.aafp.org**

Child Health Day
(First Monday in October)

National Institute of Child Health and Human Development
31 Center Dr.
MSC 2425
Building 31, Room 2A32
Bethesda, MD 20892
Phone: 301-496-5133
Website: **http://www.nih.gov/nichd/**

November

National Diabetes Month

American Diabetes Association
1660 Duke St.
Alexandria , VA 22314
Phone: 703-549-1500
Toll-free: 800-232-3472
Website: **http://www.diabetes.org**

"Turkey Trot" events
(held throughout the month, close to Thanksgiving)

various organizations

December

World Festival of Traditional Sports

TAFISA (see May page 312)

Note: Resource G includes selections from *Chase's 1995 Calendar of Events* and events verified by the sponsoring organizations. This resource is not intended to be a complete listing of all possible physical activity-related events. Add to this list as you become aware of additional special events.

To obtain the annually published *Chase's Calendar of Events*, check with your community library, or contact:

NTC Contemporary Publishing Co.
4255 W. Touhy Ave.
Lincolnwood, IL 60046
Phone: 800-USA-READ

Also available is *The Health Events Calendar* published by the Health Information Resource Center, a national information clearinghouse for consumer health information. Phone: 800-828-8225; e-mail: **hlthinfo@aol.com.**

Resource H

Healthy Communities 2000: Model Standards

The following is reprinted from the American Public Health Association, and represents the physical activity components throughout the document:

Healthy Communities 2000: Model Standards; Guidelines for Community Attainment of the Year 2000 National Health Objectives. 3rd Edition. Washington, DC: American Public Health Association, 1991.

These model standards can be used as a template for your community. Simply fill in the blanks with goals that are appropriate for your specific population. The *Healthy Communities 2000* standards follow the blanks in parentheses.

Model Standards Goals. Community residents will be physically fit, thereby improving their health and vigor and reducing morbidity and mortality.

Model Standards Note: *Healthy People 2000* objectives are national in scope and are provided as a guide for action by state and local communities. As such, they have been restated in their entirety without change. The target for each of these objectives has been repeated verbatim as a reference for community use. However, communities are encouraged to establish targets based on their own situations and, where possible, establish targets that are more ambitious than the national reference.

In this edition, the word "other" has been added to each *Healthy People 2000* objective which contains a Special Population Target. The use of the word "other" is meant to suggest that communities may wish to develop special population targets for community-specific subpopulations—for example, for selected age, race, sex, income, and/or other high-risk groups.

Revised physical activity and fitness objectives are currently under development for the year 2010. To view the latest version, please visit this website: **http://web.health.gov/healthypeople/**

Healthy Communities 2000 Model Standards

Focus	Objective	Indicator of success
Risk reduction objectives		
Regular practice of light to moderate physical activity	1.3.4. By _____ (2000) increase to at least _____ (30) percent the proportion of people aged 6 and older who engage regularly, preferably daily, in light to moderate physical activity for at least 30 minutes per day. (Baseline: 22 percent of people aged 18 and older were active for at least 30 minutes 5 or more times per week and 12 percent were active 7 or more times per week in 1985) Note: Light to moderate physical activity requires sustained, rhythmic muscular movements, is at least equivalent to sustained walking, and is performed at less than 60 percent of maximum heart rate for age. Maximum heart rate equals roughly 220 beats per minute minus age. Examples may include walking, swimming, cycling, dancing, gardening and yardwork, various domestic and occupational activities, and games and other childhood pursuits.	Percent regularly engaging in physical activity
Physical activity programs	1.3.5. By _____ increase to at least _____ percent the proportion of people aged 6 and older who had the opportunity to participate in the physical activity programs of at least one community organization within the past year. Model Standards Note: The community may wish to develop special population targets, for example, by age, race, sex, income, handicap conditions, etc., for community relevant subpopulations.	a. Number/rate, and type of available physical activity programs b. Percent participating in physical activity programs c. Percent of special populations (school-aged children and adolescents, older adults, low-income adults, and people with chronic physical and mental conditions) participating in programs d. Percent engaging in regular physical activity
Physical activity for cardiorespiratory fitness	1.4.6. By _____ (2000) increase to at least _____ (20) percent the proportion of people aged 18 and older and to at least _____ (75) percent the proportion of children and adolescents aged 6 through 17 who engage in vigorous physical activity that promotes the development and maintenance of cardiorespiratory fitness 3 or more days per week for 20 or more minutes per occasion.	Percent engaging in vigorous physical activity

Focus	Objective	Indicator of success

	(Baseline: 12 percent for people aged 18 and older in 1985; 66 percent for youth aged 10 through 17 in 1984) Special Population Target Vigorous Physical Activity
	
	                      1985 2000
	                    Baseline Target
	
	a. Lower-income people aged 18 and older (annual family income <$20,000) 7% 12%
	b. Other ____ ____
	
	Note: Vigorous physical activities are rhythmic, repetitive physical activities that use large muscle groups at 60 percent or more of maximum heart rate for age. An exercise heart rate of 60 percent of maximum heart rate for age is about 50 percent of maximal cardiorespiratory capacity and is sufficient for cardiorespiratory conditioning. Maximum heart rate equals roughly 220 beats per minute minus age.	

Leisure-time physical activity	1.4.7. By _____ (2000) reduce to no more than _____ (15) percent the proportion of people aged 6 and older who engage in no leisure-time physical activity. (Baseline: 24 percent for people aged 18 and older in 1985) Special Population Targets No Leisure Time Physical Activity 1985 Baseline 2000 Target a. People aged 65 and older 43% b. People with disabilities 34% c. Lower-income people (annual family income <$20,000) 32%+ (17%) d. Other ____ ____ + Baseline for people aged 18 and older Note: For this objective, people with disabilities are people who report any limitation in activity due to chronic conditions.	Percent engaging in no leisure-time physical activity

(continued)

Healthy Communities 2000 Model Standards (continued)

Focus	Objective	Indicator of success
Muscular strength, muscular endurance, and flexibility	1.6.8. By _____ (2000) increase to at least _____ (40) percent the proportion of people aged 6 and older who regularly perform physical activities that enhance and maintain muscular strength, muscular endurance, and flexibility. (Baseline data available in 1991)	Percent engaging in physical activities for enhancing muscular strength, endurance, and flexibility
Practices for attaining appropriate body weight	1.7.9. By _____ (2000) increase to at least _____ (50) percent the proportion of overweight people aged 12 and older who have adopted sound dietary practices combined with regular physical activity to attain an appropriate body weight. (Baseline: 30 percent of overweight women and 25 percent of overweight men for people aged 18 and older in 1985)	Percent combining sound dietary practices with regular physical activity
Awareness of the benefits of physical activity and fitness	1.7.10. By _____ increase to at least _____ percent the proportion of people aged _____ and older who can identify that regular exercise reduces the risk of heart disease, helps maintain appropriate body weight, reduces the symptoms of depression and anxiety, and enhances self-esteem. Model Standards Note: The community may wish to develop special population targets, for example, age, race, sex, handicapping conditions, etc., for community relevant subpopulations.	Percent who can identify benefits of regular physical activity
	1.7.11. By _____ increase to at least _____ percent the proportion of people ages _____ and older who can identify that cardiorespiratory fitness, muscular strength, muscular endurance, flexibility, and body composition (percent body fat) are important to health. Model Standards Note: The community may wish to develop special population targets, for example, age, race, sex, handicapping conditions, etc., for community relevant subpopulations.	Percent who can list components of fitness
Awareness of practices that promote cardiorespiratory fitness	1.7.12. By _____ increase to at least _____ percent the proportion of people ages 6 and older who can identify correctly the frequency and duration of physical activity thought to most effectively promote cardiorespiratory fitness. Model Standards Note: The community may wish to develop special population targets, for example, age, race, sex, handicapping conditions, etc., for community relevant subpopulations.	Percent who can identify physical activity required to promote cardiorespiratory fitness.

Focus	Objective	Indicator of success
Services and Protection Objectives		
Comprehensive planning	1.7.13. By _____ the community will develop and implement a comprehensive plan to improve the physical activity and fitness of its residents.	a. Presence of written plan b. Documented implementation activity
Participation in daily school physical education	1.8.14. By _____ (2000) increase to at least _____ (50) percent the proportion of children and adolescents in 1st through 12th grade who participate in daily school physical education. (Baseline: 36 percent in 1984–86)	Percent participating in daily school physical education
Class time spent in physical activity	1.9.15. By _____ (2000) increase to at least _____ (50) percent the proportion of school physical education class time that students spend being physically active, preferably engaged in lifetime physical activities. (Baseline: Students spent an estimated 27 percent of class time being physically active in 1983) Note: Lifetime activities are activities that may be readily carried into adulthood because they generally need only one or two people. Examples include swimming, bicycling, jogging, and racquet sports. Also counted as lifetime activities are vigorous social activities such as dancing. Competitive group sports and activities typically played only by young children, such as group games, are excluded.	Percent of class time spent physically active
Worksite fitness programs	1.10.16. By _____ (2000) increase the proportion of worksites offering employer-sponsored physical activity and fitness programs as follows: Worksite Size 1985 Baseline 2000 Target 50–99 employees 14% ____(20%) 100–249 employees 23% ____(35%) 250–749 employees 32% ____(50%) >750 employees 54% ____(80%) Other ____ Model Standards Note: Community may wish to consider setting a standard for worksites with less than 50 employees.	Percent of worksites with programs

(continued)

321

Healthy Communities 2000 Model Standards (continued)

Focus	Objective	Indicator of success
Availability and accessibility of facilities	1.11.7. By ____ (2000) increase community availability and accessibility of physical activity and fitness facilities as follows: Facility — 1986 Baseline — 2000 Target Hiking, biking, and fitness trail miles — 1 per 71,000 people — 1 per 10,000 people Public swimming pools — 1 per 53,000 people — 1 per 25,000 people Acres of park and recreation open space — 1.8 per 1,000 people (553 people per managed acre) — 4 per 1,000 People (250 people per managed acre) Other ____	Number, rate, and type of available facilities
Patient counseling	1.12.18. By ____ (2000) increase to at least ____ (50) percent the proportion of primary care providers who routinely assess and counsel their patients regarding the frequency, duration, type, and intensity of each patient's physical activity practices. (Baseline: Physicians provided exercise counseling for about 30 percent of sedentary patients in 1988)	Percent patients assessed and counseled
Community surveillance objective	1.12.19. By ____ the community will have a baseline data set and established methodology for measuring progress for each of its physical activity and fitness objectives.	a. Presence of surveillance system b. Presence and analysis of data set c. Reports distributed to community
Physical education and competitive athletic program	8.4.39. By ____ the physical education and competitive athletic program of each school will include provision for the evaluation of each individual's appropriate level of participation, a plan for graduated conditioning, training in the prevention of injuries relevant to each type of activity, the provision of all appropriate safety equipment, and the handling of medical and dental emergencies, all in accordance with policies developed in cooperation with official health agency servicing the community.	Percent of schools having evaluation policy

Focus	Objective	Indicator of success
School-based instruction on injury prevention	9.18.29. By ____ (2000) provide academic instruction on injury prevention and control, preferably as part of quality school health education, in at least ____ (50) percent of public school systems (grades K through 12). (Baseline data available in 1991)	Percent providing injury prevention and control instruction
Protective equipment in sports and recreation	9.19.30. By ____ (2000) extend requirement of the use of effective head, face, eye, and mouth protection to all organizations, agencies, and institutions sponsoring sporting and recreation events that pose risks of injury. (Baseline: Only National Collegiate Athletic Association football, hockey, and lacrosse; high school football; amateur boxing; and amateur ice hockey in 1988)	Percent requiring use of protective equipment
Risk Reduction		
Participation in physical activities to promote cardiorespiratory fitness.	13. By ____ increase to at least ____ percent the proportion of people aged ____ and older who participate in vigorous physical activities that promote the development and maintenance of cardiorespiratory fitness 3 or more times per week for 20 minutes or more per occasion.	Percent engaging in vigorous physical activity
Mental and emotional health	14. By ____ increase to at least ____ percent the proportion of people aged ____ and older who are questioned routinely by primary care providers about their mental and emotional health, including sources of stress and coping skills.	Percent questioned
Regular practice of light to moderate physical activity	15.11.15. By ____ (2000) increase to at least ____ (30) percent the proportion of people aged 6 and older who engage regularly, preferably daily, in light to moderate physical activity for at least 30 minutes per day. (Baseline: 22 percent of people aged 18 and older were active for at least 30 minutes 5 or more times per week and 12 percent were active 7 or more times per week in 1985) Note: Light to moderate physical activity requires sustained, rhythmic muscular movements, is at least equivalent to sustained walking, and is performed at less than 60 percent of maximum heart rate for age. Maximum heart rate equals roughly 220 beats per minute minus age. Examples may include walking, swimming, cycling, dancing, gardening and yardwork, various domestic and occupational activities, and games and other childhood pursuits.	Percent regularly engaging in physical activity

Resource I

Excerpts from CDC's "Ready. Set. It's Everywhere You Go" Campaign Handbook

This resource includes excerpts from:

Centers for Disease Control and Prevention. *Ready. Set. It's Everywhere You Go.* Atlanta: U.S. Department of Health and Human Services, 1997.

Pages 329–337 provide you with condensed versions of the social marketing concepts covered earlier in *Promoting Physical Activity: A Guide for Community Action.* Pages 339–343 provide valuable information about working with the media to publicize and promote your efforts. You'll also find information about developing physical activity programs and events on pages 345–353, as well as a "Ready. Set. It's Everywhere You Go" flyer (page 354).

Ready. Set.
It's Everywhere You Go.

- ◆ Marketing Strategies for Physical Activity

- ◆ Working with the Media: Story Angles and Talking Points

- ◆ Developing Physical Activity Programs and Events

CENTERS FOR DISEASE CONTROL AND PREVENTION

Introduction

In support of the landmark Surgeon General's report, Physical Activity and Health, the Centers for Disease Control and Prevention (CDC) is taking the lead to promote physical activity. Since the release of the report, CDC has conducted epidemiological, consumer, and behavioral research. From these data, CDC has selected a target audience for a nationwide physical activity promotion campaign: adults who are currently not active enough to enjoy the health benefits of physical activity, but who are thinking about or attempting to be more active.

Part of a national initiative to increase levels of physical activity in the U.S. population, the materials in this kit share the key theme "Physical Activity—It's Everywhere You Go." This theme raises awareness that the physical activity needed for a healthier life can be found in many common activities, such as brisk walking, bicycle riding, heavy housework, and yardwork. By simply adding more of these types of activities, most people can increase their activity and therefore may improve their health.

Whether you are a local, state, or national organization, the materials collected in this kit can help you promote regular, moderate physical activity to people within this target audience. For this target audience, CDC recommends 30 minutes of moderate physical activity a day at least 5 days per week. Physical activity can substantially reduce the risk of developing or dying from heart disease, diabetes, colon cancer, and high blood pressure. Physical activity can also reduce symptoms of depression and anxiety, improve mood, and make it easier and more enjoyable for people to perform daily tasks.

The target audience's "readiness to change" means that they want to know more about the benefits of physical activity—and are eager to find out how they can overcome what may now seem insurmountable barriers to a more active lifestyle. This kit provides ample information and examples to help you meet their needs.

We think the target audience will be responsive to this theme and to the ideas presented in this kit, which was designed with input from organizations around the country. The enclosed materials provide ideas for promotion, media relations, and long-term programs to increase physical activity. No matter where you are in your program planning, we hope you will use the ideas and information provided in this kit to design program activities that meet your audience's particular needs.

Marketing Strategies for Physical Activity

Social Marketing—A Fresh Approach to Promoting Physical Activity

With the "It's Everywhere You Go" campaign, CDC takes a fresh, consumer-based approach to promoting regular, moderate physical activity. Social marketing provides the framework within which program planners can apply knowledge, theories, and techniques to improve health behaviors. Using this framework, CDC has developed the strategies, messages, and materials in this marketing kit, which were carefully crafted for maximum impact with our target audience (described below). Those of you promoting physical activity at the national, state, or local level can put these tools to work as well.

Social Marketing Concepts

Social marketing is a strategy for changing behavior in subgroups within a population. The process involves applying techniques from marketing and advertising to the analysis, planning, execution, and evaluation of programs designed to influence the behavior of a target audience. The accompanying table describes key elements of social marketing.

Consumer Orientation

Social marketing efforts are grounded in science and are consumer driven. They begin with the premise that the primary source of information for health communication efforts comes from the consumers to be reached — that is, consumers whose behaviors are the targets for change.

In social marketing, understanding the target audience is essential to developing effective messages and strategies. Of course, people are more than their age, race, and gender. Their attitudes, knowledge, and beliefs about being physically active are critically important in understanding how to motivate people to change their behavior. Knowledge of the target audience leads to more appropriate message design, more effective delivery, and better reception by the audience.

Key Elements of Social Marketing		
Concept	**Definition**	**Application**
Consumer orientation	Intervention research, planning, implementation, and evaluation are based on the consumers' perspective.	Use research methods to understand consumer perspective; pretest materials with members of the target group.
Audience segmentation	Differentiation of large groups of people into smaller, more homogeneous subgroups.	Determine behavioral, motivational, cultural, and other variables that may affect the communication strategy. Create specific target groups who share the same characteristics and are distinct from other subgroups.
Channel analysis	Determination of the appropriate methods to reach target audience members where and when they are most likely to attend to and respond to the message.	Determine those places, times, and states of mind when the target audience will most likely be thinking about the subject.
Strategy	Set of approaches that focuses the program on meeting stated objectives.	After determining the objective(s), select broad approaches that can be refined to include specific activities for reaching the target audience.
Process tracking	Mechanisms established to monitor program implementation.	Evaluate to determine if program is implemented as planned. Use results to redirect, refine, or revise implementation.

Adapted from: Lefebvre and Rochlin, 1997.

Target Audience

Below we describe the target audience selected for the "It's Everywhere You Go" campaign and share detailed demographic and psychographic (psychological attributes, values, beliefs, and attitudes toward life in general) information that was used to develop consumer messages and to guide campaign development.

The audience selected for the "It's Everywhere You Go" campaign includes physical activity **contemplators**—those who think about becoming moderately physically active—and **preparers**—individuals who plan to do moderate activity and may have tried it, but want to do more.

Audience selection for this campaign was based on the Stages of Change Model, in which Prochaska and colleagues (Prochaska, DiClemente, Norcross, 1992) define a continuum of readiness to change behavior. The model describes how individuals move through a series of stages as they progress toward their goal of adopting or altering a behavior pattern or a lifestyle. This continuum begins with pre-contemplation (not even considering change) and moves to contemplation, preparation, action, and maintenance (sustained adoption of healthy behavior).

Although people do not move through these stages in a strictly linear fashion, each stage is a predictable, well-defined experience in which particular milestones are met before the next stage is reached. Theories suggest that certain cognitive and behavioral techniques aid movement to the next stage. Research has consistently shown that people who try to make changes to reach stages they are not ready for set themselves up for failure (Prochaska, Norcross, DiClemente, 1994). In this model, then, one key to success in motivating behavior change is defining the audience according to their stage of change. This step enables us to make our strategy and tactics more specific with stage-appropriate messages, channels, and techniques.

As defined by the model, people in the contemplation and preparation stages are more ready to change than precontemplators, and are therefore more likely to be open to consumer messages about moderate physical activity (defined by CDC/ACSM as 30 minutes of moderate-level physical activity a day at least 5 days a week). Similarly, people in action and maintenance have different needs, and will be receptive to a different message. Research and experience provide us with the following insights for promoting behavior changes in contemplators and preparers:

- Contemplators for moderate physical activity are considering changing their behavior, but are still ambivalent. Barriers to being regularly active outweigh perceived benefits of physical activity.
- Promote behavior change by:
    △ Helping them identify their barriers to change and weigh the pros and cons of being moderately physically active.
    △ Increasing levels of self confidence about physical activity through motivating messages and opportunities to build the skills necessary to achieve an active lifestyle.
    △ Encouraging them to set small, specific goals that can slowly be increased toward achieving an active lifestyle.
- Preparers for moderate physical activity may have a plan and may know what to do, but their action is not consistent or regular. They may be uncertain about the outcomes of their actions. Preparers may show small signs of progress toward implementing their plan or take action with mixed or inconsistent results.
- Promote behavior change by:
    △ Recommending that they develop a plan for regular moderate activity, with an emphasis on small, specific, and realistic goals.
    △ Showing them how much fun physical activity can be and reinforcing their attempts to be more active.
    △ Encouraging them to focus on their successes and to make use of social networks to support their progress.
    △ Emphasizing learning basic skills necessary to change behavior and the importance of making a life-long commitment to change.

Target Audience Profile

A set of data called *Healthstyles* was examined to provide insight into our target audience. The *Healthstyles* data, which combines health behavior and communication-relevant questions with general lifestyle, sociopolitical, and media usage items, goes beyond traditional demographic and geo-demographic factors to provide insight into consumer "orientations to health". Healthstyles is based on the results of three mail survey questionnaires, administered in 1995, from a quota sampling of 5,000 persons representative of U.S. adults in age, gender, marital status, race/ethnicity, income, region, household size, and population density. (The average response rate across all three surveys was 67%).

Using the *Healthstyles* data, contemplators and preparers for physical activity account for 38% of the total population. This percentage has been applied to the U.S. census to estimate the number of people in our target audience.

Demographics: Who Are We Talking To?

The audience for the "It's Everywhere You Go" campaign comprises 73 million American adults with the following demographic characteristics:

- 65% are between the ages of 18 and 45 years
- 60% are women
- 71% are married
- 58% have children at home; 35% have children less than 5 years old
- 66% have a high school education or greater
- 74% are employed
- 58% have a household income greater than $30,000

This information alone tells us that effective communication would likely promote physical activity as a family-oriented experience that people with young children can manage. But our profile tells us much more about this audience and provides clues about what motivates them or prevents them from increasing their levels of physical activity.

Attitudes and Beliefs: What Interests and Motivates Our Audience?

The following table outlines a number of additional audience characteristics and corresponding opportunities for promoting physical activity. This list of opportunities is by no means exhaustive; it is provided to demonstrate how knowledge about the target audience can be translated into effective program ideas. The "It's Everywhere You Go" campaign capitalizes on these opportunities in its overall message and program strategies.

Motivating the Audience

Target Audience Characteristic	Promotion Opportunity
A key motivator is engaging in physical activity with family or friends; having less time for family and friends is a barrier.	Make moderate physical activity a family activity or a fun way to spend time with friends. Think about holding a physical activity event at a local gathering place such as the zoo. A day at the zoo presents an opportunity for a family to spend time together while walking for some distance.
Having more energy is the chief perceived benefit of improving health habits.	Promote moderate physical activity's positive effect on energy levels. Have target audience members chart their energy levels over the course of your physical activity intervention.
Believe themselves to be interesting, friendly, mature, fun, smart, sensitive, independent, easy-going, practical, honest and content. Believe they are NOT physically fit, athletic, rugged, winners.	Promote moderate physical activity with an image the audience will relate to: fun, upbeat, practical.
Lack of confidence in ability to be regularly physically active.	Emphasize activities that are simple and achievable. Provide target audience with the opportunity to try the desired behavior. For example, hold a walk-a-thon at a shopping mall or a cleanup and beautification project at a park. Build physical activity skills by demonstrating different types of moderate physical activity and letting the target audience practice those skills.
Absence of planning when, where, and how long to be physically active.	Teach planning and monitoring skills to target audience. Try establishing a buddy system or walking group that meets regularly.
Experience moderate to high amounts of stress.	Position moderate physical activity as a way to reduce stress. Introduce the idea of physical activity stress breaks or a mini-recess for adults.

Target Audience Characteristic	Promotion Opportunity
Feel too tired or believe that it is too late after work to engage in physical activity.	Get the message out that after work is not the only time of day when one can be physically active. Why not take a morning walk with the dog and kids or a brisk walk during the lunch hour?
Have competing demands for time.	Show your audience how to incorporate moderate physical activity into their daily lives without taking much time out of the day. Examples such as taking the stairs instead of the elevator, moving briskly when pushing a child in a stroller, or walking the dog can help the target audience get started on reaching their goals.
Believe that physical activity is too expensive.	Promote free or low-cost ways to obtain moderate physical activity, such as walking in municipal parks or in one's own neighborhood or participating in a park or river cleanup. Show the variety of activities—such as mowing the lawn, raking, gardening, and cleaning the house—that provide moderate physical activity.
Less likely to say they are satisfied with their lives.	Position moderate physical activity as something that can help enhance quality of life and an overall sense of well-being.
Want to stay thin or lose weight but are not confident in their ability to maintain a low-fat diet and to stay thin or lose weight	Show the relationship between moderate physical activity and weight management.

Media Habits: Where Can We Reach Our Audience?

When promoting your program, event, or activity, aim for advertisements and coverage in the newspaper sections and on the television programs and radio formats highlighted below, since they are likely to be accessed by the target audience. (Please see the section of this kit entitled "Working with the Media" for information on pitching stories and giving interviews.) Users of this kit should select the information that is appropriate to their own circumstances.

Media Habits		
Type of Media	**Section/Program**	**Media Opportunity**
Newspaper	News section	Offer to provide representatives from your (or your partners') organization for interviews by local reporters.
	Advertising supplements	Talk to your local paper about reproducing and including this kit's public service announcement (PSA) in their advertising supplement.
	Comics	Inquire about the possibility of placing the print PSA in the comics section of your local paper.
	Lifestyle section	Pitch a story about a family whose members have incorporated moderate physical activity into their daily lives.
Non-cable television	Local news	Invite local stations to cover your event or activities. Partner with a local station to provide nightly tips on fitting in moderate physical activity or ask them to air the television PSA. Enlist the support of a local television weather forecaster in promoting your event or activities during the broadcast.
	News interviews	Offer to provide representatives from your (or your partners') organization for media interviews on local television news.
Radio	Country Soft rock Easy listening	Place the radio PSA on local stations with these formats. Have a representative from your organization be a guest during morning or evening drive time.

References

Lefebvre RC, Rochlin L. Social marketing. In *Health Behavior and Health Education: Theory, Research and Practice, Second Edition*. San Francisco: Jossey-Bass, 1997.

Prochaska JO, Norcross JC, DiClemente CC. *Changing for Good*. New York: William Morrow and Company Inc., 1994.

Prochaska JO, DiClemente CC, Norcross JC. In search of how people change. *American Psychologist* 47:1102-1114, 1992.

More About Social Marketing

- Andreasen AR. *Marketing Social Change: Changing Behavior to Promote Health, Social Development, and the Environment*. San Francisco: Jossey-Bass, 1995.

- Lefebvre RC, Rochlin L. Social marketing in: *Health Behavior and Health Education: Theory, Research and Practice, Second Edition*. San Francisco: Jossey-Bass, 1997.

- Maibach E, Parrot RL (eds.). *Designing Health Messages: Approaches from Communication Theory and Public Health Practice*. Thousand Oaks, CA: Sage Publications, 1995.

- Sutton SM, Balch GI, Lefebvre RC. Strategic questions for consumer-based health communications. *Public Health Reports*, 110:725-733, 1995.

Working With The Media: Story Angles and Talking Points

T he media can help you recruit partners and participants and help draw attention to the goal of your program—promoting moderate physical activity. Publicity can thus add to the success of your events and increase audience recognition of your organization.

Publicity also can extend the impact of an event. For example, a Zoo Walk can be preceded and followed by publicity on radio and television stations, and in the local newspaper. Media coverage gets your message out to more people than might be able to attend your event.

If you have media relations experience, you already know how to effectively communicate your message to the media. If you have not worked with the media before, someone else in your organization or a partner organization may be familiar with media relations. If possible, find and work with this person.

What Makes News?

Use the following story angles or "news hooks" to interest your media contacts in a physical activity story. Offer story angles appropriate for each publication's and program's particular format and audience.

Community physical activity events.
Promote walks and other planned physical activity events through the media. These events provide the target audience with fun opportunities to engage in moderate physical activity and to build skills.

Community physical activity opportunities.
Our surroundings play a role in encouraging or hindering physical activity. Use the media to promote stories about how city planning, community development, traffic flow, and accessibility influence physical activity in your community. For example, highlight the increasing number of places to ride bikes; the design of new, safer walking paths; or extended hours at public recreation facilities.

Activity groups or clubs.
A feature story can be developed about clubs or groups in your area formed to create companionship for those interested in increasing their activity. Whether it's walking, gardening, biking, or in-line skating, the emphasis is on doing fun things with other people—something we know motivates our target audience.

Tips for fitting physical activity into busy lifestyles.
Media stories can provide tips for fitting moderate physical activity into busy lifestyles, such as walking at lunch with a friend or colleague, taking the stairs instead of the elevator, or being active with kids on weekends and after work. You may want to feature an "average" person who has found time to fit moderate physical activity into his or her life.

Seasonal physical activity.
Stories can be developed around moderate physical activity and the change in seasons. For example, in the fall, rake the leaves, take a walk, go apple or pumpkin picking, or chop wood; in the winter, shovel the walk, clean the house, or build a snowman; in the spring, garden, mow the lawn, take a walk, or spring clean; in the summer, wash the car or walk in the morning or early evening.

Active vacations.
Physical activity is everywhere you go. Develop stories that will help viewers or readers plan moderate physical activity during vacations. Recommend places that have riding and walking paths nearby or that offer swimming and hiking opportunities.

Worksite physical activity.
Most of our target audience is employed. Stories about companies that provide and promote physical activity opportunities may be of interest to your media contacts. Identify companies that provide on-site physical activity facilities or opportunities or sponsor community or employee physical activities.

Helpful Hints for Obtaining Media Coverage

Meet Face to Face

Whenever you can, arrange to meet face to face with reporters, editors, and producers. Bring your article, news release, or other material you want them to use. If you are asking them to cover an event, leave behind some written background information.

Emphasize the importance of promoting physical activity throughout the community. If appropriate, use this opportunity to offer your services as an expert resource on physical activity, for now or in the future. If a story does appear, send a short note of thanks.

Media Sponsorship

Media outlets may be willing to do more than provide publicity. Invite a television or radio station, local cable network, or area newspaper to cosponsor your event.

Television Weather Forecasters

An effective way to get your message out is through local television weather forecasters. They usually have a significant public following and often will mention activities on the air. It would not be unusual for them to mention your activities several times during a newscast. Encourage local weather forecasters to include a weather-appropriate physical activity tip after each forecast (e.g., a bike ride in nice weather or a mall walk during bad weather).

Giving Interviews

Prepare thoroughly for an interview. Organize your information, and write important points on notecards if necessary. Although the interviewer will have questions, keep key message points in mind and be prepared to make simple, direct, and easy-to-understand statements that reflect your key messages.

Talking Points

When conducting the interview, try to incorporate the following talking points, as appropriate.

Physical Activity in the United States

- According to *Physical Activity and Health: A Report of the Surgeon General,* a landmark review of scientific evidence linking physical activity and health:
  - △ Physical inactivity is a serious nationwide problem. It poses a public health challenge for reducing the national burden of unnecessary illness and premature death.
  - △ More than 60% of Americans are not getting enough physical activity to obtain health benefits.
  - △ Twenty-five percent of adults report no physical activity in their leisure time.

■ Based on the *Healthstyles* data set (see "Marketing Strategies for Physical Activity"), a nationally representative sample of adults:

△ About 73 million American adults are thinking about or trying to start becoming more physically active. This figure is derived from the percentage of adults who identify themselves as either planning to start doing physical activity in the near future (8.9%) or doing some moderate activity but thinking about doing more (28.6%).

Promoting Moderate Physical Activity

■ The "It's Everywhere You Go" campaign is designed to help people think differently about physical activity and show them how to fit it into their lives.

■ The audience for this campaign is thinking about becoming physically active or adding more activity to their lives. Thus, effective way to promote physical activity is to "meet these people where they are," by helping them to work moderate physical activity to their schedules. That is to say, it is not likely that many of these people will go from being inactive to competing in a triathlon without passing through a series of smaller, more achievable steps.

■ The CDC and American College of Sports Medicine have defined moderate physical activity as 30 minutes of moderate-level physical activity a day at least 5 days a week.

Benefits of Moderate Physical Activity

■ Physical activity reduces the risk of developing or dying from some of the leading causes of illness and death in the United States.

■ Regular physical activity can:

△ Substantially reduce the risk of developing or dying from heart disease, diabetes, colon cancer, and high blood pressure.

△ Reduce symptoms of depression and anxiety, improve mood, and enhance ability to perform daily tasks.

■ People who are usually inactive can improve their health and well-being by becoming even moderately active on a regular basis.

Overcoming Barriers

■ Many people will have to work up to being active for 30 minutes a day. They should start slowly with realistic goals (e.g., walking 10 minutes). Their confidence will grow, and they will soon be able to see some benefits of physical activity.

- Physical activity need not be strenuous for a person to achieve health benefits. Nor do people need to join a health club or take up jogging. The following activities can provide moderate-intensity physical activity:
    - Walking the dog, taking walking breaks during the day, or taking the stairs instead of the elevators.
    - Gardening and yard work—raking the lawn, bagging grass or leaves, digging, hoeing, weeding, planting trees and flowers, pushing a lawn mower.
    - Housework—scrubbing the floor or bathtub on hands and knees, hanging laundry on a clothesline, cleaning out the garage, washing windows.
    - Washing and waxing the car by hand.
    - Home repair—roofing, painting, wall papering, plastering, remodeling.
- Engaging in physical activity with friends or family members can improve a person's health and enhance relationships at the same time.
- Planning in advance can help people stick to a physical activity routine. They should make plans to walk with a friend or colleague regularly.
- Being prepared is not only for the Boy Scouts. Encourage people to keep comfortable shoes and a T-shirt at the office or some gear (basketball, in-line skates, tennis racquet) in their car trunk—they never know when an opportunity will arise. They should also keep a walking partner's phone number by their home or office phone.
- Be it gardening, line dancing, yoga, playing softball, or riding a bike, people should participate in moderate-intensity physical activities that they enjoy.

Developing Physical Activity Programs and Events

Physical activity is everywhere you go. The ways to promote moderate physical activity in your region, state, or community and the locations in which to do so are countless. Make a difference in your community by creating or using existing community events during which your audience can try new types of physical activity. These events can help build audience confidence and skills. They will also demonstrate that moderate physical activity can be fun and can fit into a busy lifestyle.

This guide contains ideas for non-traditional physical activity events and venues, and lists potential partners. The ideas were developed in light of the target audience characteristics, barriers, and motivators – derived from consumer research – discussed in the section of this document entitled "Marketing Strategies for Physical Activity." For example, the target audience has identified time away from family and friends as a barrier to physical activity. Thus, showing them how to do moderate physical activity *with* family and friends is a good strategy for reaching this audience and helping them change their behavior. The emphasis is on fun, family-oriented activities; overcoming barriers; and building skills among the target audience. The events and locations that follow were chosen to reach the target audience when they are likely to be attentive to moderate physical activity messages, and to demonstrate how common activities can provide moderate physical activity. You can implement one of these ideas and adapt it to fit your resources, or conduct an altogether different type of event—the choice is yours.

Of course, attendance at one event will not result in long-term behavior change for most people; however, events like those highlighted below can draw attention to the importance of physical activity and help reshape people's perceptions of physical activity. And there is no reason to stop at one event or activity. You may decide to hold physical activity events on an ongoing basis to reinforce your message and involve as many people as possible, or you might host one of the suggested events to kick off a longer-term intervention.

Consider holding your event in conjunction with an annual health or fitness observance. You might even partner with a state or local chapter of the sponsoring organization. A partial listing of these observances is provided at the end of this section.

Look for ways to incorporate the materials in this kit into your physical activity promotion activities. For example, broadcast the radio public service announcements at your event and make copies of the "It's Everywhere You Go" material available to participants. You can also create your own materials based on the "It's Everywhere You Go" message.

Program Information

Search the **Combined Health Information Database** (CHID) to find out about other programs that are successfully reaching a similar target audience. CHID can be accessed at most county or university libraries and on the World Wide Web at http:\\chid.nih.gov.

"It's Everywhere You Go"...
Park and Recreation Events

Municipal parks and recreation facilities are excellent sites for physical activity events. They are open to the public, entrance is usually free or low cost, and they are identified with the promotion of wellness, leisure, and family and group activities. Many physical activity events can be planned and implemented in conjunction with park and recreation organizations.

YOU COULD

- Start a before-work, lunch, or after-hours walking group at a park near a high concentration of businesses.
- Conduct "getting started" workshops to introduce people to new activities. The activities need not be limited to what we traditionally think of as physical activity. What about hosting an outdoor dancing lesson or a power-walking seminar?
- Sponsor a walk in a local park. The event could be conducted as a fundraiser for recreational equipment or as part of a park cleanup.
- Hold a weekend event during which members of the community can play a pickup game of basketball, volleyball, tennis, or softball.
- Sponsor a kite festival at the park. Encourage families to come to the event and to take some walking trails during the day.

Sample Park and Recreation Programs

In Colorado, Parks and Recreation Departments united with local health departments to conduct physical activity promotion activities throughout the State.

Foothills Parks and Recreation District formed a partnership with the Jefferson County Department of Health and Environment to plan a broad spectrum of creative wellness activities. With funding from the Jefferson County Commissioner's Office, they purchased and outfitted a 34-foot bus for use as a mobile wellness classroom to deliver disease prevention and health promotion and physical activity-related programs throughout the community — to schools, worksites, and hard-to-reach neighborhoods.

The Fort Morgan Parks and Recreation Department joined forces with rather unusual partners: a local cemetery administrator to allow walking programs on the grounds of the memorial park, a local motel owner to provide water aerobics classes in his under-used swimming pool, and the staff of a 240-acre wildlife preserve (formerly a dump and wasteland) to develop walking trails and educational and recreational opportunities for community members.

- Municipal park staff and officials
- Park and recreation officials
- Radio stations (live broadcast from event)
- Service organizations
- Walking groups
- Dance instructors
- Chamber of Commerce
- Hospital-based wellness programs

Zoo and Aquarium Events

Zoos and aquariums provide opportunities for families and friends to spend time together while engaging in physical activity. These locations frequently come to mind when families plan outings.

YOU COULD

- Hold a "Walk with the Animals" event that combines walking for physical activity with a family day at the zoo. Form a partnership with your local zoo, that could, for example, reduce entry fees during the event. At an information booth near the zoo's entrance, participants can receive a map highlighting places in the zoo where they can pick up information on physical activity, samples of orange juice or bottled water (free or at a reduced price), and tickets redeemable for zoo merchandise. For example, a station positioned near a particularly active animal could illustrate the importance of keeping active. At the monkey house, visitors could receive information on activities around their house or for their families. At each station, participants can estimate the distance they traveled.
- Host an aquarium event that emphasizes walking and water sports as a fun way to engage in physical activity. Set up stations around the aquarium that provide ideas for fitting physical activity into daily life.
- Conduct an event that encourages participants to search for particular animals located specific distances away from each other and the entrance. People who find a certain number of animals could receive a rebate on zoo merchandise or rebates from other event partners.
- At any of these events, use distance markers or provide maps or pedometers so that participants can track how far they have walked.

- Zoos and aquariums
- Sporting goods stores
- Pet stores
- Walking groups

Gardening Events

People might not realize that gardening provides opportunities for physical activity. Gardening can be done individually, with the family, or within a group. Often overlooked as a way to engage in physical activity, gardening can last a lifetime.

YOU COULD

- Conduct gardening workshops to introduce people to flower or vegetable gardening.
- Sponsor individual or group plots in a community garden. Workshop attendees could receive rebates on the plots or win plots in a raffle, or availability could be limited to a first come-first serve basis. You could hold a contest for the plot with the best flowers, most vegetables, best individual or group plot, etc. to heighten interest. Winners could receive rebates on gardening supplies.
- Contact farms to gauge interest in holding "glean" days. Gleaning involves collecting the fruits and vegetables that were not harvested (e.g., apples that fell off the trees) and donating them to food banks. Whoever collects the most can come back to pick their own (at a reduced rate).
- Make a day of the event. Hold sack races and scavenger hunts. Whoever walks a certain distance or finds a certain number of items can receive a prize.

POTENTIAL PARTNERS

- Flower and gardening stores
- Grocery stores
- Gardening clubs or horticultural societies
- Small resource farmers
- Farmers' markets
- Chambers of Commerce
- City councils
- Cooperative extension service

Community Service Events

You can promote the campaign's messages and activities through community efforts that tie physical activity into volunteer efforts. Not only will participants beautify their surroundings and strengthen their communities, but they will participate in activities that will boost their energy levels and build moderate physical activity skills with friends and family.

YOU COULD

- Organize a community cleanup day. Participants could help clean parks, trails, streams, or roads (i.e., adopt a highway).
- Conduct school or home cleanup, repair, and painting events.
- Conduct a community car wash. The proceeds raised could be allotted for school or community recreational equipment.

POTENTIAL PARTNERS

- Department of Transportation
- Religious and volunteer organizations
- Hardware stores
- Organizations that support persons with disabilities

Indoor Events

Indoor facilities—schools, malls, health clubs, community centers—may already offer physical activity opportunities. Many are ideal places to host a workshop or event. Indoor facilities make weather considerations less of a concern, and most are safe places to hold events.

YOU COULD

- Host a physically active back-to-school night.
- Work with a mall or shopping center to begin an early morning walking program.
- Partner with a health club or community center to host a physical activity fair that includes opportunities to try different types of physical activity, clinics on physical activity safety, and displays from activity groups (e.g., bowling and softball leagues or hiking clubs).
- Hold a series of workshops that teach members of the target audience how to use dancing to help reach their physical activity goals. It might be western dancing one week and salsa the next.

- Host a weekly family skate in the evening at an ice or roller rink.
- Start a beginner's volleyball league or host a family volleyball tournament.
- Offer a workshop designed to encourage planning for physical activity and bolster self-confidence. The workshop might explain how to fit physical activity into a busy lifestyle and the benefits of engaging in physical activity with friends or family while providing demonstrations and opportunities to try new forms of physical activity.

POTENTIAL PARTNERS

- Volleyball, racquetball, and other sports leagues
- Walking groups
- Mall management companies
- Skating rink management companies
- Parent-teacher organizations
- Hospital-based wellness programs
- Dance schools and instructors

Sample Indoor Programs

Seward, Alaska, shares its physical activity facilities and resources with the entire community. The high school and technical school make their fitness and recreation facilities available during non-school hours to community members. People can swim, lift weights, or play basketball or racquetball at low cost, and community aerobics instructors use the facilities to teach classes to the public. Even visitors to Seward can take advantage of these opportunities, which they learn about from a promotional folder left in hotel rooms.

At Hoover High School in inner-city San Diego, California, students helped develop a 2,800-square-foot fitness center at the school. The fitness center is open to students, school staff, and the community when the school day is over. This program created partnerships between high school staff and students, the school's food service, the California Governor's Council on Physical Fitness and Sport, the fast-food industry, and the local community. Hoover High School's program allows adolescents and young adults to be physically active with their friends, peers, and family in a safe and enjoyable environment, and addresses local residents' needs for recreation facilities.

Worksite Events

Since almost three-quarters of our target audience is employed, the worksite presents a likely effective location in which to spread the physical activity message. Partner with individual businesses or business associations in your area to conduct worksite-based events and interventions.

YOU COULD

- Involve businesses in a state or local "walk at lunch day" that encourages employees to take a walk during their lunch break.
- Encourage businesses to sponsor employee softball or volleyball teams or local leagues or to hold classes and workshops in small-group settings.
- Encourage employers to turn standard 10-15 minute breaks into recess or activity breaks.
- Work with companies in your area to develop "physical activity friendly" company picnics and other corporate events or to develop friendly competitions to increase employees' physical activity.

Sample Worksite Programs

Union Pacific Railroad offers health promotion programming not only at its Omaha, Nebraska, headquarters but even in the most remote company locations. The Union Pacific Railroad worksite wellness program targets the company's 27,000 employees, most of whom are blue-collar workers. At company locations where health promotion facilities are not available, old railroad cars have been converted and equipped as rolling fitness centers for use by employees. Union Pacific's program has identified key determinants of physically active lifestyles among special populations, such as blue-collar employees in remote locations, and has used this information to design and disseminate effective physical activity programs. As a founding member of the Wellness Councils of America in 1981, Union Pacific Railroad provides a model to encourage other employers to provide opportunities for employees to incorporate moderate physical activity into their daily lives by providing supportive worksite environments and policies.

The Blackfoot School District Community Wellness Program, the first such program in Idaho, targets school district employees living in or near Blackfoot, a rural Idaho community of about 10,000 people. A comprehensive education program about health and wellness laid the foundation for physical activity interventions based on goal setting, incentives, an employee walking program, and the accumulation of "physical activity miles"—a standard for measuring a variety of physical activities, including walking, gardening, bicycling, and swimming. This program illustrates how employers can provide supportive worksite environments and policies, and opportunities for employees to incorporate moderate physical activity into their daily lives.

POTENTIAL PARTNERS

- Chamber of Commerce
- Hospital-based wellness programs
- Individual companies
- State restaurant association

Physical Activity

It's at the zoo.

It's in the rain.

It's in the park.

It's in the driveway.

It's at the office.

It's at the mall.

It's in the neighborhood.

It's in the garden.

It's on the sidewalk.

It's Everywhere You Go.

Physical activity! It's in the house, in the yard, at the office, and even at the mall. Just 30 minutes of moderate physical activity a day at least five days per week is what you need. It can boost your energy and lower your stress and risk of chronic disease. It can be done as common activities – walking, gardening, and housework. They all count! If you think you can't do 30 minutes of activity, start with shorter amounts. Get more out of life with physical activity – It's Everywhere You Go!

Call 1-888-CDC-4NRG for more information.

CDC
CENTERS FOR DISEASE CONTROL
AND PREVENTION

Resource J

Sample State Promotion Activities

This resource contains sample physical activity promotion activities that were conducted in several U.S. states as a result of CDC's "Ready. Set. It's Everywhere You Go" campaign. With no federal funding and just a little encouragement, these innovative states developed successful interventions on a shoestring budget. We hope these real-world examples will give you ideas for your own intervention programs and will demonstrate the limitless opportunities for physical activity promotion that are possible when creative program planners and resourceful partners take action.

Iowa

Three projects are getting Iowans moving!

- The Iowa Department of Public Health reaches thousands of individuals nationwide with daily motivational messages about physical activity and healthy eating in an electronic listserv format known as FITNET. This daily e-mail promotion reaches over 50,000 individuals who subscribe to the listserv for their daily dose of fun and inspiration. Each message is approximately one hundred words long and combines interesting facts with common sense wisdom and humor to gently persuade people to adopt and maintain healthier lifestyles. The Iowa Department of Public Health provides FITNET free for the asking, and believes the service is an important part of its overall mission to promote good nutrition and physical activity. In addition to the listserv format, any organization can obtain an electronic file holding a year's supply of motivational messages, which businesses may personalize and redistribute to their employees. To subscribe to either service, contact FITNET's creator, Tim Lane, via e-mail at **tlane@idph.state.ia.us.**

- In the state of Iowa, 99 counties joined forces to create a list of the state's best suggestions and opportunities to be physically active, celebrating Iowa's tourism and products while relating them to healthy behaviors. First produced as flyers and posters, the Iowa map of opportunities to be active was announced in a dynamic press release in 1998, and before long the idea really caught on! In 1999, the list of 99 or more county-specific ideas led to the formation of a statewide challenge to all residents—"99 IN '99." This program encourages Iowans to improve their health by making small, sustainable changes such as consuming more fruits and vegetables or participating in physical activities at least 99 times during 1999. The motivating Iowa 99-county map serves as a progress diary. Those who participate in the challenge may check off a county on the Iowa map each time they achieve one of the desired behaviors. When all 99 counties have been checked, an individual will have completed 99 days of successful behavior to earn any one of many creative incentives that play on the 99 theme. From the start, the state department of public health worked with numerous partners to make the state activity map and poster-sized flyers available extensively. Because the program promoted Iowa towns, events, and products, numerous state agencies, local businesses, and organizations willingly became involved in what program planners hope will be an annual celebration. For example, a Holiday Inn in Cedar Falls offers bicycle and stroller rentals to patrons who wish to explore the sights.

- The Iowa Department of Public Health's *Vital Signs* is a collection of over 52 signs suitable for posting wherever people who are making healthy choices might see them (i.e., along life path points such as stairwells, elevators, and cafeterias). Originally developed in Polk County as part of the Healthy Polk 2000 "Signs of Spring" project, the idea has grown into a yearlong idea. The package of 52 time-tested messages is being shared with others for a cost of approximately $10. For more information, contact:

Tim Lane
Iowa Department of Public Health
E-mail: **tlane@idph.state.ia.us**

Texas

The Texas Department of Health, in an effort to promote physical activity and family health, developed a statewide initiative to promote walking at the zoo as a means of spending family time together in a fun and active way. As of 1999, 11 of the 12 zoos throughout the state have worked with their local health departments to set up mile markers along the zoo's major paths, with health information stations strategically placed along the way. During designated times of the year, health department employees staff the information stations and award T-shirts bearing the "Physical Activity: It's Everywhere You Go" theme to those who complete the entire zoo walk. The idea has been so successful that local health departments and zoos are exploring additional ways they can partner for better health. For more information, contact:

Texas Department of Health
Bureau of Chronic Disease Prevention and Control
1100 West 49th Street
Austin, TX 78756
Phone: 512-458-7111

Ohio

The Ohio Department of Health has partnered with the State Department of Natural Resources to promote walking for fun and fitness in 72 state parks throughout Ohio. Piloted in 1998, the program awards prizes to individuals who successfully complete a certain number of miles of walking trails during a designated time of year. Nearly 1,000 people participated in the program during the first year, a success that both agencies look forward to continuing with assistance from additional business and organizational partners. For more information, contact:

Ohio Department of Health
Bureau of Health Promotion
246 North High Street
Columbus, OH 43215

Louisiana

In 1998, the Louisiana Office of Public Health formed sunny relationships with weather forecasters at four of the major media networks across the state. Meteorologists were simply asked to include a weather-appropriate physical activity tip at the beginning or ending of their forecasts each day during the month of May. The meteorologists voluntarily complied, and their often witty and off-the-cuff comments successfully reached nearly 140,000 people with physical activity-promoting messages.

California expanded the idea by linking with radio traffic reporters who offered health-promoting and injury-preventing messages during peak drive-time traffic periods. For more information, visit the website of the Prevention Institute in Berkeley, California: **http://www. preventioninstitute.org**.

Kansas

Gardening proved to be a creative and enjoyable way for parents and children to be active together while enjoying the fruits (and vegetables) of their labor! The Learning Garden in southeast Kansas was developed in 1998 to encourage parents to be more physically active with their children while learning gardening techniques and food preparation ideas for a variety of produce. Targeting low-income families who participated in the USDA Special Supplemental Food Program for Women, Infants, and Children (WIC), the community garden project was sponsored by a community-based coalition that included participation by the local health department, cooperative extension master gardeners, the mental health center, and local media.

For 10 sessions, preschoolers enjoyed age-appropriate gardening activities while their parents met with gardening and nutrition experts. Each session included 30 minutes of instruction followed by hands-on experience in the Learning Garden, where, together, parents and children put their knowledge into action. For more information, contact:

Crawford County Health Department
Phone: 316-231-5411

or:

Kansas LEAN
Phone: 316-337-6051

Nebraska

Physical activity is "Everywhere You Go" throughout Nebraska, according to the Nebraska Health and Human Services System (NHHSS), which in 1998 blanketed the state with CDC's "Ready. Set. It's Everywhere You Go" campaign. The campaign reached thousands of residents while fostering new partnership linkages among state agencies and organizations. Following are some examples:

- A black and white 8-1/2 × 11 poster was displayed in newsletters that went out to 2,700 members of the Nebraska School Activities Association; 4,300 school personnel; and more than 3,000 coaches; and to members of Nebraska Public Health Association; the Nebraska Health and Human Services System; and the Nebraska Association for Health, Physical Education, Recreation and Dance.

- Audio and video public service announcements were played during Nebraska high school football, volleyball, gymnastics, and basketball championships. These messages reached at least 10,000 people.

- NHHSS teamed up with the Nebraska Travel and Tourism Division to create an information brochure that highlighted healthy travel tips and a variety of ways one could figuratively tour Nebraska. By following a map's suggested activities and checking them off or logging them on the map, individuals could learn a great deal about the state while taking steps to better health. Copies of this brochure were disseminated through worksites and schools and along highway rest stops throughout the state. Rest stop personnel encouraged their visitors to complete an evaluation of the brochure, and of the 96 individuals who took the time to complete evaluations, nearly everyone indicated that the information was useful, and many of the respondents even requested additional information.

- NHHSS worked with the Nebraska Press Advertising Service to create a seven-week series of newspaper advertisements featuring the graphics and messages of the "Ready. Set. It's Everywhere You Go" campaign for use in rural Nebraska. It is estimated that these ads reached 500,000 people. One year later, the ads were still being placed in the smaller newspapers throughout the state.

- Each year, a Healthy Nebraskans calendar has been produced which, in 1998, was distributed to 4,500 agencies, hospitals, schools, coalitions, local health departments, and citizens. The 1998 and 1999 calendars focused on achieving regular moderate physical activity.

- "Ready. Set. It's Everywhere You Go" campaign posters and promotional materials were shared with county cooperative extension educators, parks and recreation professionals, school teachers, and a variety of agencies across the state of Nebraska.

Barbara Scudder-Soucie
Nebraska Health and Human Services
Division of Health Promotion and Education
301 Centennial Mall South
Lincoln, NE 68509-5044
Phone: 402-471-2101

Glossary of Physical Activity Terms

aerobic capacity—The maximum amount of oxygen that can be transported from the lungs to the tissues during exercise. Aerobic capacity is influenced by age, sex, exercise habits, heredity factors, and clinical cardiovascular status. It is used as an index of an individual's capacity for sustained work performance and is commonly used to measure cardiovascular fitness. It is also referred to as maximum oxygen consumption ($\dot{V}O_2$max).[1]

aerobic exercise—Exercise in which aerobic (oxidative) metabolism is used to generate the energy required to perform an activity. Regular aerobic exercise increases the functional capacity of the cardiovascular system. Aerobic exercises include activities such as running, jogging, brisk walking, cycling, and swimming.

body composition—The relative amounts of muscle, fat, bone, and other anatomical components that contribute to a person's total body weight. Body composition differs markedly between men and women. Simple methods for determining body composition are often stated as percent body fat, pounds of fat, or lean body mass. Body composition comprises one of the five health-related components of physical fitness.

body fat—The total amount of fat deposited in the body as "storage fat" (which accumulates in adipose tissue) and "essential fat" (which is required for normal physiologic functioning and is stored in bone marrow as well as in major organs and tissues). Essential fat is about four times higher in women than in men.

cardiorespiratory fitness—The ability of the circulatory and respiratory systems to supply fuel during sustained physical activity. Cardiorespiratory fitness is one of the five health-related components of physical fitness.

cardiovascular endurance—The capacity of the heart, lungs, and blood vessels to deliver nutrients and oxygen to the tissues and to remove waste, thereby allowing continuation of strenuous tasks involving large muscle groups for long periods of time. Cardiovascular endurance is one of the five health-related components of physical fitness.

coronary heart disease—A condition in which blood flow is restricted through a coronary artery by the thickening of the arterial wall from deposits of plaque. It is also known as coronary atherosclerosis.

coronary risk factors—Factors associated with a higher incidence of coronary heart disease. These factors include tobacco use, high blood pressure, high blood cholesterol, a family history of heart disease, diabetes, and physical inactivity.

estimated maximum heart rate—An estimation of maximum heart rate when a heart rate stress test is not performed. It is calculated by the following formula: 220 – age = maximum heart rate.

exercise—Physical activity that is planned, is structured, and provides for repetitive bodily movement. It is done to improve or maintain one or more components of physical fitness.[2]

flexibility—The range of motion available at a joint. The length of the muscles, ligaments, and tendons largely determine the amount of movement possible at each joint. Lack of flexibility may result in impaired movements and increased susceptibility to injury. Flexibility is one of the five health-related components of physical fitness.

intensity—The level of energy required to perform a specific activity. It is often described as maximum oxygen consumption ($\dot{V}O_2$max), percent maximum heart rate reserve (HRR), or multiples of resting metabolism (METs).

lean body mass—Total body weight minus the weight of storage fat. Lean body mass is estimated using skinfold calipers or underwater (i.e., hydrostatic) body weight. See also body composition.

light-intensity physical activity—Any activity requiring less than 3 METs of energy expenditure or performed at less than 50% of maximum heart rate.

metabolic equivalent (METs)—A unit used to estimate the metabolic cost (i.e., oxygen consumption) of physical activity. One MET equals the resting metabolic rate (i.e., the energy expended as someone sits very quietly or rests while awake), approximately 3.5 ml $O_2 \times kg^{-1} \times min^{-1}$. To expend more than 1 MET requires physical activity. As the intensity of the activity increases, so does the MET numeric score.

moderate amount of physical activity—An amount of activity sufficient to burn approximately 150 kilocalories of energy per day, or 1000 kilocalories per week. The duration of time it takes someone to achieve a *moderate amount* of activity depends on the intensity of the activities chosen. The more intense the level of activity, the less time is needed to burn 150 kilocalories.

moderate-intensity physical activity—Any activity requiring 3 to 6 METs of energy expenditure or performed at 50 to 69% of maximum heart rate. It is equivalent to sustained walking, is well within most individuals' current physical capacity, and can be sustained comfortably for a prolonged period of time (at least 60 minutes). A person should feel some exertion but also should be able to carry on a conversation comfortably during the activity.

muscular endurance—The ability of muscle groups to exert external force through repetitive motion or sustained exertion. It is one of the five health-related components of physical fitness.

muscular strength—The amount of external force that a muscle can exert against resistance in a single effort (i.e., how much weight a person can lift or how much tension can be exerted). It is one of the five health-related components of physical fitness.

physical activity—Any bodily movement produced by skeletal muscles that results in an energy expenditure and is positively correlated with physical fitness.[2]

physical fitness—A set of attributes that people have or achieve relating to their ability to perform physical activity. The health-related components of physical fitness include the following: (1) body composition, (2) cardiovascular endurance, (3) flexibility, (4) muscular endurance, and (5) muscular strength.

regular physical activity—A level of physical activity done frequently enough to reap some health benefit (i.e., an accumulated 30 minutes or more of moderate-intensity activity on 5 or more days of the week or an accumulated 20 minutes or more of vigorous-intensity activity on 3 or more days of the week).[3,4]

sedentary lifestyle—A lifestyle characterized by little or no physical activity.

target heart rate—Though exercise professionals do not agree on the usefulness of this formula, a target heart rate can be defined as the desired heart rate to maintain during physical activity, based on an individual's maximum heart rate (220 – the individual's age) and the desired level of intensity for exercising. The formulas for calculating the two primary zones of intensity are as follows: moderate intensity = 50 to 70% of maximum heart rate; vigorous intensity = 70 to 85% of maximum heart rate.

For example, a 55-year-old's recommended target heart rate zone for moderate-intensity activity would be in the range of 83 to 116 bpm.[1] This was determined using the following calculations:

> 220 – 55 = 165 bpm
>
> 165 × .50 = 83 bpm
>
> 165 × .70 = 116 bpm

In order for persons to know whether they are exercising within their target heart rate zone, they will need to determine their exercise heart rate. The heart or pulse rate can be obtained by having a person place his or her index and middle finger on the radial artery, which is on the wrist, palm up, just below the thumb. A person should stop exercising briefly, measure his or her pulse rate for six seconds, and multiply that number by 10 to obtain the number of beats per minute (bpm).

vigorous-intensity physical activity—Hard or very hard physical activity requiring sustained, rhythmic movements and greater than 6 METs of energy expenditure (i.e., performed at 70% or more of maximum heart rate according to age.[4,5] Vigorous activity is intense enough to represent a substantial physical challenge to an individual and results in significant increases in heart and respiration rate.

1. Centers for Disease Control and Prevention, San Diego State University Project. *Project PACE: Physician Manual.* Atlanta: Centers for Disease Control and Prevention, Division of Chronic Disease Control and Community Intervention, 1992.

2. Caspersen CJ, Powell KE, Christenson GM. Physical activity, exercise, and physical fitness: definitions and distinctions for health-related research. *Public Health Reports* 1985; 100(2): 126–131.

3. American College of Sports Medicine. Summary statement: workshop on physical activity and public health. *Sports Medicine Bulletin* 1993; 28(4):7.

4. U.S. Department of Health and Human Services. *Physical Activity and Health: A Report of the Surgeon General.* Atlanta: Centers for Disease Control and Prevention, 1996.

Glossary of Program Planning Terms

audience analysis—Use of a variety of methods to study certain characteristics, attitudes, or practices of a target audience and to obtain information on the relevance or importance of certain issues to members of the target audience, their involvement in the issue, and their access to various communication channels. Audience analysis strives to identify the target audience's needs, document the perceived costs and benefits of addressing those needs, and formulate a program or campaign that appropriately addresses these needs.

audience profile—A thorough description of the target audience. Based on both quantitative and qualitative information, it includes demographic characteristics; psychographic characteristics; product usage habits; media habits; beliefs and behaviors as they relate to the desired health behavior (what the target audience might find beneficial and costly about the healthy behaviors); the alternative behaviors with which the desirable behaviors compete; and the skills, enablers, barriers, facilitators, and sense of efficacy that help the target audience assess the healthy behaviors. The richer the profile, the more opportunities it provides the program strategist to develop a program and communications plan that will engage the intended audience and move them to the desired action.

audience segmentation—Division of a population into homogeneous subsets in order to more effectively communicate a message or distribute a product to a population. Ultimately, segmenting a target audience helps health promotion planners predict behavior and formulate tailored messages or programs to meet specific needs.

campaign—A planned, organized, and integrated set of activities with a clearly defined purpose that uses multiple strategies and channels. Campaigns are waged during a defined time and are usually long (e.g., six weeks to a year or more) and sustained. In addition to mass communication activities, a campaign may consist of grassroots programming, community organization, and legislative advocacy.

communication channel—Any route used to deliver a message. Any person, organization, or institution having access to a definable population is a potential channel. Examples include mass media (e.g., radio, television, newspaper), person-to-person contacts, spokespersons, nonprofit agencies, places frequented by members of the target audience (e.g., schools, worksites, churches, a physician's office, post offices, grocery stores, restaurants, shopping malls, laundromats), public events, direct mail, outdoor advertising, printed materials, product labels, and telemarketing.

channel analysis—Specification of which channels, singly or in combination, will best reach or serve the needs of each target audience segment. Channel analysis includes not only the medium through which messages, products, and services pass but also when and how they pass.

community—A social unit that usually encompasses a geographic region in which residents live and interact socially, such as a political subdivision (e.g., a county, city, or town) or a smaller area (e.g., a section of town, a housing complex, or a neighborhood). A community may be a social organization (a formal or informal group of people who share common concerns or interests). Very often, a community is a composite of subgroups defined by a variety of factors, including age, sex, occupation, socioeconomic status, physical activity history, and current physical activity preferences.[1]

consumer-based health communication—Applying a social marketing approach to the creation of effective health information dissemination strategies. It incorporates the expressed opinions of members of the target audience (the consumer) into the process of transforming scientific recommendations—based on clinical, epidemiologic, and other empirical evidence—into messages relevant to the target audience.

consumer-based research—The research (e.g., interviews, surveys, focus groups, and mall intercept studies) conducted to assess the social norms, values, beliefs, attitudes, priorities, motivations, and other factors—both health- and nonhealth-related—that influence the consumer's behavior. Such research is fundamental when taking a social marketing approach to program planning.

environment—The entirety of the physical, biological, social, cultural, and political circumstances surrounding and influencing a specified behavior.

focus groups—A small group of people (about 8 to 10) who together respond to a set of questions and undertake a discussion on a selected topic. All participants represent the target audience and are encouraged to express their views related to the topic.

formative research—Research conducted during the developmental stages of a project or campaign. It may include reviews, pretesting messages or materials, and pilot testing programs on a small scale before full implementation. The primary purpose of formative research is to maximize the likelihood of effective intervention; it can suggest improvements in message or program content and delivery as well as identify potentially misleading or misunderstood messages and intervention strategies before more costly implementation occurs.

gatekeeper—Someone to work with or through in order to reach the intended audience or accomplish a task. These individuals stand "at the gate" between the health promotion planner and the target audience and often determine whether the health promotion planner gains access to others. Examples are policymakers, decision makers, homemakers, and heads of households.

intermediaries—Organizations (such as professional, industrial, civic, social, or fraternal groups) that serve as a channel for distributing program messages and materials to members of the target audience.

intervention—An organized or planned activity that interrupts a normal course of action within a targeted group of individuals or the community at large so as to diminish an undesirable behavior or to enhance or maintain a desirable one. In health promotion, interventions are linked to improving the health of the population or to diminishing the risks for illness, injury, disability, or death.

media advocacy—The strategic use of media to apply pressure for changes in public policy. One of the main purposes of media advocacy is to increase the capacity of communities to develop and use their voices in order to be heard and seen.[2]

partnership—A group of individuals or organizations that work together on a common task or goal.

primary audience—Those persons whom any health promotion program is most specifically designed to reach and affect.

program—A set of planned activities over time designed to achieve specified objectives.

psychographic characteristics—Describing individuals or groups according to psychological attributes, values, beliefs, and attitudes toward life in general. Psychographic characteristics include personality type or tendencies; lifestyle choices; exhibited behaviors, such as risk-taking tendencies; self esteem; level of self efficacy; locus of control; IQ; Myers Briggs Indicator Type; receptivity to new information; and Stage of Change. Psychographic measures, like demographic measures, can be used to segment audiences and choose test markets.

reach—In communications, an estimation of the number of people or households exposed to a specific media message during a specific period of time. When describing a program, it is the number of people attending or exposed to an intervention, program, or message.[3,4]

safe environment—Surroundings that are physically safe (i.e., that minimize the potential for bodily injury or harm) as well as emotionally safe (i.e., free from ridicule or harassment). In the process of behavior change, people need opportunities to practice newly acquired behaviors or skills in an environment that allows them to perform imperfectly, free from the potential danger of physical or emotional harm.

secondary audience—The persons or organizations who are in a position to reach or influence the primary audience (for example, people who work with the target audience, gatekeepers, intermediaries, etc.).

secondary data sources—Indirect public or private sources of information that may or may not represent the opinions or practices of the target population. Information is collected prior to and apart from a program. Such information may include census data, national polls or surveys, Behavioral Risk Factor Surveillance data, U.S. Food Consumption data, National Health and Nutrition Examination Survey data, etc.

self-efficacy—Believing in one's own ability to make a lifestyle change and committing to those beliefs.[5] It can also be described as the cognitive and behavioral factors related to a person's perception of his or her own ability to make lifestyle changes.

social marketing—Applying advertising and marketing principles and techniques (i.e., applying the planning variables of product, promotion, place, and price) to health or social issues with the intent of bringing about behavior change. The social marketing approach is used to increase the acceptability of a new idea or practice within a target population.[6]

stakeholder—An individual or organization that has something to gain or lose as a result of health promotion program efforts or ideas. This person or group has a stake in the outcome of the program and a unique appreciation of the issues or problems involved.

survey—A standard list of questions to obtain information, either directly or indirectly, from a selected group of individuals regarding their opinions, attitudes, knowledge, or practices.

target audience or target population—A group of individuals or an organization, community, subpopulation, or society that is the focus of a specific health promotion effort.

1. Green LW, Kreuter MW. *Health Promotion Planning: An Educational and Environmental Approach.* 2d ed. Mountain View, CA: Mayfield, 1991:262.

2. Wallack L, Dorfman L, Jernigan D, Themba M. *Media Advocacy and Public Health: Power for Prevention.* Newbury Park: Sage 1993:xi.

3. National Cancer Institute, DHHS. *Making Health Communication Programs Work: A Planner's Guide.* NIH Publication, No. 89-1493, Appendix E, 1989.

4. Green LW, Lewis FM. *Measurement and Evaluation in Health Education and Health Promotion.* Palo Alto, CA: Mayfield, 1986:365.

5. For a comprehensive discussion of self-efficacy and factors that influence it, see Bandura A. *Social Foundations of Thought and Action: A Social Cognitive Theory.* Upper Saddle River, NJ: Prentice-Hall, 1986:390–453.

6. For more information about social marketing, refer to Manoff RK. *Social Marketing: New Imperative for Public Health.* Westport, CN: Praeger, 1985.

References

Introduction

American Academy of Pediatrics, Committee on Sports Medicine and Fitness. 1992. Fitness, activity, and sports participation in the preschool child. *Pediatrics* 90: 1002–1004.

American Academy of Pediatrics, Committee on Sports Medicine and Fitness. 1994. Assessing physical activity and fitness in the office setting. *Pediatrics* 93: 686–689.

American College of Sports Medicine. 1975. *Guidelines for Graded Exercise Testing and Exercise Prescription.* Philadelphia: Lea and Febiger.

American College of Sports Medicine. 1978. The recommended quantity and quality of exercise for developing and maintaining fitness in healthy adults. *Medicine and Science in Sports* 10: vii–x.

American College of Sports Medicine. 1990. Position stand: the recommended quantity and quality of exercise for developing and maintaining cardiorespiratory and muscular fitness in healthy adults. *Medicine and Science in Sports and Exercise* 22: 265–274.

American Heart Association. 1972. *Exercise Testing and Training of Apparently Healthy Individuals: A Handbook for Physicians.* Dallas: American Heart Association.

American Heart Association. 1975. *Exercise Testing and Training of Individuals with Heart Disease or at High Risk for Its Development: A Handbook for Physicians.* Dallas: American Heart Association.

American Medical Association, Elster AB, Kuznets NJ. 1994. *AMA Guidelines for Adolescent Preventive Services (GAPS): Recommendations and Rationale.* Chicago: Williams and Wilkins.

Centers for Disease Control and Prevention. 1997. Guidelines for school and community programs to promote lifelong physical activity among young people. *Morbidity and Mortality Weekly Report: Recommendations and Reports* 48 (RR-6) (March 7): 1-36. Atlanta, GA: U.S. Department of Health and Human Services, Public Health Service, Centers for Disease Control and Prevention.

Harris SS, Capersen CJ, DeFriese GH, Estes EH Jr. 1989. Physical activity counseling for healthy adults as a primary prevention intervention in the clinical setting: report for the U.S. Preventive Services Task Force. *Journal of the American Medical Association* 261: 3588–3598.

National Institutes of Health. 1996. Physical Activity and Cardiovascular Health, NIH Consensus Development Panel on Physical Activity and Cardiovascular Health. *Journal of the American Medical Association* 276(3): 241–246.

Pate RR, Pratt M, Blair SN, et al. 1995a. Physical activity and public health: a recommendation from the Centers for Disease Control and Prevention and the American College of Sports Medicine. *Journal of the American Medical Association* 273(5): 402–407.

President's Council on Physical Fitness. 1965. *Adult Physical Fitness: A Program for Men and Women.* Washington, DC: U.S. Government Printing Office.

Public Health Service. 1991. *Healthy People 2000: National Health Promotion and Disease Prevention Objectives.* Washington, DC: U.S. Department of Health and Human Services, Public Health Service, Publication No. (PHS) 91–212.

Sallis JF, Patrick K. 1994. Physical activity guidelines for adolescents: consensus statement. *Pediatric Exercise Science* 6: 302–314.

U.S. Department of Health and Human Services. 1996. *Physical Activity and Health: A Report of the Surgeon General.* Atlanta: U.S. Department of Health and Human Services, Centers for Disease Control and Prevention, National Center for Chronic Disease Prevention and Health Promotion.

U.S. Preventive Services Task Force. 1989. *Guide to Clinical Preventive Services.* Baltimore: Williams & Wilkins.

U.S. Preventive Services Task Force. 1996. *Guide to Clinical Preventive Services* (2nd Edition). Baltimore: Williams & Wilkins.

Chapter 1

Arroll B, Beaglehole R. 1992. Does physical activity lower blood pressure? A critical review of the clinical trials. *Journal of Clinical Epidemiology* 45: 439–447.

Blair SN, Goodyear NN, Gibbons LW, et al. 1984. Physical fitness and incidence of hypertension in healthy normotensive men and women. *Journal of the American Medical Association* 252: 487–490.

Blair SN, Kohl HW III, Paffenbarger RS Jr. et al. 1995. Physical fitness and all-cause mortality: a prospective study of healthy and unhealthy men. *Journal of the American Medical Association* 273: 1093–1098.

Caspersen CJ, Merritt RK. 1995. Physical activity trends among 26 states, 1986–1990. *Medicine and Science in Sports and Exercise* 27: 713–720.

Centers for Disease Control and Prevention. 1995. *Healthy Eating and Physical Activity: Focus Group Research with Contemplators and Preparors.* Atlanta: Nutrition and Physical Activity Communications Team, National Center for Chronic Disease Prevention and Health Promotion, Centers for Disease Control and Prevention.

Centers for Disease Control and Prevention. 1998. *1996 BRFSS Summary Prevalence Report.* Atlanta: Behavioral Surveillance Branch, Office of Surveillance and Analysis, National Center for Chronic Disease Prevention and Health Promotion, Centers for Disease Control and Prevention.

Dishman RK, Sallis JF. 1994. Determinants and interventions for physical activity and exercise. In *Physical Activity, Fitness, and Health: International Proceedings and Consensus Statement* edited by C. Bouchard, R.J. Shephard, and T. Stephens. Champaign, IL: Human Kinetics.

Jones DA, Ainsworth BE, Croft JB, et al. 1998. Moderate Leisure-Time Physical Activity: Who Is Meeting the Public Health Recommendations? A National Cross-Sectional Study. *Archives of Family Medicine* 7 (May/June): 285–289.

Kann L, Kinchen SA, Williams BI, Ross JG, Lowry R, Hill CV, et al. 1998. Youth Risk Behavior Surveillance—United States, 1997. In CDC Surveillance Summaries, August 14, 1998. *Morbidity and Mortality Weekly Report* 47(No. SS-3): 1–89.

Kelley G, McClellan P. 1994. Antihypertensive effects of aerobic exercise: a brief meta-analytic review of randomized controlled trials. *American Journal of Hypertension* 7: 115–119.

Lee I, Paffenbarger RS. 1998. *Physical Activity and Stroke Incidence: The Harvard Alumni Health Study.* Report no. LXI (October): 2049-2054. Boston: Harvard School of Public Health.

Minnesota Heart Health Program. 1989. *Lifetime Fitness Participant Manual.* Minneapolis: University of Minnesota.

Paffenbarger RS, Hyde RT, Wing AL, et al. 1993. The association of changes in physical activity level and other lifestyle characteristics with mortality among men. *New England Journal of Medicine* 328: 538–545.

U.S. Department of Health and Human Services. 1996. *Physical Activity and Health: A Report of the Surgeon General.* Atlanta: U.S. Department of Health and Human Services, Centers for Disease Control and Prevention, National Center for Chronic Disease Prevention and Health Promotion.

Chapter 2

Ainsworth BE, Haskell WL, Leon AS, et al. 1993a. Compendium of physical activities: classification of energy costs of human physical activities. *Medicine and Science in Sports and Exercise* 25(1): 71–80.

Ainsworth BE, Richardson M, Jacobs DR, et al. 1993b. Gender differences in physical activity. *Women in Sport and Physical Activity Journal* 2(1): 1–16.

Åstrand, P-O, Grimby G. 1986. *Physical Activity in Health and Disease.* Sweden: Almquist and Wiksell, Acta Medica Scandinavica Symposium Series, No. 2.

Borg, G. 1998. *Borg's Perceived Exertion and Pain Scales.* Champaign, IL: Human Kinetics.

Jones DA, Ainsworth BE, Croft JB, et al. 1998. Moderate Leirsure-Time Physical Activity: Who Is Meeting the Public Health Recommendations? A National Cross-Sectional Study. *Archives of Family Medicine* 7 (May/June): 285–289.

The mistakes exercisers make. *Health* July/August 1998:18.

Pate RR, Pratt M, Blair SN, et al. 1995a. Physical activity and public health: a recommendation from the Centers for Disease Control and Prevention and the American College of Sports Medicine. *Journal of the American Medical Association* 273(5): 402–407.

Patrick K, Sallis JF, Long B, et al. 1994. A new tool for encouraging activity: project PACE. *The Physician and Sportsmedicine* 22(11): 45–52.

Pratt M. 1995. Exercise and sudden death: implications for health policy. *Sport Science Review Journal* 4(2): 106–122.

U.S. Department of Health and Human Services. 1996. *Physical Activity and Health: A Report of the Surgeon General.* Atlanta: U.S. Department of Health and Human Services, Centers for Disease Control and Prevention, National Center for Chronic Disease Prevention and Health Promotion.

U.S. Department of Health and Human Services. 1996. *Physical Activity and Health: A Report of the Surgeon General At-A-Glance.* Atlanta: U.S. Department of Health and Human Services, Centers for Disease Control and Prevention, National Center for Chronic Disease Prevention and Health Promotion.

Chapter 3

Abrams DB, Elder JP, Carleton RA, et al. 1986. Social Learning Principles for Organizational Health Promotion: An Intergrated Approach. In *Health and Industry: A Behavioral Medicine Perspective* edited by T.J. Coates and M.F. Cataldo. New York: John Wiley and Sons.

Abrams DB. 1991. Conceptual models to integrate individual and public health interventions: the example of the workplace. In *Proceedings of the International Conference on Promoting Dietary Change in Communities.* Seattle: The Fred Hutchinson Cancer Research Center, 170–190.

Andreasen AR. 1995. *Marketing Social Change: Changing Behavior to Promote Health, Social Development, and the Environment.* San Francisco: Jossey-Bass Publishers.

Balch G. University of Illinois at Chicago. 1996. Personal Communication.

Covey S. 1989. *The Seven Habits of Highly Effective People.* New York: Simon and Schuster.

Fishbein M. 1995. Developing effective behavior change interventions: some lessons learned from behavioral research. In: Backer TE, David SL, Soucy G, editors. *Reviewing the Behavioral Science Knowledge Base in Technology Transfer.* Rockville, MD: National Institutes of Health, National Institute on Drug Abuse, 246–261.

Francese, P. 1995. America at Mid-Decade. *American Demographics.* (February) 17(2): 23–31.

Glanz K, Rimer BK. 1995. *Theory at a Glance: A Guide for Health Promotion Practice.* Washington, DC: National Cancer Institute and National Institutes of Health. NIH Publication No. 95–3896.

Goodman RM, Steckler A, Kegler MC. 1997. Mobilizing Organizations for Health Enhancement: Theories of Organizational Change. In *Health Behavior and Health Education: Theory, Research, and Practice,* Second Edition, edited by K. Glanz, F.M. Lewis, and B.K. Rimer. San Francisco, CA: Jossey-Bass Publishers.

Jones DA, Ainsworth BE, Croft JB, et al. 1998. Moderate leisure-time physical activity: who is meeting the public health recommendations? A national cross-sectional study. *Archives of Family Medicine* (May/June); 7: 285–289.

Kann L, Kinchen SA, Williams BI, Ross JG, Lowry R, Hill CV, et al. 1998. Youth Risk Behavior Surveillance—United States, 1997. In CDC Surveillance Summaries, August 14, 1998. *Morbidity and Mortality Weekly Report* 47(No. SS-3): 1–89.

King AC. 1991. Community intervention for promotion of physical activity and fitness. *Exercise and Sport Sciences Reviews* 19: 211–259.

McLeroy KR, Bibeau D, Steckler A, Glanz K. 1988. An ecological perspective on health promotion programs. *Health Education Quarterly* 15: 351–377.

Maibach EW, Maxfield A, Ladin K, Slater M. 1996. Translating health psychology into effective health communication: the American Healthstyles Audience Segmentation Project. *Journal of Health Psychology* 1: 261–278.

Meredith G, Schewe C. 1994. The power of cohorts. *American Demographics* 16(12): 22–31.

Mergenhagen, P. 1995. *Targeting Transitions: Marketing to Consumers During Life Changes.* Ithaca, NY: American Demographics Books.

Prochaska JO, DiClemente CC, Norcross JC. 1992. In search of how people change: applications to addictive behaviors. *American Psychologist* 47(9): 1102–1114.

Smith JW, Clurman A. 1997. *Rocking the Ages: The Yankelovich Report on Generational Marketing.* New York: Harper Business.

Smith W. Academy for Educational Development. Washington, DC. 1998. Personal Communication.

Smith W. 1998. "Social Marketing: What's the Big Idea?" *Social Marketing Quarterly* (Winter) IV(2): 5–17.

Sutton SM, Balch GI, Lefebvre RC. 1995. Strategic questions for consumer-based health communications. *Public Health Reports* 110(6): 725–733.

Thomas V, Wolfe DB. 1995. Why won't television grow up? *American Demographics* 17(5): 24–29.

U.S. Department of Health and Human Services. 1996. *Physical Activity and Health: A Report of the Surgeon General.* Atlanta: U.S. Department of Health and Human Services, Centers for Disease Control and Prevention, National Center for Chronic Disease Prevention and Health Promotion.

Chapter 4

Abrams DB, Elder JP, Carleton RA, et al. 1986. Social Learning Principles for Organizational Health Promotion: An Intergrated Approach. In: *Health and Industry: A Behavioral Medicine Perspective,* edited by M.F. Cataldo and T.J. Coates. NY: John Wiley and Sons.

Abrams DB. 1991 Conceptual models to integrate individual and public health interventions: the example of the workplace. In *Proceedings of the International Conference on Promoting Dietary Change in Communities.* Seattle: The Fred Hutchinson Cancer Research Center, 170–190.

Ajzen I, Fishbein M. 1980. *Understanding Attitudes and Predicting Social Behavior.* Englewood Cliffs, NJ: Prentice-Hall.

Andreasen. Q & A Interview With Alan Andreasen. 1998. S*ocial Marketing Quarterly* Spring; IV(3): 22–39.

Bandura A. 1986. *Social Foundations of Thought and Action: A Social Cognitive Theory.* Englewood Cliffs, NJ: Prentice-Hall.

Becker MH, ed. 1974. The health belief model and personal health behavior. *Health Education Monographs* 2: 324–473.

Burden D. 1997. *Walkable Communities: A Search for Quality.* Introduction and Planning Sections, Walkable Communities Course, Slides and Text. (March).

Crow LD, Crow A, eds. 1963. *Readings in Human Learning.* New York: McKay.

Farquhar JW. 1987. *The American Way of Life Need Not Be Hazardous to Your Health.* New York: W.W. Norton & Co.

Fishbein M, Bandura A, Triandis HC, et al. 1992. *Factors Influencing Behavior and Behavior Change: Final Report—Theorist's Workshop.* Rockville, MD: National Institute of Mental Health.

Fishbein M. 1995. Developing effective behavior change interventions: some lessons learned from behavioral research. In *Reviewing the Behavioral Science Knowledge Base in Technology Transfer* edited by T.E. Backer, S.L. David, and G. Soucy. Rockville, MD: National Institutes of Health, National Institute on Drug Abuse, 246–261.

Glanz K, Rimer BK. 1995. *Theory at a Glance: A Guide for Health Promotion Practice*. Washington, DC: National Cancer Institute and National Institutes of Health. NIH Publication No. 95–3896.

Glanz K, Lewis FM, Rimer BK (editors). 1997. *Health Behavior and Health Education; Theory, Research, and Practice. Second Edition*. San Francisco, CA: Jossey-Bass Publishers.

Gottlieb NH, McLeroy KR. 1994. Social health. In *Health Promotion in the Workplace* (2nd Edition) edited by M.P. O'Donnell and J.S. Harris. Albany, NY: Delmar Publishers.

Green LW, McAlister AL. 1984. Macro-intervention to support health behavior: some theoretical perspectives and practical reflections. *Health Education Quarterly* 11: 322–339.

King AC. 1991. Community intervention for promotion of physical activity and fitness. *Exercise and Sport Sciences Reviews* 19: 211–259.

King AC, Jeffery RW, Fridinger F, et al. 1995. Environmental and policy approaches to cardiovascular and disease prevention through physical activity: issues and opportunities. *Health Education Quarterly* 22(4): 499–511.

Knowles MS. 1984. *The Adult Learner: A Neglected Species* (3rd Edition). Houston: Gulf Publishing Co.

Lasater T, Abrams D, Artz L, et al. 1984. Lay volunteer delivery of a community-based cardiovascular risk factor change program: the Pawtucket Experiment. In *Behavioral Health: A Handbook of Health Enhancement and Disease Prevention* edited by J.D. Matarazzo, S.M. Weiss, and J.A. Herd. New York: Wiley, 1166–1170.

Lefebvre RC, Lasater TM, Carleton RA, et al. 1987. Theory and delivery of health programming in the community: the Pawtucket Heart Health Program. *Preventive Medicine* 16: 80–95.

McLeroy KR, Steckler A, Goodman R, et al. 1992. Health education research: theory and practice—future directions. *Health Education Research: Theory and Practice* 7(1): 1–8.

Prochaska JO, DiClemente CC, Norcross JC. 1992. In search of how people change: applications to addictive behaviors. *American Psychologist* 47(9): 1102–1114.

Rogers EM. 1983. *Diffusion of Innovations* (3rd Edition). New York: The Free Press/ Macmillan Publishing Company.

Sallis JF, Hovell MF. 1990. Determinants of exercise behavior. *Exercise and Sport Science Reviews* 18: 307–330.

Sallis JF, Hovell MF, Hofstetter CR. 1992. Predictors of adoption and maintenance of vigorous physical activity in men and women. *Preventive Medicine* 21: 237–251.

U.S. Department of Transportation Federal Highway Administration. 1994a. *A Compendium of Available Bicycle and Pedestrian Trip Generation Data in the United States: A Supplement to the National Bicycling and Walking Study* (October). Chapel Hill, NC: University of North Carolina, Highway Safety Research Center.

U.S. Department of Transportation Federal Highway Administration. 1994b. *Final Report: The National Bicycling and Walking Study. Transportation Choices for a Changing America.* FHWA-PD-94-023. Washington, DC.

Chapter 5

Abrams DB, Elder JP, Carleton RA, et al. 1986. Social learning principles for organizational health promotion: An intergrated approach. In: *Health and Industry: A Behavioral Medicine Perspective,* edited by M.F. Cataldo and T.J. Coates. NY: John Wiley and Sons.

Ajzen I, Fishbein M. 1980. *Understanding Attitudes and Predicting Social Behavior.* Englewood Cliffs, NJ: Prentice-Hall.

Balch G. University of Illinois at Chicago. 1996. Personal Communication.

Bandura A. 1986. *Social Foundations of Thought and Action: A Social Cognitive Theory.* Englewood Cliffs, NJ: Prentice-Hall.

Baranowski, T. 1989–90. Reciprocal determinism at the stages of behavior change: an integration of community, personal and behavior perspectives. *International Quarterly of Community Health Education* 10(4): 297–327.

Bloom BS, ed. 1956. *Taxonomy of Educational Objectives, Handbook I: Cognitive Domain.* New York: Longmans, Green.

Carmody T, Senner J, Manilow M, et al.1980. Physical exercise rehabilitation: long-term dropout rate in cardiac patients. *Journal of Behavioral Medicine* 3: 163–168.

Centers for Disease Control and Prevention. 1995. *Healthy Eating and Physical Activity: Focus Group Research with Contemplators and Preparers* (June). Atlanta, GA.

Chapman LS. 1994. Awareness strategies. In *Health Promotion in the Workplace* (2nd Edition) edited by M.P. O'Donnell and J.S. Harris. Albany, NY: Delmar Publishers, 163–184.

Cotton D, Javis D. 1993. Part 1: The transtheoretical model: A conceptual framework for behavior change. In: CDC. *Hemophilia Behavioral Intervention Evaluation Projects: Adult Intervention Manual.* Atlanta, GA.

DiClemente C, Prochaska J, Fairhurst S, et al. 1991. The process of smoking cessation: an analysis of precontemplation, contemplation and preparation stages of change. *Journal of Consulting and Clinical Psychology* 59: 295–304.

Dishman R. 1988. *Exercise Adherence.* Champaign, IL: Human Kinetics.

Farquhar JW, Fortmann SP, Maccoby N, et al. 1984. The Standford Five City Project: an overview. In *Behavioral Health: A Handbook of Health Enhancement and Disease Prevention* edited by J.D. Matarazzo, S.M. Weiss, J.A. Herd, et al. New York: Wiley, 1154–1165.

Fishbein M, Bandura A, Triandis HC, et al. 1992. *Factors Influencing Behavior and Behavior Change: Final Report—Theorists' Workshop.* Rockville, MD: National Institute of Mental Health.

Fishbein M. 1995. Developing effective behavior change interventions: some lessons learned from behavioral research. In *Reviewing the Behavioral Science Knowledge Base in Technology Transfer* edited by T.E. Backer, S.L. David, and G. Soucy. Rockville, MD: National Institutes of Health, National Institute on Drug Abuse, 246–261.

Glanz K, Lewis FM, Rimer BK (editors). 1997. *Health Behavior and Health Education; Theory, Research, and Practice.* Second Edition. San Francisco, CA: Jossey-Bass Publishers.

Karoly P, ed. 1985. *Measurement Strategies in Health Psychology.* New York: Wiley.

Kibler RJ, Cegala DJ, Miles DT. 1974. *Objectives for Instruction and Evaluation.* Boston: Allyn & Bacon.

Knowles, MS. 1984. *The Adult Learner: A Neglected Species* (3rd Edition). Houston, TX: Gulf Publishing Co.

Marcus BH, Banspach SW, Lefebvre RL, et al. 1992a. Using the stages of change model to increase the adoption of physical activity among community participants. *American Journal of Health Promotion* 6(6): 424–429.

Marcus BH, Rossi JS, Selby VC, et al. 1992b. The stages and processes of exercise adoption and maintenance in a worksite sample. *Health Psychology* 11(6): 386–395.

Marcus BH, Emmons KM, Simkin LR, et al. 1994. Evaluation of stage-matched versus standard self-help physical activity interventions at the workplace. *Annals of Behavioral Medicine* 16: S–035.

Marcus BH, Emmons KM, Simkin LR, et al. 1998. Evaluation of motivationally tailored versus standard self-help physical activity interventions at the workplace. *American Journal of Health Promotion* 12: 246–253

Owen N, Bauman A, Booth M, et al. 1995. Serial mass-media campaigns to promote physical activity: reinforcing or redundant? *American Journal of Public Health* 85(2): 244–248.

Parcel G, Baranowski T. 1981. Social learning theory and health education. *Health Education* 12: 14–18.

Pate RR, Pratt M, Blair SN, et al. 1995a. Physical activity and public health: a recommendation from the Centers for Disease Control and Prevention and the American College of Sports Medicine. *Journal of the American Medical Association* 273(5): 402–407.

Prochaska JO, DiClemente CC, JC Norcross. 1992. In search of how people change. Applications to addictive behaviors. *American Psychologist* (Sept) 47: 1102–1114.

Rogers EM. 1983. *Diffusion of Innovations* (3rd Edition). New York: The Free Press/ Macmillan Publishing Company.

Rosenstock IM, Strecher VJ, and Becker MH. 1988. Social learning theory and the health belief model. *Health Education Quarterly* 15(2): 175–183.

U.S. Department of Health and Human Services. 1989. *Making Health Communication Programs Work.* (April). Bethesda, MD: National Institutes of Health, National Cancer Institute, Office of Cancer Communications.

U.S. Department of Health and Human Services. 1996. *Physical Activity and Health: A Report of the Surgeon General.* Atlanta: U.S. Department of Health and Human Services, Centers for Disease Control and Prevention, National Center for Chronic Disease Prevention and Health Promotion.

Wallston KA. 1994. Theoretically based strategies for health behavior change. In: O'Donnell MP, Harris JS, editors. *Health Promotion in the Workplace* (2nd Edition). Albany, NY: Delmar Publishers, 185–203.

White SL, Maloney SK. 1990. Promoting healthy diets and active lives to hard-to-reach groups: market research study. *Public Health Reports*; 105(3): 224–231.

Wilson DK, Purdon SE, Wallston KA. 1988. Compliance to health recommendations: a theoretical overview of message framing. *Health Education Research, Theory and Practice* 3: 161–171.

Chapter 6

Ajzen I, Fishbein M. 1980. *Understanding Attitudes and Predicting Social Behavior.* Englewood Cliffs, NJ: Prentice-Hall.

Baranowski T, Perry CL, Parcel GS. 1997. How individuals, environments, and health behavior interact. In *Health Behavior and Health Education: Theory, Research, and Practice* (2nd Edition) edited by K. Glanz, F.M. Lewis, and B.K. Rimer. San Francisco: Jossey-Bass Publishers, 153–178.

Burden, D. 1997. *Walkable Communities: A Search for Quality.* Introduction and Planning Sections, Walkable Communities Course, Slides, and Text. (March).

Harris L. 1995. *Between Hope and Fear: Teens Speak Out on Crime in the Community.* Washington, DC: National Teens, Crime, and the Community Program.

Heaney CA, Israel BA. 1997. Social networks and social support. In *Health Behavior and Health Education: Theory, Research, and Practice* (2nd Edition) edited by K. Glanz, F.M. Lewis, and B.K. Rimer. San Francisco: Jossey-Bass Publishers, 179–205.

House JS. 1987. Social support and social structure. *Sociological Forum* 2: 135–146.

Israel BA. 1982. Social networks and health status: linking theory, research, and practice. *Patient Counseling and Health Education* 4: 65–79.

Knowles MS. 1984. *The Adult Learner: A Neglected Species* (3rd Edition). Houston, TX: Gulf Publishing Co.

Linegar JM, Chesson CV, Nice DS. 1991. Physical fitness gains following simple environmental change. *American Journal of Preventive Medicine* 7: 298–310.

MMWR 1999. Neighborhood safety and the prevalence of physical inactivity—selected states, 1996. *Morbidity and Mortality Weekly Report.* Atlanta, GA: Centers for Disease Control and Prevention, February 26; 48(7): 143–146.

Pedestrian Federation of America. 1995. *Walk Tall: A Citizen's Guide to Walkable Communities.* Emmaus, PA: Rodale Press.

Rogers EM. 1983. *Diffusion of Innovations* (3rd Edition). New York: The Free Press/ Macmillan Publishing Company.

Sharp D. 1998.Fitness Friendly Award: Portland, Oregon. *Health* (July/August), 76–77.

U.S. Department of Transportation. Federal Highway Administration. 1992. National Bicycling and Walking Study. *Case study no. 14: Benefits of bicycling and walking to health.* Publication no. FHWA-PD-93-025.

U.S. Department of Transportation. 1997. *Walkability Checklist.* DOT HS 808 619. Washington, DC, (September).

U.S. Environmental Protection Agency. 1998. The Effects of Urban Form on Travel and Emissions: A Review and Synthesis of the Literature. HVIX Reference C611-005. Washington, DC, (April).

Chapter 7

American Public Health Association. 1991. *Healthy Communities 2000. Model Standards: Guidelines for Community Attainment of the Year 2000 National Health Objectives* (3rd Edition). Washington, DC: American Public Health Association.

Fawcett SB, Sterling TD, Paine-Andrews A, et al. 1995. *Evaluating Community Efforts to Prevent Cardiovascular Diseases.* Atlanta, GA: U.S. Department of Health and Human Services, Public Health Service, Centers for Disease Control and Prevention, National Center for Chronic Disease Prevention and Health Promotion.

Green LW, Kreuter MW. 1991. *Health Promotion Planning: An Educational and Environmental Approach.* Mountain View, CA: Mayfield Publishing Company.

Kibler RJ, Cegala DJ, Miles DT, Bark LL. 1974. *Objectives for Instruction and Evaluation.* Boston: Allyn and Bacon.

Public Health Service. 1991. *Healthy People 2000: National Health Promotion and Disease Prevention Objectives.* Washington, DC: U.S. Department of Health and Human Services, Public Health Service. DHHS Publication No. (PHS) 91–50212.

Rohn J. 1993. *The Art of Exceptional Living.* Chicago, IL: Nightingale Conant, (May).

Chapter 8

American Heart Association, Georgia Affiliate. 1991. *Community Site Handbook.* Marietta, GA: American Heart Association, Georgia Affiliate.

Ames EE, Trucano LA, Wan JC, et al. 1992. *Designing School Health Curricula: Planning for Good Health.* Dubuque, IA: William C. Brown Publishers.

Bracht N. 1990. *Health Promotion at the Community Level.* Newbury Park, CA: Sage Publications.

Health Resources and Services Administration. 1998. Are Consortia/Collaboratives Effective in Changing Health Status and Health Systems? A Critical Review of the Literature. *Health 2000.* Atlanta, GA: Health 200, Inc.

Himmelman A. 1996. *Collaboration for a Change: Definitions, Models, and a Guide to the Collaborative Process.* Minneapolis, MN: Arthur T. Himmelman Consulting Group.

National Cancer Institute. 1989. *Making Health Communication Programs Work: A Planner's Guide.* Washington, DC: U.S. Department of Health and Human Services, Public Health Service, National Institutes of Health. NIH Publication No. 89–1493.

Peisher, A. 1991. Partnership model. In: *Community Site Handbook* by the American Heart Association, Georgia Affiliate. Marietta, GA: American Heart Association, Georgia Affiliate.

Van Hulzen C. 1992. *Coalition-Building at the Community Level to Address Public Health Issues.* Atlanta: U.S. Department of Health and Human Services, Public Health Service, Centers for Disease Control and Prevention.

Chapter 9

Abrams DA. 1991. Conceptual models to integrate individual and public health interventions: the example of the workplace. In: *Proceedings of the International Conference on Promoting Dietary Change in Communities.* Seattle: The Fred Hutchinson Cancer Research Center, 170–190.

Bellingham R, Isham D. 1990. Enhancing CVD related behavioral changes in the workplace: corporate comparisons and cultural issues. *American Association of Occupational Health Nurses Journal* 38: 433–438.

Brownson R, Schmid T, King A, et al. 1998. Support for policy interventions to increase physical activity in rural Missouri. *American Journal of Health Promotion* 12(4) (March/April): 263–266.

Centers for Disease Control and Prevention. 1993. Physical activity and the prevention of coronary heart disease. *Morbidity and Mortality Weekly Report* 42(35): 669–672.

Chapman LS. Awareness strategies. 1994. In *Health Promotion in the Workplace* (2nd Edition) edited by M.P. O'Donnell and J. S. Harris. Albany, NY: Delmar Publishers, 163–184.

Chapman LS. 1996. *Using Wellness Incentives: A Positive Tool for Healthy Lifestyles.* Seattle: Summex Corporation.

Glaros TE. 1997. *Health Promotion Ideas That Work.* Champaign, IL: Human Kinetics, 47.

Gottlieb NH, McLeroy KR. 1994. Social health. In *Health Promotion in the Workplace* (2nd Edition) edited by M.P. O'Donnell and J.S. Harris. Albany, NY: Delmar Publishers, 459–493.

Grosch J, Alterman T, Petersen M, Murphy L. 1998. Worksite health promotion programs in the U.S.: factors associated with availability and participation. *American Journal of Health Promotion* 13(1) (September/October): 36–56.

IRSA, The Association of Quality Clubs. 1992. *The Economic Benefits of Regular Exercise.* Boston: IRSA, The Association of Quality Clubs. To obtain a copy of this publication, contact The Association at 253 Summer Street, Boston, MA 02210, 617-951-0055.

Leatt P, Hattin H, Wests C, et al. 1988. Seven year follow-up of employee fitness program. *Canadian Journal of Public Health* 79(1): 20–25.

Marcus BH, Emmons KM, Simkin-Silverman LR, et al. 1998. Evaluation of motivationally tailored vs. standard self-help physical activity interventions at the workplace. *American Journal of Health Promotion* 12 no. 4 (March/April): 246-253.

Marcus BH, Rossi JS, Selby VC, et al. 1992. The stages and processes of exercise adoption and maintenance in a worksite sample. *Health Psychology* 11(6): 386–395.

Marcus BH, Simkin LR, Rossi JS, et al. 1996. Longitudinal shifts in employees' stages and processes of exercise behavior change. *American Journal of Health Promotion* 10(3): 195–200.

Pelletier KR. 1993. A review and analysis of the health and cost-effective outcome studies of comprehensive health promotion and disease prevention programs at the worksite: 1991–1993 update. *American Journal of Health Promotion* 8(1): 50–62.

Public Health Service. 1991. *Healthy People 2000: National Health Promotion and Disease Prevention Objectives.* Washington, DC: U.S. Department of Health and Human Services, Public Health Service.

Public Health Service. 1995. *Healthy People 2000: Midcourse Review and 1995 Revisions.* Washington, DC: U.S. Department of Health and Human Services, Public Health Service.

Sharratt MT, Cox M. 1988. Employee fitness: state of the art. *Canadian Journal of Public Health* 79(2): S40–S43.

Shephard RJ. 1992. A critical analysis of work-site fitness programs and their postulated economic benefits. *Medicine and Science in Sports and Exercise* 24(3): 354–370.

Taylor W, Baranowski T, Rohm Young D. 1998. Physical activity interventions in low-income, ethnic minority, and populations with disability. *American Journal of Preventive Medicine* 15 (November): 255–440.

The Wellness Councils of America, The Wellness Councils of Canada. 1998. *Health Promotion: Sourcebook for Small Businesses.* Omaha, NE: Wellness Councils of America (WELCOA).

U.S. Department of Health and Human Services. 1993. *1992 National Survey of Worksite Health Promotion Activities.* Washington, DC: U.S. Government Printing Office.

Wanzel RS. 1994. Decades of worksite fitness programmes: progress or rhetoric? *Sports Medicine* 17(5): 324–337.

Chapter 10

American Alliance for Health, Physical Education, Recreation and Dance. 1999. *Physical Education for Lifelong Fitness.* Champaign, IL: Human Kinetics.

American Heart Association. 1995. Strategic plan for promoting physical activity. Dallas: American Heart Association.

Bailey DA, Martin AD. 1994. Physical activity and skeletal health in adolescents. *Pediatric Exercise Science* 6: 330–347.

Bedini LA. 1990. Separate but equal? Segregated programming for people with disabilities. *Journal of Physical Education, Recreation and Dance* 61: 40–44.

Brown M, Gordon WA. 1987. Impact of impairment on activity patterns of children. *Archives of Physical Medicine and Rehabilitation* 68: 828–832.

Calfas KJ, Taylor WC. 1994. Effects of physical activity on psychological variables in adolescents. *Pediatric Exercise Science* 6: 406–423.

Centers for Disease Control and Prevention. 1997. Guidelines for school and community programs to promote lifelong physical activity among young people. *Morbidity and Mortality Weekly Report* 46(RR-6): 1–36.

Collins JL, Small ML, Kann L, et al. 1995. School health education. *Journal of School Health* 165(8): 302–311.

Fitness Fever website. **http://www.fitnessfever.com**. 20 October 1998.

Human Kinetics. 1998. *Active Youth: Ideas for Implementing CDC Physical Activity.* Champaign, IL: Human Kinetics.

Joint Committee on National Health Education Standards. 1995. *National Health Education Standards: Achieving Health Literacy. An Investment in the Future.* Atlanta: American Cancer Society.

Kann L, Kinchen SA, Williams BI, Ross JG, Lowry R, Hill CV, et al. 1998. Youth Risk Behavior Surveillance—United States, 1997. In CDC Surveillance Summaries, August 14, 1998. *Morbidity and Mortality Weekly Report* 47(No. SS-3): 1–89.

Kelder SH, Perry CL, Peters RJ Jr, et al. 1995. Gender differences in the Class of 1989 Study: the school component of the Minnesota Heart Health Program. *Journal of Health Education* 26(2 Suppl): S36–S44.

McKenzie TL, Sallis JF, Faucette N, et al. 1993. Effects of a curriculum and inservice program on the quantity and quality of elementary physical education classes. *Research Quarterly for Exercise and Sport* 64(2):178–187.

Morrow JR, Freedson PS. 1994. Relationship between habitual physical activity and aerobic fitness in adolescents. *Pediatric Exercise Science* 6: 315–329.

National Association for Sport and Physical Education. 1998. *Physical Activity for Children A Statement of Guidelines*. Reston, VA: NASPE Publications.

Pate RR, Small ML, Ross JG, et al. 1995b. School physical education. *Journal of School Health* 165(8): 312–318.

"Physical Dimensions" brochure.

Program Adds New Dimensions to School Health. *Health Issues* October 1997, 5(3).

Public Health Service. 1991. *Healthy People 2000: National Health Promotion and Disease Prevention Objectives*. Washington, DC: U.S. Department of Health and Human Services, Public Health Service.

Ross JG, Pate RR. 1987. The National Children and Youth Fitness Study II. A summary of findings. *Journal of Physical Education, Recreation and Dance* 58(9): 51–56.

Sallis J. 1997. San Diego State University. Personal Communication.

Sallis JF, McKenzie TL. 1991. Physical education's role in public health. *Research Quarterly for Exercise and Sport* 62(2): 124–137.

Sallis JF, Patrick K. 1994. Physical activity guidelines for adolescents: consensus statement. *Pediatric Exercise Science* 6: 302–314.

Silverman S. 1991. Research on teaching in physical education. *Research Quarterly for Exercise and Sport* 62: 352–364.

Simons-Morton BG, Taylor WC, Snider SA, et al. 1994. Observed levels of elementary and middle school children's physical activity during physical education classes. *Preventive Medicine* 23: 437–441.

Tappe MK, Duda JL, Menges-Ehrnwald P. 1990. Personal investment predictors of adolescent motivational orientation toward exercise. *Canadian Journal of Sport Science* 15(3): 185–192.

U.S. Department of Health and Human Services. 1996. *Physical Activity and Health: A Report of the Surgeon General*. Atlanta: U.S. Department of Health and Human Services, Centers for Disease Control and Prevention, National Center for Chronic Disease Prevention and Health Promotion.

Index